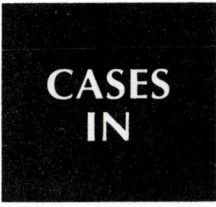

CASES IN

Production/Operations Management

Edited by
Roger W. Schmenner

The Fuqua School of Business, Duke University

Contributing Authors

Robert D. Landel
Roger W. Schmenner
John Haywood-Farmer
Michiel R. Leenders
Edward W. Davis
Robert R. Britney
James A. Erskine
D. Clay Whybark

Christopher Piper
David A. Collier
Albert R. Wood
James R. Freeland
Alexander B. Horniman
John L. Colley, Jr.
John L. Snook

SCIENCE RESEARCH ASSOCIATES, INC.
Chicago, Henley-on-Thames, Sydney, Toronto

A Subsidiary of IBM

Acquisition Editor: David S. McEttrick
Development Editor: Molly Gardiner
Composition and Production Management: CRACOM Corporation

Library of Congress Cataloging-in-Publication Data
Main entry under title:

Cases in production/operations management.

   Includes index.
   1. Production management—Case studies.
I. Schmenner, Roger W., 1947-   . II. Landel,
Robert D.
TS155.C317   1986   658.5′092′6   85-27762
ISBN 0-574-19560-2

Printed in the United States of America.

10   9   8   7   6   5   4   3   2   1

CONTENTS

PREFACE

This book brings together 29 cases on mainstream topics in Production and Operations Management. These cases were written at several schools, although most are from either the Colgate Darden Graduate Business School at the University of Virginia or the School of Business Administration at the University of Western Ontario. Both of these institutions share rich case method traditions, and these contributions represent some of the best work of their most talented case writers in operations management. With just a few exceptions, the cases in the volume are full-bodied, flesh-and-blood depictions of actual situations in a variety of manufacturing and service settings. These cases required permission for publication from the companies and managers involved. Some of the names, characters, and figures are disguised because of proprietary interests, but the points of view and stories told by these cases are true-to-life management situations filled with insights for all students of operations management.

The cases chosen for this volume are meant to appeal to the fundamental, core interests of production and operations management in both manufacturing and services businesses. This volume purposely avoids issues of new capacity, vertical integration, and manufacturing strategy that are the fortes of other casebooks. Instead, we have tried to be as nitty-gritty as possible, choosing cases designed to do well what many other casebooks either skirt or address with weaker, armchair-fabricated cases and situations. Among the issues addressed in these cases are the following:

- Analyzing processes and bottlenecks
- Understanding worker problems and incentives
- Developing and using work standards
- Redesigning processes and layouts
- Determining manpower requirements
- Planning production over extended periods of time
- Recognizing the appropriateness of various lot sizing schemes
- Scheduling production over the near term
- Assessing production control systems and improving them
- Judging the suitability of MRP systems and how they should be implemented
- Evaluating distribution systems
- Learning about statistical quality control and its effective application
- Exploring other aspects of quality management
- Assessing and justifying new production technology

The cases addressing these issues are organized into four general categories:
1. Process Analysis, Job Design, and Standards,
2. Production Planning, Scheduling, and the Management of Materials,
3. Quality Management,
4. Management of Technology.

While the cases can be used in this order, there is no need for them to follow precisely the sequence outlined in the table of contents.

PART 1

PROCESS ANALYSIS, JOB DESIGN, AND STANDARDS

Carmen Canning Company (B) (R)

In January, 1982, Mr. Thompson, general manager of the Carmen Canning Company, Ltd., Jamaica, was reviewing the past year's operations. He was particularly concerned with the can making, filling and packing departments which seemed to be limiting the capacity of the cannery. During 1981, these departments were forced to operate at more than ten overtime hours per week to meet sales demands. In addition to direct labour costs, this practice had added 35% of direct labour to overhead costs. With a forecast increase of 5% in demand for 1982, Mr. Thompson knew substantial investment in space and equipment would be required unless he could find some means to increase output from the existing facilities.

COMPANY BACKGROUND

In 1940, the Carmen Canning Company began operations with a plant in Christiana, Manchester Parish, Jamaica, an area of large fruit groves. The company was a subsidiary of International Canneries, with head offices in London, England.

The new cannery processed 60,000 cases of orange juice (four dozen 14 fl. oz. tins per case) in 1941 and employed 60 production workers. In 1942, the employees voted for representation by the Fruit Workers Union (F.W.U.). During the following eight years, the company grew slowly because of difficulties in getting adequate supplies of fresh oranges and sluggish post-war demand.

Steady expansion came in the 1950s as the Jamaican economy prospered. New equipment increased capacity and versatility. In 1953, grapefruit juice, paw-paw nectar, and mango nectar were produced for the first time. The export market proved profitable and, by 1963, production had climbed to 300,000 cases. With the exception of a few slow years, the 1960s and 1970s followed a steady growth pattern and in 1981 volume had grown to a million cases.

Past company policy had been not to lay off workers displaced by technological changes. In 1981, there were 172 production workers including 36 females. Wages were the highest paid by any company in the area, except for those paid by a bauxite company about 15 miles away. The average hourly wage at the cannery was $2.25 for men and $1.13 for women. Employees received time and a half for the first three hours of overtime each day (double time for over three hours) and a shift premium of 10 cents per hour.[1]

[1]Government regulations stipulated that female employees could not work before 6 A.M. or after 10 P.M. but could work shifts between 6 A.M. and 10 P.M. Women could only work 200 overtime hours per year unless the company requested permission from the Jamaican Ministry of Labour.

EXHIBIT 1
Product Flow

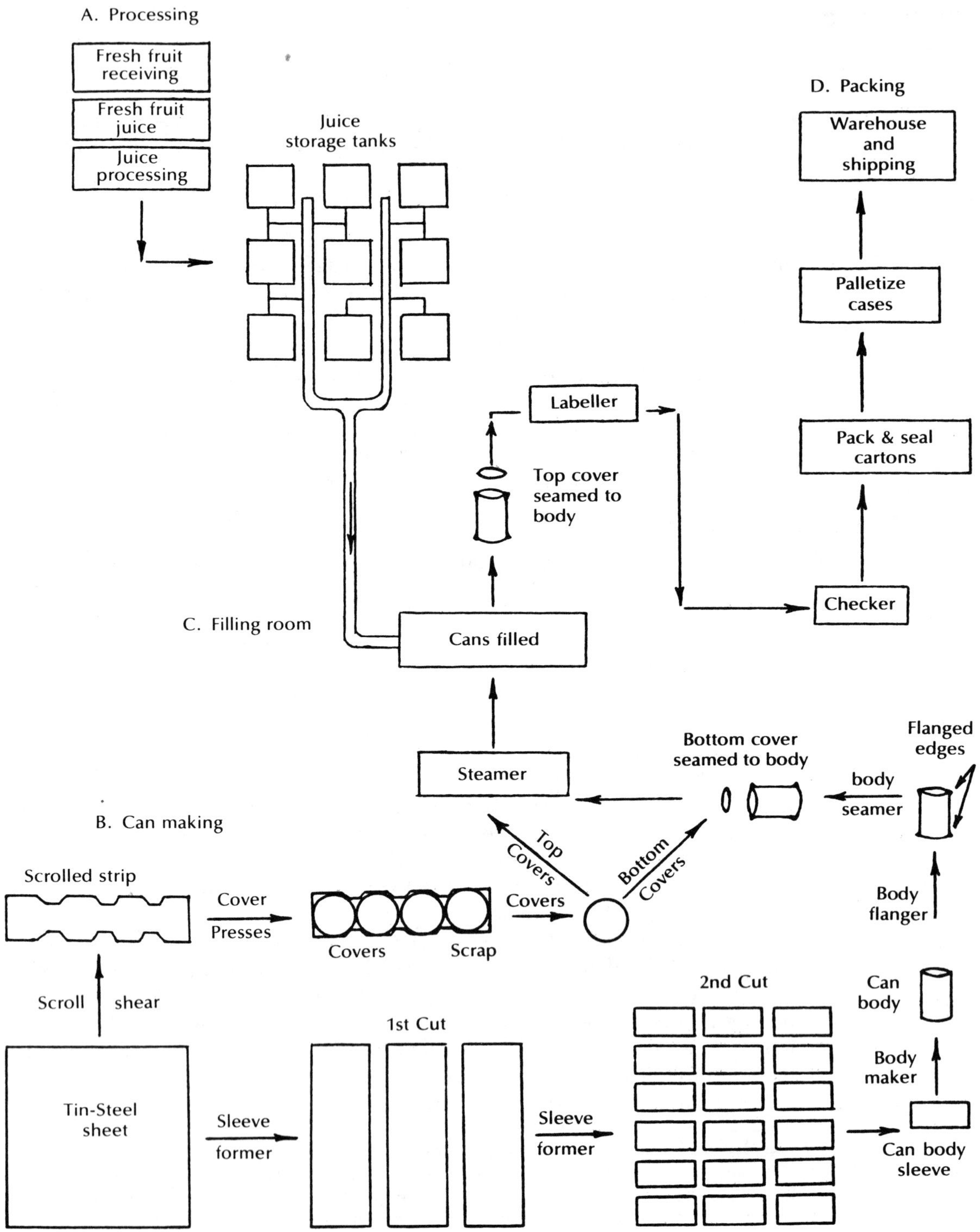

A. Processing

Fresh fruit receiving

Fresh fruit juice

Juice processing

Juice storage tanks

C. Filling room

Cans filled

Labeller

Top cover seamed to body

Steamer

Bottom cover seamed to body

body seamer

Flanged edges

Body flanger

B. Can making

Scrolled strip

Cover Presses

Covers   Scrap

Covers

Top Covers

Bottom Covers

Scroll shear

Tin-Steel sheet

Sleeve former

1st Cut

Sleeve former

2nd Cut

Can body

Body maker

Can body sleeve

D. Packing

Warehouse and shipping

Palletize cases

Pack & seal cartons

Checker

EXHIBIT 2
Work Flow in Can Making, Filling, and Packing

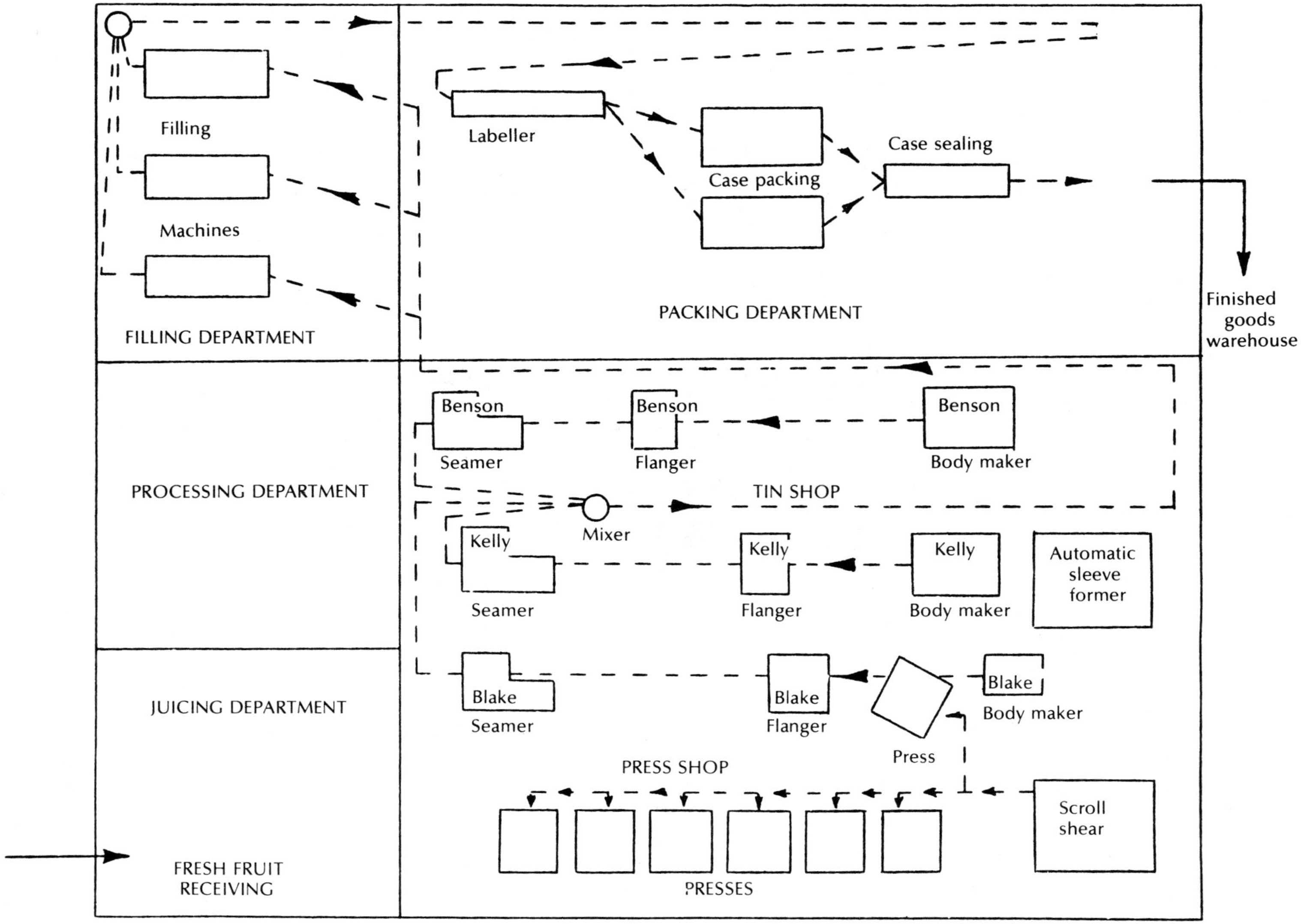

The five major production departments were juicing, processing, can making, filling and packing. Processing was the only department operating three shifts; all the others operated one eight-hour shift five days per week with overtime when necessary.

PLANT OPERATIONS

Product flow started from fruit receiving through juicing to processing and filling. In processing, nine storage tanks held juices for direct delivery to three filling machines in the filling department. An overhead conveyor carried tin cans from can making to the filling room. From the filling room, a conveyor transported the canned juices to the packing room for labelling, case packing, sealing and palletizing for delivery to the finished goods warehouse. (See Exhibit 1.) During 1981, packing room production was one million cases.

CAN MAKING

Can making was divided into two major operations: the press shop for cover punching and the tin shop for can fabrication (see Exhibits 1 and 2). In the press shop, a scroll shear cut tin-steel sheet into strips from which the seven presses punched out the covers.

In the tin shop, sheet for the can bodies was cut on the automatic sleeve former and fed into one of the three body makers (Kelly, Benson or Blake models). The body makers formed the cylindrical portion of the can. An elevator and gravity feed runway carried the bodies to the automatic flangers and a similar runway carried the bodies to the seamers (see Exhibit 3). In the flanger, the edges on both ends of the cylinder or body were turned out so that covers could be attached to the can. The seamer attached the bottom covers to the can body. The runways from each of the three seamers led to a mixing operation and a single overhead conveyor carried the cans to the filling room.

EXHIBIT 3
Can Making Conveyor System

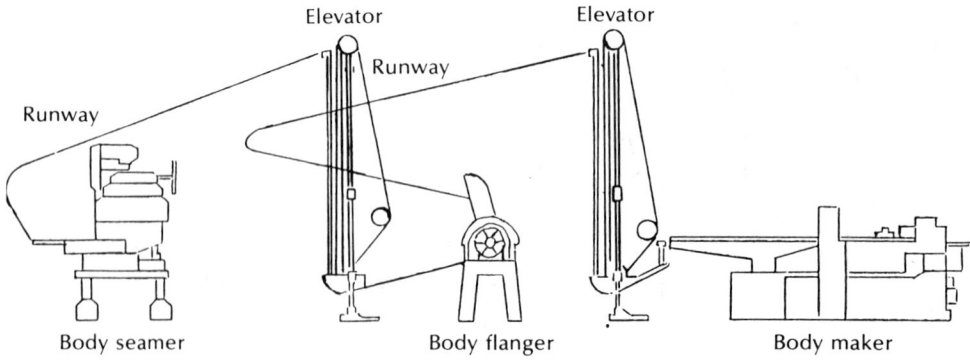

(Not to scale)

Assigned Jobs

Thirteen operators were employed in the press shop. The three male employees worked as scrap collectors (2) and mechanic (1). The ten women ran the scroll shear (2) and the presses (8). Covers were stacked in cases (53,000 covers per case). A fork lift truck operator delivered the cases to the body seamers, to the filling room or to the warehouse as production demanded. Eleven people worked

EXHIBIT 4
Can Making Equipment and Labour

Equipment		Labour		
		Employees		
Machine	Rated capacity covers/min	Male	Female	Job function
A. Press shop				
Scroll shear	20 shts/min (64 cov/sht)		2	1 to feed sheets—1 to remove strips
Presses				
1	140		2	1 to feed strips—1 to remove covers
2	140			
3	140		2	"
4	140			
5	140		2	"
6	160			
7	160		2	"
		2		Scrap collectors
		1		Mechanic
Maximum production	1,020	3	10	
B. Tin shop	*Cans/min*			
Automatic sleeve former	600		2	1 to feed sheets—1 to remove sleeves
Kelly				
Body maker	280	1		Feed body maker, check runways.
Flanger	280			
Seamer	270		1	Feed seamer, check runways.
Benson				
Body maker	200	1		Feed body maker, check runways
Flanger	200			
Seamer	190		1	Feed seamer, check runways
Blake				
Body maker	74		1	Feed body maker, check runways
Flanger	74			
Seamer	70		1	Feed seamer, check runways
			1	Add or take off cans (Ave. 48/min.)
			1	Open or close cartons
			1	Stack cartons
Maximum production	530	2	9	

in the body shop. The two men operated body makers. The women worked at the automatic sleeve former (2), body maker (1), seamers (3) and the mixer (3).

The body making operators were responsible for feeding the body sleeves and checking the elevator and runway to the automatic flanger for jams. When jams occurred, the operators either cleared the stoppage quickly or shut off the machines. Slight variations in tin-steel plate specifications forced the operators to make machine adjustments quickly to reduce the delays and maintain a steady flow of can bodies. These operators also kept an eye on the automatic flanger.

Body seaming operators fed the covers into the machine. They were also responsible for clearing jams in the runway and elevator from the flanger. If the jam could not be cleared quickly, seamer operators shut off the equipment.

A team of three mixing operators was responsible for balancing the can making delivery conveyor to the filling room. When any of the body makers or seamers slowed down or stopped, this team fed completed tins into the mixer. When a slow-down or a stop occurred in the filling department, they removed tins from the mixer. On the average, one operator could remove or add one case of 48 tins per minute while the other two operators prepared the full or empty cartons.

FILLING DEPARTMENT OPERATIONS

Filling room operations involved can sterilizing and cooling, filling and seaming, and checking (see Exhibit 5). The conveyor from the tin shop branched into three inclined lines at the filling room. As the cans passed each branch, they rolled down the incline past a set of fifteen open-flame steam jets and were immediately air-cooled before filling. Covers were similarly heated and cooled before entering the enclosed, controlled-atmosphere filling room. In the filling room, the cans were filled and sealed and the three lines again converged into a single conveyor for delivery to the packing room.

Assigned Jobs

Seven women and one man worked in the filling department. The man was responsible for general maintenance. The women sterilized top covers (2), operated the filling machines and sealers (3), checked weights (1) and checked cans for leaks (1). (See Exhibit 6.) The two sterilizer operators were also responsible for clearing the frequent jams which occurred at the open steam sterilizer. Tins became stuck on the corner of the incline leading to the jets and these operators had to leave their stations and take a wooden stick to clear the jam. This periodic stoppage prevented tins from reaching the filling room and also caused a back-up of cans into the tin shop. Normally, after two hours of operation, a filling machine was stopped, cleaned and changed over to another of the nine process storage tanks. The filling machine operator warned the mechanic a few moments ahead of time as she noticed interruptions in the incoming flow. The mechanic then prepared to close the direct feed valve. After closing this main valve, he went to the empty process storage tank, closed the out-flow valve and opened the valve on a fresh tank. In the meantime, the filling operator cleaned her machine for the next batch. This tank changeover normally took five minutes and was usually

EXHIBIT 5
Layout Filling Department and Sterilizing Equipment

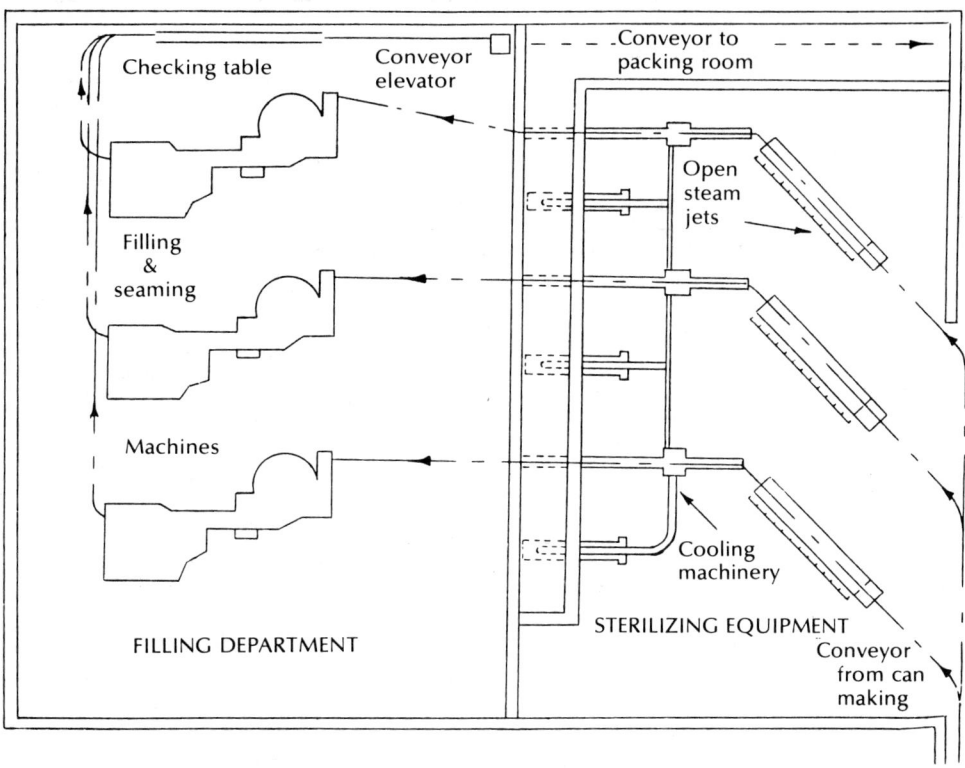

EXHIBIT 6
Filling Room Equipment and Labour

Equipment		Labour		
		Employees		
Machine	Rated capacity cans per minute	Male	Female	Job function
Sterilizer and runways			2	Feed covers to sterilizer, check jamming at can sterilizer.
Filling machine				
No. 1	170		1	Operate filler and seamer, stop
No. 2	170		1	line for tank change, clean tanks.
No. 3	170		1	
		1		Change process storage tanks plus general maintenance.
			1	Check can weight
			1	Check for leaks
Maximum production	510	1	7	

EXHIBIT 7
Packing Room Equipment and Labour

Equipment		Labour		
		Employees		
Machine	Rated capacity	Male	Female	Job function
Labelling machine	540 cans/min	1		Feed labels and glue
			1	Check labels for size and glueing, feed packing runways.
Carton packing Line No. 1	14 cs/min	1		Prepare cartons,
No. 2	14 cs/min	1		Feed cartons.
Carton sealer		2		Palletize cases
		1		Operate fork lift truck, deliver pallets to finished goods warehouse
Maximum production	540 cans/min	6	1	

EXHIBIT 9
Can Making Stoppage Analysis

Equipment studied	Stoppage elements	Missing tins machine not filled	IBID	Jamming feed	Adjust feed	Clean suction discs
Kelly Body Seamer	Number of stops	4-2 min. 180 tins	3-2 min. 135 tins	8	1	1
Capacity: 270 cans/min	Time (centi mins)	75	55	675	165	145
Study time: 90 min.	Percentage of total stops	2.8	2.0	25.2	6.2	5.4
Kelly Body Maker	Number of stops			2		
Capacity: 280 cans/min	Time (centi mins)			125		
Study time: 40 min.	Percentage of total stops			26.5		
Benson Body Maker	Number of stops			2		
Capacity: 200 cans/min	Time (centi mins)			45		
Study time: 30 min.	Percentage of total stops			9.8		
Benson Body Seamer	Number of stops	4-2 (60 tin)		2		
Capacity: 190 cans/min	Time (centi mins)	35		110		
Study time: 30 min	Percentage of total stops	4.8		15.4		

EXHIBIT 8
Conveyor Analysis Including Elevators and Machine Space

Conveyor	Length (ft)
Benson Body maker to flanger	44
Benson Flanger to seamer	44
Benson Seamer to mixer	12
Blake Body maker to flanger	30
Blake Flanger to seamer	30
Blake Seamer to mixer	20
Label machine No. 1 packer	42
No. 1 Packer to case sealer	20
Kelly Body maker to flanger	40
Kelly Flanger to seamer	40
Kelly Seamer to mixer	4
Tin shop mixer to filling department	172
Filling room mixer to label machine	164
Label machine No. 2 packer	55
No. 2 Packer to case sealer	20

NOTE: Can diameter = 3″

Change suction discs	Wrong estimation (Consequence = stop)	Elevator behind body maker	Runway to flanger	Flanger jamming	Elevator behind flanger	Runway to seamer	Seamer	Mixer	Fill room refuse acceptance	TOTALS	Percentage of machine running time
1	3	1	3		1		3	1	8		
550	35	130	70		45		180	50	505	2660	
20.4	1.3	4.9	2.6		1.7		6.8	1.9	19.0	100	29.6
			6	1					4		
			30	45					270	470	
			6.4	9.6					57.5	100	11.9
1			4						2		
115			165						135	460	
25.0			35.9						29.3	100	15.4
					1	1	1		4		
					135	10	135		305	730	
					18.4	1.4	18.4		42.0	100	24.4

confined to one machine at a time. Exhibit 6 summarizes the filling room equipment and labour.

PACKING DEPARTMENT OPERATIONS

The first operation in the packing department was labelling. (See Exhibit 2.) The cans then went up an inclined conveyor and divided into two branches, one for each packing line. The lines converged again as the filled cases were finally stacked on the pallets for delivery to the finished goods warehouse.

Assigned Jobs

Seven operators were employed in the packing department: a male label machine operator, one female checker, two male case packing operators, two male operators to palletize the cases, and one male fork-lift truck operator to transport the cases to the warehouse (see Exhibit 7).

The labelling machine operator was responsible for feeding and adjusting the pick-up tension of the machine. The quality of the locally purchased labels varied considerably, sometimes by ⅛" either under or oversize. With oversized labels, the tension feed would be too great and no labels would be picked up (too many for undersized labels). In this case, the female checker positioned beside the inclined conveyor would take off about a case of cans before informing the label machine operator. He would then stop the machine, remove the inferior labels and insert a new batch. Correct adjustment to the glue feed was also an important responsibility of the label machine operator: Too much or too little and the labels would not stick. Again, the checker would inform the label operator to make adjustments. Dust from the ink embossing and the labels also prevented the glue from sticking. At present, the quality of the glue was excellent but government policy to reduce imports and increase domestic manufacture would soon force the company to buy locally. To date, three local suppliers had been tried, but the label operator had considerable difficulty getting any of the glues to work satisfactorily. After each shift, overtime maintenance was necessary to clean the label dust from the equipment bearings and lubricate the machine.

The checker also separated the cans for delivery to the packing machines. The packing operators prepared the cardboard cartons and positioned the cases in the automatic packing machine to receive 48 cans of processed juice. Exhibit 8 summarizes conveyor lengths in the tin shop filling and packing departments.

CONCLUSION

To assist him in his analysis of can making, filling and packing departments, Mr. Thompson had a time-study man take some random studies in the can making lines and note the number of stops and the times taken with each stop (see Exhibit 9). With this information, he hoped to achieve some immediate improvements to increase efficiency and reduce costs.

CASE

2

Missanabie Mining Company (R)

In April, 1975, Mr. G.L. Hovi, the Mine Superintendent of Missanabie Mining Company, was preparing for a meeting with the Company's General Superintendent of Operations, Mr. T.L. King. Both Mr. Hovi and Mr. King were concerned about the question of handling loaded ore trucks during operating delays of the ore crusher at the mine. This was a problem that had plagued mine supervisors for several years. Mr. Hovi knew that some action was urgently required and that he would be asked for his recommendation at the forthcoming meeting.

COMPANY BACKGROUND

The Missanable Mining Company (MMC) operated a large open-pit iron-ore mine in Northern Ontario. Besides the mine itself, the Company operated an ore handling facility on Lake Superior, loading ocean-going ships and lake freighters. The mine was accessible by aircraft, railroad and by a 60 mile winter road from the Trans-Canada Highway. The region had a cool climate with snow beginning in November and disappearing in June.

The mine was located in a crescent-shaped ore deposit which is shown in Exhibit 1. Exhibit 2 shows a cross-section of the deposit and indicates how the waste was removed in order to expose the deposit itself. As excavation of the pit progressed, the principal waste-removal operations were located further and further from the actual ore deposit. As seen in the cross-section, waste removal could occur at left benches 3, 4 and 5, plus right benches 2 and 3. Ore removal, on the other hand, could only occur at bench 5 and right bench 4. An overall view of the mine is shown in Exhibit 4.

Production was scheduled on a year-round, twenty-four-hour-per-day basis to produce over 50 million tons of crude ore per year, yielding about 23 million tons of high grade concentrate. To accommodate this production, a concentrator was built with a capacity of about 2,310 cubic yards per hour. It was the policy of the mine to operate the concentrator at capacity at all times.

EXHIBIT 1
Plan of Ore Deposit, Overhead View

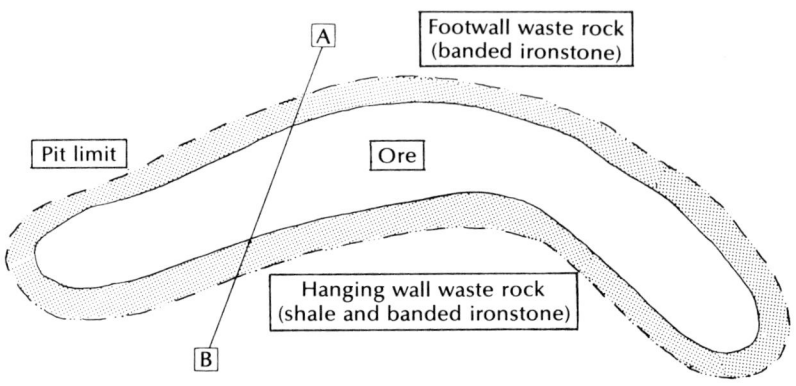

EXHIBIT 2
Cross Section A–B

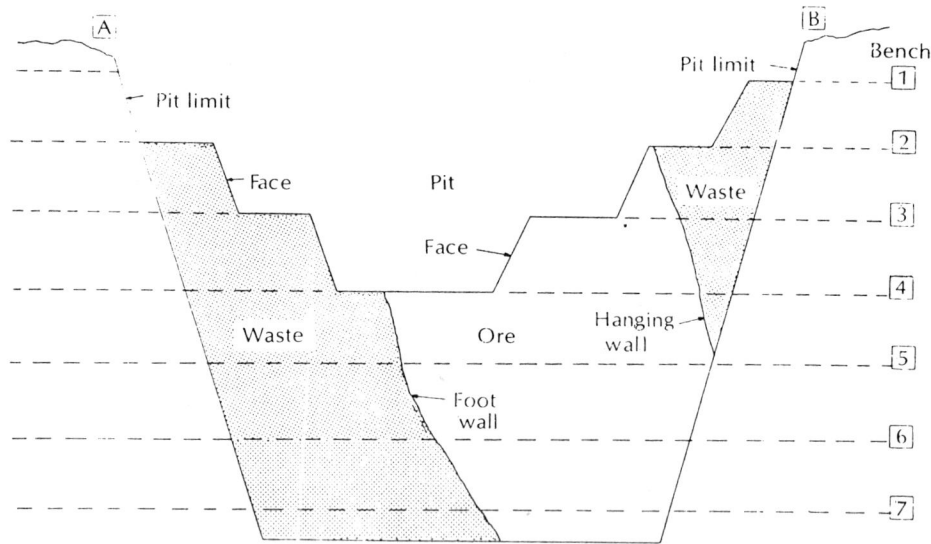

THE PRODUCTION PROCESS

The production process (Exhibit 3) began with large drills cutting forty-foot holes into the solid rock along the face of a bench. These holes were filled with an explosive slurry of ammonium nitrate and fuel oil. When the explosive charge was detonated, the solid rock shattered into forty-foot-high piles of loose material known as "muck."

EXHIBIT 3
Schematic Diagram of Production Process

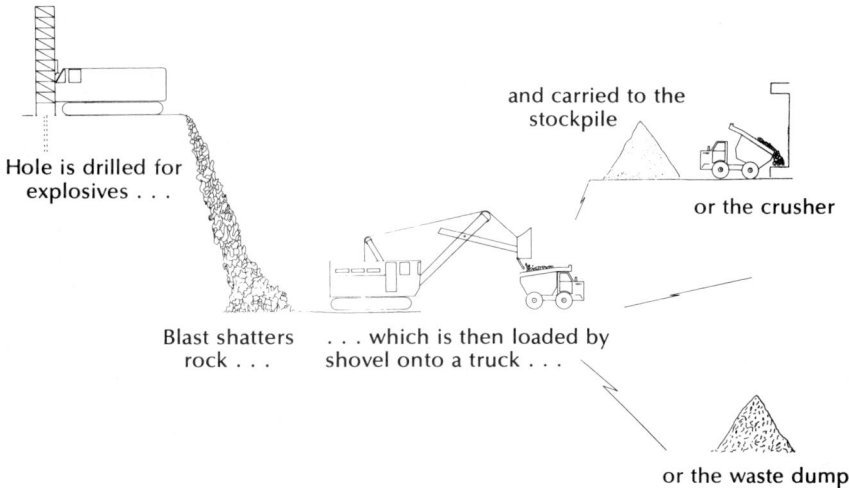

Hole is drilled for
explosives . . .

and carried to the
stockpile

or the crusher

Blast shatters
rock . . .

. . . which is then loaded by
shovel onto a truck . . .

or the waste dump

EXHIBIT 4
Overall View of the Mine

After a blast, large electric shovels moved into position to load diesel powered trucks (Exhibit 5). These hauling units carried waste material to a **waste dump** outside the mine, while ore was hauled to the crusher. Every day, about **141,000** tons of ore and about **94,000** tons of waste rock were hauled to the crusher and waste dumps respectively.

EXHIBIT 5
The Loading Operations

EXHIBIT 6
Tractor Clearing Loose "Muck" around Shovel

The ore, containing about 30% iron, entered the crusher, where large rocks were reduced in size by jaw and gyratory crushers. After being crushed, the material passed by conveyor to the concentrator where it was further ground and separated into waste tailings and 66% iron concentrate.

The concentrate thus produced was collected and loaded aboard railroad trains. After a ten-hour trip to the port facility, the train was unloaded automatically, and the ore was loaded aboard ships bound for European and North American customers.

Shovels

In 1975, MMC operated electric-powered shovels at various bench faces in the mine, with one unit assigned full time to the crude-ore stockpile. Average operating costs and capacities appear in Exhibit 7. All shovels were equipped with 15-cubic-yard-capacity buckets. Recent time studies indicated that shovels loaded an average of 627 cubic yards per hour. WHile all shovels were located in active ore or waste locations in the mine, there were usually only seven shovels available on any given shift. Unavailable shovels were usually undergoing scheduled maintenance. This maintenance rarely required more than one shift to complete. An eighth available shovel, located at the crude-ore stockpile, was an older unit with a very weak undercarriage. Mine operators had decided to retire the unit, but then resolved to use it on the stockpile where very little moving about was required.

Tractors

Tractors were assigned to operating shovels for the purpose of smoothing the loading area to reduce truck tire wear. The tractor cleared loose rock from the loading area while the shovel was waiting for trucks. (See Exhibit 6.) One tractor was also assigned to the stockpile shovel. MMC's Accounting Department assumed that this tractor worked one hour for each hour worked by the stockpile shovel, plus 1.5 minutes per load dumped on the stockpile. Appropriate hourly operating costs appear in Exhibit 7.

Trucks

MMC also owned a fleet of off-highway rear-dump trucks. Average costs, availabilities, and carrying capacities appear in Exhibit 7. Usually, four trucks were assigned to each shovel, with the remaining units undergoing preventive maintenance or repairs.

EXHIBIT 7
Average Mining Costs and Capacities

	Shovels	Tractors (one per shovel)	Trucks
Labour ($/hour)	$12.05 (12.05)*	$ 7.72 (7.72)	$ 7.72 (7.72)
Maintenance ($/hour)	63.45 (12.69)	12.25 (2.45)	12.26 (2.45)
Fuel/Electricity ($/hour)	5.34 (5.34)	5.50 (0.55)	6.50 (0.65)
Supplies ($/hour)	16.00 (3.20)	3.25 (0.65)	11.50 (2.30)
Overhead ($/hour)	3.16 (0)	2.02 (0)	2.02 (0)
TOTAL ($/hour)	$100.00 (33.28)	$30.74 (11.37)	$40.00 (13.12)
Number owned	11	N/A	41
Number available	7	N/A	28
Capacities	15 cu. yds/bucket 627 cu. yds/hour	N/A	47 cu. yds/load 168 cu. yds/hour

*Cost of idle time

During a typical operating cycle, a truck assigned to a shovel working in ore began by travelling about a mile from the crusher to the shovel-loading area at a bench face in the mine. The truck would turn at the shovel, wait for any trucks being loaded to leave, and then "spot" or back into position beside the shovel, which would then load the truck. Once his truck was loaded, the operator would leave the shovel area, turn onto the haul road and drive up out of the mine to the crusher. On arrival, he would turn, back up to one of the two open dumping lines, dump, and return to the mine.

The Crusher

The crusher was capable of handling a maximum of 10,400 tons per hour. It required an average of 1.7 minutes for each truck to dump, and two trucks could dump simultaneously into one line. The ore subsequently entered a series of jaw crushers, screens, and gyratory crushers. Because of the weight and hardness of the rock, there was considerable wear and tear on the machinery in the crusher. It was, therefore, necessary to carry out a continuing program of repairs and preventive maintenance. To this end, one crusher line was closed throughout the day shift, reducing the intake capacity of the crusher from 10,400 tons per hour to 5,200 tph. (Once loaded on a truck, one cubic yard of ore weighed 2.55 tons while one yard of waste weighed 2.00 tons.) During the afternoon and night shifts, both crusher lines remained open.

As well as the daily 8-hour shutdown for repairs and maintenance on one line, the crusher was prone to brief holdups caused by "bridging" and other operating delays. Bridging occurred when a large rock jammed between the jaws of the jaw crusher, blocking one line completely. Once a line was blocked, it would remain closed until the rock was removed or shaken loose. Delays of this nature could last from one minute to over an hour, and sometimes (very rarely) continued throughout a complete shift. During the afternoon and evening shifts, it was rare for both crusher lines to be "down" (closed) simultaneously, but during the day shift, when one line was down for maintenance, it was not uncommon to have a complete temporary shut-down while blockage of the one serviceable line was removed. Exhibit 8 shows a distribution of the duration of crusher delays during the day shift.

The Stockpile

When the mine began operations in 1970, Mr. Hovi's predecessor noted that trucks often arrived from the mine with a full load of ore only to find both crusher lines closed. Trucks then turned around and returned to the mine (a distance of about 5,000 feet) dumping the ore beside the shovel which had originally loaded it. The entire shovel-truck crew then moved from an ore zone until the crusher was re-opened. Unfortunately, it took the shovels 15 minutes to move from an ore zone to a waste zone.

Recognizing the inefficiency of this type of operation, the Superintendent decided to start a stockpile about 400 feet from the crusher, where loaded ore

EXHIBIT 8
Distribution Showing Duration of Crusher Delays During Day Shift

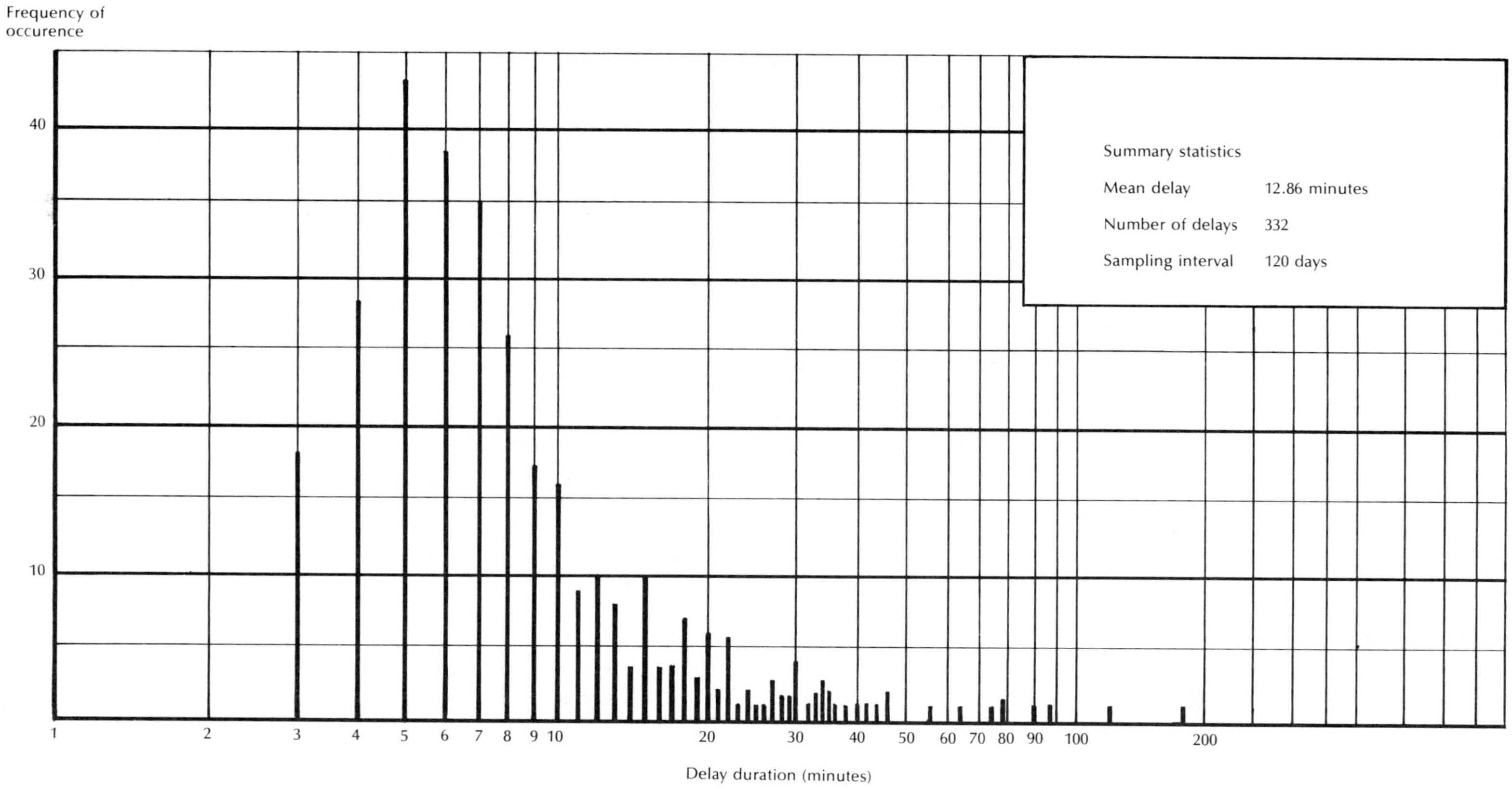
Frequency of occurence
40
30
20
10
1
2
3
4
5
6
7
8
9 10
20
30
40
50
60 70 80 90 100
200
Delay duration (minutes)
Summary statistics
Mean delay 12.86 minutes
Number of delays 332
Sampling interval 120 days

trucks could dump, rather than return loaded to the mine when the crusher was down.

For several years, this stockpile was always used whenever the crusher was down. It was thought to be cheaper to station a shovel, which would otherwise be "spare," at the stockpile, and move the ore from the stockpile to the crusher later, than send loaded ore trucks back to the mine.

In order to signal to hauling units when the crusher was closed, a flashing yellow light was located above each of the two crusher lanes. The appropriate light was turned on by the crusher dumpman when a line was closed. Seeing both yellow lights flashing, truck drivers would proceed directly to the stockpile with their loads of ore.

The time required for a loaded truck to come from a shovel in the mine, turn, and dump on the stockpile was effectively the same as the time needed to carry ore to the crusher, turn, and dump into an open line. Therefore, the cost of ore reaching the stockpile was the same as the cost of ore entering the crusher.

Any ore dumped on the stockpile, however, would ultimately have to be moved from the stockpile to the crusher. For this purpose, the electric shovel mentioned previously was stationed at the stockpile. When this shovel was not in use, it stood idle at the stockpile. Trucks could haul 330 cubic yards per hour over the short distance to the crusher. Time was spent reducing the stockpile during periods of blasting when all production trucks were moved out of the mine, and during shovel breakdowns which freed trucks. When necessary, stockpile removal could be carried out during the afternoon and night shifts.

OPERATING OPINIONS

Mr. Hovi felt that once a shovel-truck "team" began to produce, it was important that the team remain on the go. He believed that a rhythmic cycle was set up which it was undesirable to break. Workers in the mine might conceivably feel frustrated and lose enthusiasm for their work, if their cycle were periodically disrupted. Long periods of waiting at the crusher, he believed, might break the rhythm, causing a considerable reduction in efficiency and productivity in the mine. However, Mr. Hovi knew that the cost of the resulting inefficiency could not be measured accurately.

Accountants had suggested, however, that when a truck or bulldozer was forced to wait idle, the engine be slowed to reduce fuel consumption to 10% of the normal amount. Maintenance expense incurred was thought to be about 20% of normal, as was the supplies expense. A temporarily idle shovel consumed electricity at its normal rate, and incurred maintenance and supplies expenses at about 20% of normal rates. Costs of idle time are summarized in Exhibit 7.

On the other hand, Mr. Hovi wanted to use the stockpile as little as possible because of the additional cost of re-handling ore. He was aware that the Mine General Foreman might be tempted to use the stockpile during *any* crusher delay, since the Foreman was motivated to produce as many *truck trips* per shift as possible. Mr. Hovi thought that the stockpile was not necessary for providing an in-process inventory because the concentrator was equipped with twelve silos for storing crushed crude ore. These silos, holding about six hours live storage of crude ore production, could continue to supply the concentrator during long mine delays or slow-downs.

It had also been suggested that the stockpile be used for storing various grades of ore, ranging from 27% Fe to 35% Fe. The varying grades of ore could then be used for blending to maintain constant grade control of the finished concentrate. Such a practice was considered impractical because of the lag between the input of crude ore and the production of finished concentrate. However, the stockpile was useful for ensuring a continuous flow of ore to the crusher during blasting,[1] poor road conditions, and power-shovel breakdowns.

Mr. Hovi had to evaluate the courses of action open to him. He and Mr. King had agreed that there was an optimum point at which total waiting and stockpile re-handling costs would be minimized, and further agreed that the current rule failed to minimize these costs. He knew he would be called on to recommend a new plan to Mr. King.

---

[1]Blasting occurs once a day and lasts 30 to 40 minutes.

Deans Brewery (AR)

In February, 1982, Mr. Simpson, chief engineer at Deans Brewery, Trinidad, was completing the design of a new bottling line. The last remaining major issue dealt with the materials handling situation at the end of the line. Currently, the company was using manual labor to put the full cases of beer on pallets. Mr. Simpson was considering the possibility of using automatic equipment.

COMPANY BACKGROUND

Deans Brewery was located in the southern Caribbean island of Trinidad. Founded by John Deans in 1924, the company had established a high reputation. Deans beer had also become a favorite with tourists, and as a result a modest export business to the United States had started in 1959. In February, 1982, sales reached the highest level in the company's history.

Four sales peaks occurred during the year: Carnival,[1] Christmas, Easter, and Independence.[2] Carnival was the highest sales period, but each peak caused the company to operate on tight schedules during which Deans hired more labor and scheduled extra shifts.

BREWING PROCESS

Beer brewing started with extraction of sugar from malt by an enzymic process. This sugar was boiled with hops, producing a sterilized and concentrated solution. The resins extracted from the hops during boiling acted as a preservative and gave the beer its bitter flavor. The hops were then removed, and the solution was cooled to a temperature of 50°F for bottom fermentation lasting seven days, during which yeast converted the sugar to alcohol and CO_2. After fermentation the beer was cooled to 30°F and stored for ten days (during which the yeast separated out) and then roughly filtered through diatomaceous earth. After 24 hours storage it was put through a polish filtration process and was artificially carbonated ready for bottling. After bottling and case packing, the beer was stored in the finished goods warehouse ready for delivery to retail outlets.

Copyright © 1982, The University of Western Ontario and The University of the West Indies.

Case material of the Western School of Business Administration is prepared as a basis for classroom discussion. This case was prepared by Professors M.R. Leenders and J.A. Erskine.

[1]Carnival took place two days before Ash Wednesday, which normally occurs during February and occasionally in early March.

[2]Trinidad gained its independence from Britain on August 31, 1962.

CURRENT OPERATIONS IN BOTTLING AND WAREHOUSING

The bottling department and warehouse were part of the same building separated by a wire fence (see Exhibit 1). The current bottling line had a capacity of 400 bottles per minute and usually operated two eight-hour shifts, five days a week at 85-percent efficiency. For the past three months it had run at three shifts per day. This had meant that maintenance, previously done at night, had begun to interfere with production time. The third shift was difficult to staff and supervise, but the expanded bottling capacity would eliminate this need. At 1,000 bottles per minute demand could be met by a one-shift operation with occasional overtime.

The last operation on the current bottling line was the manual stacking of full cases (24 bottles per case) on wooden pallets. Each case weighed 45 pounds, and each pallet held 40 cases (5 layers high of 8 cases per layer). Two men were employed at this task; normally it took 7½ seconds to load each case. Each man loaded his own pallet and earned $120.00 a week.

Currently two fork lifts carried the full pallets to the warehouse where they were stacked three high. The company owned 12 fork lifts and usually had at least two in the repair shop at any one time. The warehouse (ceiling height 15½ ft.) had four storage bays in total, and usually two were being unloaded while the other two were being loaded. Space was reasonably plentiful except before peak sales periods when extra pallets were stacked in the aisles for inventory build-up.

EXHIBIT 1
Warehouse Layout Showing Proposed Automatic Palletizing System

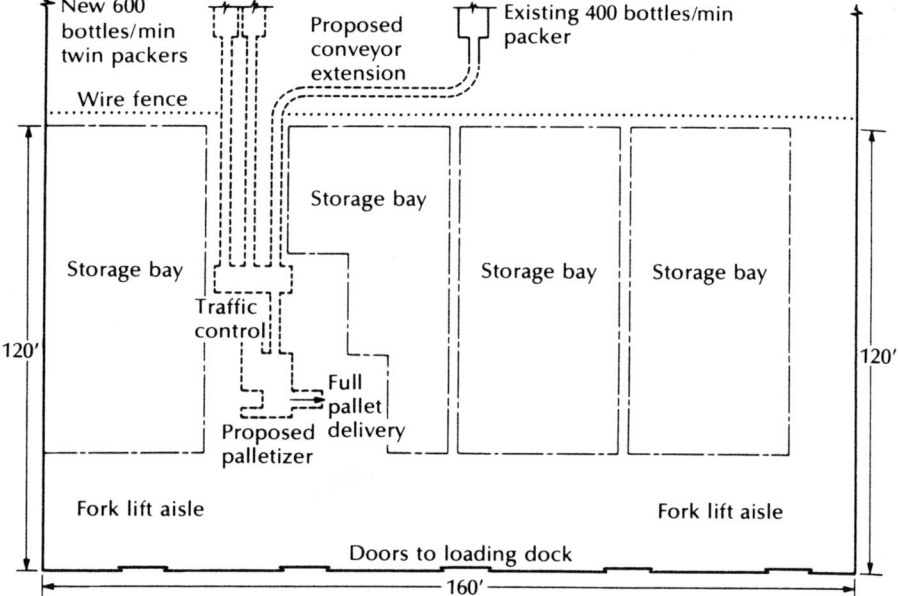

NEW BOTTLING LINE

The bottling line which Mr. Simpson had designed called for major changes in the bottling shop. Line capacity was to be increased by 600 bottles per minute with the addition of twin packers which would unload onto two exit conveyors. Aside from this, a new empty bottle conveyor feed-in system was planned and would occupy all existing space between the bottling shop and the warehouse. As a result it would be necessary to move the unloading and palletizing operation into the warehouse. (See Exhibit 1.) The required conveyor system from the three bottling lines to the warehouse for hand loading of pallets would cost $54,000 including installation. One advantage of the move to the warehouse was the shortening of the fork lift route. Mr. Simpson calculated that turnaround time from the new location would range from 35 seconds to 3 minutes and would probably average 1 minute.

AUTOMATIC PALLETIZER

Mr. Simpson was considering the possibility of substituting an automatic palletizer for the hand loading operation in the new location (see Exhibit 2). The machine's operation was similar in concept to the manual loading procedure. It would take eight cases at a time and feed them onto the pallet in a predetermined pattern. The pallet was then lowered for the next layer. The full pallet was put onto the discharge conveyor which could hold up to three full pallets. The machine required one operator whose primary function was to make sure the machine shut off in case of trouble and to clear jams if they occurred at the feed-in point. He would probably be paid $150.00 per week. The palletizer would require a different feed-in system from manual loading because of the counting operation and machine height.

EXHIBIT 2
Automatic Palletizer Pallet Stacking Pattern

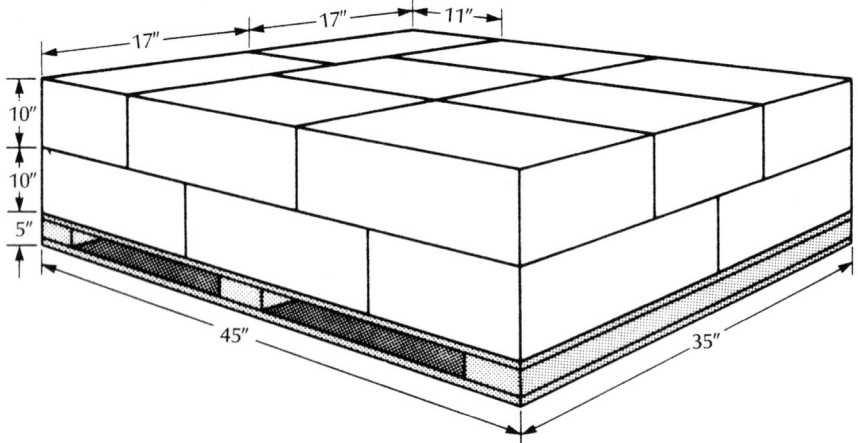

Mr. Simpson was considering two different makes of equipment, Perrin and Clark. He had received literature on both and had talked with sales representatives and also with executives in North American breweries. He was not sure how to choose between the two makes. Mr. Simpson wanted a palletizer which could handle 45 cases per minute, operate on a 50-Hz electrical supply, load at least 40 cases per pallet and have a stacking pattern identical to the present system. Both Perrin and Clark sales representatives said they could produce satisfactory equipment.

Perrin Conveyors, Ltd., was a Canadian subsidiary of an American firm. It handled all Canadian and Commonwealth sales and operated relatively autonomously from its parent. For over 50 years Perrin had enjoyed a high reputation for its conveyor systems which were light, easy to install, durable, and efficient. An additional feature was the ready convertibility of all conveyors to any of three basic types—live roller, gravity, or belt. Perrin had designed and manufactured many of the conveyor systems for Canadian grain handling and mineral processing installations. Perrin manufactured a variety of materials handling equipment including palletizers, although it had never built one which met all of Mr. Simpson's specifications. Maximum capacity was determined by the number of cases the machine could handle in a given amount of time, and Perrin had never manufactured a unit faster than 40 cases per minute. In answer to Mr. Simpson's request, Perrin had said they would design a machine especially for him, which could handle 45 cases per minute and stack five, six, or seven layers high with 8 cases per layer. The machine would be strictly mechanical, consisting of gears, belts, etc., and would not require a foundation of any sort. It would require an air line at a pressure of 120 psi. which exceeded the 90 psi. in the current general shop lines, and, therefore, a separate small compressor would have to be added at a cost of about $1,200. Perrin would supply a skilled technician for ten days to help with installation after delivery. The equipment would carry a standard guarantee of one year. Deans Brewery had purchased Perrin conveyors in the past and had been fully satisfied. Perrin's quotation for the palletizer was $162,000,[3] including the air compressor.

Clark Loading Systems was an American company of high reputation in the palletizer field. It could supply a standard model which met all of Mr. Simpson's specifications and could stack five, six or seven layers high. The Clark palletizer would be hydraulic, with few mechanical parts, requiring a 12-foot hole in the floor for the piston in the pallet lift. The general shop air line pressure would be sufficient for the machine. Service and guarantee terms would be the same as Perrin's. Clark also manufactured conveyors which tended to be heavier, bulkier, and more difficult to install than Perrin's but which also enjoyed an excellent reputation for quality and durability. Clark quoted a price of $204,000 for the palletizer.

If Mr. Simpson decided to use an automatic loader, he would have to combine

---

[3] All prices quoted represent landed cost to Deans, including freight and duty but not including installation.

the three exit lines into one line for delivery into the loader. He had asked both Perrin and Clark to quote on a traffic control system to join the lines. This system would have to jockey the cases into the single line and automatically count eight cases for delivery to the loader for each layer on the pallet.

Clark indicated that a traffic control unit would cost $36,000, plus $30,000 for conveyors leading from the end of the bottling lines to the control unit and from the unit to the loader. Perrin quoted $36,000 for the control and $24,000 for the conveyors.

Two mechanics would have to be trained to service a loader, and Mr. Simpson felt training could be done when one of the suppliers' technicians was at Deans for installation and start-up. A palletizer was not a complex machine and servicing should not be difficult for a skilled mechanic. Spare parts would be available from the makers, but with normal maintenance, costs would be negligible. Mr. Simpson felt that two of the mechanics already employed to service the bottling shop at about $180 per week could be trained to handle a palletizer as part of their regular duties.

Both palletizers under consideration would require electric power from lines extended into the warehouse from the bottling department. Each palletizer had a 12.75 h.p. motor; power consumption would probably cost $1,500 per year.

Installation costs would be substantial for either palletizer-conveyor system. Mr. Simpson estimated that a total Perrin System with traffic control could be installed by a local engineering contractor for $45,000. A complete Clark system would require $54,000.

Mr. Simpson wondered if he should change to a seven-layer pallet if an automatic palletizer were purchased, but he was not sure how he could quantify the advantages and disadvantages of such a move. In any case he wanted to find the best system possible for handling finished goods. Mr. Simpson was concerned about his lack of familiarity with this kind of equipment, but he realized he could not turn easily for help elsewhere. It had been standard practice at Deans Brewery to justify certain investments on the basis of meeting future demand. These investments would also have to show a reasonable return in the long run.

Marriott In-Flite Services Division

It was a warm June day in Washington, D.C. and Marv Thorenstein was trying to keep his mind on the problem at hand, and not on the fact that the air conditioner was malfunctioning. Marv was an MBA summer intern with the In-Flite Services Division of the Marriott Corporation. He had just completed a month-long study of Shoppe #060, an airline catering kitchen operated by the Division at Baltimore-Washington International Airport (BWI). The study was part of the Resource Management Program that had recently been instituted by upper management of In-Flite Services. Marv's boss, Bill Valenti, was the Director of the program. Mr. Valenti was expecting by the end of the week a report from Marv on the daily operations of Shoppe #060, including any specific recommendations that Marv might have concerning increased productivity.

CORPORATE HISTORY

In Washington, D.C. in 1927, J. Willard Marriott and his wife Alice opened a nine-seat root beer stand named the Hot Shoppe. From this humble beginning, the present day Marriott Corporation evolved to include three major business units which provided 92% of the sales in 1980: Hotels, Restaurants, and the Contract Food Services of which In-Flight Services was a portion. Additionally, the firm owned and operated two amusement parks and a cruise line. In 1980, the corporation had sales of over $1.5 billion, a 21% increase over the previous year.

IN-FLITE SERVICES DIVISION

The airline catering business was begun in 1937 when J. Willard Marriott contracted with Eastern, American, and Capital Airlines to provide box lunches to their passengers departing Washington, D.C. Hot meals soon appeared which were kept warm by a heated brick and the airline catering industry was on its way. In 1980, the Marriott In-Flite Service Division was the largest independent airline food caterer in the world, servicing over 100 different airlines on four continents with 43 domestic In-Flite kitchens and 20 foreign catering operations. Eastern Airlines was the largest single account for U.S. operations, with Delta and American not far behind.

Copyright © 1985 by the Colgate Darden Business School Sponsors, University of Virginia, Charlottesville, Virginia. Reproduced by permission.

This case was prepared by John M. McCahon and revised by G. Steven Waters and R.D. Martin under the supervision of Professor Edward W. Davis.

Each of the 43 In-Flite kitchens in the U.S. was run as a profit center by a general manager, who ensured the correct preparation of airline menus by his catering operation. Each airline specified the type of meal or snack and its preparation in terms of quality and quantity. Specifications were maintained by each airline catering guide and updated periodically. Quality control was maintained by Marriott supervisors as well as periodic kitchen inspections by airline food service representatives. Also, passenger or flight attendant complaints concerning badly prepared food or missing meal tray items were investigated by airline food service representatives. If a departing flight was delayed due to meal catering, the airline could charge the In-Flite kitchen for lost time at the departure gate, which could amount to thousands of dollars per flight-hour.

Although individual contracts for airline food service were negotiated by a marketing department within the division, it was each general manager's responsibility to keep his kitchen's operations at the highest quality and service level possible. The importance of high quality and good service was underscored by the fact that an airline could cancel a contract for a particular location with only 30 days notice.

Each general manager's performance was judged by comparing his annual budget with yearly financial results. The three major areas of concern for management were food and labor costs (comprising 75% of total costs), and other non-food controllable costs such as gasoline, uniforms, and utilities. The domestic catering operations were divided into seven regions with each supervised by a regional vice-president who in turn reported to the In-Flite Services Division vice-president at corporate headquarters in Washington, D.C.

RESOURCE MANAGEMENT PROGRAM

The Resource Management Program was initiated in November, 1978 by the In-Flite Service Division in an effort to halt the decline in profit margins caused by rapidly inflating food and labor costs. The purpose of the program was to achieve increased productivity for each catering operation by analyzing daily work operations, identifying idle time that could be effectively utilized, and then streamlining operations with no decrease in the expected service level. Streamlining of operations could be accomplished by the elimination of work positions if an employee in another position could assume the added workload, or by an increase in productivity due to automation. As a summer intern in the Resource Management Program, Marv's efforts were focused in this area.

SHOPPE #060, BWI AIRPORT

Shoppe #060 serving the Baltimore-Washington International Airport (BWI) was typical of one of Marriott's smaller domestic airline catering operations. There were nearly 100 full-time employees at the In-Flite kitchen which operated seven days a week (part-time workers were not used). As of May, 1980, the weekly total of flights catered by the kitchen was roughly 300. Weekly gross sales figures averaged $80,000 (a compilation of charges for food, beverages, and delivery of the items to the airplane). In addition, fees were charged for the cleaning of

EXHIBIT 1
Organization of Shoppe #060

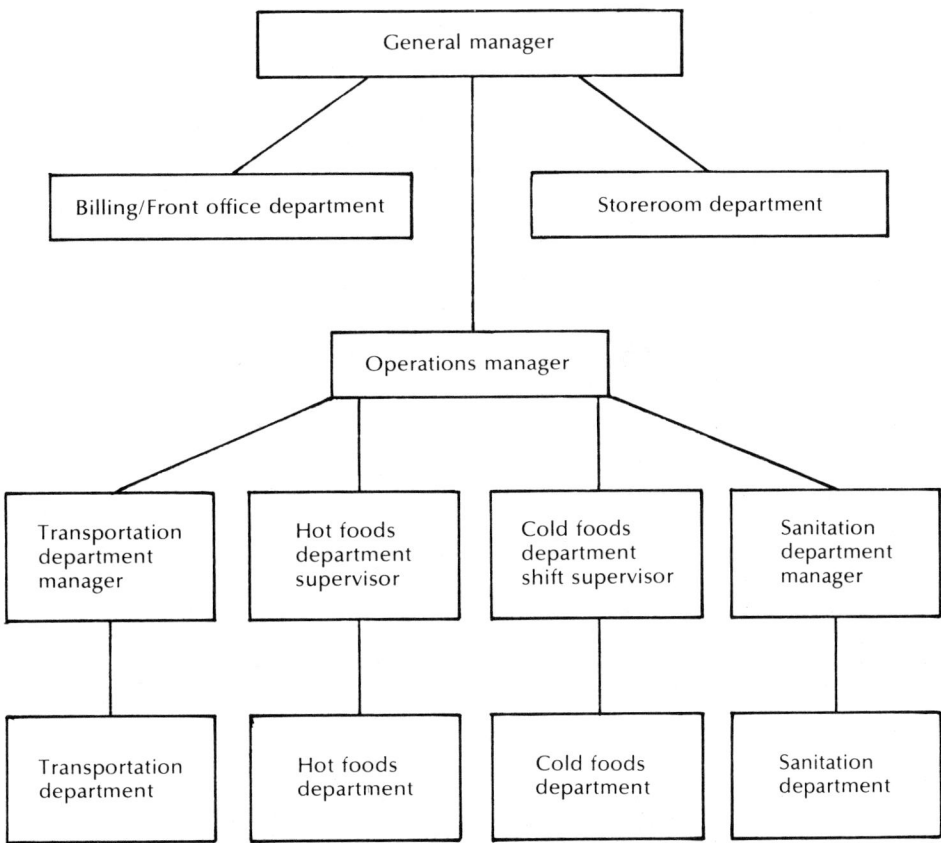

reuseable food service items (trays, etc.). In-Flite kitchen operations were divided into six activities overseen by the general manager and an assistant, the operations manager. The six activities were: Transportation, Hot Foods, Cold Foods, Sanitation, Storeroom, and Administration/Billing. Exhibit 1 shows the managerial organization of the kitchen.

Due to the short time available to spend on the project at BWI, Marv chose to restrict his analysis to the Transportation and Cold Foods Departments—the two largest in terms of number of employees and opportunities for improvement. A brief description of the two departments follows.

TRANSPORTATION DEPARTMENT

The Transportation Department was responsible for the delivery and loading of meals and snacks to BWI outbound flights, and the unloading of dirtied reuseable food service equipment from inbound flights. Under the supervision of the trans-

EXHIBIT 2
Organizational Chart—Transportation Department—Shoppe #060

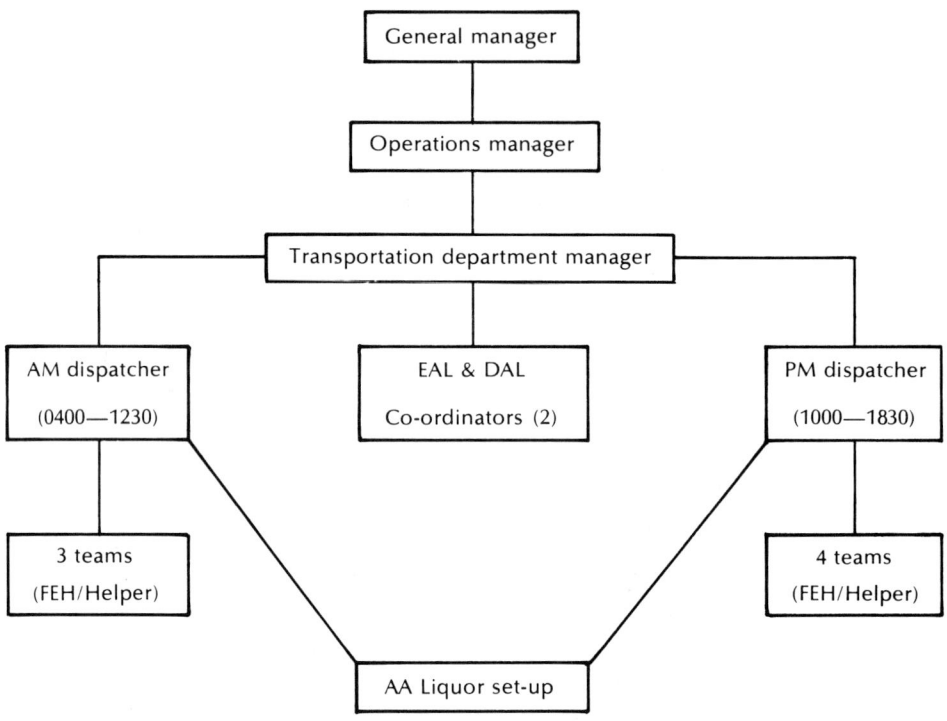

portation manager, there were seven teams composed of one food and equipment handler (FEH) and one helper. Each team worked an 8½ hour shift including a 45 minute lunch break and each worker was paid for eight hours per shift. In addition there was a dispatcher at the kitchen who ensured that the teams left for the airfield on time and with the proper number of meals requested by the airline. There were also two coordinators, one for Eastern flights and one for Delta, who supervised those airline's catering operations. Exhibit 2 contains an organization chart for the Transportation Department.

The FEH and helper positions were the highest paid in the kitchen ($7.51 average hourly wage and benefit rate), due to the heavy responsibility of maneuvering their delivery trucks alongside a multi-million dollar aircraft. (See Exhibit 3.) In order to service the airliner through the galley hatch, the body of the truck was hydraulically raised to hatch level and meals were transferred. Prior to departing the kitchen to cater assigned flights, each of the seven teams was required to set up these flights. This function entailed the bagging of ice cubes, assembly of specified amounts of beer and wine, coffee, milk, orange juice, and creamers, and a double check that meals were ready to be transported. Normally, this activity took no longer than 30 minutes, except in the case of wide-body jets (such as DC-

EXHIBIT 3

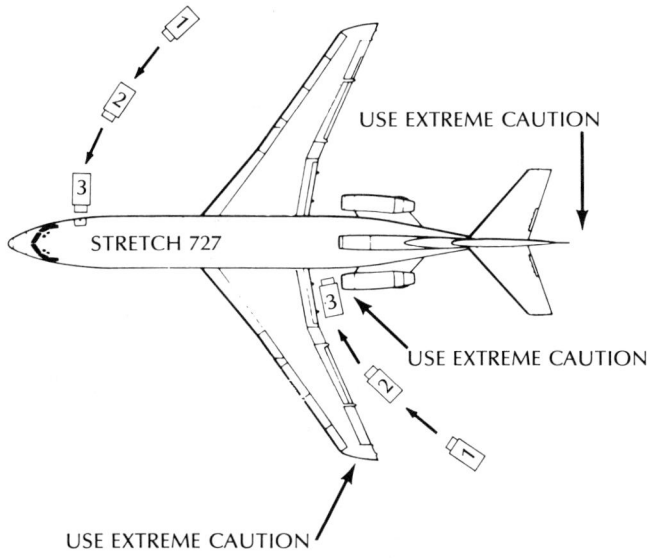

USE EXTREME CAUTION

STRETCH 727

USE EXTREME CAUTION

USE EXTREME CAUTION

10 and American 747 flights) where it could take as long as one hour. Often, the FEH and helper would set up two or more flights at one time, then transport the trays out to several planes in one trip. This resulted in batching efficiencies that reduced average setup time, and also reduced some of the travel time for driving from the kitchen to the airfield.

COLD FOODS DEPARTMENT

The Cold Foods Department was responsible for the preparation and the packing of all cold snacks, salads, fruit plates, and desserts specified by the airlines' menus. Various shifts of 8 or 8½ hours were worked in the department. Each shift included a 30 minute lunch break and another 15 minute break. Employees were paid for 7½ or 8 hours depending on the length of the shift.

Exhibit 4 is a bar chart of the activities performed by each worker on each shift. As shown in Exhibit 4, each shift contained some workers who staffed one or more packing belts. Each packing belt was a straight conveyor line at which three or four workers set up and loaded individual meal trays with cups, silverware, salads, rolls, butter, and desserts prior to loading onto a meal carrier for transportation to the aircraft. Four belts were used for tourist class flights, with an additional belt used exclusively for the first class trays. Each shift had a floor supervisor and a lead person who filled in wherever the need was greatest.

ANALYSIS OF SHOPPE #060 OPERATIONS

In his analysis of the Transportation Department, Marv first compiled a chart to determine how long it should take an FEH and helper to cater each of six different

EXHIBIT 4

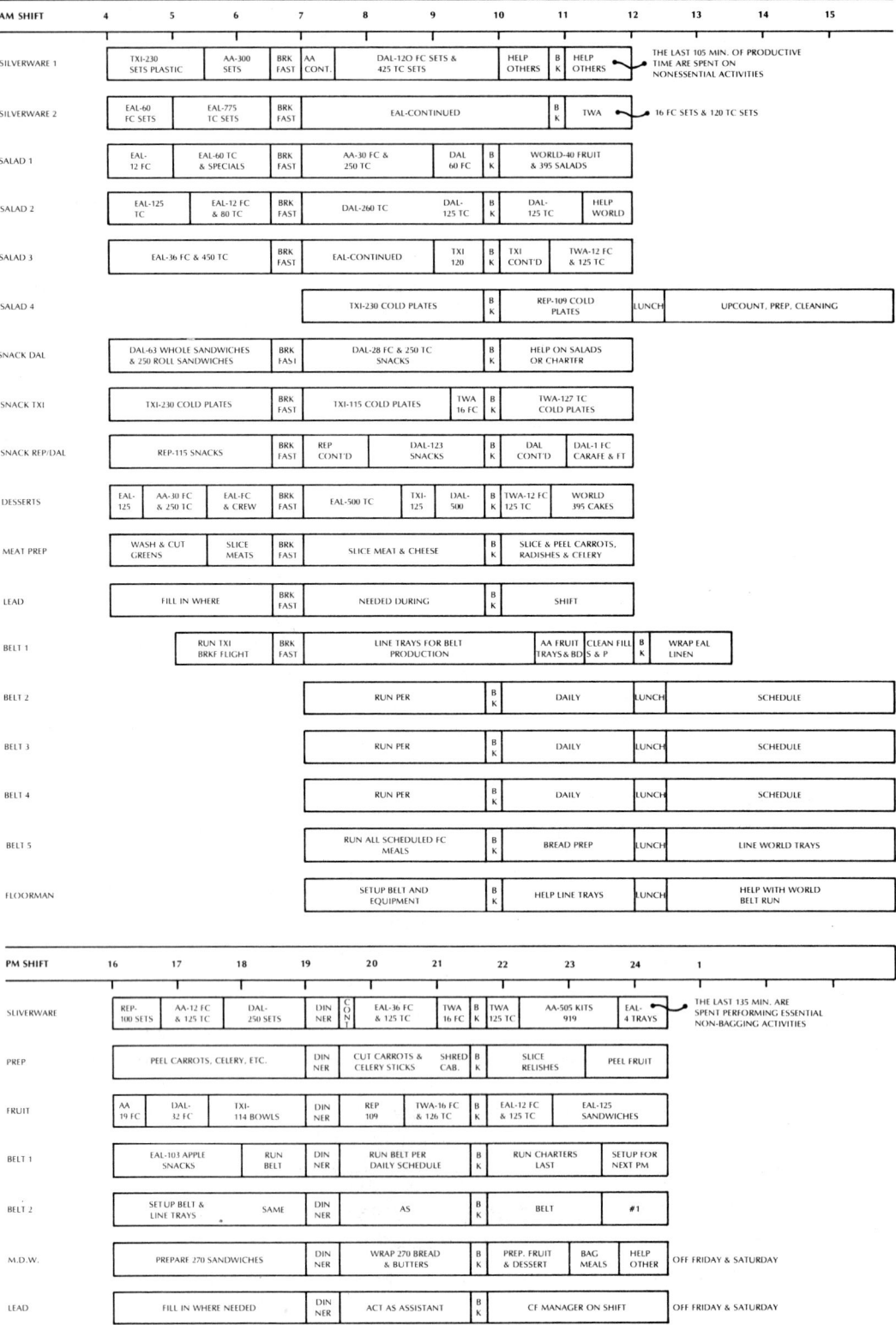

AM SHIFT	4	5	6	7	8	9	10	11	12	13	14	15
SILVERWARE 1	TXI-230 SETS PLASTIC	AA-300 SETS	BRK FAST	AA CONT.	DAL-120 FC SETS & 425 TC SETS		HELP OTHERS	B K	HELP OTHERS	THE LAST 105 MIN. OF PRODUCTIVE TIME ARE SPENT ON NONESSENTIAL ACTIVITIES		
SILVERWARE 2	EAL-60 FC SETS	EAL-775 TC SETS	BRK FAST	EAL-CONTINUED				B K	TWA	16 FC SETS & 120 TC SETS		
SALAD 1	EAL-12 FC	EAL-60 TC & SPECIALS	BRK FAST	AA-30 FC & 250 TC		DAL 60 FC	B K	WORLD-40 FRUIT & 395 SALADS				
SALAD 2	EAL-125 TC	EAL-12 FC & 80 TC	BRK FAST	DAL-260 TC		DAL-125 TC	B K	DAL-125 TC	HELP WORLD			
SALAD 3	EAL-36 FC & 450 TC		BRK FAST	EAL-CONTINUED		TXI 120	B K	TXI CONT'D	TWA-12 FC & 125 TC			
SALAD 4				TXI-230 COLD PLATES			B K	REP-109 COLD PLATES	LUNCH	UPCOUNT, PREP, CLEANING		
SNACK DAL	DAL-63 WHOLE SANDWICHES & 250 ROLL SANDWICHES		BRK FAST	DAL-28 FC & 250 TC SNACKS			B K	HELP ON SALADS OR CHARTER				
SNACK TXI	TXI-230 COLD PLATES		BRK FAST	TXI-115 COLD PLATES		TWA 16 FC	B K	TWA-127 TC COLD PLATES				
SNACK REP/DAL	REP-115 SNACKS		BRK FAST	REP CONT'D	DAL-123 SNACKS		B K	DAL CONT'D	DAL-1 FC CARAFE & FT			
DESSERTS	EAL-125	AA-30 FC & 250 TC	EAL-FC & CREW	BRK FAST	EAL-500 TC	TXI-125	DAL-500	B K	TWA-12 FC 125 TC	WORLD 395 CAKES		
MEAT PREP	WASH & CUT GREENS	SLICE MEATS	BRK FAST	SLICE MEAT & CHEESE			B K	SLICE & PEEL CARROTS, RADISHES & CELERY				
LEAD	FILL IN WHERE		BRK FAST	NEEDED DURING			B K	SHIFT				
BELT 1		RUN TXI BRKF FLIGHT		BRK FAST	LINE TRAYS FOR BELT PRODUCTION			AA FRUIT TRAYS & BD	CLEAN FILL S & P	B K	WRAP EAL LINEN	
BELT 2				RUN PER			B K	DAILY		LUNCH	SCHEDULE	
BELT 3				RUN PER			B K	DAILY		LUNCH	SCHEDULE	
BELT 4				RUN PER			B K	DAILY		LUNCH	SCHEDULE	
BELT 5				RUN ALL SCHEDULED FC MEALS			B K	BREAD PREP		LUNCH	LINE WORLD TRAYS	
FLOORMAN				SETUP BELT AND EQUIPMENT			B K	HELP LINE TRAYS		LUNCH	HELP WITH WORLD BELT RUN	

PM SHIFT	16	17	18	19	20	21	22	23	24	1
SLIVERWARE	REP-100 SETS	AA-12 FC & 125 TC	DAL-250 SETS	DIN NER	C O N T	EAL-36 FC & 125 TC	TWA 16 FC	B K	TWA 125 TC	AA-505 KITS 919	EAL-4 TRAYS	THE LAST 135 MIN. ARE SPENT PERFORMING ESSENTIAL NON-BAGGING ACTIVITIES
PREP	PEEL CARROTS, CELERY, ETC.			DIN NER	CUT CARROTS & CELERY STICKS	SHRED CAB.	B K	SLICE RELISHES	PEEL FRUIT	
FRUIT	AA 19 FC	DAL-32 FC	TXI-114 BOWLS	DIN NER	REP 109	TWA-16 FC & 126 TC	B K	EAL-12 FC & 125 TC	EAL-125 SANDWICHES	
BELT 1	EAL-103 APPLE SNACKS		RUN BELT	DIN NER	RUN BELT PER DAILY SCHEDULE		B K	RUN CHARTERS LAST	SETUP FOR NEXT PM	
BELT 2	SETUP BELT & LINE TRAYS	SAME		DIN NER	AS		B K	BELT	#1	
M.D.W.	PREPARE 270 SANDWICHES			DIN NER	WRAP 270 BREAD & BUTTERS		B K	PREP. FRUIT & DESSERT	BAG MEALS	HELP OTHER	OFF FRIDAY & SATURDAY
LEAD	FILL IN WHERE NEEDED			DIN NER	ACT AS ASSISTANT		B K	CF MANAGER ON SHIFT		OFF FRIDAY & SATURDAY

EXHIBIT 5
Times to Strip Old Equipment and Load New Equipment on A/C—Shoppe #060-BAL

	S&L	Load only	Strip only
Delta			
DC-9	25 min.	15 min.	15 min.
727-S	25 min.	15 min.	15 min.
Eastern			
DC-9	15 min.	10 min.	10 min.
727	20 min.	15 min.	15 min.
727-S	25 min.	20 min.	20 min.
American			
707	45 min.	25 min.	25 min.
TWA			
707	40 min.	25 min.	25 min.
727-S	30 min.	20 min.	20 min.
Republic			
DC-9	20 min.	—	—
Ozark			
DC-9	20 min.	15 min.	15 min.
Texas Intl.			
DC-9	—	—	—
World			
DC-10	50 min.	40 min.	40 min.
Air Florida			
727	25 min.	—	—
American Eagle			
DC-8	50 min.	—	—

types of aircraft that flew into BWI (Exhibit 5). This chart used established time standards and was organized by different seating and galley configurations for each airline. Using the catering times and the daily team schedule (excerpt shown in Exhibit 6), Marv next constructed a bar chart of the daily activities of each team (Exhibit 7). Included on the chart when necessary were a ten-minute drive from the kitchen to the airfield, a ten-minute drive between planes, and flight set up times. The chart accurately represented the current team schedule, but Marv knew that airlines made minor flight schedule changes almost every month and major schedule changes quarterly, so any schedule he could devise would only be in effect for a relatively short time. Marv wanted to determine if the existing catering schedule could be accomplished with fewer than seven teams without incurring additional overtime costs or delayed flights while allowing for a flexible response to late arriving flights. Instead of immediately creating a new schedule, Marv wanted to look at each team's idle time to determine if one or more teams could be eliminated. He used the bar chart of daily activities to compile a table of idle times for each team on a daily basis (Exhibit 8); he thought this information would help him determine the answer to his question. Management felt that up to thirty minutes idle time per shift might be required for flexibility in responding to airline schedule variations, and present labor contracts specified that no more than eight hours of overtime could be scheduled per employee each week.

EXHIBIT 6
Transportation Department Team Daily Schedules—Shoppe #060

	Airline	FLT #	ETA	ETD	Frequency	A/C	Task/service
Team #1							
0400-	Delta	152	0215	Term	Daily	727-S	Strip
	Delta	106	Orig	0700	Daily	727-S	Load
	Delta	138	Orig	0720	Daily	727-S	Load
	Eastern	631	Orig	0800	Daily	DC-9	Load
	Republic	367	0738	0820	Daily	DC-9	Strip & Load
	Delta	203	1010	1040	Daily	727-S	Strip & Load
	Delta	1717	Orig	1159	Daily	DC-9	Load
Team #2							
0500-1330	Eastern	385	Orig	0645	Daily	727	Load
	Eastern	983	0704	0735	Sat.-Only	727-S	Strip & Load
	Texas Intl.	751	Orig	0750	Daily	DC-9	Drop Off @ TXI
	Eastern	947	Orig	0915	Daily	727-S	Load
	Air Florida	Charter	0940	1020	Sat.-Only	727	Strip & Load
	Eastern	147	Orig	1036	Daily	DC-9	Load
	Eastern	291	1259	1325	Daily	DC-9	Strip & Load
Team #3							
0500-1330	American	207	Orig	0745	Daily	707	Load
	TWA	025	Orig	0800	X-Sun	727-S	Load
	World	14	0735	0835	Daily	DC-10	Strip & Load
	Eastern	173	0936	1049	Daily	727-S	Strip & Load
	American Eagle	Charter	1005	1200	Wed.-Only	DC-8	Strip & Load
	Delta	130	1052	1117	Daily	727-S	Strip & Load
	Eastern	809	1159	1224	Daily	727-S	Strip & Load

While evaluating the team workload situation, Marv knew he must consider some external factors. First, any decision he made should not lead to delayed flights. Under their service contract, which was extended on a yearly basis, any costs incurred from flight delays caused by the transportation department would be charged to Marriott. Currently the cost of a delayed flight could be as much as $5,000/hour. In addition to the threat of added costs, Marv had to consider labor issues. Shoppe #060 was a non-union shop, but he had heard that one kitchen in Boston had recently unionized.

In the Cold Foods Department, Marv was particularly interested in silverware bagging activities. As Exhibit 4 shows, the two silverware bagging positions on the A.M. shift bagged 1,095 and 971 sets of silverware per day. The actual time spent to bag the sets was 330 and 435 minutes, respectively. The P.M. shift position bagged 789 sets per day in 330 minutes. On this basis, the baggers' production rates appeared to be considerably less than the standard rate of 4 sets per minute. This standard had been set several years earlier by division staff personnel based on time studies and management expectations. Marv wondered what the overall labor savings would be if the standard rate could be achieved. He noted that the average hourly wage and benefit rate was $5.73 in the Cold Foods Department.

EXHIBIT 7

Marriott In-Flite Services Division—Transportation Department Team Schedules (Bar Charts)

HOURS

4	5	6	7	8	9	10	11	12	13	14	15	16	17	18	19	20	21	22	23	24

TEAM

1 — DAL | SET-UP | DAL | EAL | REP | SET-UP | DAL | DAL | LUNCH
152 727-S S | 106; 138; 367 | 106; 138 727-S L | 631 DC-9 L | 367 S¦L | 203; 1717 ALSO, AIR FLA. CHARTER. SAT ONLY | 203 727-S L | 1717 DC-9 S¦L

2 — SET-UP | EAL | TXI | EAL | SET-UP | EAL | S-U | FLA. | EAL | LUNCH | S-U | EAL
386; 751; 983 SAT ONLY | 386; 751 727 L DO | 767 DC-9 | 983 727-S S¦L SAT ONLY | 947 727-S L | 947 S¦L SAT ONLY | 147 QUART. 727 S¦L | 147 DC-9 L | 281 DC-9 S¦L

3 — SET-UP | AA | TWA | WORLD | S-U | AA | DAL | S-U | EAL | LUNCH
207, 015, 17 | 207 707 L (X-SUN) | 015 727-S L | 14 DC-10 S¦L WED. | 173; 130 ALSO AHLEG WED. | 173 727-S S¦L | EAGLE 107 WED | 130 727-S S¦L | 809 727-S S¦L

4 — AA | LUNCH | SET-UP | DAL | OZA | EAL | TWA | TXI | EAL | EAL
605 707 S¦L | 534,331,169 393,131,703 | 534 DC-9 S¦L X-SAT | 331 727-S S¦L | 169 DC-9 S¦L | 393 707 S¦L | 765 DC-9 DO X-SAT | 131 727-S S¦L | 703 727-S S¦L

5 — SET-UP | EAL | REP | TX | OZA | DAL | SET-UP | DAL | LUNCH | EAL | DAL
335 ALSO 847 SAT¦MON | 847 727 S¦L SAT¦MON | 335 DC-9 S¦L | 485 DC-9 DO S | 528 DC-9 S | 761 S¦L X-SAT | 237, 946 439, 877 | 237 727-S S¦L | 946, 499 DC-9, 727-S S¦L | 877 DC-9 S¦L

6 — SET-UP | AA | AA | LU. | REP | TWA | LU. | EAL | TWA | AA
341, 305 ALSO, 841 FR-WED | 341 ALSO, 841 FR-WED 707 S¦L | 305 DC-9 S | 361 707 S¦L | 843 707 S | 172 727-S S¦L | 026 727-S S | 414 727-S S | 394 DC-9 S | 889 DOR S | 162 DOR 727-S S | 50 S

7 — SET-UP | DAL | WORLD | LUNCH | EAL | EAL | SET-UP | EAL
AA 605 FOR TEAM 4 | 60,33 727-S S¦L | 60 727-S S¦L | 33 DC-10 S¦L | 616 DC-9 S¦L | 492, 816 727-S S¦L SAT MON ONLY | 32 EAL SODA KITS

DAL DAL

EXHIBIT 8
Marriott In-Flite Services Division Transportation Department—Team Idle Times

	Idle times[1]							
	Sun.	Mon.	Tues.	Wed.	Thur.	Fri.	Sat.	Total
Team 1	60	60	60	60	60	60	30	390
Team 2	115	115	115	115	115	115	30	720
Team 3	100	65	65	25	65	65	65	450
Team 4	35	35	35	35	35	35	100	310
Team 5	110	45	110	110	110	110	70	665
Team 6	120	120	120	30	120	120	120	750
Team 7	0	0	0	0	0	0	0	0
TOTAL	540	440	505	375	505	505	415	3285

[1]Up to 30 minutes per team per day has been deducted from these figures to allow for prompt service to late-arriving planes.

He also noted that the P.M. bagger spent 135 minutes per day on essential, non-bagging activities, as indicated in Exhibit 6.

In addition, Marv had learned of a semi-automatic silverware bagging machine costing $6,000 that was available. Using this machine, an operator was supposed to be able to bag seven sets of silverware per minute. At this rate, based on 435 minutes of productive time on the A.M. baggers' shifts, a single worker should be able to bag up to 3,045 sets per day; however, at that time, only 2,305 sets could be machine bagged since some sets had to be linen-wrapped (with the same standard applicable). With this constraint in mind, Marv wanted to determine what the annual labor savings would be if he could eliminate one or two of the silverware bagging positions. Also, since there was some question of whether the quoted machine rate of 7 sets per minute was realistic, he wanted to determine what rate the machine would have to meet to produce a 2-year payback.

CONCLUSION

Marv had to decide what his recommendations for increasing productivity would be to Bill Valenti. He knew that the criteria for investing in capital equipment at the In-Flite Services Division included an after-tax ROI of at least 15% and a payback period of two years or less. With all these facts in mind Marv wiped the perspiration from his brow, loosened his tie and settled back in his chair to think his ideas through one more time before beginning his report.

Dayton Instruments Corporation

Sarah Henderson ran through the rain to meet her car pool. Normally, Friday afternoon was a happy occasion—it was payday at the Dayton Instruments plant where Sarah was employed. Lately, however, payday had become just another reminder of how difficult it was to make ends meet these days. As she climbed into the rear seat of the car she noticed once again how much newer it was than what she and her husband could afford. They were still making payments on a five-year-old used car. With food prices increasing as they were, Sarah's family would have a tough time with the rent payments, let alone thinking of a new car. Perhaps it was a desire for sympathy that caused her to speak as the car headed out of the plant compound. "Today's paycheck," she said, "was spent before I got it. How can anyone survive on what they pay here?" Homer Bergin put his elbow over the front seat and turned around. "I reckon," he said, "you'll just have to work a little harder." With that, he produced his paycheck for Sarah to see. At first she couldn't believe it—his check was more than double what she was being paid. Homer chuckled as he turned around and put the check back into his pocket. Sarah was sorry she had said anything in the first place, and resolved to say nothing more. How could it be, she wondered, that Homer made twice as much as she made? She knew he was in a higher labor grade, and that he did work some overtime occasionally, but that couldn't account for the whole difference. The explanation, she concluded, must lie in the wage incentive plan.

Under this plan workers who increased their productivity were rewarded proportionately higher wages. Sarah understood the plan, she also knew that she worked every bit as hard as Homer, if not harder. She was clearly being short-changed, and as she settled back for the ride home, she resolved to give her foreman a piece of her mind the first thing Monday morning.

DAYTON INSTRUMENTS CORPORATION—BACKGROUND

The Plant

The Dayton Instruments plant was located in Fairborn, just to the northeast of and adjoining Dayton, Ohio. The company had been founded by a German im-

Copyright © 1985 by The Colgate Darden Graduate Business School Sponsors, University of Virginia, Charlottesville, Virginia. Reprinted by permission.

Case originally prepared by C.M. Mayer, under the supervision of Professor Robert D. Landel. Names, places, and figures have been disguised. Case rewritten for classroom purposes by Amit Mukherjee and Robert D. Landel.

migrant during the early 1950s and currently produced a wide line of electronic instruments such as frequency counters, recorders, oscilloscopes, and test metering devices. Early growth had been good, but not exceptional. However, in the early 1970s, the firm became one of the leaders in an industry which experienced spectacular growth.

The company built its reputation by offering high quality products priced consistently below its competition. Growth continued even when that of the rest of the industry slowed, and from 1977 to 1981 the company had a sustained rate of growth of nearly 20% each year. Further, because most of its customers were

EXHIBIT 1
Organization Chart

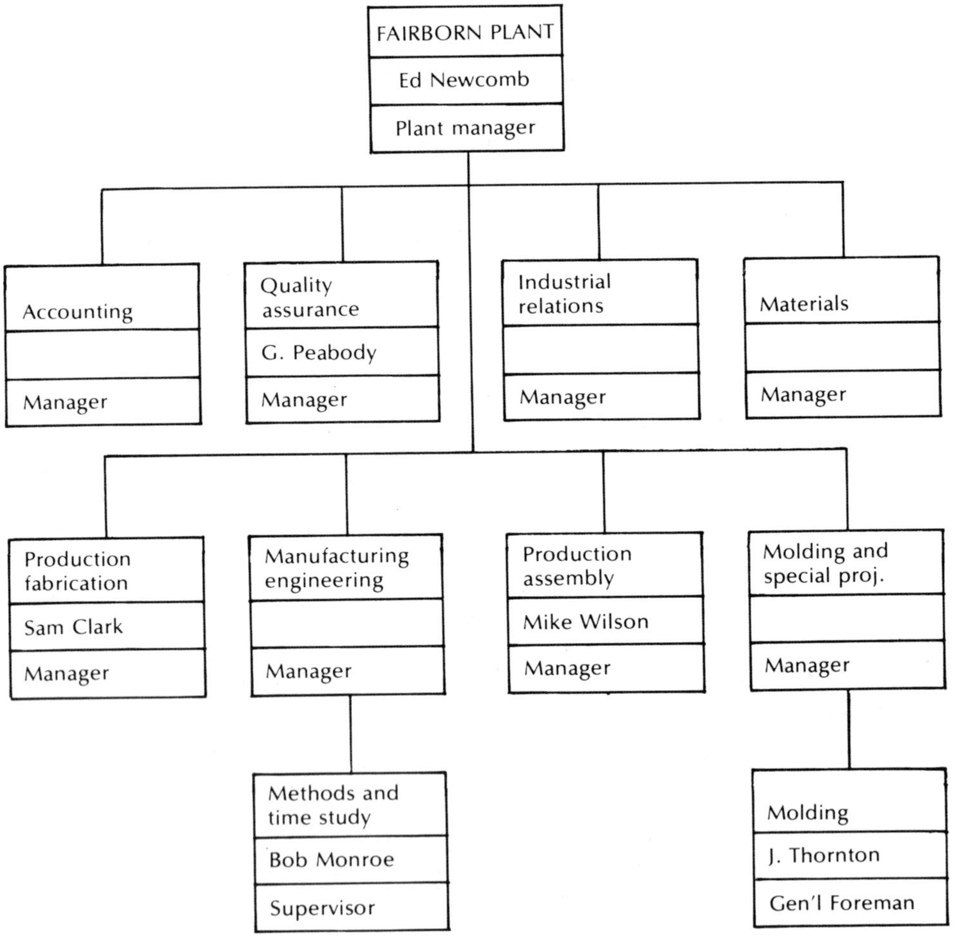

Source: Company files.

institutions whose capital expenditure plans were made well in advance of need, most top-level executives considered the company nearly "recession-proof."

In 1978, the company was absorbed by American Econodynamics (AE), a conglomerate with interests running from meat to steel production. AE merged Dayton's marketing and research departments and most of its engineering function with those of another of its divisions in San Jose, California. Consequently, the Fairborn plant was reduced to a purely manufacturing facility. However, it retained its name, for AE wanted to capitalize on Dayton's excellent reputation. The new electronics division of AE, therefore, came to be called "Dayton Instruments Corporation, a subsidiary of American Econodynamics Corporation." The division's organizational chart is given in Exhibit 1.

The plant had been expanded almost continuously for the best part of a decade and in 1981 covered nearly 300,000 square feet. An 85,000 square feet addition was under construction. All plant facilities were properly maintained, well-lighted, and the general noise level in the plant was not objectionable. Visitors to the plant received an overall impression of cleanliness, order, and constant, fast-paced motion.

In June, 1981, the plant employed 1,300 workers, of whom 73% were direct-labor employees and primarily, female. Relations between management and workers were good. The plant could, therefore, work without time clocks; worker promptness was dependent only upon the cooperation of employees and the effectiveness of supervisors. The plant had never been unionized, although attempts had been made by two different unions. The latest attempt had been in the Spring of 1981, when workers rejected the union by a margin of nearly 4 to 1, though virtually every other manufacturing company in the area was unionized. Company executives attributed this situation to several factors: a well defined and effective grievance procedure; competitive wages; periodic meetings at which the plant manager talked to, and fielded questions and complaints from every employee in the plant; and the plant's wage incentive plan. Without doubt, however, the recession which had plagued the economy since mid-1980 had influenced the workers' opinions.

The Fairborn plant was the only AE facility which had a wage incentive plan. The plan had been designed by and installed with the aid of a consulting firm during the early 1970s. It was meant to boost productivity and increase worker motivation. It was, primarily, the success of this plan which had enabled Dayton Instruments to produce products highly valued by the market, and so establish itself as an industry leader. On some product lines, Dayton Instruments had, over the years, reduced its prices without sacrificing profit margins despite increased labor and raw material expenses.

The Manufacturing Operations

Component production was one of the two major categories of manufacturing operations carried out at the plant. Almost all mechanical and electrical components were manufactured at Fairborn, though most electronics components were purchased. This fact accounted for the unusually large assortment of metal cutting and forming machines, plastic molding machines and coil winders on the production floor. Only a few types of components were used in Dayton's products. These tended to remain unchanged over the years and made for a highly repetitive manufacturing process.

Assembly operations constituted the other major type of work. All assembly work, barring that of a small speaker which was imported from Japan, was done within the plant. Two assembly lines and numerous batch work stations were supplied with components directly from the production floor; only raw materials and finished goods were held in inventory. Despite an extensive product line, products were differentiated only during the final stages of assembly.

With the exception of the plastic molding department, the plant worked one shift a day, five days a week. The molding department worked three shifts a day, six days a week. This was because the molding department did not have the physical capacity to supply the plant's needs on a single shift production schedule. At the same time, AE had placed a moratorium on capital expenditures. Thus, in the event of further increase in demand for the plant's products, the non-availability of plastic molded parts would constrain its ability to service the demand.

WAGE INCENTIVE ADMINISTRATION

The Wage Incentive Plan

The purpose of the Dayton Instruments Corporation's Wage Incentive Plan was to provide an opportunity for extra pay, in fair proportion to extra efforts. Employees were given a booklet explaining the wage incentive plan. This booklet is reproduced as Exhibit 2. By studying this booklet and referring to the examples contained in it, most employees were able to predict very closely what their earnings would be each week. Sarah Henderson's and Homer Bergin's total pay (net of deductions) is shown in Exhibit 3.

Most experts in wage incentive administration feel that the average efficiency under a daywork compensation system is only 50 to 60 percent. With work standards, but without wage incentives, efficiency rises to 85 to 95 percent. At Dayton Instruments, under a full fledged incentive plan, productivity had averaged 120% of the standard rate of work over the last several years.

The incentive plan was set up as a Straight Line (Standard Hour) Plan. Under this plan, which is also called a 100% or a 1:1 plan, incentive payments were made in direct proportion to the output of work. Thus, an employee who produced at 110% of standard received 10% more than base pay. The company, therefore, did not make any direct labor savings, but profited from the better utilization of its fixed assets and indirect labor resources. Management expected the average, well-trained worker would earn 125% of the base pay at the occupational rate (defined in the glossary of Exhibit 2) by working at an incentive pace.

Responsibility for administration of the plan was divided. Timekeeping and payroll aspects were the responsibility of the Accounting Department. Time studies and standards were the responsibility of the Manufacturing Engineering Department, particularly of the Supervisor of Methods and Timestudy, R. L. Monroe.

EXHIBIT 2
Wage Incentive Plan for Hourly Employees

INTRODUCTION

Our company is in a highly competitive business. Therefore, we must produce a high quality product at a competitive cost. To accomplish this the Company must have able, efficient employees who are well paid for their efforts.

Everyone can realize benefits with proper use of our wage incentive plan. This booklet describes the ground rules of the incentive plan. Do not hesitate to ask questions or make suggestions through your supervisor.

GENERAL RULES

1. The Company guarantees that each employee will be paid for the hours reported per day at personal rate plus any adjustment due to overtime premiums and shift differentials. The employee will have an opportunity to earn incentive bonus if the work is covered under the incentive plan.

2. The Company will provide incentive opportunity where wage incentives can be based on practical measurements of the work performed.

3. The employee will be paid incentive bonus in direct proportion to the extra amount of production of acceptable quality above the established amount of production.

4. Time standards will be set for specific methods and will be guaranteed (except for obvious clerical errors or temporary standards) as long as no change is made in the operation. When any change is made which affects the time required to do a job, such as material, methods, tooling, machine feed or speed, molding machine cycles, tolerances or quality; the old standard will be canceled and a new standard established.

Changes in time standards that are made for these reasons will be confined to those elements of the operation which are affected by the change. Such changes may increase or decrease the standard time for the job.

5. Time standards are expressed as pieces per hour and standard hours per 100 units of production. Time standards will be established by competent personnel, thoroughly trained in time study techniques and wage incentive practices. Time standards are set from direct time studies and from predetermined time standard analysis.

6. When idle time is available during the machine-controlled elements of an operation, manual work may, where practical, be assigned to utilize this time. The job time standard will not be affected by such assignments as long as the work can be readily performed within the machine-controlled time.

7. Employees will be paid at their personal rate for lost time due to major delays beyond their control. Delays must be reported immediately to the supervisor or credit for such lost time will not be allowed. Claims for minor delays will not be allowed where such interruptions are inherent in the operation and appropriate allowances have been included in the standard.

8. All incentive earnings will be calculated on the occupational rate, except where the personal rate is higher than the occupational rate. Day work, which is work performed off standard, will be paid for at the employee's personal rate.

9. Incentive earnings will be based on each individual day's production.

10. Periodic audits will be performed to determine if the plan is being administered by the set criteria.

EXHIBIT 2, cont'd

TIME STANDARD PROCEDURES

1. **Time Study.** Time study engineers will study, time, and record each element of an operation. While timing the operation, the engineers will rate the performance of the operator.

2. **Rating.** Variations in the operator's performance must be considered in establishing fair incentive standards. The actual time used for each element is adjusted to the time an experienced, qualified operator uses, working at a normal pace. If the operator works faster than a normal pace, the time used for each element is increased proportionately. Normal performance is rated 100% and needs no further adjustments.

   Examples of the adjustments in observed time are as follows:

   If the actual time taken is .16 minutes at 125% rating, the time allowed will be increased — .16 x 125% = .20 normal minutes.

   If the actual time taken is .25 minutes at 80% rating, the time allowed will be decreased — .25 x 80% = .20 normal minutes.

   If a machine is operating at optimum speed, the incentive wage opportunity is allowed in the range of 125%.

3. **Normal Performance (100%).** Normal performance is an experienced operator's pace, which is neither slow nor fast, but rhythmical, consistent, continuous and maintainable throughout the day. The normal pace of 100% is considered fair and equitable at this plant.

4. **Personal and Fatigue Allowances.** During the work day, all employees are allowed time for personal and fatigue needs. This allowance is a factor in determining the time standard for an operation. For manual work a factor of 15% is allowed. A 5% factor is used for operators on machine controlled elements.

5. **Quality.** The job standard will provide adequate time to maintain established standards of quality.

6. **Small Lot Incentive Coverage.** A "small lot" is a short run or one-time operation. In this situation the standard is good for one run only.

7. **Temporary Standard.** A temporary standard is a time standard on an operation where limited information of the method is available and/or where the operator performing the task is new to the work. A temporary standard will remain until studies are made on experienced operators with firmly established methods.

8. **Blanket Coverage.** A blanket coverage number is a three digit operation number assigned by timestudy. This number puts the operator on an incentive standard when the operator in certain cases is unable to report against the regular operation number. The numbers are used for small lot coverage, for non-operator caused rework, and for regular operations coverage if the standard is set after Wednesday. The coverage is good for Thursday and Friday, only until the standard can be submitted to the computer.

   Example:

Oper. #	Incentive Hrs./100 pcs.	Pcs./Hr.
380	0.8340	120

   a. The timestudy engineer studies an operation and issues a standard immediately.

   b. He assigns the operation number that corresponds to the standard in the computer and both he and the supervisor initial the time sheet entry.

   c. The timestudy engineer records the part number, operation description, date, operation number, and the standard he allows for the job.

9. **Allowance Over Standard.** Additional time can be applied to existing standard, usually for a short period of time. An allowance may be required due to faulty tools or parts and/or slower machine cycles.

   Example:

	Oper. #	Std. Hrs. Per Piece	Pcs./Hr.
Regular	05	.0100	100
Allowance	05-1	.0020	
Combined	05/05-1	.0120	83.3

10. **Work Codes.** Work codes are used primarily to cover work performed off standard, such as cleanup time or waiting time. They can also be used for training time, for protecting a bonus, or for deducting from the bonus when operator errors are detected.

EXHIBIT 2, cont'd

Two work codes, 58 and 60, can directly affect an employee's bonus. If an operator is working on a new job, work code 58 can be used to protect any bonus earned on other jobs that day. If an operator must rework his/her own mistakes, work code 60 can be used to deduct previously earned bonus.

11. **Group Incentive.** On moving line assembly operations and certain other jobs, it may be necessary to provide a standard for a group of people. These standards are set in the following manner:

1. All elements of the job are studied.

2. Total number of finished pieces desired per day is determined from production schedules.

3. Line speed is calculated.

4. Number of work stations needed to produce the desired number of finished pieces is figured.

5. Work stations are balanced as closely as possible to provide an equal amount of work at each station.

6. Incentive wage opportunity is allowed in the range of 125%.

7. Most down-time is clocked out as day work.

   Example: Broken screwdrivers, waiting for parts, etc.

Work codes should be applied, with the supervisor's approval, to properly account for waiting time or other indirect time. Normally, delays beyond 5 minutes should be charged to the work codes.

Operators transferring temporarily must show the department number where the work is done in order to get incentive credit.

Each week a performance report is distributed to all departments. This report indicates by operator clock number: the actual hours on standard, the standard hours produced, the performance percentage, hours worked and the percent of hours on standard. The performance is found by dividing the actual hours on standard into the standard hours produced.

Clock No.	Act./Hrs. on/Std.	Std./Hrs. Prod.	% Performance	Total Hrs.	% Hrs. Std.
888	32	40	125	40	80

Each week department supervisors will distribute to each employee a weekly performance card.

GLOSSARY

EMPLOYEE TIME RECORDING

Employees are required to fill in a time sheet each day. Each entry is important and should be checked before being turned in at the end of the shift.

Time should be reported as accurately on non-standard jobs as it is on standard.

Occupational Rate: The hourly rate normally attained by employees within their classified labor grade.

Personal Rate: The hourly rate assigned to an employee.

Hours on Standard: The hours worked on incentive jobs.

Standard Hours Earned: Pieces of acceptable quality produced multiplied by the standard hours per piece.

Day Work Hours: Hours worked on non-incentive jobs and hours allowed for delays, breakdowns, etc.

Performance: Standard hours earned divided by hours on standard.

EXHIBIT 2, cont'd

A. **The employee's "Personal rate" is the same as his/her "Occupational rate." The employee is at the top of the labor grade.**

EXAMPLE: Personal rate: $4.20; Occupational rate: $4.20

	(a)	(b)	(c)	(d) (a) × (b)	(e) (d) ÷ (c)	(f) (c) × $4.20	(g) (d) × $4.20	(h) (g) − (f)
Job number	Production	Std. hrs. per piece	Hours worked	Std. hrs. earned	Job per- formance %	Min. pay	Standard earnings	Bonus earned
1	500 pcs.	.0110	4.5	5.50	122%	$18.90	$23.10	$4.20
2	200 pcs.	.0045	.9	.90	100%	$ 3.78	$ 3.78	-0-
3	100 pcs.	.0200	1.6	2.00	125%	$ 6.72	8.40	$1.68
Hours on std.			7.0					
Daywork			1.0			$ 4.20		
Total hours			8.0	8.40		$33.60		$5.88

$$\text{Performance} = \frac{\text{Std. hrs. earned}}{\text{Hours on std.}} = \frac{8.40}{7.00} = 120\%$$

Total earnings = Min. pay + Bonus = $39.48

B. **The employee's "Personal rate" is less than as his/her "Occupational rate."**

EXAMPLE: Personal rate: $3.35; Occupational rate: $4.20

	(a)	(b)	(c)	(d) (a) × (b)	(e) (d) ÷ (c)	(f) (c) × $3.35	(g) (d) × $4.20	(h) (g) − (f)
Job number	Production	Std. hrs. per piece	Hours worked	Std. hrs. earned	Job per- formance %	Min. pay	Standard earnings	Bonus earned
1	500 pcs.	.0110	4.5	5.50	122%	$15.07	$23.10	$8.03
2	200 pcs.	.0045	.9	.90	100%	$ 3.02	$ 3.78	$ .76
3	100 pcs.	.0200	1.6	2.00	125%	$ 5.36	8.40	3.04
Hours on std.			7.0					
Daywork			1.0			$ 3.35		
Total hours			8.0	8.40		$26.80		$11.83

$$\text{Performance} = \frac{\text{Std. hrs. earned}}{\text{Hours on std.}} = \frac{8.40}{7.00} = 120\%$$

Total earnings = Min. pay + Bonus = $38.63

Time standards used in the incentive plan were set by company industrial engineers on the basis of either time and motion studies or predetermined standards data. In Exhibits 4, 5 and 6, the results of three time studies for the same welding operation are shown. In this particular operation, the worker used a specialized machine known as a "Wikstrom" Welder to weld two contacts onto a spring blank. The operation was studied by three different industrial engineers.

Exhibit 5 shows the observations listed by one of the industrial engineers. The industrial engineer observed the worker producing three batches of 100 pieces of a job in 3.17 minutes, 3.26 minutes and 3.12 minutes respectively. He computed

EXHIBIT 2, cont'd

C. The employee performs his/her regular jobs at a sub-standard level.

EXAMPLE: Personal rate: $3.35; Occupational rate: $4.20

Job number	(a) Production	(b) Std. hrs. per piece	(c) Hours worked	(d) (a) × (b) Std. hrs. earned	(e) (d) ÷ (c) Job performance %	(f) (c) × $3.35 Min. pay	(g) (d) × $4.20 Standard earnings	(h) (g) − (f) Bonus earned
1	350 pcs.	.0110	4.5	3.85	85%	$15.07	—	0
2	100 pcs.	.0045	.9	.45	50%	$ 3.02	—	0
3	70 pcs.	.0200	1.6	1.40	88%	$ 5.36	—	0
Hours on std.			7.0					
Daywork			1.0			$ 3.35		
Total hours			8.0	5.70		$26.80		0

$$\text{Performance} = \frac{\text{Std. hrs. earned}}{\text{Hours on std.}} = \frac{5.70}{7.00} = 81\%$$

Total earnings = Min. pay + Bonus = $26.80

*Bonus is only paid if performance is 100% or greater.

D. The employee performs *some* of his/her regular jobs at a sub-standard level.

EXAMPLE: Personal rate: $3.35; Occupational rate: $4.20

Employee performs all jobs regularly, but job #2 at a sub-standard level.

Job number	(a) Production	(b) Std. hrs. per piece	(c) Hours worked	(d) (a) × (b) Std. hrs. earned	(e) (d) ÷ (c) Job performance %	(f) (c) × $3.35 Min. pay	(g) (d) × $4.20 Standard earnings	(h) (g) − (f) Bonus earned
1	500 pcs.	.0110	4.5	5.50	122%	$15.07	$23.10	$8.03
2	100 pcs.	.0045	.9	.45	50%	$ 3.02	$ 1.89	−$1.13
3	100 pcs.	.0200	1.6	2.00	125%	$ 5.36	8.40	$3.04
Hours on std.			7.0					
Daywork			1.0			$ 3.35		
Total hours			8.0	7.95		$26.80		$9.94

$$\text{Performance} = \frac{\text{Std. hrs. earned}}{\text{Hours on std.}} = \frac{7.95}{7.00} = 114\%$$

Total earnings = Min. pay + Bonus = $36.74

the mean production time, 0.0318 minutes per piece. Since he had estimated that the operator had been working at 120% of her normal pace, he multiplied the average production time (0.0318) by the pace estimate (120%) to obtain the normal time, 0.0381 minutes. Exhibit 6 shows that the normal times determined by the three industrial engineers was averaged to obtain a standard expressed as 0.0748 hours per 100 pieces or, equivalently, as 1333 pieces per hour. A factor of 15% of the normal time was added as a personal and fatigue allowance. Exhibit 7

EXHIBIT 2, cont'd

E. The employee performs a new job at sub-standard, but makes standard on other jobs.

EXAMPLE: Personal rate: $3.35; Occupational rate: $4.20

Employee performs jobs 1 and 3 regularly; job 2 is a new job. When a sub-standard performance is due to a lack of experience on a new job, the supervisor can use work code 58 for the time spent on this job to protect the employee's bonus on other jobs. In this example for job 2, the supervisor uses work code 58 to protect earlier bonus.

Job number	(a) Production	(b) Std. hrs. per piece	(c) Hours worked	(d) (a) × (b) Std. hrs. earned	(e) (d) ÷ (c) Job performance %	(f) (c) × $3.35 Min. pay	(g) (d) × $4.20 Standard earnings	(h) (g) − (f) Bonus earned
1	500 pcs.	.0110	4.5	5.50	122%	$15.07	$23.10	$8.03
2	100 pcs.	.0045	.9	.45	50%	$ 3.02	—	—
3	100 pcs.	.0200	1.6	2.00	125%	$ 5.36	8.40	$3.04
Hours on std.			7.0					
Daywork			1.0			$ 3.35		
Total hours			8.0	7.95		$26.80		$11.07

$$\text{Performance} = \frac{\text{Std. hrs. earned}}{\text{Hours on std.}} = \frac{7.95}{7.00} = 114\%$$

Total earnings = Min. pay + Bonus = $37.87

EXHIBIT 3
Calculation of Worker Paychecks

	Henderson	Bergin
Personal rate	$ 5.11	$ 6.07
Occupational rate	5.48	6.07
Base pay	204.36	242.62
Bonus	39.87	211.07
Gross pay	244.23	453.69
Federal withholding	38.88	18.61
State withholding	5.11	4.04
FICA	14.28	26.54
Charity	2.17	0.54
U.S. savings bond	2.72	4.35
Credit union	10.87	21.74
Net pay	$170.20	$377.87

EXHIBIT 4

Dept. ___6760___ Date _____ Study No. _____

Part No. __200721-455__ Name _____ Matl. _____

Operation No. ___10___ Name _____

Operator's No. _____ Name __E. Saunders__

Machine No. ___3___ Type __2 contacts__

Tool _____ Speed _____ Feed _____

Time started _____ Time stopped _____ Total time __ES__

Department No.	Element Description	Actual	Rating	Normal
	Cycle:	.030	120	
	30/10 30/10 30/10 30/10		=	.03
	29/10 30/10 32/10 31/10			
	29/10 30/10 30/10 29/10 30/10			
	Box: 62/			
	/2500			

EXHIBIT 5

Dept. _____6760_____ Date _____ Study No. _____

Part No. _200721-455_ Name _____ Matl. _____

Operation No. _____10_____ Name _____

Operator's No. _____ Name _____E. FOX_____

Machine No. _____3_____ Type _____

Tool _____ Speed _____ Feed _____

Time started _____ Time stopped _____J.M.W._____ Total time _____

Department No.	Element Description		Actual	Rating	Normal
	PLACE PARTS IN MACHINE, WELD				
	2 HITS PER PC.				
	21820-22020	3.17/100	.0318	120	.03
	22020-22220	3.26/100			
	22220-22420	3.12/100			

EXHIBIT 6

Dept. ___*6760*___ Date _____ Study No. _____

Part No. ___*200721-455*___ Name _____ Matl. _____

Operation No. ___*10*___ Name ___*WELD (2) CONTACTS*___

Operator's No. _____ Name ___*W. SPROUSE*___

Machine No. ___*#3*___ Type _____

Tool _____ Speed _____ Feed _____

Time started _____ Time speed _____ Total time ___*JKS*___

Department No.	Element Description	Actual	Rating	Normal
	Cycles: 1.53/ 1.49/			
	/50 /50	.0302	125	
			=	.03
	.0378 (from Exhibit 6)			
	.0360 (from Exhibit 4)			
	.0381 (from Exhibit 5)			
	3 /.1119			
	.0373 × 115% = .0429 (115% is allowance for personal time)			
	PKG. & MAT'L HANDLING .0020			
	.0449 STD MINS			
	1333 PCS/HR			
	.0748 HRS/100 PCS			

EXHIBIT 7

PROCESS DETAIL

☐ ELECTRO-MECHANICAL   ☐ ELECTRONIC

DATE 6/26/80	ISSUE NO 8	SHEET 1 OF 1	FAB CODE 13	PRIMARY USE CODE	DESCRIPTION Spring Assembly		PART NUMBER 200721-455	

Dept.	Mach. group	Oper. number	Operation name		Special instructions Tools, jigs, fixtures req'd	LG	STD Hrs./100	STD Fcs./Hr.	Current labor value
~~6790~~	~~84~~	~~05~~	~~Degrease~~	Void					
6760	52	10	Assemble & Weld		39-109502	3	.0743	1333	
6220		15	Inspection						
6433		999	Store						

MATERIAL REQUIRED PER M	REMARKS		PREP BY OWT	CHKD BY WBC

MATERIAL REQUIRED PER M
(8855-826) S-21-P Form #32
Contact tape
.2808 Troy oz./M
1000 EA. 300975-041 SPRING

DRAWING ISSUE 2	DRAWING NUMBER 200721-455	USED ON 306012-581
DESCRIPTION Spring Assembly		PART NUMBER 200721-455

Oper 05
Degrease 300975-041 Spring
Degrease springs only as required for welding each day.

Oper 10
Assemble & Weld two contacts form 32 per S-21-P on Wikstrom Contact Welder
Dial Feed Tooling 39-109502
Pack in 200989-851 Carton

Oper 15   Inspection
Finished size, shape and location of contacts

Correcting Die
70900-4884

EXHIBIT 8

PAGE ____ OF ____ DAILY PRODUCTION AND TIME REPORT DATE _____ SHIFT _2_

EMPLOYEE NAME __L. F. GREENE__ CLOCK NUMBER __3452__ DEPARTMENT NUMBER __6610__

CHARGE NUMBER						DASH	WORK CODE	FORE-MAN'S INITIALS	PART NUMBER OR OPERATION DESCRIPTION									OPERATION NUMBER	PART COUNT	% ONLY	START TIME
4	5	3	1	8	6				7	0	0	0	6	0	2	5	8	11	40		4:30
							32														4:40
3	9	6	6	2	6		9-A		7	0	3	0	1	6	8	7	4	461	5,290		5:00
							12														12:52
													O	U	T				———		1:00

PAGE ____ OF ____ DAILY PRODUCTION AND TIME REPORT DATE _____ SHIFT _2_

EMPLOYEE NAME __L. F. GREENE__ CLOCK NUMBER __3452__ DEPARTMENT NUMBER __6610__

CHARGE NUMBER						DASH	WORK CODE	FORE-MAN'S INITIALS	PART NUMBER OR OPERATION DESCRIPTION									OPERATION NUMBER	PART COUNT	% ONLY	START TIME
H	5	3	1	8	6				7	0	0	0	6	0	2	5	8	11	2,170		4:30
							12														12:30
													O	U	T				———		1:00

__L. F. Greene__
EMPLOYEE'S SIGNATURE

TOTAL HOURS __8__

EXHIBIT 9

Incentive Coverage—Historic Data (all figures are percents)

	1978	1979	1980
January	84	85	89
February	84	86	90
March	80	85	91
April	74	88	90
May	79	91	90
June	82	90	90
July	79	89	88
August	81	89	88
September	81	90	90
October	81	90	93
November	80	90	92
December	82	89	

Source: Company records.

EXHIBIT 10

	1978	1979	1980
Standard Hours Produced on Incentive—Jan. 1978 to Nov. 1980			
January	75,609	95,061	112,416
February	77,034	95,155	118,272
March	90,739	111,250	151,736
April	69,506	87,788	116,183
May	69,426	89,075	126,488
June	88,421	107,332	160,766
July*	32,867	39,327	58,967
August	81,977	96,053	141,292
September	98,747	103,846	169,683
October	89,515	116,477	138,058
November	92,515	110,295	112,616
December	112,495	131,602	
Hours Worked on Incentive—Jan. 1978 to Nov. 1980			
January	61,202	80,143	93,847
February	62,751	79,673	99,005
March	74,460	92,482	127,367
April	58,004	74,774	98,559
May	57,931	77,832	108,066
June	73,895	95,026	137,057
July*	27,997	34,496	50,941
August	69,528	81,502	118,500
September	85,497	89,522	142,777
October	79,301	101,766	116,709
November	80,896	94,834	101,417
December	96,406	112,879	

Source: Company records.
*The Fairborn plant closed for two weeks each July for vacations.

presents a description of the proper method of using the Wikstrom Welder to perform the job studied in Exhibits 4, 5 and 6.

Payroll accounting was accomplished by the Daily Production and Time Report, shown in Exhibit 8. Each day workers completed this report which detailed the time they had expended on various parts or manufacturing operations. The forms were collected by the timekeeper and computer data cards were keypunched daily. A timekeeping program collated and summarized this data and provided a weekly printout, in which the details of each worker's time were shown, and his weekly pay was computed.

In June, 1981, 27,700 hours per week, or about 90% of the available direct labor hours, were on standards, and were, therefore, eligible for incentive payments. In fact, this meant that more than 90% of the direct labor employees received incentive pay since many of them worked on standard rates for a part of the day and on day rates for the rest. Exhibit 9 shows the historic coverage rates of the incentive plan and Exhibit 10 the historic data on standard hours worked and hours produced by direct labor employees. Exhibit 11 gives the result of a random sample of performance efficiency for 100 direct labor workers in June. Indirect labor employees had no opportunity to earn incentive bonuses.

EXHIBIT 11
Weekly Efficiency Percentages: Random Sample of 100 Workers, June 1981

Worker number	Rate	Worker number	Rate	Worker number	Rate	Worker number	Rate
1067	135	3032	93	2718	132	1836	189
0985	157	1266	146	2292	126	2823	154
0623	137	4116	81	3441	124	3637	137
0852	136	3312	112	3119	169	3101	126
2115	105	3328	126	0903	171	2429	106
2637	117	3694	132	4364	48	4024	136
1912	162	2713	132	2991	126	3531	109
2612	117	2954	131	3033	105	2616	56
3737	123	1727	132	2842	120	3468	149
3122	132	2603	138	3559	82	4213	130
1115	174	4143	115	3829	134	1132	134
3418	49	4320	93	2641	149	2944	109
2163	119	2531	134	2025	131	0321	154
3337	114	1262	151	3436	104	3981	108
2881	130	2933	139	2222	172	2145	149
1969	113	1948	144	3762	100	2802	102
0990	206	3321	130	3582	116	3229	127
1900	123	3514	129	3021	145	3763	74
4286	59	4093	133	2120	192	3239	126
1563	137	2615	149	1014	139	0612	123
1628	121	3801	125	2005	126	4515	116
3857	66	3216	125	4012	81	3051	147
2277	118	3654	127	2814	96	3488	113
3184	89	2717	126	1538	174	0809	131
2213	114	1631	166	1150	157	2210	113

Source: Company records.

Typical Problems in Administering the Plan

Though the plan was well understood and appreciated by the workers, implementation problems did crop up occasionally. Most of these had to be resolved by the Manufacturing Engineering Department, and in particular, by Bob Monroe.

Methods changes gave rise to the most common difficulties Bob Monroe encountered. An alert worker would often find a quicker way to do a job, despite the fact that most jobs were fairly simple and most had been studied by an industrial engineer. By making a surreptitious methods change, the employee could effectively increase her productivity beyond the expected incentive pace, and thus receive large bonus payments. Such a change could go undetected by supervisors and result in long periods of excessive incentive payments. Bob Monroe sought to counter this practice by offering cash awards for suggestions which improved productivity. His hope was that the expectation of cash in hand today would encourage workers to report methods changes.

Another problem was that of older employees. Some had been at the same basic work station for nearly 20 years and were simply slowing down as they advanced in age. They also fatigued more easily, yet were dedicated and dependable employees. Few in this class were able to work at the expected incentive pace, and most did well to work at normal pace for eight hours. On the other hand, management felt that some allowance should be made for longevity, and that such employees had a legitimate claim to special consideration.

Other employees, who had only partial or no ability to earn incentive bonuses, demanded the opportunity. Some employees refused a transfer, even at a higher labor grade, if it meant working without a standard. The testing and repair area, for instance, had posed problems for the plant management. Traditionally no standards had been considered possible in this area because workers were required to troubleshoot for the cause of a malfunction and then repair it. While most repairs could be standardized easily, it was difficult to predict the time required for troubleshooting. After numerous appeals from the workers in this area, most of whom were valued employees, Bob Monroe solved the problem by mounting a clock at each station. Workers switched the clock on while making repairs, and off while troubleshooting. At the end of the day, total elapsed clock time was eligible for 125% incentive payments and the balance of the day was paid at the daywork rate.

Since the company paid incentives to workers on the moving lines, a persistent problem was that of balancing the load at each work station on the line so that all workers would contribute equally to the productivity of the line. Any engineering, design, or methods change was likely to affect the balance. In fact, a change in the supplier of a part could potentially upset the balance, if the tolerances on new parts were even slightly different from those on the old one.

Attitudes of Foremen

In dealing with problems such as these, a critical factor was the attitude of the shop foremen. The more senior foremen usually supported the incentive plan, and recognized that they were a key element in its success. Generally, senior foremen would report methods improvements to the Manufacturing Engineering Department.

The management, however, was uncertain about the junior foremen. In May, 1981, approximately 20 workers had been promoted to foremen. An orientation and training session lasting a week had been held for them. For most of one morning Bob Monroe spoke to the class on the subject of time study and incentives. Unfortunately, he wasn't sure that he had got the positive response that he had sought.

Generally, most foremen felt that their major problems were in such areas as ensuring that sufficient component parts were available to sustain production and accommodating malfunctions and breakdowns of equipment ranging from pneumatic screwdrivers to the plant air conditioning. Most considered the wage incentive plan a motivator that significantly reduced problems in their relationships with workers. Finally, most were quite familiar with the plan since they had worked under it before being promoted to their present positions, and were well aware of such opportunities as existed for employees to exploit the plan.

Most of the industrial engineers felt that the foremen made adequate efforts in support of the incentive plan. One of them estimated that no more than 10% of the 50 foremen were problems in this regard.

Employee Attitudes Towards the Plan

In administering the wage incentive plan, another critical factor was the sensitivity of employees and the amount of personal feeling and emotion attached to the plan. This was only to be expected since the actions of the industrial engineers would be immediately reflected in a worker's paycheck. Information on incentive earnings flowed quickly through the plant. Bob Monroe cited one example:

> We had a case here one time where we had some people on a job and they were most unhappy with their standard. Yet, we felt the standard was good. We didn't know why they weren't making it and we kept looking at it to find out. Well, the daughter of one of the ladies on this job started here on the night shift in a different job. She was going to high school during the day and working this particular job at night. The second night she made 150% and she said, "Hey, Mother, what does this mean that I had to do 100 and I can do 150—all night I did 1,200 of these things?" Her mother looked at her—she was an old pro—and said, "It just means you made yourself time and half last night plus your shift premium." Of course, Mother told all of her friends on *her* job (this jealousy factor is really a problem), "I told you our standard was too tight. Over there, my daughter started, and second night made 150%."
>
> It doesn't matter what the conditions were—or what other factors were present—I heard 20 times the next day: "150% . . . 150% . . . 150% . . ." So they do get the word around.

In June, 1981, the "word" had gotten to Sarah Henderson. The problem brought to light by her complaint proved to be a difficult one for the administrators of the wage incentive plan.

SARAH HENDERSON'S COMPLAINT

The Decision to Pay Incentive Rate on the Machine Cycle

The problem that had bothered Sarah was fundamentally one of compensating workers who operated machines with fixed cycle times. If, for example, a particular machine operation had a standard time of 1.0 minute, and the machine cycle time was fixed at 0.8 minute, the job was said to be "machine-paced." Under some incentive plans, a worker on a machine-paced job would be eligible for incentive payments on only 0.2 of each minute. Consequently, she would have a lesser opportunity for incentive gains than another worker who set her own pace. When translated into dollars, 125% of 1 is, of course, more than 125% of 0.2.

Consequently, most workers were reluctant to accept assignment to machine-paced jobs when alternatives were available. Because of the need to voluntarily attract good workers to these jobs, the management had made the decision several years ago to pay the incentive rate of 125% on machine cycle time. Thus, an employee who worked at 125% of standard during that portion of an operation which she paced would be paid 125% of the entire operation. Although this represented a major change, Bob Monroe recalled that those involved had unanimously supported the decision.

The Welder Problem

While it reduced employment reluctance to transfer, the decision to place machine-paced jobs on incentive pay created a new problem. An operator might very well change the cycle time of her machine from, say, one minute to 0.63 minute and so increase her incentive rate from 125% to 200%.

The problem that occurred with the Wikstrom Welders illustrated how the incentive scheme for machine-paced jobs could be abused. Bob Monroe reported that when the company first acquired these specialized machines, time standards had been formulated assuming that the welders would be operated on a semi-automatic basis. However, as some of the operators gained experience and came down the learning curve, they were able to manipulate the welder more or less automatically. The situation reached the point where one welding worker was making 300% of standard. When the company's weekly productivity reports repeatedly showed excessively high performance for the workers in the unit, the industrial engineers decided to perform another study and establish a new standard. As described by Monroe,

> We reestablished the standard at the cycle time the operators were using.[1] The people were reasonable and accepted it. We were fair, and the new standards were presented to the operators, and their collective opinion was, "Well, it was nice while it lasted, but you still took too much away." However, over time they've gotten back up to 150%—at least a couple have. And everything was fine until this molding thing.

Sam Clark, who was in charge of the Wikstrom Welders (see Exhibit 1), supported the reestablishment of the standards. Sarah Henderson, who operated

---

[1]Exhibits 4, 5, and 6 are sample time study sheets from this study.

one of the welders, did not. But, she accepted the new standard reluctantly—until she saw Homer Bergin's paycheck.

The Molding Room Situation

As she had promised herself, Sarah approached her foreman first thing Monday morning. "People in the molding room are doing a lot better than 125%," she said. "I saw a paycheck Friday that would knock your eyes out. If our standards get tightened up, why the devil don't theirs?"

The foreman replied that there might be other factors that Sarah hadn't considered, and suggested some of them. He promised, however, to look into the matter further, and said he would talk to her about it later. She was, if not satisfied, at least willing to wait. She went to her welder, and the foreman went to the morning staff meeting held by Sam Clark. Despite what he told Sarah, this wasn't the first complaint he had heard, and he mentioned it to Mr. Clark.

"Has anyone else had complaints on this?" Clark asked. The other foremen replied that they had. "Something is obviously wrong, and I know what it is," he said as he dialed Bob Monroe's number. "Bob, those S.O.B.'s in molding have cranked up the cycle times on their machines. What's fair for us is fair for them, and my people are complaining. I'm going to bring this up at the staff meeting with the plant manager this morning, but I thought I'd give you some advance notice. How about getting that outfit shaped up?"

The molding room contained several very expensive machines. The controls of the machines were exposed, and adjusting the cycle time was not difficult. Bob Monroe had suspected that workers in this area were shortening the cycle times because of scattered reports on quality control problems with molded plastic parts. A quick check of the weekly Worker Productivity Report confirmed that performance was abnormally high. However, he had personally checked these machines a couple of times, and the controls were always set properly. Over the next week, the controversy grew.

Reactions to the Problem

Bob Monroe (Supervisor of Methods and Time study) suspected that the molding department's general foreman was secretly warning his people to reset their machines to specifications whenever he saw industrial engineers heading toward his area. Bob was upset. "Our wage incentive system depends heavily on fairness. This situation has to be corrected, and quickly."

Sam Clark (Manager of Production Fabrication) was equally concerned. He had allowed the standards on the Wikstrom Welders to be adjusted. Now he demanded that something be done about the molding machines.

George Peabody (Manager of Quality Assurance) agreed. "We've been getting more 'sink-ins'[2], warped housing, discolorations, and poorly trimmed parts lately," he said. "When speed goes up, quality goes down. Period."

---

[2]A "sink-in" is a depression in the surface of a molded plastic part caused by insufficient "cure" time in the molding cycle.

Mike Wilson (Manager of Production Assembly) was not as certain. He had been transferred from San Jose to his present job only two weeks previously. While he felt that the overall quality of molded plastic parts could be improved, he was more concerned with having parts available when his department needed them. Shutting down a moving line for lack of parts could be an expensive proposition.

Jerry Thornton (General Foreman of Molding) was aware of what was being said of his operation. He denied that there was a quality problem, and insisted that the major concern was not the wage incentive plan, but whether the plant could produce to meet demand. He insisted that he had quotas to achieve and was determined to meet them.

Homer Bergin (a molding machine operator) had a similar view. "This is hot, sweaty, boring work. I'm entitled to what I can make. As it is, I'm working six days a week while these other people have their Saturdays off."

Ed Newcomb (the Plant Manager) had mixed emotions. While he recognized the need for fairness, he was also aware of the critical need for parts. He was reluctant to take any action which could result in the plant having to purchase molded plastic parts because of an inability to produce sufficient quantities in-house. However, as matters stood, he did not feel that the incentive problem was important enough to deserve his personal intervention. He was content to let Bob Monroe propose an equitable solution.

Bob Monroe had four options:

1. He could ignore the problem. If the plant workload eased, the workers would probably stop tampering with the cycle time settings.
2. He could insist upon reestablishing the standards.
3. He could demand that the specified cycle times be maintained, by proper supervision.
4. He could purchase large, elapsed-time clocks and wire them to the machines in such a way as to record cycle times. Then, the total machine cycle time could be paid at the daywork rate and the off-cycle could be paid at the incentive rate.

Monroe wanted to analyze each of these possibilities in terms of the objectives of the incentive plan and make a recommendation at the next staff meeting.

Knox Electronics

While he was on his way to the cafeteria for lunch, Phil Chase, Chief Industrial Engineer for Knox, was stopped by a visibly upset Scott Pagent. Scott, with four months in time study, was the newest member of the Industrial Engineering Department. He had been hired immediately upon his January, 1980, graduation from Virginia Tech, with a degree in Industrial Engineering. Just the previous month Scott had been given the responsibility for maintaining and establishing time standards for Section 6750 of the Switches and Relays Department. The foreman for the section was John Ransom.

"Phil, I can't work with John Ransom," Scott said. "He is bucking any changes I make in his section and is encouraging the operators to take a hostile attitude towards me. I thought I was hired to bring new ideas for improving productivity, but I can't even set simple standards without his interferences!"

Scott Pagent's complaint was one of many that Phil had been hearing concerning the establishment of the revised work standards in the Switches and Relays Department. The Department's production had dropped considerably since the introduction of the new standards six weeks previously and the workers in that department were very unhappy. Phil wondered whether the company should stand fast behind the new standards, return to the old standards, or reach a compromise somewhere between the two extremes.

Two factors complicated the problem. First, old standards which still covered 85% of the units produced in the Switches and Relays Department had been set as far back as seven years ago using the stopwatch method. Recently, industrial engineers had restudied various jobs and set new standards using predetermined times from the Movement Time Study (MTS) Program. Management recognized that the old standards covering the various units in the Switches and Relays Department had been very loose but the company had been reluctant to change them up until the MTS program was adopted. Second, methods changes had been instituted for the assembly of many of the relays and switches produced in the department. In many cases, these methods changes had been made simultaneously

Copyright © 1985 by The Colgate Darden Graduate Business School Sponsors, University of Virginia, Charlottesville, Virginia. Reproduced by permission.

This case was prepared by Professor Robert D. Landel, The Colgate Darden Graduate School of Business Administration. Revised, 1982, by Robert D. Landel and Amit Mukherjee.

with the change in the technique used for setting the work standards. Thus, the effects of each were difficult to judge individually.

"I catch it from both sides," Phil explained. "Management keeps harping about work improvements and productivity; they want the standards to be tightened. The workers, however, complain about any increase we make in the standards. Several foremen in the department are after us, too. They insist that their production will never get back to normal, unless we slow down the pace of our activities of revising the old standards. I know some foremen would not care if we stayed out of the Switches and Relays Department for the next year. We industrial engineers who set the work methods and time standards are caught in the middle!"

COMPANY HISTORY

Knox Electronics was a medium-sized manufacturer of small electronics parts for sale to original equipment manufacturers, wholesalers, and large retail electronic parts dealers. The company produced over 2,500 different parts such as capacitors, resistors, relays and switches out of its plant at Gambier, Ohio.

The company had been founded by James Hayes in 1932 to supply relays used in telephone exchange switching equipment. From World War II up until the late 1960s its reputation for high-quality products promoted rapid sales growth which in turn required the company to expand production capacity. The company also diversified its product line to include a wide variety of electrical parts.

By 1970, however, overseas manufacturers were able to produce parts comparable in quality at lower costs, due mainly to their use of cheaper foreign labor in the construction of such hand-assembled items as switches and relays. Once its quality advantage was neutralized by these producers, Knox Electronics attempted to compete in the market-place by lowering its selling prices. This strategy placed a severe strain on its once healthy profit margins. Several cost reduction programs were put into action, including one for salaried employees called Foreman's Methods Improvement Program. Another, called Worker Suggestion Bonus, gave any hourly employee offering a methods improvement or any other cost-reducing suggestion 10% of the annual savings resulting from the suggestion. Both of these programs were successful in reducing manufacturing costs, but management now felt that even more substantial reductions were necessary in order to compete.

Approximately 400 of the company's 900 employees performed some type of hand-assembly work. The majority of hand-assembly workers were women with children in school, working to supplement their husbands' incomes. Although some of the products were assembled on a line with each worker performing only one or two steps, most of the products were assembled at individual work stations.

Under the company's wage incentive plan all hand-assembly workers were guaranteed a certain base hourly wage. Group incentives were used for line workers, but individual incentives were given for those jobs requiring complete assembly by a single worker. Production standards for the various assembly operations were pegged to the worker's base pay. For every percentage point that output exceeded standard, the worker received an equal percentage of her base pay as incentive. For example, if a worker was guaranteed $3.50 an hour for a standard hourly production of 100 pieces, she was still paid $28.00 per day if she produced less than 800 pieces. If she produced 1600 pieces in a day, however, she was paid $56.00, with $28.00 of this amount being the bonus of incentive compensation. Individual production records were not posted, but section production records within the various departments were posted weekly (i.e., switch assembly sections, relay sections).

The average guaranteed wage at Knox Electronics was $3.91. The average wage per hour, including incentives, however, was $5.17, above the community average of $4.76 per hour for workers performing similar type work. During the past two year period, management had given all employees a cost of living increase of 9% each year. These increases were expected to be continued.

The company was not unionized, despite repeated attempts by local union representatives. The issue had been put to a vote twice and defeated both times. Management claimed that the relatively high wages and benefits, combined with the "family-type" atmosphere of the plant worked to keep out the union.

TIME STANDARDS AT KNOX ELECTRONICS

Formal Industrial Engineering methods, in the form of time standards, first came into use at the company in 1947. By the 1970s, the Company had an industrial engineering staff of twelve men. Phil Chase described the development of standards at Knox:

"The company has relied heavily on time standards since their introduction here. We depend on them for production scheduling, determination of incentive wages, making make vs. buy analyses, and pinpointing methods improvements. Up until this year, we used the stopwatch method to determine standard times. We would make observations of a worker assembling a unit and time each element necessary for assembly. This old analysis sheet from one of the jobs in the Switches and Relays Department will illustrate what I mean. The operator was assembling a relay spring combination used in various forms of electrical equipment while she was seated at a desk with a special fixture designed to hold four of these relays at once. (See Exhibits 1, 2, and 3.) The workers got each of the pieces used to assemble the spring from the raised bins on the desk behind the fixture.

"As you can see, from this standard time analysis, we had six industrial engineers study two operators—Hannah Moore and Doris Crozier. The figures have been boiled down somewhat from the original observations. First of all, each analyst observed approximately 100 assembly cycles. The figures shown here were the average times for each element in the assembly cycle. Second, since the spring assemblies were built on a 4 station fixture, the original times have been divided by four. The industrial engineer who compiled this sheet, took each of the six individual observations and found the average time for each element, and the average time for the entire cycle (Exhibit 3, Column 7). If only one analyst were making this study, he would have included a performance rating to adjust the time to what he considered a normal pace. In other words, if the industrial engineer felt that Hannah Moore was only working at 80% of the normal pace while he was

EXHIBIT 1

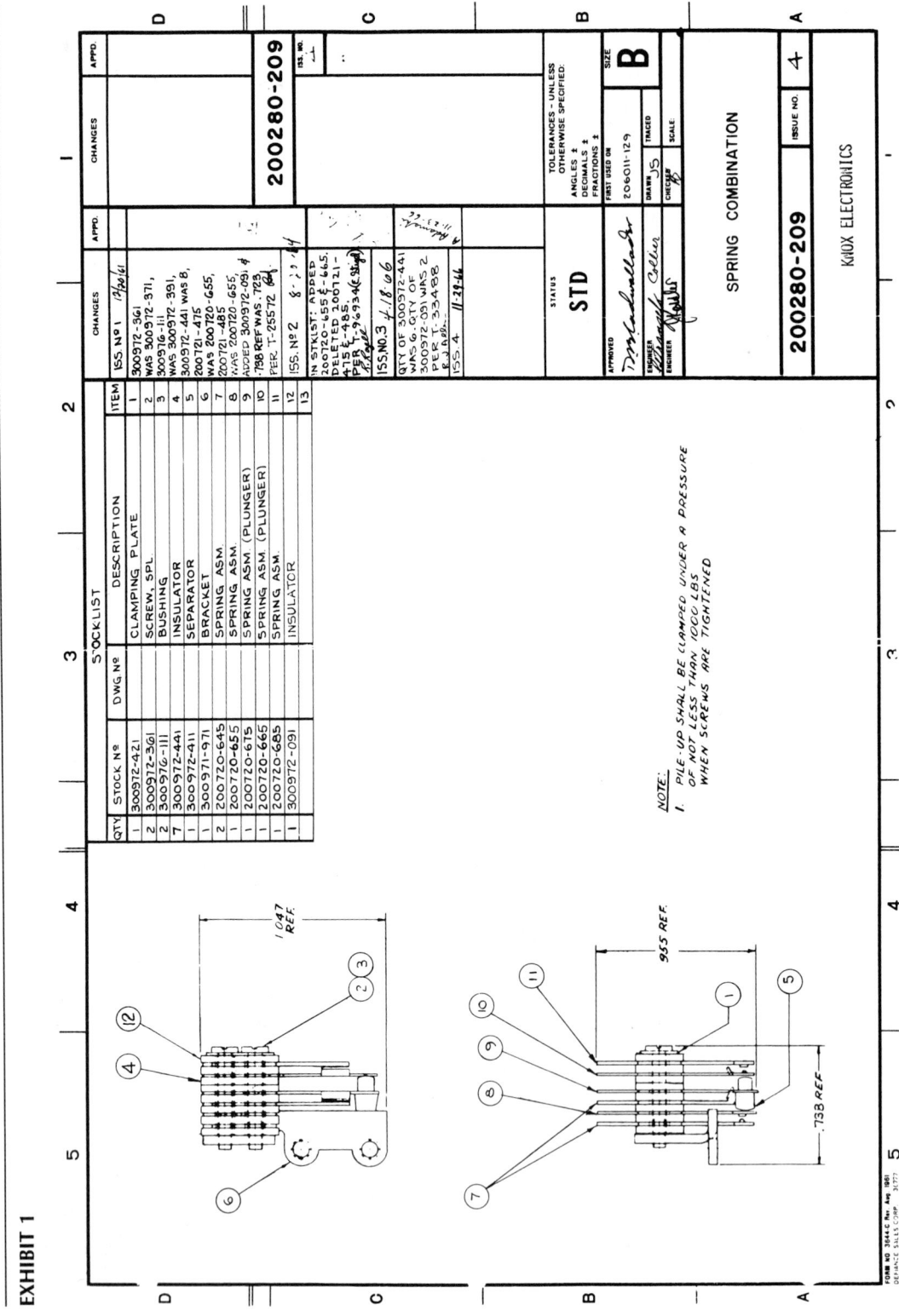

EXHIBIT 2
Lay-Out for Operation #2 (Pile-Up Assembly)

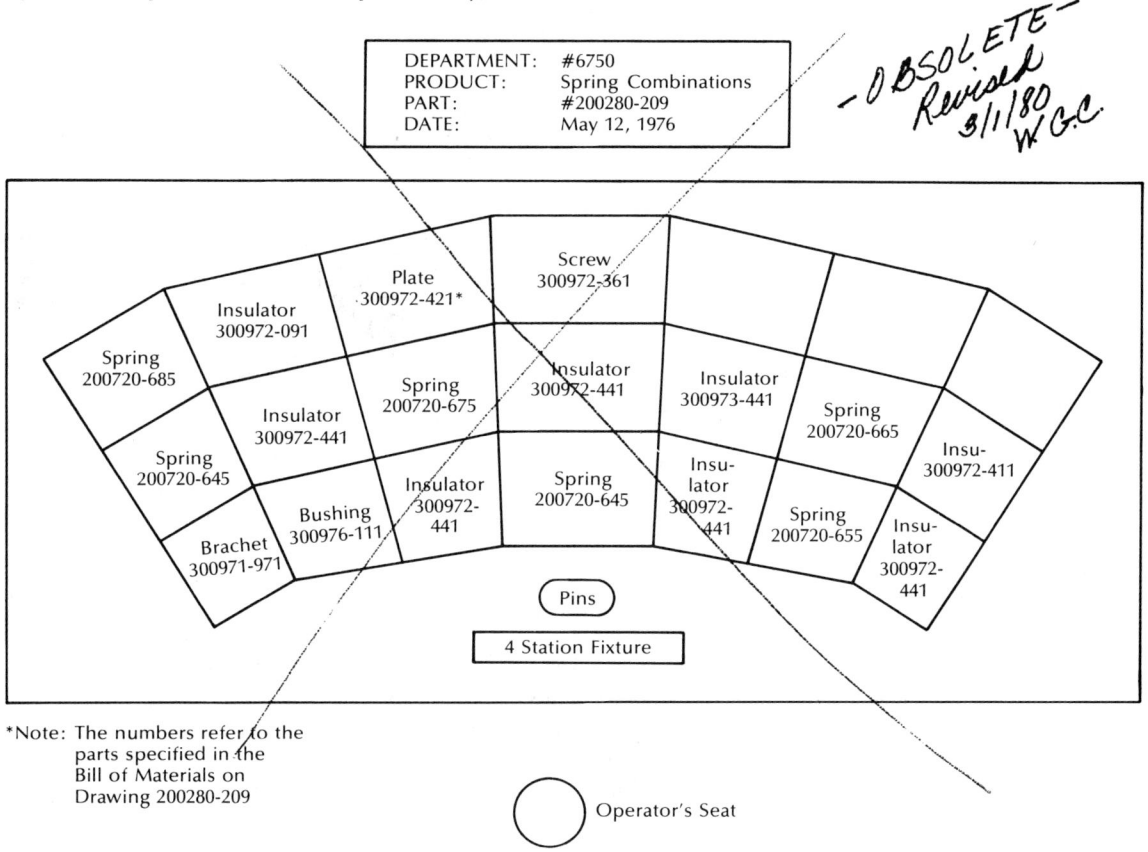

DEPARTMENT:	#6750
PRODUCT:	Spring Combinations
PART:	#200280-209
DATE:	May 12, 1976

*Note: The numbers refer to the parts specified in the Bill of Materials on Drawing 200280-209

timing her, he would have adjusted the times accordingly. In most time study situations we believe, however, that by averaging six observations on two workers, no performance rating is necessary.

"The average minutes per piece total was multiplied by 115% to allow for delay, rest and fatigue. These final figures (Exhibit 3, Column 8) gave us the standard time for each element and the total cycle. The standard for part #200280-209, operation #2 established under the stopwatch system became 74.4 pieces per hour.

"All our standards were established by stopwatch until six months ago, when we began to use MTS. This is a predetermined times system which was developed by a group of British engineers to overcome some of the difficulties usually found in the use of other predetermined times systems like MTM. The engineers found that it was far easier to think of hand-assembly motions not in terms of distances, but in terms of limb movements. They were able to classify six major movements which had surprisingly constant times (see Exhibit 4). In addition to these, they were able to identify several actions as the termination of the movements. These, too, they

EXHIBIT 3
Pile-Up Assembly Data—200280-209—Operation #2 (Department 6750)

Date	(1) 5-19-74	(2) 5-19-74	(3) 5-19-74
Operator Operator # Analyst	H. Moore 0654 P.B.C.	D. Crozier 0983 M.A.H.	D. Crozier 0983 K.C.O.
Get & Place Bracket.	.0298	.0292	.0400
Get & Place Guide Pins.	.0440	.0564	.0542
Get & Place Bushings.	.0552	.0548	.0528
Get & Place Insulators (300972-441)	.1092	.1242	.1296
Get & Place Spring Assembly.	.1830	.1980	.1698
Get & Place Insulators (300972-091)	.0182	.0207	.0216
Place Plate, Remove Pins, Insert Screws.	.1191	.1612	.1411
Drive Screws w/Air Driver.	.0616	.0400	.0482
Remove from Fixture, mark, check, & put aside.	.0416	.0574	.0417
Machine times	.009	.010	.011
TOTAL CYCLE	.6707	.7519	.7100

.8064 std. min/pc.; 1.344 hours/100 pcs.; 74.4 pcs./hr.
*Times are for 1 piece done on a 4-station fixture.

found, had fairly constant times. Thus, if a worker has to reach out and pick up a screw, there are only two times involved: the reach and the pick.

"We found this system intriguing because it did not involve taking measurements of hand travel, etc. as is required with the Motion-Time-Measurement technique. One industrial engineer can now sit at his desk, follow a planned work-method, and use the MTS predetermined times to develop a standard time for the job. That is the advantage of a predetermined time system: you don't involve lots of engineers and you don't have to guess how fast the operator is working. We purchased the rights to use MTS from the consulting firm which suggested it to us. Six other industrial engineers and I went to their MTS training school for two weeks.

"The company did put quite a bit of money into the MTS program. We feel that the savings in time required to develop standards would justify the expense. One man at his desk could develop a work standard using MTS while earlier we used six men out in the shop with stopwatches.

"We welcome MTS because of its time-savings aspects. We have asked for more men in the department because we are swamped with work, but the company's current belt-tightening just won't allow us to hire any more men. We hope MTS will help us out. In addition, many of the loose production standards are being modified with MTS in an effort to boost productivity.

"Six months ago, we instituted new MTS based standards in two smaller departments with no difficulties. But this trouble we are having in the Switches and Relays Department concerns me. The old standards there were easy to beat. However, they were firm standards; they weren't something we could just walk in and change to suit ourselves, because we could not do that unless we had an

(4) 5-19-74	(5) 5-19-74	(6) 5-19-74	(7)	(8)
H. Moore 0654 P.J.D.	D. Crozier 0983 W.G.C.	H. Moore 0654 K.N.Y.	Average minutes per piece	(7) × 115% = STD. MIN./Pc.
.0260	.0380	.0220	.0308	.0354
.0502	.0420	.0440	.0484	.0557
.0572	.0420	.0420	.0508	.0584
.1476	.1440	.1500	.1338	.1539
.2322	.1500	.1680	.1836	.2111
.0246	.0240	.0250	.0223	.0256
.1164	.1438	.0786	.1267	.1457
.0442	.0480	.0400	.0470	.0541
.0533	.0540	.0390	.0478	.0550
.011	.009	.010	.010	.0115
.7625	.6948	.6186	.7012	.8064

(Handwritten annotation across column (6): "OUTDATED changed 3/11/80 W.G.C.")

obvious clerical error or methods change. Now that we have the new MTS technique we can quickly restudy an assembly procedure. If this results in a higher standard, the industrial engineer can claim a cost reduction, thus, he will be saving the company money by revising a loose time standard."

SWITCHES AND RELAYS

John Ransom, the foreman of Section 6750 in the Switches and Relays Department, explained his view of the current difficulty:

"I just don't understand what is going on! Many of the old standards for producing relays had lasted for seven years and many of my girls were producing 150% of standard. Thus, they knew that eventually the standards would be tightened, but this amount of change is too much!

"Well, anyway, this all started when Hannah Moore was transferred from my section to the switches section. She was barely on the job two weeks when her new foreman made a methods change by moving several of the compartments to a recessed area directly in front of the operator. This decreased the head and eye movement necessary to locate the parts and the foreman got a bonus for the methods improvement under the Methods Improvement Program. Hannah realized that the same improvement could be made on her old assembly job in my section, so she put the idea in and received a Worker Suggestion Bonus for it.

"Less than a week after that methods improvement was adopted, Scott Pagent sent out a new MTS based standard for the eight jobs affected by Hannah Moore's suggestion. Well, the girls here got all upset, since most of their standards increased over 30%. The MTS program was new to me, and so I gave my

EXHIBIT 4

Examples of Movement Time Standards (time in minutes)

	Allowed time in modules	Allowed time in minutes
Movement class		
1—finger movement only	1	.00215
2—movement of hand from the wrist	2	.00430
3—movement of forearm from the elbow	3	.00645
4—movement of the entire arm (no shoulder movement)	4	.00860
5—movement of entire arm and shoulder	5	.01075
7—any movement longer than "5" which requires no steps or side steps	7	.01505
Action type		
G = *Get*		
G0—simple contact (touch)	0	0
G1—simple grasp	1	.00215
G3—normal get (pick up object)	3	.00645
P = *Put*		
P0—contact put-toss-or-drop	0	0
P2—visually aided put (place)	2	.0043
P5—specific put (more difficulty)	5	.01075
Special		
R2—regrasp (shift fingers)	2	.0043
E2—use eyes	2	.0043
A4—apply pressure	4	.0086

*Any movements in parentheses are simultaneous movements and are therefore not added to total time.
NOTE: Each module of time is .00215 minutes.

EXHIBIT 4, cont'd

Illustration of the Use of MTS in Determining the New Time Standards for Assembling Spring Combination No. 200280-209

EXAMPLE: Element 2, Exhibit 6

Motion codes	Movement class	Action type	Modules allowed
2G3	2	G3	5
(R2)	This move is simultaneous and is therefore not included in time		
2P2	2	P2	4
(2P0)	Simultaneous		
1G3	1	G3	4
(R2, 2P0)	Simultaneous		
1P2	1	P2	3
		SUBTOTAL	16
		× frequency	4
		TOTAL MODULES	64

64 modules × .00215 minutes per module = .1376 minutes for element 2

permission for the rate increases after examining Scott's new time sheets and observing the new method of assembly; but I didn't understand those "reference book" produced standards (see Exhibit 6 for an example of one such sheet). Why, Scott didn't even come out on the shop floor to observe the new methods. You can bet that I will get myself into the action the next time Pagent comes around here with his clipboard and a new MTS standard sheet for me to review."

Doris Crozier, one of the six women assigned to assembling part #200280-209, the spring combination, had this to say about the new methods and standards:

"I really don't understand how they expect us to produce at the new standard of 97 pieces an hour when the old standards was only 74.4. This methods improvement hasn't made that big a difference! I know that some of us more experienced assemblers can often produce over standard, but not 30% over all the time! With the new work station layout, I never get a chance to look up and around to speak to other girls. My husband and I are remodeling our basement into a den and I was counting on the little bit of bonus I do make to help make the payments. I'll try my best, but I think this new standard is unreasonable!"

EXHIBIT 5
Revised Lay-Out for Operation #2 (Pile-Up Assembly)

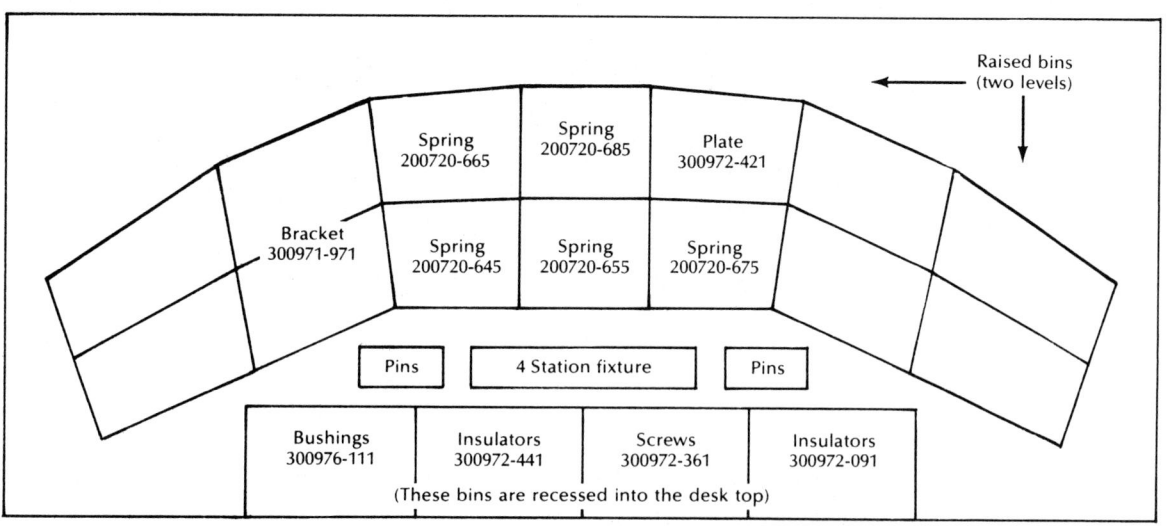

EXHIBIT 6
MTS Analysis Sheet

PAGE _1_ OF _2_

Department: SWITCHES AND RELAYS			Dept. #: 6750		
			Part #: 200250-209		
Product: SPRING COMBINATION					
			Operation #: 2		
Operation: ASSEMBLE SPRING COMBINATION PILE-UP					
Machine: 4-STATION FIXTURE # 39-104577			Machine #:		
AIR-DRIVEN SCREWDRIVER			Speed-Cycle:		

Ele.	Element description	Hand	Motion codes	FEQ	MODS
		B — R / L			
1	GET 2 BRACKETS ↑ PUT ONE EACH IN 2 STATIONS	Ⓑ — R / L	3G3 (R2), 3P5, 3P0, 1G3, (R2, 3P0), 1P5	2	54
		B — R / L			
2	GET FIXTURE PINS ↑ PUT 2 IN EACH STATION	Ⓑ — R / L	2G3 (R2), 3P3, (2P0) / 1G3, (R2, 2P0), 1P2	4	64
		B — R / L			
3	GET 2 BUSHINGS ↑ PUT ON PINS	Ⓑ — R / L	3G3, (R2) 3P2, (3PC) / 1G3, (R2, 3P0), 1P2	4	72
		B — R / L			
4	GET INSULATORS (300972-441) ↑ PUT ON PINS (7 PER SPRING PILE-UP)	Ⓑ — R / L	2G3, (R2), 2P2, (2P0) / 1G3, (R2, 2PC), 1P2	14	224
		B — R / L			
5	GET SPRING ASM. ↑ PUT ON PINS (6 PER SPRING PILE-UP)	Ⓑ — R / L	3G3, (R2, E2) 3P5, (3PC) / 1G3, (R2, E2, 3PC), 1P5	12	288
		B — R / L			
6	GET 2 INSULATORS (300972-091) ↑ PUT ON PINS (1 PER SPRING PILE-UP)	Ⓑ — R / L	3G3, (R2) 3P2, (3PC) / 1G3, (R2, 3PC), 1P2	2	36
		B — R / L			
7	GET 2 CLAMPING PLATES ↑ PUT ON PINS (1 PER SPRING PILE-UP)	Ⓑ — R / L	3G3, (R2), 3P2, (3PC) / 1G3, (R2, 3P0), 1P2	2	36
		B — R / L			
8	WITHDRAW ONE PIN FROM PILE-UP ↑ PUT ASIDE. HOLD PILE-UP. GET ONE SCREW AND PUT IN PILE-UP	B — ⓇR / L	2G1, 2P0, 2P0 (2G1, R2), 3G3, (R2), 3P2	4	72
		B — R / L			
9	GET AIR DRIVER	B — Ⓡ R / L	3G1	1	4
		B — R / L			

REMARKS OR SPECIAL CONDITIONS:	TOTAL CYCLE MOD UNITS	=	
	NORMAL MINUTES (×.00215)	=	
	PROCESS TIME = ×	=	
	TOTAL NORMAL TIME	=	
	ALLOWANCES-REST =	% =	
	−NOMINAL DELAY =	% =	
	− =	% =	
DATE SET: 3-1-80 DATE APPROVED:	TOTAL STANDARD	=	
ANALYST: S. Parent APPROVED:	RATE FOR %-PIECES/HOUR		

EXHIBIT 6, cont'd

PAGE 2	OF 2

Department: SWITCHES AND RELAYS			Dept. #: 6750		
Product: SPRING COMBINATION			Part #: 200 280-209		
Operation: ASSEMBLE SPRING COMBINATION PILE-UP			Operation #: 2		
Machine: 4-STATION FIXTURE #39-104577 AIR-DRIVEN SCREW DRIVER			Machine #: Speed-Cycle:		

Ele.	Element description	Hand	Motion codes	FEQ	MODS
		B R / L			
10	PUT DRIVER ON SCREW & DRIVE SCREW GET SECOND PIN IN HAND (3 PINS ONLY)	B (R) / L	3P2, A4 (2G1, 2PO, R2)	4	36
		B R / L			
11	PROCESS TIME	B R / L			
12	PUT DRIVER ASIDE & POSITION HAND GET LAST PIN IN HAND & PUT ALL PINS ASIDE	B R / (L)	(1PO, 3PO) 2G1, 2PO, 2PO	1	7
		B R / L			
13	GET 2 SCREWS & PUT ONE EACH IN TWO PILE-UPS	(B) R / L	3G3, (R2)3P2, (3PO) 1G3, (R2,3PO),1P2	2	36
		B R / L			
14	GET AIR DRIVER	B (R) / L	3G1	1	4
15	PUT DRIVER ON SCREW & DRIVE SCREW GET PILE-UP & PLACE ASIDE (DO 3 TIMES)	B R / L B (R) / L	3P2, A4 (2G1, 2PO, R2)	4	36
16	PROCESS TIME	B R / L			
17	PUT DRIVER ASIDE GET LAST PILE-UP & PUT ASIDE	B R / (L)	(1PO), 2G1, 2PO (R2), 4PO	1	9
		B R / L			978
		B R / L	TOTAL:		4
		B R / L			
		B R / L			
		B R / L			
		B R / L			

REMARKS OR SPECIAL CONDITIONS: PROCESS TIME OF .0065 MIN. PER SCREW	TOTAL CYCLE MOD UNITS	=	244.5
4 PILE-UPS ARE BUILT AT A TIME ON A 4-STATION FIXTURE	NORMAL MINUTES (×.00215)	=	.525
	PROCESS TIME = .0065 × 2	=	.013
.612 STD. MIN./PIECE 97.0 PCS./HR	TOTAL NORMAL TIME	=	.538
	ALLOWANCES-REST = 15 %=	=	.080
	−NOMINAL DELAY =	%=	
	− =	%=	
DATE SET: 3-1-80 DATE APPROVED: 3/22/80	TOTAL STANDARD MINUTES	=	.618
ANALYST: S. Parent APPROVED: L.C. Ramsey	RATE FOR 100 %-PIECES/HOUR	=	97.0

EXHIBIT 7
Hourly-Employees Earnings (Sample) 1/8/80 thru 1/15/80

Employee number	Actual hours	Incentive pay	Premiums for overtime	Minimum guarantee adjustment	Total weekly pay
0098	40	180.00			180.00
0158	40	204.80			204.80
0187	37.5	194.29		4.46	198.75
0311	31.9	159.50			159.50
0416	40	196.31		20.09	216.40
0635	46	285.66	18.63		285.66
0744	40	190.40			190.40
0802	40	207.49		12.11	219.60
0877	40	204.80			204.80
0983 (D Crozier)	46	331.20	21.60		331.20
1046	46	228.62	14.95		228.62
1139	40	239.60			239.60
1265	38	186.09		3.91	190.00

Earnings for Doris Crozier (Employee #0983) and other workers in the Switches and Relays Department for the week of January 8, 1980 (before the methods and standards changes) are shown in Exhibit 7. Payroll records for the six women assembling spring combination #200280-209 showed that although their old guaranteed wage was $4.24 an hour, their actual wages averaged $5.47. For the period following the establishment of the new standard on the spring combination, however, their average wages earned were only $2.85 an hour. The company had to make-up the difference to the guaranteed $4.24 an hour.

PERFORMANCE EVALUATION CRITERIA FOR SCOTT PAGENT

An industrial engineer, for purposes of the annual performance-and-raise review, was judged on the following items: the standard coverage in his departments and the cost reduction which he is able to submit.

Scott, who was 22, commented on his entry position in the Industrial Engineering Department: "This job is an excellent position to gain exposure to the plant's operations. As I am assigned to different areas in the plant it allows me to see the entire manufacturing process from simple soldering to the molding of plastic parts. I see this job as a springboard, a foundation which should stand me in good stead in any attempt to get into a line management position, whether at this company or another."

Scott was aggressive, and he decided that the fastest way to gain recognition was by obtaining cost reductions. He further realized that it was easier to track loose existing standards and MTS them, as opposed to the more difficult and time consuming approach of devising new fixtures and elaborate work stations to gain a cost reduction. He, therefore, turned his attention to the loose standards in John Ransom's section of the Switches and Relays Department.

EXHIBIT 8
Sample Productivity Report February 11–15, 1980

Worker no.	ACTHR	HRSTD	STDHRS	%
0187	39.80	27.31	29.51	108
0311	40.00	39.42	37.30	95
0416	40.00	38.00	49.00	129
0744	39.80	36.52	31.20	85
0983	40.00	34.80	58.00	166
(D. Crozier)				
1139	40.00	32.40	40.10	123
1591	40.00	32.00	36.00	113
1833	40.00	25.40	29.30	115

Explanation of column headings:
Worker no.—Individual's reporting number
ACTHR —Actual hours worked
HRSTD —Total hours worked on standard items
STDHRS —Standard hours earned
% —STDHRS/HRSTD

Scott followed a set procedure in determining standards to review. First, he looked at the weekly department production report which gave the previous week performance for each operator by clock number (Exhibit 8). If he noticed that an operator had produced a high number of standard hours while working a comparatively low number of actual hours on piece rate work, he identified the individual by the clock number and checked if that individual worked in his area of responsibility. If the employee was assigned to John Ransom, then he obtained a copy of the job report, which listed all the jobs that a worker had completed during the week, for that person. He checked this report to determine the jobs on which the employee was "beating the system". For example, Scott noted that D. Crozier, worker number 0983, was working at 166%. He checked her job report and found that she had been on piece rate only on part no. 200280-209.

Next, he contacted production control about each part which raised his interest to determine how many pieces of that part were used in production the previous year, and the current year, to date. With this information he was able to estimate, roughly, the cost reduction that could be realized.

Finally, Scott usually observed the operator at work before he made his decision on whether or not to MTS the job. If he did restudy the job using MTS and a cost reduction resulted, he submitted a cost reduction proposal and a revised time standard would be implemented.

JOB EVALUATION CRITERIA FOR JOHN RANSOM

John Ransom, age 26, had been working at Knox since his graduation from high school. His first job had been in the machine shop. Tim Jocobs, who had been responsible for the shop when John first started work, remembered him:

"John is ambidextrous and smart as hell. He would give us fits in the shop. Any job that he was placed on he would bust the standard. I would go out and observe the job, and convince myself that the standard was good; John would get on the job and run 200%. He is just one of those people who would work smart and take advantage of everything to ensure his getting a large bonus. Mind you everything he did was near legal. In fact I bet you he was taking home more pay in the shop than he is making on his present salary."

The Manager of Manufacturing, Kit Watson, primarily was looking for John to improve departmental efficiency and morale. He was hoping that if John could accomplish these goals, the increased sales in the current year could be handled by the department without further taxing an already strained manufacturing budget.

Before being named foreman, John had spent time in production control and worked six months as a time study man. He had recently completed the company's five week in-house management development program.

PHIL CHASE'S PROBLEM

Phil Chase, after having lunch with Scott Pagent, returned to his office. He wanted all differences between John and Scott aired and settled before their dispute escalated into a confrontation between the production foremen and the industrial engineers. Phil said:

"The introduction of MTS into this plant has been a full-time job for me. I believe that this system will in time improve our wage incentive plan. I have tried to spend time informing and educating the foremen and managers about the program in order to gain their acceptance. A full blown interdepartmental squabble could seriously hurt this program."

Phil decided to set up a meeting with John and Scott in one of the conference rooms for 8:30 the next morning. Over the phone, Phil told John that the meeting would provide him with an opportunity to talk about the problems concerning standards in his section. Later, Phil wondered how easy it would be to act as a referee between the two young bucks.

SELECTED COMMENTS FROM THE MEETING

John:

"Scott comes into the area and resets standards. His new ones are not even reasonable. My operators are unable to even run 100% against his standards . . . It's hurting my weekly department productivity report. Last week my department ran 84%, the plant average was 118% . . . I thought the incentive system was set up to give an operator a chance at 125% . . . How can I explain a low figure like this to my boss, who is expecting production from me . . . I refuse to believe that my people are so bad, or that I'm doing such a poor job that my department runs this low . . . Look at this standard on part number 200280-209, operation number 2. The old standard was 74.4 pieces per hour. Scott comes in and raises it by almost one-third. Sure, you can set the standard and walk away, but I have to try and work with these people. It's hard to tell a person who is used to taking home a bonus, who considers it part of her income, and sets up her budgeting accordingly, that she no longer can get it. In fact, she will have to work harder just to meet the standard. It's ridiculous, this standard is too tight and there are more like this out in the department . . . Small wonder my department morale is shot to hell . . . I thought you guys were staff, but you walk in and work on standards at times when I'm not even in the department. Staff, hell, you have the power over the operators because you control the purse strings."

Scott:

"As far as part number 200280-209, if you will look at the productivity report for week no. 567 (See Exhibit 8) you'll see that D. Crozier ran 166% on the old standards for almost five days. I know she can make the new standard . . . I'm doing what I was hired for, I am new here and don't have friends on the production floor who might influence my judgment . . . The standards in your department are loose . . . Once I set a standard, I have no authority to make sure that the proper methods are used. If an operator or foreman decide they don't like a standard, they can effectively undo my work. It's being in this staff position that is frustrating. I have been told by some operators in your department that you are encouraging them to drag their feet on the new standards in the hope that the Vice-President of Manufacturing will enter the picture on your side."

The Vice-President of Manufacturing, Tom Edwards, later commented on the situation:

"For the past several years we have been highly concerned with our manufacturing costs. We have to meet the selling prices of our foreign and domestic competitors. The primary differential is in the cost of labor. Foreign manufacturers pay only one-third as much for their labor; therefore, we must be as productive and efficient as possible. Direct labor is now 17.6% of total manufacturing costs, down from 19.3% five years ago.

We must walk a thin line, however, because our people are not machines. We have kept the union out so far, but it gets tougher all the time. I saw the local union representative at the gate again yesterday, trying to find enough dissatisfied workers to get something going. We have tried to establish a good working relationship between labor and management. I am proud to admit that I know most of the workers here, or at least I am able to recognize them. When I walk through the plant, I like to stop and chat with different people on all levels. I think I find out the "mood" of the workers that way.

"This difficulty in the Switches and Relays Department worries me. We let those loose standards exist for too long. When we tried to tighten them up, the workers complained. I hope this slowdown in production there will last only during a period of adjustment. Perhaps the new standards are too tight. But that is a decision that has to be made by industrial engineering and approved by each foreman, though, if it does get out of hand, I'll have to step in."

Century National Bank

Ted Chandler, Vice President of Management Development at Century National Bank (CNB), hunched intently over the papers on his desk. Before him were the results from the first ten months of the Profit Improvement Program (PIP). The bank's outside consultant, aided by three internal analysts, had completed work measurement and manpower staffing studies in three of the bank's largest branches. These three branches were reporting monthly performance data, but, so far, top management had not insisted on corrective action in the poor performance areas identified by the program.

Ted Chandler stretched and leaned back in his chair. What, he wondered, should be the future of PIP? Reactions within the bank had been mixed. Many people felt that the work measurement methodology of PIP was not appropriate for the bank's planning needs.

Ted knew that as the bank officer in charge of PIP he had to develop a recommendation for the Profit Control Committee meeting the next day. Specifically, he had to recommend whether to drop the program or to extend it to the bank's other thirteen branches. If he wanted to keep PIP, should he recommend hiring Frank Parkinson, the outside consultant, to work for the bank as a full-time planning officer?

Ted picked up a sheet showing some of the consultant's recommendations. He wondered if he should insist on corrective action in the areas where PIP results had identified poor performance.

PROFIT IMPROVEMENT PROGRAM: MAY 1980-JUNE 1981

Background

In September of 1980, Ted Chandler compared recent banking industry operating costs with those of CNB. He became concerned about the fact that payroll costs were a larger percentage of the bank's gross income than other banks of similar size and that these payroll costs had been increasing at a disturbing rate.

Century National Bank was the largest bank in a group of ten banks owned by a multibank holding company. Within the general economic and financial environment of the state, "Century National Bank was able to achieve a considerably greater percentage increase in total deposits and in total loans than the average of all weekly reporting banks in the state . . . and a percentage increase in deposits and loans nearly three times greater than that experienced by all weekly reporting banks in the United States."[1] CNB's return on assets had steadily improved from .66% in 1977 to .93% in 1979 and its return on equity rose from 8.5% to 12.5% over the same period.

Century's primary objective was continued growth in deposits and loans. Area and regional managers, working with individual branch managers, annually pre-

---

[1]Annual Report, Century National Bank.

EXHIBIT 1
Partial Organization Chart

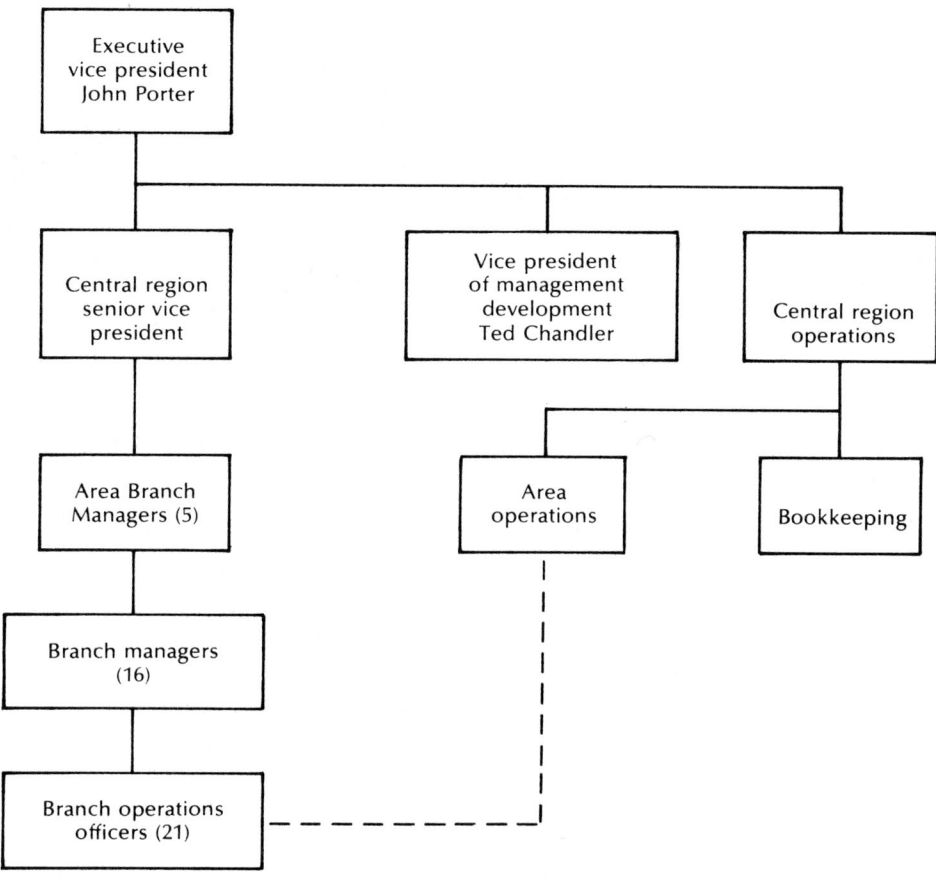

Numbers in parentheses represent the number of managers/officers.

pared their budgets based on desired sales growth. Branch managers were measured against how well they achieved sales (deposits and loans) objectives. Branch managers were expected to make outside calls on commercial customers. Also, they encouraged their employees to increase the sale of new accounts and loans by using prizes and recognition as incentives.

Because of his concern with rising payroll costs, Mr. Chandler, then the officer in charge of management development (Exhibit 1), initiated the idea of employing an outside consulting firm to set up a work measurement program. After contacting eight companies, a large nationally known management consulting firm was selected. The potential net annual savings were estimated by the consulting firm to be $1,352,000.

Profit Improvement Program Organization

The work measurement program was named the Profit Improvement Program and was put under the direction of the Executive Vice President, John Porter. Ted Chandler was designated as the bank officer in charge of the program. He felt that the PIP group should be a staff group whose function was to aid the branch managers. This went along with the bank's concept of centralized organization where such things as accounting, purchasing, and personnel matters were controlled from the main office.

The consulting firm assigned Frank Parkinson to the job on a full-time basis. Mr. Parkinson was very quantitatively skilled and enjoyed his technical work very much. CNB assigned three young men from the management training program to work under Mr. Parkinson. One of these three "analysts" was designated head analyst. He had an MBA from the University of North Carolina and had been with CNB for a little over one year. The other two analysts were also new with the bank, one having been there for three months and the other for two weeks. The three analysts were trained in work measurement techniques by Mr. Parkinson for one week. Progress was reported by Mr. Parkinson weekly at a meeting of the bank's Profit Control Committee. It was composed of Mr. Porter, who was the chairman of the committee, two bank officers from the Commercial Lending Department, the Corporate Secretary, and Mr. Chandler. Exhibit 2 is the memorandum that introduced the Profit Improvement Program to the bank officers and managers.

To assist the analysts in the branch studies, Mr. Parkinson recommended that the branch operations officer should be the direct contact for the analysis. The operations officer was equivalent to an assistant branch manager and was responsible for the day-to-day operation of the office as well as being a loan officer. He reported both to the branch manager and to the area operations officer. All operations officers attended eight two-hour training sessions on the various aspects of PIP.

PIP was separated into two areas: (1) a work measurement program designed to set standards on the various tasks performed in a branch and to measure performance against man power budgets based on those standards, and (2) a waiting line analysis to schedule tellers.

EXHIBIT 2
Memorandum

December 14, 1980

To: All Officers & Managers
Subject: Profit Improvement Program

Our Profit Improvement Program is now well under way in several areas of the bank. As you realize, this is an ambitous undertaking, and we are sure you know how anxious we are to show real improvement as soon as possible.

We are assured by our consultant that actual accomplishment of reduced costs lies entirely in your hands, both now and in the future. It is recognized that until studies are completed in your areas, the full complement of work standards and other control techniques will not be available to you. At the same time we are confident that you are willing and able to take appropriate improvement action based on your own knowledge of your operations in anticipation of the new performance controls.

Each time you contemplate requesting a newly authorized position for your staff, the filling of a vacancy or replacement for a terminated employee, there is an opportunity for profit improvement. Perhaps there are other ways in which the problem can be solved. Consider all the possibilities you can think of and ask the PIP staff for their assistance before taking final action. For example, some of the following alternatives may forestall the need for adding staff:
- Reapportionment of routine duty assignments among several employees.
- Identification and postponement of selected low-priority work to low volume periods.
- Cross training of employees to handle non-recurring special work.
- Reasonable use of overtime to handle short-term spurts in workload.
- Borrowing and lending available employee time between sections for routine work.

In addition, review whatever interim arrangements you would make assuming a delay in filling the vacancy. If such arrangements will work during a short period, they may well become part of the permanent routine.

In order to assure that every effort is made to maintain economical staffing levels, we are asking Dave Durrill and our consultant, Frank Parkinson, to review all current personnel requisitions with you as they are received to provide you with every possible assistance.

As you know, a good portion of the money we save will revert back to you through increased salaries and profit sharing.

Chairman of the Board

WORK MEASUREMENT PROGRAM AND PERFORMANCE ANALYSIS

The work measurement program consisted of the four elements described in Exhibit 3. The jobs to be studied were first determined. Tellers, new account clerks, a vault custodian, a receptionist, loan interviewers, and supervisors performed the major work activities. The tasks performed within each job were identified next, and these tasks were listed on flow process charts and broken down into minute, timeable elements. The predetermined time value technique was employed using the consulting firm's table of motion-time values (Exhibit 4). An example of the work measurement program for the signature card action is shown in Exhibit 5 and 6. Exhibit 5 is the Process Analysis Chart. Exhibit 6 gives

EXHIBIT 3
Basic Elements of the Work Measurement Program

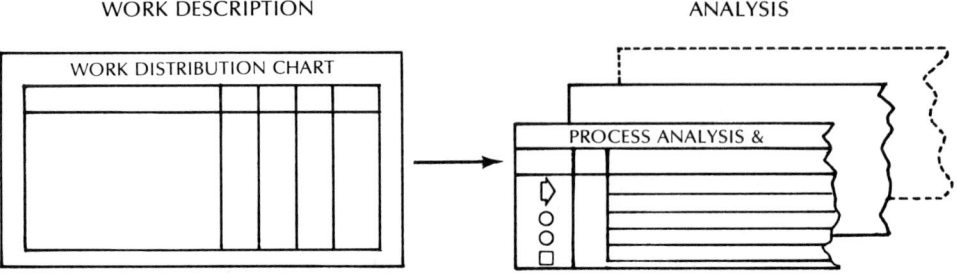

WORK DESCRIPTION

ANALYSIS

- Purpose of the Work Distribution Chart is to identify and describe major and secondary work processes and the approximate time spent by various persons or groups on each.

- It provides the basic information for subsequent analytical and measurement work.

- In itself may suggest certain desirable improvements

- Purpose of process analysis is to describe the WHO, WHAT, WHERE, HOW, WHEN, and WHY of the work performed.

- Takes each major process from the WDC and breaks into the step-by-step sequence of operations, beginning to end.

- Work is analyzed for possibility of:
  – eliminating
  – simplifying
  – combining
  – changing sequence

(see Exhibit 5 for example)

the calculation of the work standard. The standard is broken down into two segments, the constant time and the variable time. The constant time, for signature card actions, 130.8 hrs/month, is the amount of time which must be spent regardless of the volume of signature cards. On the other hand, total variable time (variable standard time of .224 hours/unit times transactions per month) is directly variable with signature card requests.

The Standard Work Distribution Chart

Standards were determined in a similar way for all other major work processes in the branch. They were then transformed to the Standard Work Distribution Chart (Exhibit 7). Based on projected monthly volume, the standard hours necessary for each job category, such as teller, could be determined. In order to arrive at total budget hours for a branch, various allowances were made. For instance, employees were not expected to work at 100%, or to perform 100 standard hours work in 100 actual hours; rather, the objective was to get a group of people to work at 85% effectiveness, or to perform 85 standard hours of work in 100 actual hours. The full-time equivalents were reached by dividing total paid hours by the

EXHIBIT 3, cont'd

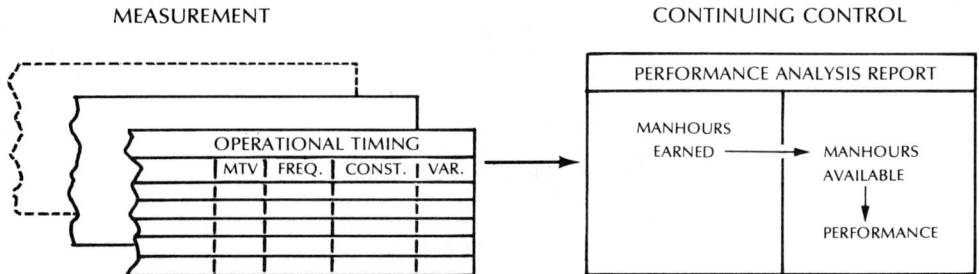

MEASUREMENT

CONTINUING CONTROL

OPERATIONAL TIMING

| MTV | FREQ. | CONST. | VAR. |

PERFORMANCE ANALYSIS REPORT

MANHOURS EARNED → MANHOURS AVAILABLE

PERFORMANCE

- Purpose of the Operational Timing portion of the process chart is to break each operation into timeable segments.
- Predetermined and other standard time values are assigned to arrive at a standard time for each operation and for each process.
- In combination with volume counts provides the data necessary for performance analysis and control reporting.

(see Exhibit 5 for an example)

- The Performance Analysis Report brings together on one form a summary of section activity for any given period.
- This is a basic tool for continuing controls, and provides data from which management can:
  - plan work
  - control work
  - evaluate effectiveness
  - plan improvement
    - scheduling
    - distribution
    - staffing
    - budgeting
    - cost analysis

(see Exhibit 8 for an example)

number of working hours in the month (based on 7.5 hours per day). Two part-time employees were considered equal to one full-time employee. The difference between a staff of 19 full-time employees and two part-time employees and a staff of 14 full-time employees and four part-time employees, based on a salary of $13,000 per year per employee, would result in an annual payroll savings of $52,000.

The standard work distribution chart was the main exhibit used in the presentation to branch management. Mr. Parkinson and the analyst assigned to the particular branch made the presentations to the branch manager, the branch operations officer, and the bank's personnel officer. After the findings and recommendations were presented, branch management was given a written report discussing the staffing recommendations of the PIP group and a copy of all the data leading up to the recommendations. Then the PIP group requested a memorandum from the branch manager indicating the extent of his agreement with the PIP recommendations and the manner in which he planned to achieve the identified savings. The extent of the branch manager's agreement was usually less than what PIP recommended.

Text continued on page 87.

EXHIBIT 4
Motion-Time Values for Clerical Work Measurement

Ref.	Read and visual examination	MTV*	Unit**
RD	(Values include eye shift)		
−1	Read typed or printed material	3.3	Word
−2	Read longhand material	3.5	"
−3	Read numbers, 1 or 1st digit	6.6	Digit
−4	Add, per additional digit in number	1.6	"
−5	Read aloud	7.0	Word
−6	Move eyes and focus on specific location	13.0	Occ.
−7	Scan or interpret data w/i range of vision	6.3	"
	Proofread		
−8	*Text, 1 person	8.2	Word
−9	2 persons	15.4	"
−10	*Tapes or list, 1 person, 1st digit	20.2	Digit
−11	—Additional digit	3.2	"
−12	—2 persons	14.0	"

	Write, print, post		
WR	(Values do not include "Get" and "Aside" pencil)		
−1	Write	8.2	Letter
	*Average of 5 letters/word	41.0	Word
−2	Print, letter or character	14.0	Letter
−3	*Digit	11.3	Digit
−4	Read and write (copy work)	46.0	Word
−5	Read and print (posting entries)	24.9	Digit
−6	*Per digit after 1st	12.9	"
−7	Underscore, freehand, up to 3″	14.0	Occ.
−8	Get rule from desk top, underscore up to 5″, aside ruler	61.0	Occ.
−9	Make check mark (√)	2.5	Occ.
−10	Pencil erasing, ½″ or less	60.0	Occ.
	Each additional ½″	7.0	Occ.
−11	Ink eradication	200.0	Applic.

	Sort papers manually		
SO	(Values do not include "Get")		Full sheet
−1	Sort, 8½ × 11 or larger, desk top ⎫ 10 piles	26.0	"
−2	Sort, smaller than 8½ × 11, desk top ⎭	22.0	"
−3	Pocket sort (multisort, sortagraph)	23.0	"
−4	Pigeon hole sort (mixed documents, variable location, includes walking)	35.0	"

*MTV = ¹/₁₀₀₀ minute
**Unit of Application (e.g., word, digit) or frequency of application (e.g., occasionally)

EXHIBIT 4, cont'd

	Get, jog and cross-stack		
JO	Get, jog and cross-stack regular weight paper		
−1	*2-10 sheets	52	Batch
−2	*11-20 sheets	64	"
−3	*over 20 sheets	76	"
	Get, jog and cross-stack onion skin weight paper		
−4	*2-10 sheets	66	"
−5	*11-20 sheets	102	"
−6	*over 20 sheets	126	"
	Get and lay aside		
GT	(Values include placing at work center)		
	Get easily grasped objects (G1)		
−1	*Short reach (15″ or less)	17	Occ.
−2	*Long reach (more than 15″)	25	"
	Get difficult to grasp objects (G2)		
−3	*Short R, unobstructed	19	"
−4	*Long R, unobstructed	27	"
−5	*Short R, obstructed	25	"
−6	*Long R, obstructed	33	"
−7	Get sheet paper requiring search	64	Sheet
−8	Get batch papers	30	Batch
LA			
−1	Lay aside object to desk	9	Occ.
−2	Lay aside object to out basket (up to 18″)	11	"
−3	Aside to waste basket	94	
	Walking and related body motions		
WK	(Values include minor obstructions of an average office)		
−1	Walk on level surface	4	Foot
−2	Walk (29″ to 33″)	9	Pace
−3	Arise and reposition chair	68	Occ.
−4	Sit, position well at desk	66	"
−5	Open door to walker	36	"
−6	Open door away f/walker	32	"
−7	Ascend steps, 8″ riser	11	Step
−8	Descend steps, 8′ riser	11	"
−9	Turn in chair without arising (90° turn)	39	Occ.
−10	Bend to knee level and arise	34	"
−11	Stoop (squat) to floor level and arise	40	"

EXHIBIT 5

	CLERICAL PROCESS ANALYSIS CHART		Department No. and name 602 Marion		Process No. and Name Signature Card Actions
Oper. No.	Flow	Outside	Pos. No.		Operation description
				Make ready & put away	
1				Receive customer & converse Rise & sit WK3 + WK4	
				Escort customer to desk WK1 Ask & listen (100 wds) RD5	
2				Determine type account Explore customer needs (100 wds) RD5	
3				Explain service charges on interest Talk (300 wds) RD5	
4				Forms completion & disposal (See spread sheet)	
5				Display checks & covers if checking	
6				Check references if necessary	
7				Escort customer to window Rise and sit WK3 + WK4	
				Walk WK1	
				Wait in line at window	
8				Introduce customer to officer Arise and sit WK3 + WK1	
				Walk WK1	
				Talk 30 wds RD5	
				Wait	
9				Reconcile account	

Prepared By: P. DeVivi					
Date: October 1980			**Item being counted: Signature cards**		
Constant variable	**Unit MTV**		**Frequency multipliers**	**Constant**	**Variable**
C	13,043		3	Occasion frequency*	39,129	
V	134			1A .986		132.1
V	7	100		1A .986		690.2
V	7	100		1B .799		545.3
V	7	300		1B .779		1635.9
V	5755.4			1		5755.4
C	3408.3			1	3408.3	
V	1500	1D .45		1E .779		525.8
V	20.000			2A .025		500.0
V	134			1B .779		104.4
V	4	2B 30		1B .779		93.5
V	1500			1B .779		1168.5
V	134			2C .005		.7
V	4	2D 60		2C .005		1.2
V	7			2C .143		1.0
V	500			2C .005		2.5
V	10.000			2E .02		200.0

EXHIBIT 5, cont'd

	CLERICAL PROCESS ANALYSIS CHART		Department No. and name 602 Marion		Process No. and Name Signature Card Actions
Oper. No.	Flow	Outside	Pos. No.		Operation description
10				New accounts report preparation	
				A,L,R,S	SAV ORIG & 1 = 255
					CK ORIG & 3 = 395
				L.P.R. (Back) TP30	
				Type date and office #2 (10TP + 3TP9)	
				L/A LA$_2$	
				Type NA information 66(TP4) + 3TP9	
				Fold & stuff NA report MO4	
11				Receive copy NA report from customer service	
				Open env. Remove contents, unfold and stack MT1	
				Open and close desk drawer FD3 + FD5	
				Get savings report of same date GT3	
				Staple checking and savings together	
				File FA7 − 4A1	
				FC16	
12				Deliver NA report to loan dept.	
				Arise and sit WK3 & WK4	
				Walk WK1	
				L/A report LA$_2$	
13				Receive new accounts report from loan dept. and file	
				Get NA report GT1	
				Place NA report in drawer by date FD7	
14				Settle debits to statement form	
				Check printer (2 hrs/2 wks)	
15				Time spent on reports other than NA	
16				Time spent in meetings	
17				Reception	

*Occasion frequency: Multiplier selected by the analyst.

Date: October 1980				
Prepared By: P. DeVivi			**Item being counted: Signature cards**	
Constant variable	**Unit MTV**	**Frequency multipliers**	**Constant**	**Variable**
		Occasion frequency*		
C	650	1	650	
C	128	1	128	
C	260	1	260	
C	11	1	11	
V	358.2	.856		306.6
C	132	1	132	
C	128	1	128	
C	35	1	35	
C	19	1	19	
C	24	1	24	
C	225	1	255	
		Occasion frequency*		
C	134	1	134	
C	4	4A 120	480	
C	11	1	11	
C	17	1	17	
C	110	1	110	
C	4B 8868	1	8868	
C	4C 54131		54131	
C	4D 2856	4	11424	
C	177408		177408	
		TOTAL CONSTANT	296,732	
		TOTAL VARIABLE		11,663.1

EXHIBIT 6
Standard Calculations Work Sheet

DEPARTMENT 602	BY RDG	DATE Nov. 12, 1980
PROCESS Signature Card Actions	PRIMARY Action	

	VARIABLE	CONSTANT
1. Total Operational Time (in MTVs) (As Shown on the Operational Timing Sheet)*	11,663.1	296,732.3
2. Allowance (15% of Total Operational Time) for Fatigue and Personal Delay	1,749.5	44,509.8
3. Total Operational Time and Allowance (in MTVs)	13,412.6	341,242.1
4. Monthly Constant Time (23.0** times Total in 3.)	xxxxxxxx	7,848,568.3
5. *Variable Standard Time* per unit (Divide Total in 3. by 60,000)***	.224	xxxxxxxxxxx
6. *Constant Standard Time* in hours (Divide Total in 4. by 60,000)***	xxxxxxxx	130.8

7. Estimated Hourly Rate (EHR)

$$EHR = \frac{1.000 - \frac{\#6}{\#6 + (\#5 \times mo.\ volume)}}{\#5} = Items/Hr.$$

REVIEWED AND APPROVED BY: *D. W. Logan* Supervisor   DATE 11/15/80

*See Case Exhibit 5 Totals
**Average Number of Working Days/Month
***1 MTV = 1/1000 Minute

The Performance Analysis Report (PAR)

Monthly, branch management submitted a Performance Analysis Report (PAR). This report gave the earned standard hours of work during the month in the branch, and the actual hours worked. Earned standard hours were based on the actual monthly volume in each process (e.g., signature card action) and the constant and variable time standards.

An up-to-date trend chart (Exhibit 8) was maintained for each branch by Mr. Porter and the bank's personnel officer, Mr. Randall. This chart of the branch performance compared the actual man hours worked against earned standard man hours. Earned standard hours represented the amount of standard time allowed for the actual volume of work processed at the branch during the month.

TELLER STAFFING STUDY

The second area of PIP was for the analysts to develop a means of determining the optimal teller staff assignments for various customer loads. The Marion Branch, CNB's largest, was chosen for this study. The method used was based on the relationship between customers served per unit of time and customer line length experienced at different levels of customer demand. Teller log sheets were kept by each teller for three weeks. During these same three weeks, a person was assigned the task of recording total customers at the teller windows at 10 random times per hour. It was determined by the analysts that if a criterion of a maximum of two persons in any teller line 95% of the time were desired, this service level would result in low teller utilization. If a criterion of a maximum of four persons in the line 95% of the time were used, teller utilization would be very high but customers might object to the resulting waiting time. Thus, Mr. Parkinson adopted the criterion of a maximum of three persons in any line 95% of the time which would result in a teller utilization that was workable and a line length that would be competitive with other banks' service levels (see Exhibit 9).

Using this criterion the consultant developed a rule that called for a teller window to be opened for every 14 additional customers (assuming a random arrival pattern of customers). The analysts found that a teller could service an average of 16 customers per half hour. The surveys also showed that the number of customers coming into a branch would vary depending on the time of day (busy at lunchtime), the day of the week (busy on Mondays and Fridays), and other special days (busy on payday or the day before a holiday). From this information an open window schedule was developed for each day of the week (example in Exhibit 10a and 10b). In Exhibit 10a, the first column shows the number of customers expected, the second column shows the number of windows necessary to be open to provide the desired service level, and the third column shows the recommended teller staff. Exhibit 10b was to be used by the branch operations manager in making personnel assignments.

Ted was concerned about the validity of the staffing schedule. He had thought about testing the schedule out at several branches, but he was not certain about the design or even the feasibility of such a test. He wondered if he could use

EXHIBIT 7

	BUDGET HOURS REQUIRED FOR FORECAST		MONTHLY VOLUME
Process description	Variable std. time hours/unit	Forecasted monthly vol. of units	Constant time per month (hours)
Signature card actions	.224	304	130.8
Paying & receiving trans.	.0117	37,188	311.8
Currency & coin handling	.024	7,975	—
Collecting & issuing	.057	1,366	30.7
Loans	1.171	128	31.0
Safe deposit box entries	.064	363	27.4
Savings cert. actions	.071	347	.6
Secretarial	—	—	—
Commecial development	1.500	10	
Total standard hours*			
Provision for 85% performance			
Necessary available hours			
Provision for vacation & training			
Supervision			
Necessary paid hours			
Provision for customer service			
Total budgeted hours			
Full-time equivalents (Paid hours − 172.5)**			
Recommended employee staffing (full-time—part-time)			
Present employee staffing (full-time—part-time)			

*Includes 15% Fatigue and Personal Delay Allowance
**172.5 = 23.0 days × 7.5 hours

waiting line tables from Queuing Theory to check the validity of the teller window schedules shown in Exhibit 10a.

SITUATION IN JULY, 1981

The PIP group had completed studies and presented their recommendations in three of the largest branches of the bank. Performance was being reported by these three branches but top management had not as yet taken any action for poor branch performance. Potential savings had been identified at the rate projected by the consulting firm, but these savings had not yet been achieved.

Top management of the bank was considering offering Mr. Parkinson the position of Planning Officer of the bank. He would head up the PIP group and report directly to the Executive Vice President. In trying to determine what he thought the future of PIP should be at CNB, Mr. Chandler talked to some of the people who were involved with the program. The following are some of the comments he received.

TOTAL HOURS			DISTRIBUTION OF STANDARD HOURS			
	Teller	Vault	Secretary	Loan interviewers	Clerical	Management
198.9		198.9				
746.9	746.9					
191.4	191.4					
108.6	108.6					
180.9		23.9		157.0		
50.6		50.6				
25.2		25.2				
107.8		107.8				
15.0						15.0
1625.3	1046.9	406.4		157.0		15.0
286.7	184.7	71.7		27.7		2.6
1912.0	1231.6	478.1		184.7		17.6
166.3	107.1	41.6		16.0		1.5
258.8	103.5					155.3
2337.1	1442.2	519.7		200.7		174.4
254.4	167.4	2.6		84.4		
2591.5	1609.6	522.3		285.1		174.4
15.0	9.3	3.0		1.7		1.0
14-4	7-4	3-0		2-0		2-0
19-2	9-2	5-0		3-0		2-0

Approval date: 11/20   By: G. W. Logan

Executive Vice President, John Porter:

"The Profit Improvement Program is good for the bank because it will make the branch managers better managers by giving them a means to measure the efficiency of their people as the bank grows. It will give us (top management) a quantitative means of controlling payroll costs and comparing the performance of the branches."

Personnel Officer, Mr. Randall:

"I think the program will be useful to my department, but I do not think that it was introduced correctly; the central office operations people were not involved and they should have been. Instead the program went directly into the field. There is a close informal relationship, you know, between central office operations people and branch operations people."

Area Branch Manager:

"This program is good because it will get our people to be more concerned with costs; until now we have had no way of quantifying a need for additional personnel."

EXHIBIT 8
Marion Branch, December 1980–June 1981

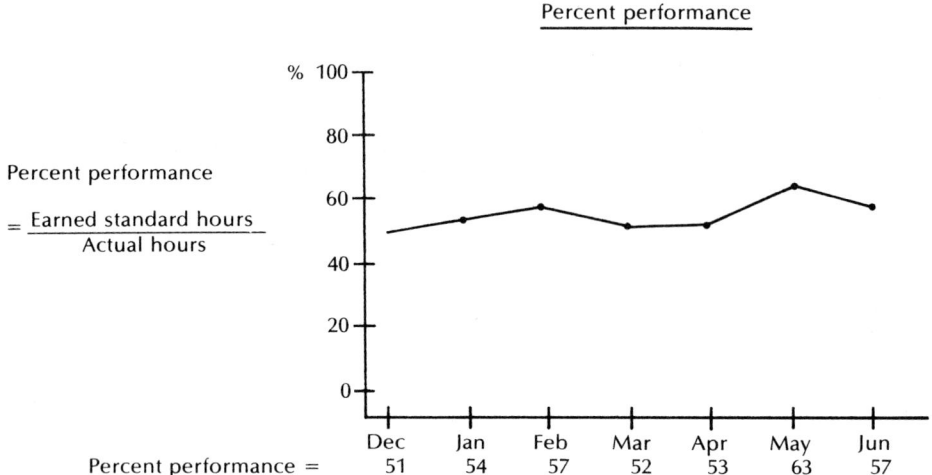

Percent performance

Percent performance

$= \dfrac{\text{Earned standard hours}}{\text{Actual hours}}$

	Dec	Jan	Feb	Mar	Apr	May	Jun
Percent performance =	51	54	57	52	53	63	57

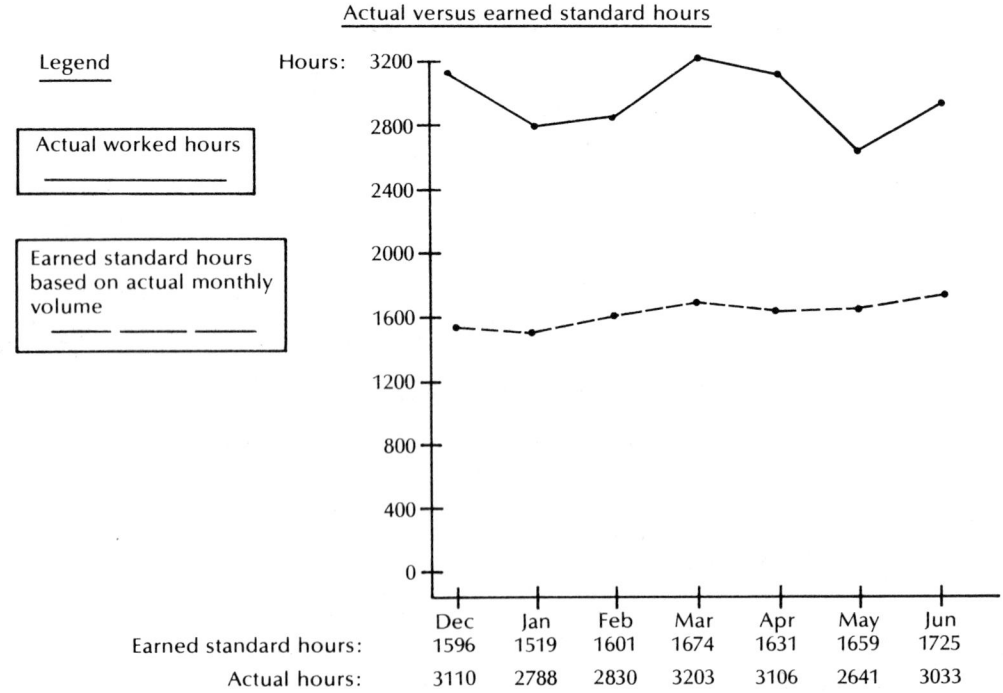

Actual versus earned standard hours

Legend

Hours:

Actual worked hours

Earned standard hours based on actual monthly volume

	Dec	Jan	Feb	Mar	Apr	May	Jun
Earned standard hours:	1596	1519	1601	1674	1631	1659	1725
Actual hours:	3110	2788	2830	3203	3106	2641	3033

EXHIBIT 9

Effects of Planned Customer Service Level on Customer on Line Time and on Teller Utilization

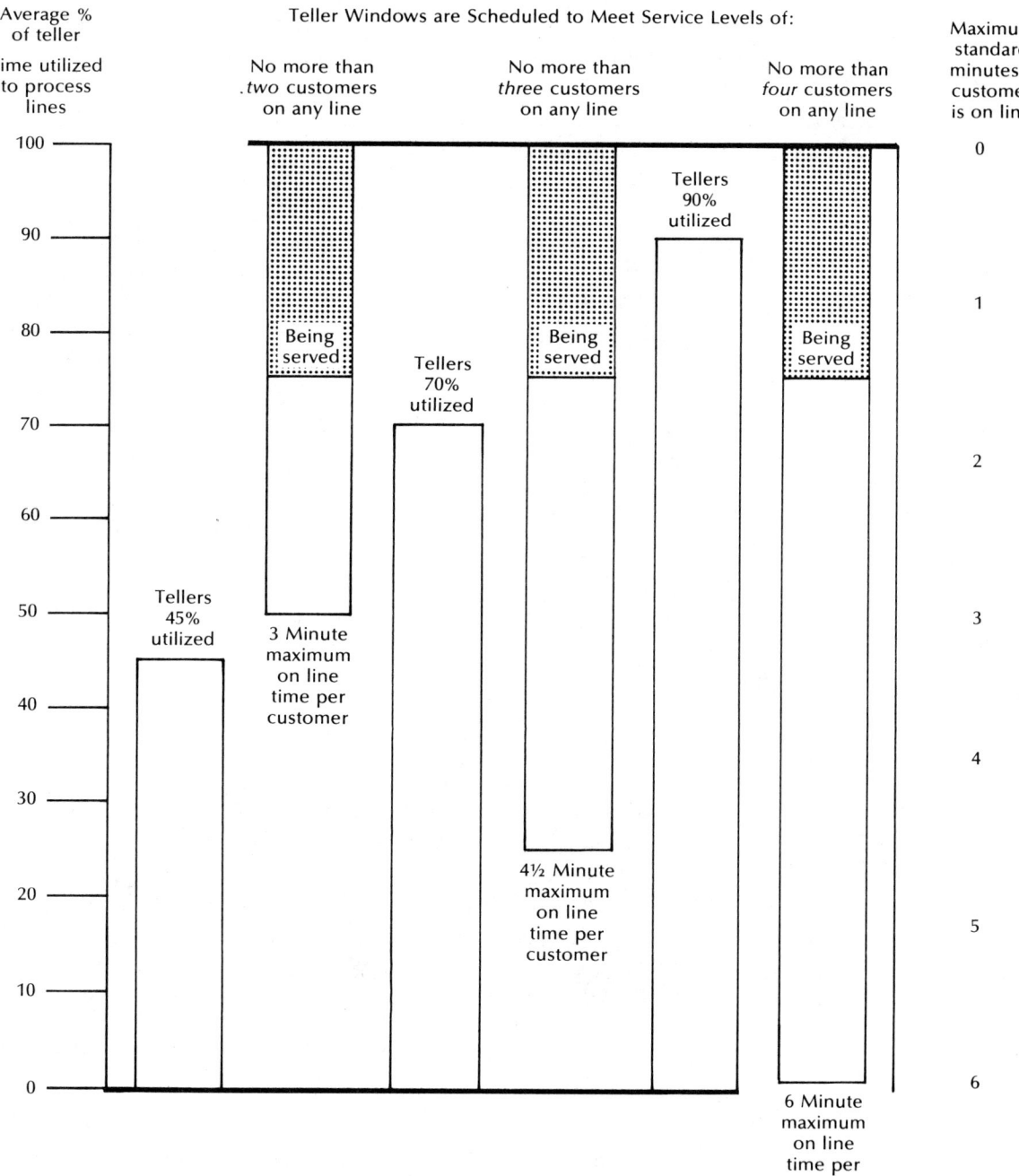

EXHIBIT 10a
Tuesday's Open Window Schedule

Time of day	NORMAL			PAY DAY			PRE-HOLIDAY		
	Average customer count	Teller* window positions	Teller staffing plan	Average customer count	Teller* window positions	Teller staffing plan	Average customer count	Teller* window positions	Teller staffing plan
9:00	93	7	7	131	10	9	112	9	8
9:30	85	7	7	120	9	9	102	8	8
10:00	77	6	7	108	8	9	93	7	8
10:30	92	7	7	129	10	9	111	9	8
11:00	84	7	7	112	9	9	101	8	8
11:30	76	6	7	107	8	9	91	7	8
12:00	78	6	7	110	9	9	94	7	8
12:30	79	6	5	111	9	7	95	7	6
1:00	54	4	5	76	6	7	65	5	6
1:30	57	5	5	80	6	7	69	6	6
Subtotal Customers	775			1084			933		
4:00	129	10	9	181	14	9	155	12	9
4:30	140	11	9	197	15	9	168	13	9
5:00	124	10	9	174	13	9	149	11	9
5:30	135	10	9	190	14	9	162	12	9
6:00	127	10	9	179	14	9	153	12	9
6:30	135	10	9	190	14	9	162	12	9
7:00									
7:30									
Subtotal	790			1111			949		
TOTAL	1565			2195			1882		

*Based on PIP studies and the Service Criterion of no more than three customers on any line 95% of the time.

Marion Branch Manager:

"I was not really aware of what these people (PIP group) were doing. I mean I knew they were working in my branch, mostly with my operations officer. I was surprised when I found out how much savings potential they identified in my branch."

Marion Branch Operations Officer:

"The branch personnel were a little nervous when they (PIP group) came around; however, I think they have done a pretty good job in getting along with the branch personnel. Personally, I think they are nice guys and all their figures and recommendations look fine on paper, but I just don't think they will work. You just cannot predict, at least the way they say you can, when customers will come in and what they will want."

Branch Manager 2:

"I don't really understand all their figures. That consultant is really smart, but I don't understand what he says. The analyst working in my branch is only 23 years old; I've been in banking for 33 years and am a vice president. How can he help

EXHIBIT 10b
Personnel Assignments

	Teller scheduled hours			Normal		Pay day		Pre-holiday	
#	Name	FT/PT	Start	Stop	Start	Stop	Start	Stop
1								
2								
3								
4								
5								
6								
7								
8								
9								
10								
11								
12								
13								

me run my branch? We've always done alright in the past, and I just don't think we need PIP."

PIP Analyst:

"I think this program is very important for the bank; it can really save money if handled in the proper way. It's very frustrating, though, to know you're right and not be able to convince the people you're trying to help. Political problems seem to get in the way."

Head Teller:

"Those boys (PIP analysts) don't really know what it's like to handle customers all day. You have to go out of your way and take some extra time to please customers or to sell them a new service."

CASE
8

Chandler Trust Company

Alexander Chase was winding down his 1981 summer internship in the Banking Operations Division of Chandler Trust Company and would soon return to his second year at the well-known southern business school he attended. His boss, Judith Stoddard, asked to see him as soon as possible. Alex knew from his brief experience at Chandler that when the boss came looking for him it had to be important. Ms. Stoddard was a First Vice President of the Bank and was in charge of a staff group that supported the Operations Division. This group, of which Alex was a part, was responsible for all automation projects undertaken in the Division. To date this had included word processing, micrographics, and some computer system automation.

"Alex," said Ms. Stoddard, "since you are almost finished with your other projects and you will be with us for another two weeks, I'd like you to undertake a special project. This is very different from anything you've done before, and as you will see when I outline the problem further, it is essential that we have your report within one week. As you probably know, the CHIPS (Clearing House Interbank Payments System) system is changing on October 1, 1981 to a same day settlement system instead of its current next day settlement.[1] This means that our transactions will all have to be processed by 4:00 P.M. on the day that they are received, if we are to settle with our clearing banks by the time the Federal Reserve closes at 6:30. You've been in that department before and have seen how things are done now, so you know that the present system is unlikely to work. I want you to come up with a plan for meeting these new CHIPS deadlines.

"I'm sure that David Winter or Brett Johnson will be able to give you some background information on the department. They have come up with some ideas on what might be done but I'll count on you to develop a comprehensive proposal."

---

[1]Banks' positions with each other are determined by their net credit or debit position vis-à-vis every other bank at the end of the banking day. These positions are "settled" by transferring funds on deposit with the Federal Reserve System to balance out the accounts. Federal Reserve funds are transferred by means of an electronic payment system called the Fedwire. See Exhibit 1 for additional definitions.

This case was prepared by Kelley S. Platt, under the supervision of Associate Professor Roger W. Schmenner, solely as a basis for class discussion. It is not intended to describe either good or bad management practice.

EXHIBIT 1

Definition of Terms

Same day funds are funds available for transfer today in like funds or withdrawal in cash, subject to the settlement of the transaction through the payment system used.

Next day funds are funds available for transfer today in like funds and available the next business day for transfer in same day funds or withdrawal in cash, subject to the settlement of the transaction through the payment system used.

Federal funds are funds on deposit at a Federal Reserve Bank in the United States. They are a subset of same day funds and only those funds transferred via the Fedwire are immediately collected. All other federal funds payments are subject to final settlement/collection.

Immediately Available Funds—see Federal funds (settlement is simultaneous with the execution of the transaction.)

Settlement refers to the balance amounts (resulting from payments drawn on and made to banks through a payment system) that are presented to the Federal Reserve System for debiting or crediting the lawful reserve accounts of the banks on the payment system that settle in this manner. Settlement is completed when all of the appropriate debit or credit entries have been made across the Lawful Reserve Accounts.

The worldwide definition of *value date* is the date when the receiving bank has use of the funds. In the U.S. we also made the funds available to the beneficiary at the same time. This is due to our accounting procedures which have not been geared to posting future values as is customary in other countries.

Source: Internal memorandum 9, Chandler Trust Company.

EXHIBIT 2

The following times will be strictly adhered to after October 1, 1981.

	EASTERN TIME
7:00 A.M.	CHIPS opens for storage and sending of payment messages.
9:00 A.M.	Fedwire opens nationwide for funds transfer
11:00 A.M.	
	Exchange of fedwire payments and CHIPS messages.
1:00 P.M.	
3:00 P.M.	
4:30 P.M.	CHIPS cut-off for payment messages.
	Fedwire cut-off (nationwide) for interdistrict transfers between federal districts.
	Fedwire cut-off (2nd district) for intradistrict 3rd-party transfers. (Each district's option.)
	(Use of Fedwire for bank settlements continues.)
4:45 P.M.	CHIPS completes providing net settlement information to participants.
5:00 P.M.	CHIPS settlement process begins.
5:45 P.M.	CHIPS cut-off time for any settling participant to notify New York clearing house that it is unwilling to settle net position of any participant for which it settles.
6:00 P.M.	CHIPS settlement.
	Fedwire cut-off (all districts) for intradistrict third-party fedwire payments.
6:30 P.M.	Fedwire closes for all transactions, (including two-party bank settlements).

Source: Internal memorandum 10, Chandler Trust Company.

COMPANY BACKGROUND

The Chandler Trust Company was a small wholesale bank. Headquartered in New York, Chandler had an Edge Act subsidiary in Miami which could only carry out international banking activities. Its overseas operations included branch offices, affiliated banks (that were part of the Chandler Group, the parent organization of Chandler Trust Company, but were separately incorporated and capitalized), and subsidiaries of the Chandler Group.

Chandler's customers included small to medium-sized multi-nationals, foreign companies, local and regional banks in the U.S., and many foreign banks and government agencies. Because of its emphasis on international business, Chandler's operations were geared to processing large volumes of foreign exchange transactions, loans, and securities investments denominated in Eurodollars[2] or foreign currencies. Much of the Eurodollar activity was channeled, for tax purposes, and to avoid interest rate restrictions imposed by the Federal Reserve Board, through Nassau or the Cayman Islands.

The Chandler Trust Company had built its reputation on customizing its services to meet its client's needs. Prompt and efficient response to customer inquiries was of utmost importance. Many of Chandler's customers relied on the Bank to invest all of their available funds every night. These amounts changed from day to day and, as a consequence, the investments had to be made over again every day. To do this, the bankers had to have accurate and timely information on their client's balances.

The headquarters office of Chandler employed approximately 500 people.

---

[2]Eurodollars, euroyen, or euromarks for example, are any currency which is deposited in a bank outside of its home country, e.g., U.S. dollars on deposit in U.S. banks' foreign branches or in foreign banks.

EXHIBIT 3
Floor Plan—Funds Transfer Department

Current floor plan is from blueprint of the area. All fixtures are to scale. The following are key items:

A. Exterior doorways onto open corridor. Free access through these doorways.
B. Interior doorway to machine room.
C. Wall 36" in height with glass panel to ceiling to block off machine room. Machine room has raised floor.
D. CHIPS machines for entering and deleting payments from the CHIPS system. Must remain on a raised floor.
E. Back-up CHIPS machines
F. Fedwire machines for fed payments. Do not have to be on a raised floor.
G. Department head's office.
H. All desks are of a standard size and freely moveable. Titles identify function performed at that desk and do not necessarily correspond to individual employees.

Source: Blueprints of the area.

EXHIBIT 3, cont'd

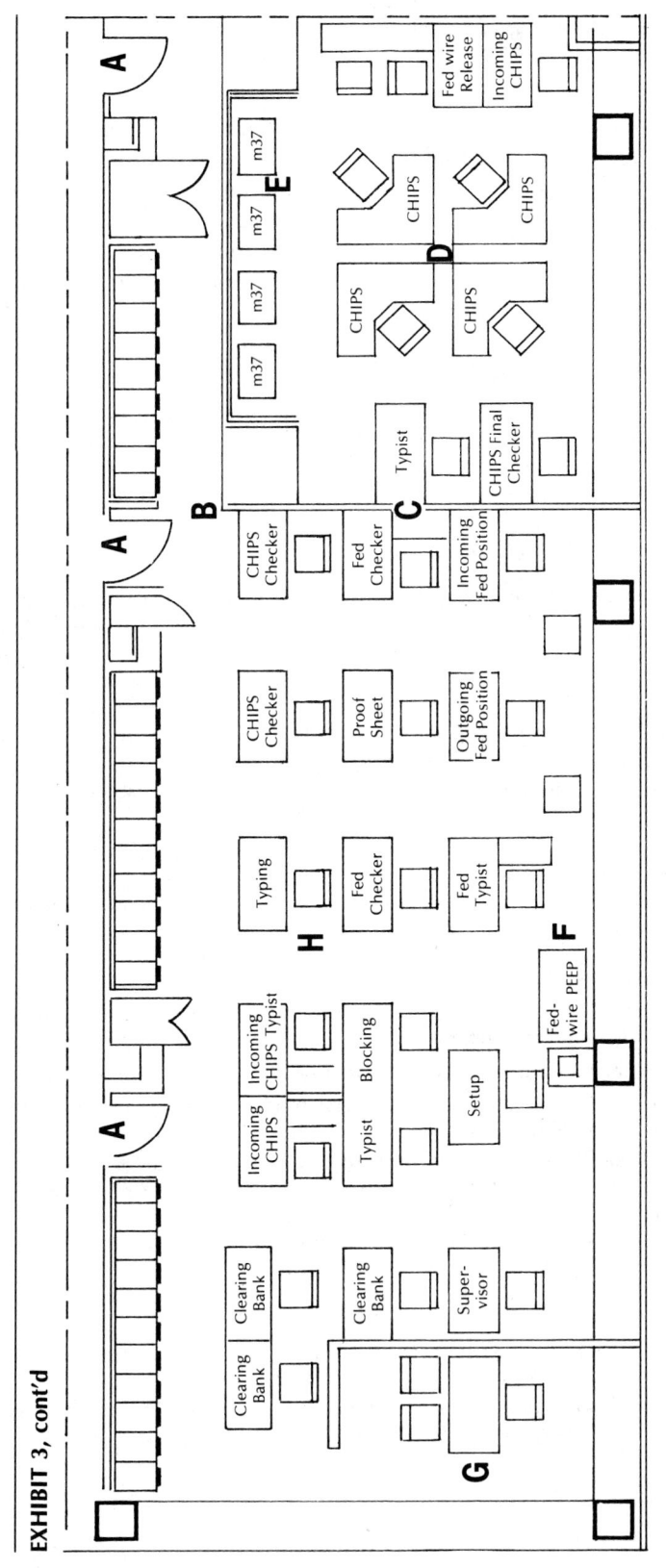

One-third of these were actually involved in the company's operating divisions. The operating departments of Chandler were divided according to the function that they performed. For example, the foreign Exchange department processed the paper work to support all the foreign currency deals that the bank or its clients made. The actual transferring of funds from one account to another or to other banks was done by the Funds Transfer Department. It acted as a service center for the other operating departments.

EXHIBIT 4
Funds Transfer Department Staffing

Job Description (current staffing levels)   Total 24

CHIPS Terminal Operator (4) Enter all CHIPS payments into terminals, release payments after verification, give incoming tickets to incoming clerk. Requires training in terminal operations.

CHIPS Checker (2) Checks the written copy of stored CHIPS payments against the cable or written instructions for accuracy. Errors are corrected by deleting the whole transaction from the system and reentering it.

CHIPS Final Checker (1) Second check on all payments before they are released.

CHIPS Incoming Clerk (2) Receives incoming CHIPS tickets from CHIPS terminal operator. Matches against advice if the bank has been told the money is coming. Prepares cables to advise of receipt if none exists. Prepares credit forms for account to receive money.

Setup Clerk (1) Receives all payment and receipt instructions. Highlights key information, i.e., names, addresses, account numbers, type of transaction.

Blocking Clerk (1) Ensures sufficient funds available for transfer by monitoring the accounts of the Bank's clients (manual process).

Clearing Bank Clerk (2) Maintain ledgers to monitor balance of all banks that use Chandler as their access to the CHIPS network.

Balance Reporting Clerk (1) Monitors balance and records transactions of a large foreign bank. Advises bank by cable of all transactions.

Fed Funds Clerk (1) Separates all fed funds payment tickets. Types necessary advices.

Fed Funds Checker (2) Checks all machine Federal funds entries against payment instructions before release from Federal funds terminal.

Fed Funds Position Sheet (2) One incoming, one outgoing, records and tallies banks' own position at the Federal Reserve by adding all payments in and subtracting all transfers out. Advises senior management of position throughout the day.

Proof Sheet Clerk (1) Posts all internal payments and transfers for data entry into demand deposit accounting system.

Fedwire Operators (2) Enter all Federal Funds Transfers into system. After verification, release payments into system.

Typists (2) Prepare cables. Type payments tickets. Break apart multipart forms and distribute to parties involved in transaction. File copies of all transactions.

Supervisors (2) One is a Fed Funds position sheet clerk and one is a Clearing Bank clerk. Responsibilities split into Fed Funds staff and CHIPS staff.

DEPARTMENTAL BACKGROUND

David Winters, Assistant Treasurer, was part of the Operations Division staff group at Chandler. When Alex asked about the functions of the Funds Transfer Department, David explained that, "the prime function of the department is to transfer and receive funds on behalf of the bank's customers and operating departments. The department interfaces with two automated systems to perform its function; the Clearing House Interbank Payment System (CHIPS) and the Federal Reserve Funds Transfer System (Fedwire). Treasurers' checks are also used to make payments. The choice of payment method is dictated by the payment instructions and the nature of the transaction.

"In addition, the department performs a wide range of other services including:

—teller facilities such as check cashing, check certification, accepting deposits, and receiving documents.

—monitoring the balance of our accounts at other banks and keeping those balances at levels specified by senior management.

—monitoring continually our balance at the Federal Reserve Bank and keeping senior management and the money traders apprised of the bank's position as necessary.

"Since the department's activities involve direct communication with the bank's customers and correspondents, careful attention to detail and a high degree of accuracy are mandatory."

"How many of these transfers or payments does the department make, David?"

"I believe those figures run about 17,000 Fed payments and 20,000 CHIPS payments per month. Our Financial Control Department produces a monthly production activity report for the Fed section and the CHIPS section of the department. (See Exhibit 7.) We've experienced an historical growth of 10-15%

EXHIBIT 4a
Production Activity Report (Banking Operations Division)

Department: <u>Funds Transfer</u>
Section: <u>Federal Funds</u>   Month ending: _____

Tasks	Actual activity			Standard activity		Task unit cost	
	Current month	Prior month	Year to date	Current month	Year to date	Actual	Standard
Incoming payments	4,644	3,991	13,033	4,337	12,986	$ 1.69	$ 1.62
Outgoing payments	3,753	3,297	10,410	3,505	10,378	3.84	3.69
Control fed funds	8,397	7,288	23,443	7,843	23,367	.63	.62
Proof sheet	22	18	61	21	61	239.03	228.40
Collection	174	187	367	162	554	10.90	10.49
Return items	1	1	3	1	3	467.74	571.58
Certification	1	1	3	1	3	262.21	320.73

EXHIBIT 4b
Production Activity Report (Banking Operations Division)

Department: <u>Funds Transfer</u>
    Section: <u>CHIPS   </u>   Month ending: _____

	Actual activity			Standard activity		Task unit cost	
Tasks	Current month	Prior month	Year to date	Current month	Year to date	Actual	Standard
Payment and transfer	7,818	7,179	14,997	9,229	28,350	$5.02	$3.67
Payment check	666	647	1,313	787	2,494	6.48	4.76
Clearpay draft	59	67	126	70	285	9.39	6.86
Clearpay memo	111	74	185	131	344	5.14	3.73
Federal funds (setup)	3,083	2,468	5,553	3,637	10,699	1.02	.74
Incoming payment	8,094	7,272	15,366	9,552	28,664	1.13	.83
Certification	104	55	159	122	326	3.97	2.92
Clearing accounts	2,603	2,164	4,767	3,072	8,779	7.74	5.68
Special accounts	678	546	1,242	800	2,285	7.63	5.61

annually over the last four years. I expect that this rate will double when we move to same day settlement. Our operation is pretty hectic on a busy day.

"The biggest problem I see with this same day settlement thing is maintaining a high level of accuracy. If we make a mistake and don't transfer the right amount of funds, or don't make the cut-off time, we can be liable for paying compensation claims because somebody else should have been earning interest on that money. It doesn't sound like much, but with interest rates at 18%, the overnight interest on a $10 million transfer is $4,931.51, and we transfer hundreds of millions every day.

"Accuracy is also important to our internal auditors. They are always after us to improve our internal processing controls. Sometimes I think the only way we could ever satisfy them is to track each transaction every step of the way through the department with checks and counterchecks along the way. Lately, they've been complaining about the department's security. All of the doors are open to the hallway and there is no door to the machine room."

Brett Johnson was an Assistant Treasurer. Part of his responsibilities included coordinating the plans for same day settlement, the upcoming change in the CHIPS payment system. Alex approached Brett for advice on the current status of the Funds Transfer Department. "The work flow in the department is fairly standardized, Alex. David and I did a situation analysis of the area last spring. We drew flow charts that trace the processing of the four major types of transactions they handle: CHIPS payments, CHIPS receipts, Fed payments, and Fed receipts. (See Exhibit 6.) The current processing is broken down by task within the payment process.

"In a typical payment one clerk receives the payment instructions in the form of a cable, a telephone message, or written instructions from another department

EXHIBIT 5
Capacity Planning Data

Activity	Average time required per transaction
Setup	1 minute
Block	60-75 seconds
Check	45 seconds
Process payment	2-5 minutes*
Verify payment	1 minute
Final check	2 mintues

Source: Case writers estimates based on internal work measurement study.
*Approximately one-third of all payments are of a simple nature which require substantially less processing time. Average 90 seconds each.

in the bank. The setup clerk "sets up" the payment by highlighting or underlining the pertinent information which includes the type of payment (Fed or CHIPS), the amount, the debit party, the paying bank, the beneficiary, and any references. Next the blocking clerk verifies that there are sufficient funds in the account to cover the transaction (blocking). If the funds are not there the clerk will check to see if there is an advice[3] of funds to be transferred into the account on that day. If not, and the transfer exceeds the client's overdraft facility, then the clerk must call the account officer to have the transfer approved.

"If the transaction involves a Fed payment or receipt then the Fed position clerk will record it on their position sheet. This is a large ledger on which they keep a tally of the bank's deposits and withdrawals in its account at the Federal Reserve.

"CHIPS and Fed payments must be entered into their respective automated payment systems. This is done by the CHIPS terminal operators and the Fedwire operator respectively. In both systems the information is entered into the machine and a paper copy or CRT screen image is created. This copy will be verified twice before the payment message is actually sent electronically.

"There are separate clerks to check the accuracy of CHIPS and Fed payments against the cable or other instructions which created the payment. Final checkers also check only CHIPS or Fed payments although there is very little training needed to learn to check either type of payment.

"The next step involves entering the proper information into the automated system to release the payment so that it can be sent. This is done by one of the terminal operators, but not the one that entered the message originally.

"Finally, the paper ticket that is the bank's record of the payment is separated ("broken down") into nine pieces that are then sent to various parts of the bank for safekeeping. Some customers have standing orders that they are to be cabled

---

[3]An "advice" is a written record verifying that a payment has been made or received.

EXHIBIT 6
Funds Transfer Department—CHIPS Payment Flow

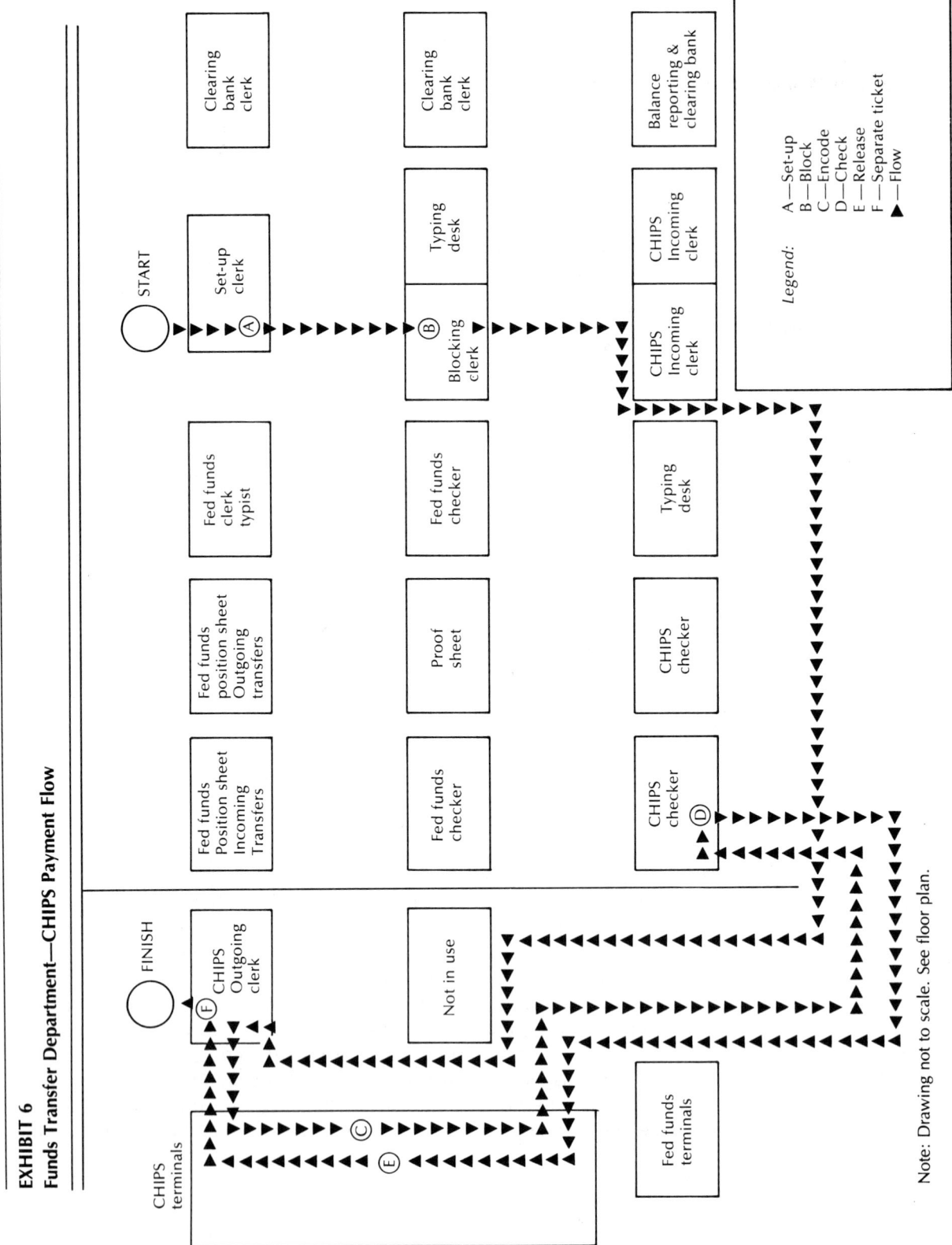

Note: Drawing not to scale. See floor plan.

Funds Transfer Department—CHIPS Receipt Flow

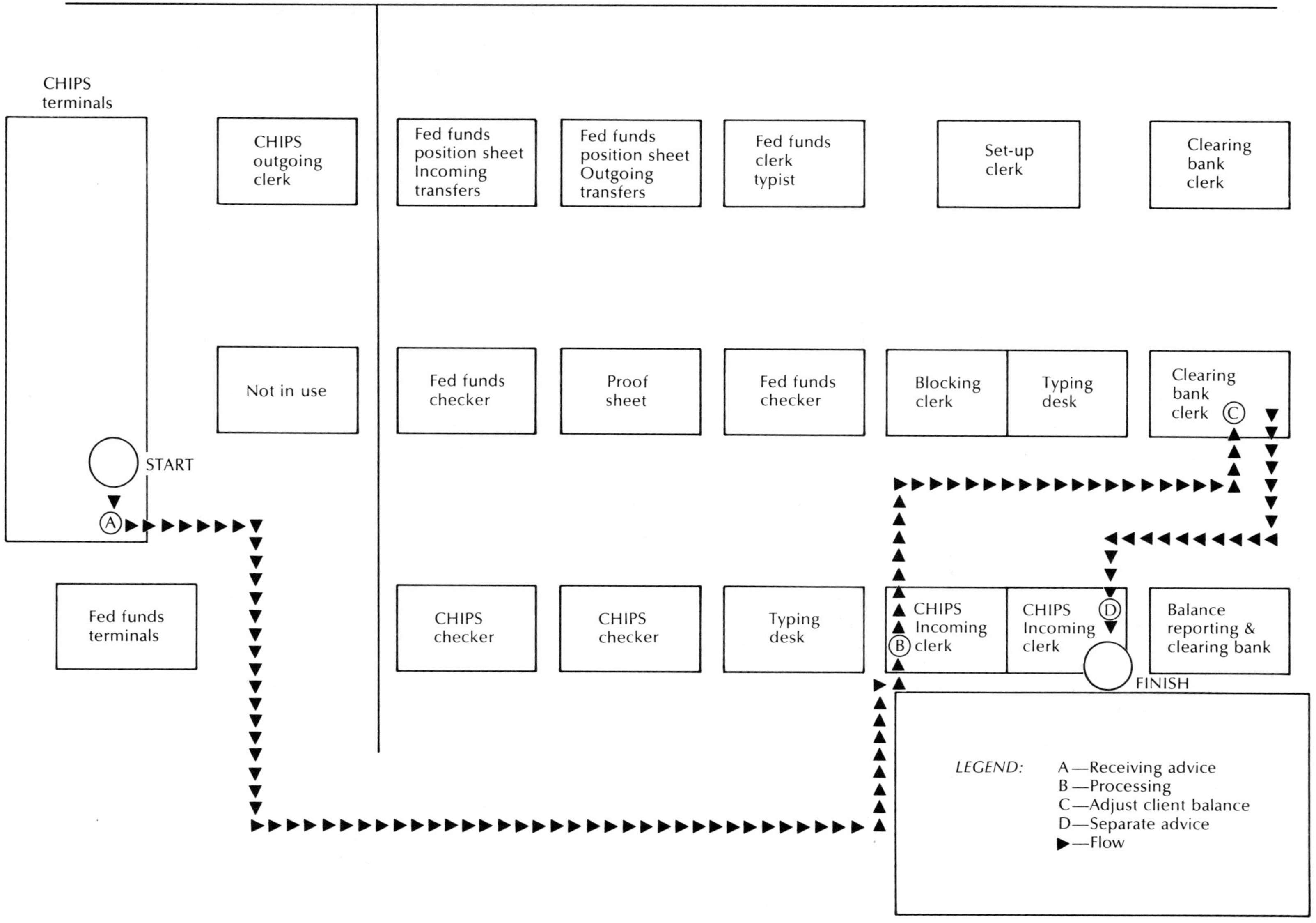

| CHIPS terminals | CHIPS outgoing clerk | Fed funds position sheet Incoming transfers | Fed funds position sheet Outgoing transfers | Fed funds clerk typist | Set-up clerk | Clearing bank clerk |

| Not in use | Fed funds checker | Proof sheet | Fed funds checker | Blocking clerk | Typing desk | Clearing bank clerk (C) |

| Fed funds terminals | CHIPS checker | CHIPS checker | Typing desk | CHIPS Incoming clerk (B) | CHIPS Incoming clerk (D) | Balance reporting & clearing bank |

START (A)

FINISH

LEGEND:

A—Receiving advice
B—Processing
C—Adjust client balance
D—Separate advice
▲—Flow

EXHIBIT 6, cont'd
Funds Transfer Department—Federal Funds Payment Flow

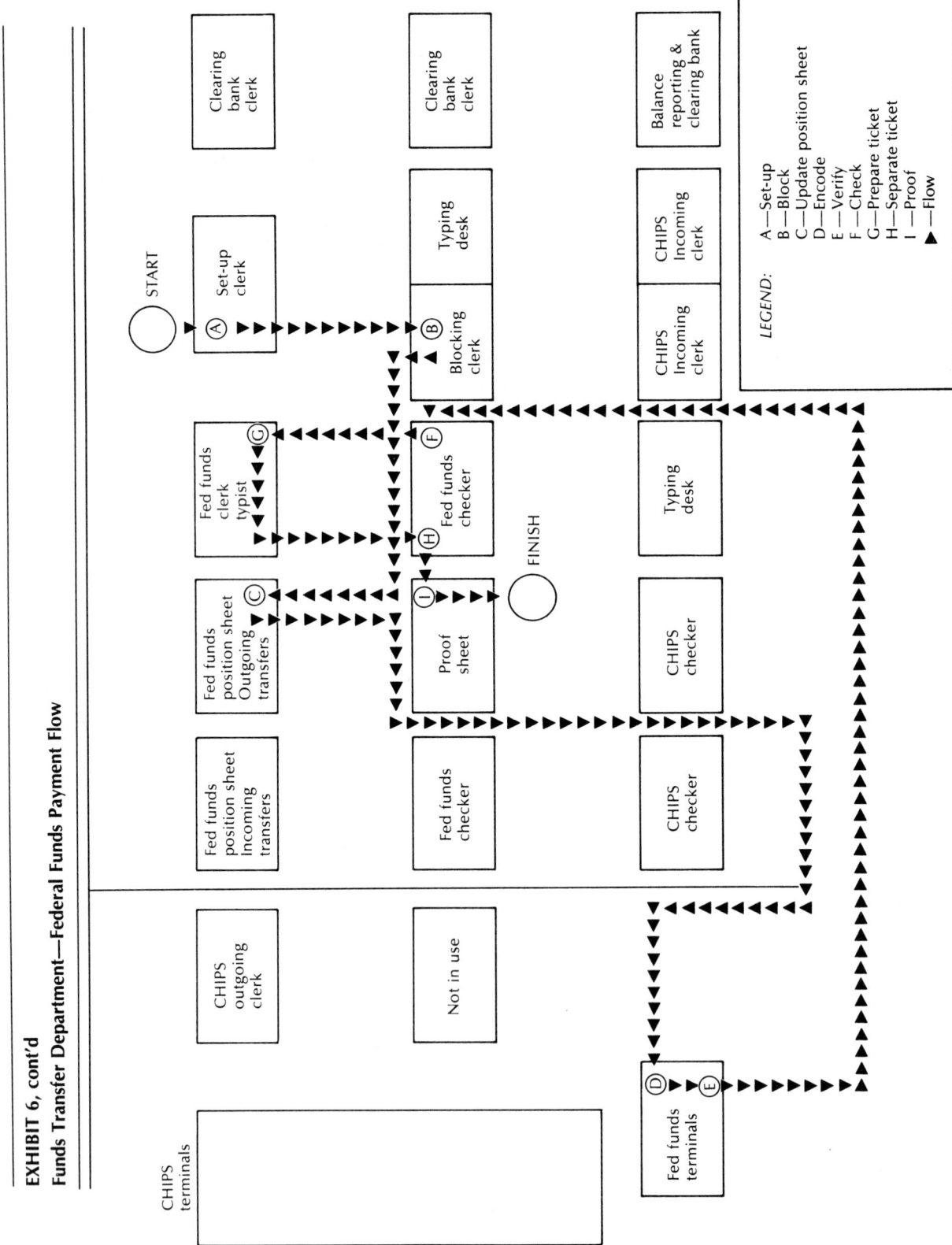

LEGEND:
A—Set-up
B—Block
C—Update position sheet
D—Encode
E—Verify
F—Check
G—Prepare ticket
H—Separate ticket
I—Proof
▲—Flow

Funds Transfer Department—Federal Funds Receipt Flow

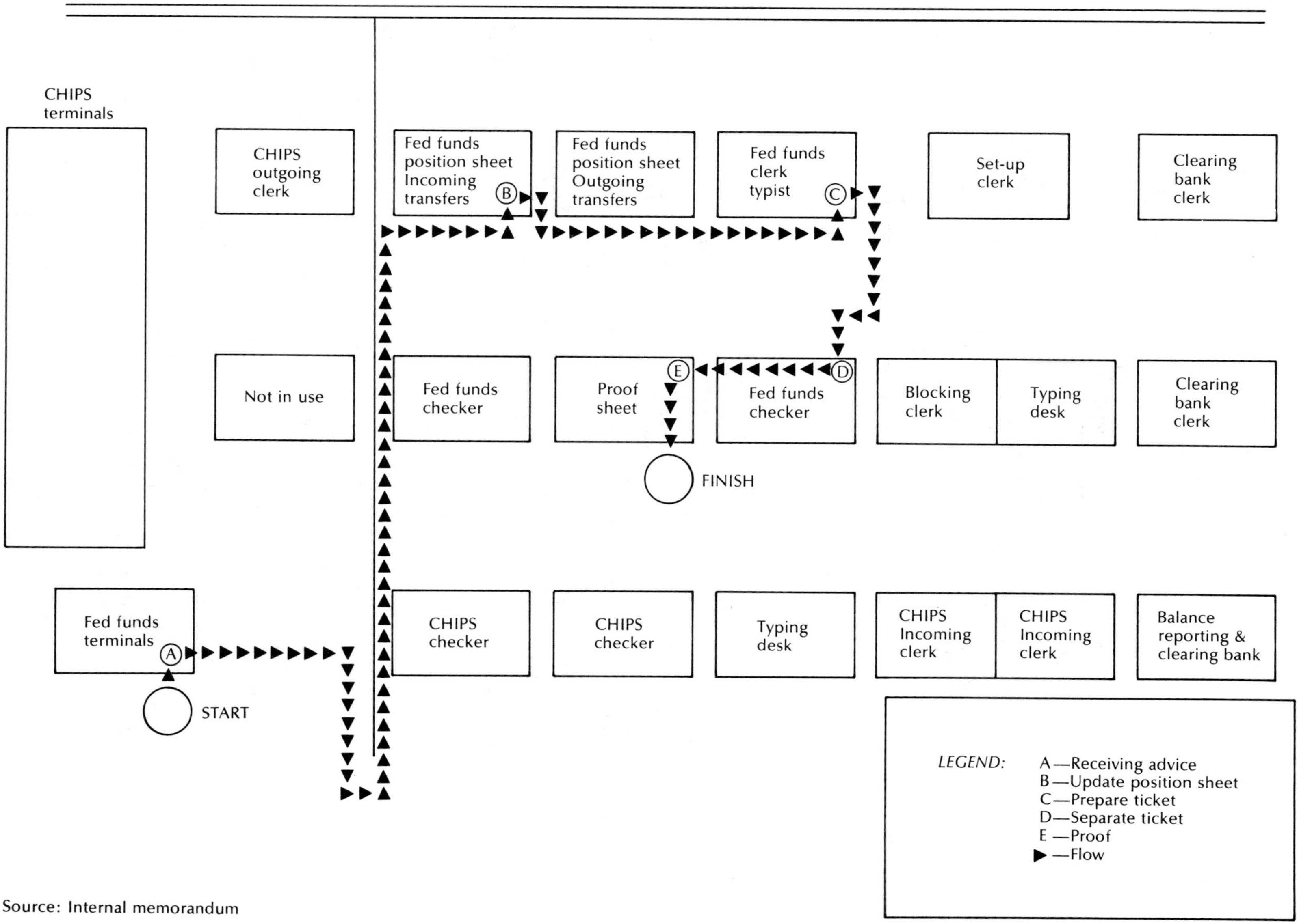

LEGEND:

A—Receiving advice
B—Update position sheet
C—Prepare ticket
D—Separate ticket
E —Proof
▲—Flow

Source: Internal memorandum

EXHIBIT 7
Funds Transfer Department—CHIPS Activity (Monthly Production Activity Report)

| Tasks | Actual activity | | | Standard activity | | Task unit cost | |
	Current month	Prior month	Year to date	Current month	Year to date	Actual	Standard
Payment and transfer	7,818	7,179	14,997	9,229	28,350	$ 5.02	$ 3.67
Payment check	666	647	1,313	787	2,494	6.48	4.76
Clearpay draft	59	67	126	70	285	9.39	6.86
Clearpay memo	111	74	185	131	344	5.14	3.73
Federal funds (setup)[1]	3,083	2,468	5,553	3,637	10,699	1.02	.74
Incoming payment	8,094	7,272	15,366	9,552	28,664	1.13	.83
Certification	104	55	159	122	326	3.97	2.92
Clearing accounts	2,603	2,164	4,767	3,072	8,779	7.74	5.68
Special accounts	678	546	1,242	800	2,285	7.63	5.61

[1]Done by CHIPS setup clerk.

EXHIBIT 7, cont'd
Funds Transfer Department—Federal Funds Activity (Monthly Production Activity Report)

| Tasks | Actual activity | | | Standard activity | | Task unit cost | |
	Current month	Prior month	Year to date	Current month	Year to date	Actual	Standard
Incoming payments	4,644	3,991	13,033	4,337	12,986	$ 1.69	$ 1.62
Outgoing payments	3,753	3,297	10,410	3,505	10,378	3.84	3.69
Control fed funds	8,397	7,288	23,443	7,843	23,367	.63	.62
Proof sheet	22	18	61	21	61	239.03	228.40
Collection	174	187	367	162	554	10.90	10.49
Return items	1	1	3	1	3	467.74	571.58
Certification	1	1	3	1	3	262.21	320.73

whenever any funds are moved into or out of their accounts. When this is the case, the CHIPS or Fed checker who has broken down the ticket will indicate that on the ticket and give it to a typist to type up the cable.

"You can see that several people must handle each transaction that the department processes. The processing starts and stops many times as the message is moved from the top of one pile to the bottom of the next pile at every step along the way. The floor plan indicates the physical flow of each transaction. You can see how many times it "walks" across the room before it is finished. (See Exhibits 3 and 6.) It didn't used to be that way when we were smaller and one person could do several of the steps as long as someone else checked the accuracy of her work. I think our clerks are going to need track shoes come October 1st if we don't do something about the work flow in here."

"Several ideas have been suggested for what to do in that department, Alex. Maybe they'll help you with your recommendations.

—First, we could move some desks around so the clerks don't have to do so much walking. Keep in mind though that the CHIPS machines have to stay in their own room and that security in the department is key.

—Second, we can add extra people to help with the processing, but it would be hard to justify without an increase in volume. The question then is where to add them. The Financial Control department did a time and motion study in there last year which gives some figures on how long it should take to do each job. (See Exhibit 5.)

—Third, we could add word processors to replace some of the manual record keeping. I really think they would help for maintaining our position at the Fed and for maintaining our clearing and foreign bank accounts. Having those balances anytime during the day is going to make a difference to the customers. Of course this option raises the question of what to do with the clerks' time if it's quicker to maintain balances on a word processor than a ledger sheet. In any case we can't afford to lose any business because of same day settlement.

"I'm sure you must be full of ideas of what we can do in there, Alex. I hope this information will be of some help to you in making your recommendations."

SAME DAY SETTLEMENT[4]

CHIPS (Clearing House Interbank Payment System) was a group of 100 financial institutions in New York. It served as an electronic payment mechanism for its participants to make payments to each other. All transactions were currently processed one day and the funds became available about 10:00 A.M. the next day. A bank's net position with other banks was balanced out by transferring funds over the Fedwire before 10:00 A.M. on the second day. Fedwire transfers were for immediately available funds because the transfer involves only a movement of funds from one bank's account at the Fed to another.

CHIPS is important because of its size—55,000 transactions totalling $150 billion to $160 billion dollars per day. Over 90% of the world's foreign exchange business was done through CHIPS. It was the major vehicle for the world's Eurodollar market, including Eurodollar loans, speculative investments, and time deposits. CHIPS was also an important settlement system for international trade transactions.

The growth of the Eurodollar market had led to instability in foreign exchange and Eurodollar interest rates because of the present next-day settlement system. Funds invested on Friday earned an extra two days interest because the trade would not be completed (settled) until Monday. There existed many opportunities for arbitrage because of the time zones and the one day lag between processing a transaction and actually having the funds available for use. To eliminate the

---

[4]*Source:* Chase Manhattan, N.A. publication.

arbitrage opportunities, the CHIPS system was to begin same day settlement of all transactions on October 1, 1981.

Same day settlement would require that all transactions be processed by 4:30 each day. At that time the participants would have two hours (4:30–6:30 P.M. EST) to settle with each other over the Fedwire. At the same time the banks would have to settle their reserve deposit requirement with the Federal Reserve Bank. The primary result would be the standardization of Eurodollar and foreign exchange rates.

The implications of same day settlement for the processing of funds transfers centered on the reliability and timeliness of the transfer and advising systems.[5] Input processing deadlines would be earlier. It would be more difficult to make corrections in transactions while they were being processed. Error corrections the next day, after the transaction was settled, would be about six times more expensive than currently because compensation would have to be paid for the interest that the injured party would have earned overnight had the transfer been properly made.

---

[5]The advising systems generate written records that verify a payment has been made or received. The output is an "advice."

Schmitt Optical Instruments (A)

On January 20, 1981, Bill Ross, Vice President and General Manager of Schmitt Optical Instruments (S.O.I.) in Kitchener, was estimating the man power requirements of a new product line being taken from R & D to production. Earlier in January, Marketing had announced to distributors and customers a line of three photon counting instruments, promising first deliveries in April.

Ross and other senior managers in the company felt it was important to the company's continued sales growth and corporate image to get their new product line to customers on time. Complicating this objective was the lack of historical data about how many units could actually be produced for delivery, given untested standards for the man-hours of assembly time per unit required for the new line.

GENERAL COMPANY BACKGROUND

As a high-growth, high-technology producer of quality electro-optical instruments, it was S.O.I.'s product policy to develop and manufacture innovative products in the field of light generation, detection, and analysis. The firm aggressively pursued sales through its agents and distributors around the world.

S.O.I. products were recognized by customers and promoted by their marketing department as being of the highest quality measured in dependability, accuracy, and convenience to operate. Their image, plus the prohibitive cost of servicing equipment in geographically distant markets, made rigorous quality control and exhaustive pre-production design and testing company policy.

S.O.I. was experiencing a large number of backorders for its products. It was the company's policy to turn over or at least modify all its product lines once every 5 years. New product development was considered crucial to S.O.I.'s success. By supplying a continuous stream of unique products to the marketplace, S.O.I. not only avoided competition with larger firms, but also maintained the high margins required to finance the firm's continued growth. Exhibit 1 presents additional sales and cost figures and estimates for future product lines.

Sixty full-time employees worked at the Kitchener office and manufacturing facility. Exhibit 2 shows S.O.I.'s total payroll by function and management's expectation of additional man power requirements over the next three years.

Copyright © 1981, The University of Western Ontario.

Case material of the Western School of Business Administration is prepared as a basis for classroom discussion. This case was prepared by David Johnston. Research Assistant, under the direction of Robert R. Britney, Professor.

EXHIBIT 1
Sales and Cost Forecasts by Product Line (in 000's of dollars)
(for year ended September 30, 1980, 1981, 1982, 1983)

	1980 Actual	1981	1982	1983
Product Group I				
High Energy Light Sources	19	130	250	500
CGS	11	79	138	250
CGS (%)	(58)	(61)	(55)	(50)
Product Group II				
Photon Counting	332	1,110	1,700	2,000
CGS	169	700	1,020	1,200
CGS (%)	(51)	(63)	(60)	(60)
Product Group III				
Pulsed Light Sources	388	500	500	500
CGS	306	461	450	450
CGS (%)	(79)	(92)	(90)	(90)
Product Group IV				
Custom Manufacturing/Consulting	355	626	1,430	2,000
CGS	134	269	644	800
CGS (%)	(38)	(43)	(45)	(40)
Product Group V				
Synchronous Lasing Inst.	334	360	500	750
CGS	244	235	325	450
CGS (%)	(73)	(65)	(65)	(60)
Product Group VI				
Mass Spectrometer Systems	—	—	120	600
CGS	—	—	72	300
CGS (%)	—	—	(60)	(50)
Product Group VII				
Medical Related Instruments	—	—	—	900
CGS	—	—	—	450
CGS (%)	—	—	—	(50)
Product Group VIII				
New Laser Group	—	—	—	200
CGS	—	—	—	100
CGS (%)	—	—	—	(50)
Product Group IX				
Fiber Optics Units	—	—	500	1,250
CGS	—	—	300	625
CGS (%)	—	—	(60)	(50)
Total sales	$1,428	$2,726	$5,000	$8,700
Total CGS	$ 864	$1,744	$2,949	$4,625
Total CGS (%)	(61)	(64)	(59)	(53)

EXHIBIT 2
Projected Employment Schedule

	Actual at Sept. 30/80	Employees added		
		1981	1982	1983
Administration				
Secretary	3	—	1	2
Management	3	—	—	1
Clerk	—	—	—	2
Accounting	1	—	1	2
Programmer	1	1	1	1
	8	1	3	8
Marketing				
Sales	2	1	2	3
Secretary	1	—	1	2
Management	4	1	—	1
Clerk	1	—	1	2
	8	2	4	8
Production				
Assembly	7	1	6	8
Machinist	4	1	3	4
Indirect labour	2	—	3	4
Management	4	1	—	1
Traffic	1	1	1	2
	18	4	13	19
Research & Development				
Engineer/Manager	9	2	—	1
Machinist	3	—	1	—
Technologist	10	1	—	1
Secretary	—	—	2	—
Programmer	1	—	—	—
Research associate	3	—	—	—
Draftsman	2	—	1	2
	28	3	4	4
Grand total	62	10	24	39

Note: In high-technology companies the general rule-of-thumb is one person for every $50,000 in sales. The above equipment projection is therefore conservative.

PRODUCTION AT S.O.I.

Half of S.O.I.'s twenty thousand square feet was dedicated to product assembly. Seven of the 18 people working in this area did the actual assembly. These unskilled employees were paid a wage higher than average for manufacturing industries and worked an 8-hour shift a day, 5 days a week.

The production process involved the precision assembly of complex subassemblies. A subassembly usually consisted of a small, custom-designed circuit board that required individual soldering at the plant of an intricate web of electronic components, such as resistors and capacitors. Delicate integrated circuit (I.C.) chips, fine ground lenses, and machined fittings required careful handling. The instrument housings, all circuit boards, and advanced subassemblies such as I.C. chips were manufactured by outside suppliers. Lead times on parts and subassemblies ranged from 1 day to 8 months. Price escalations, limiting quotas, late deliveries, and stockouts by suppliers were not uncommon in the volatile electronic components industry. The two women in S.O.I.'s stockroom used a Min/Max system to control the 10,000 item parts and subassembly inventory. Minima and maxima were set for different inventory items based on each item's lead times and the demands of the master production schedule. S.O.I. in 1980 purchased $700,000 worth of materials from suppliers for its products. Over the course of 1980, an estimated average sum of $750,000 in inventories was on hand at any one point in time. Of this average, approximately 40 percent represented raw materials, 35 percent finished product, and 25 percent work in progress.

Each product was assembled in small batches ranging from 1 to 50 units in a run depending on the product complexity. Because sophisticated products, such as the nanosecond fluorometer, often required a week for one man to assemble, excluding quality control testing which could take another half a week, the size of the run was limited to 4 or 5, with existing capacity. The average number of units per run was 20. Each assembly worker learned new unit assembly by consulting assembly blueprints and copying a prototype under the close supervision of an R & D technician or the project manager. Each unit, in order to conform to high quality standards, was tested rigorously by Quality Control. Often simultaneously with the assembly of the finished product, R & D and Quality Control were modifying the product's design either to solve problems encountered in assembly or to incorporate new features.

The assembly worker ordered parts for the whole run through the completion of a bill of materials handed to the stockroom at the start of the shift. If the parts and subassemblies were not in stock, the problem was reported to the assembly supervisor, Sue Burke, who reassigned the worker.

Daily stockouts in at least one or two items of either minor or major importance required the assembly worker to stop assembly of one product and work temporarily on another. Ross gave Burke a yearly master production schedule from which she determined daily schedules (Exhibit 3), but the master was subject to sudden change, due to design modification by R & D, rework demanded by Quality Control, inventory stockouts, or rearrangement of product priorities by management.

EXHIBIT 3
S.O.I. Production Schedule* (1979-80)

Product	Beg. Inv.	1979			1980									No. made	End inv.
		Oct.	Nov.	Dec.	Jan.	Feb.	Mar.	Apr.	May	Jun.	Jul.	Aug.	Sept.		
M301	15				16			14						30	
M302	1		6			10								16	
M303X	49						15		15					30	
301M	15													0	
M305						5								5	
301/S	32				13		15							28	
1611	9					10		6					10	26	
TX 5	17					15					7			22	
TX 5 PD	17					15					7			22	
300 PP	7						8							8	
LN 100			10	5	15	10			20	10	10	10	10	120	
ALH 1	2	10	10					25						45	
ALH 6		10			10						10			30	
ALH 7		10			10				20					40	
ALH 8					MADE TO ORDER										
610A					MADE TO ORDER										
610B					MADE TO ORDER										
610C			5				5						4	14	
ALH 215	2	10	10		16			16		17				69	
ALH 220	1	10		10			5		10			10		45	
510B			1	3				3						7	
510C			1	1				3		3				8	

*Schedule in units of product.

EXHIBIT 4

Specifications and Interconnections of the Signal Preamplifier, the AMP/Discriminator, and the Photon Counter

The SOI Model 1763 preamplifier features the versatility of two switch selectable gain positions. The maximum gain of 40 db represents a tenfold increase over other competitive units. A bandwidth of 400 MHz means unmatched performance in its class.

The SOI Model 1762 Amplifier/Discriminator combines for the first time high maximum count rate (100 MHz) and wide range gain selection (7 position). The low threshold discriminator circuitry is preceeded by a 400 MHz amplification section that insures optimum performance. When experimental conditions warrant that signal processing be remote from the experiment, the combination of the Model 1763 preamplifier and the Model 1761 Discriminator offers an attractive alternative to the Model 1762 Amplifier/Discriminator. TTL output from the 1761 and 1762 extends versatility without extending cost.

In the design of its Model 1770 Counter/Timer SOI has incorporated the most requested features in a convenient double width NIM module. Maximum count rate is 100 MHz with two counters and, unlike some 100 MHz counters, every event is displayed. The 1770 offers the versatility of three output modes including an analog output with adjustable scaling and smoothing. This is a standard feature that eliminates costly add-ons like D/A convertors. The SOI 1770 Counter/Timer—the most features of any counter available at comparable price and size.

SOI can also provide PMT housings, power supplies, bins, monochromators and other accessories necessary to assemble a state-of-the-art photon counting system.

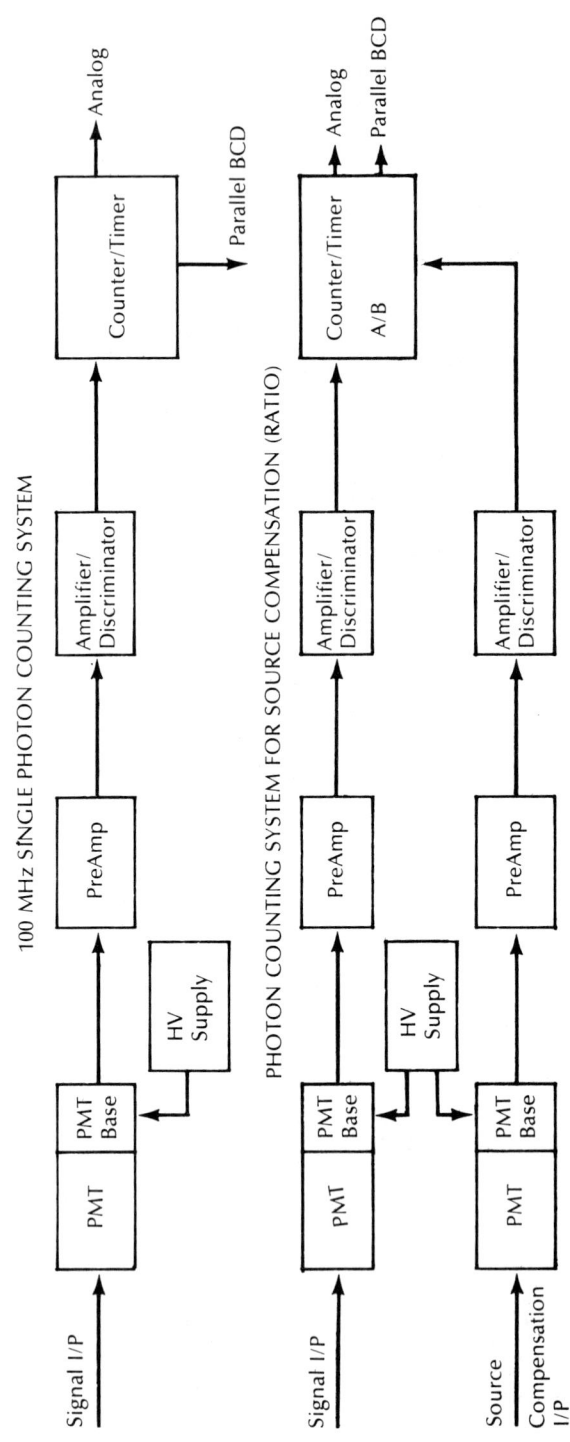

APPLICATIONS

100 MHz SINGLE PHOTON COUNTING SYSTEM

PHOTON COUNTING SYSTEM FOR SOURCE COMPENSATION (RATIO)

EXHIBIT 4, cont'd
Model 1763 Fast Preamplifier

The SOI Model 1763 low noise, fast risetime preamplifier has been designed for use with photo-multipliers, electron multipliers, and other detectors employed in photon counting, ion counting, or fast timing applications. The 50Ω input provides the ac load impedance for the detector current pulse.

The preamplifier has a fast risetime of <1 nsec and switched gain settings of 10 and 100. It is compact in design to allow for mounting close to the detector, reducing the effect of noise pickup or interference. The 1763 boosts the low-level signal for connection to either the 1761 Discriminator or the 1762 Amplifier/Discriminator.

Specifications:

Input Risetime ≤ 1 nsec

Input Protection Diode clamped ± 0.45V

Input Impedance 50Ω ac coupled

Voltage Gain ×10 or ×100

Input Reflections <10% for 2 nsec risetime

Input RMS Noise Equivalent <25 μV

Output Impedance 50Ω

Output Dynamic Range > ± 0.4V across 50Ω

Nonlinearity <1%

Input and Output Connections BNC

Power Requirements +24V @ 70mA, from rear panel of 1761 or 1762 discriminators

Power Connector Amphenol # 17-90090-15 with # 17-529 latch and # 17-310-01 shell

Dimensions 11 cm × 6 cm × 3 cm

THE PHOTON COUNTING LINE

The three instruments involved in the photon counting line detected low-level light in research and industrial applications. Exhibit 4 shows the specifications and the interconnections of the three units: the signal preamplifier (#1763), the amp/discriminator (#1761), and the photon counter (#1770). The 1770, the most complex unit ever designed by S.O.I., used two intricate circuit boards involving 2,000 separate solder points in its assembly.

Marketing predicted that in 1981 S.O.I. would have 15 percent of the 2-million-dollar market for photon counting equipment. The price for the line was $3,400: $300 for the preamplifier, $900 for the preamp/discriminator, and $2,200 for the photon counter. Exhibit 5 contains the sales predictions for the line in 1980–81.

Text continued on page 119.

EXHIBIT 4, cont'd
Model 1761 AMP/Discriminator

The SOI Model 1761 Amplifier/Discriminator features a wideband, high gain amplifier and a fast leading edge discriminator capable of count rates to 100MHz, housed in a single width module.

The amplifier section has a 50Ω input impedance with switch selectable voltage gain of 1, 2, 5, 10, 20, 50 and ×100. Risetime is less than 1 nsec.

The discriminator will accept negative inputs. Discriminator level can be adjusted from −10 mV to −300 mV by means of a front panel control. Pulse Pair Resolution is <10 nsec and Time Walk over a 10:1 range is less than 3 nsec.

Specifications:

AMPLIFIER

Input Signal Fast negative pulses which when amplified by gain selected are between threshold and −0.5V maximum.

Gain Switch selectable ×1, 2, 5, 10, 20, 50, 100

Input Impedance 50Ω ac coupled

Input Reflections <10% for 2 nsec risetime

Input Protection Diode clamped to ± 0.45V

Amplifier Risetime <1 nsec

Input Noise Equivalent <25 μV RMS

Nonlinearity <1%

Input Connector BNC front panel

DISCRIMINATOR

Threshold −10mV to −300mV continuously adjustable

Stability 0.2% per °C

Double Pulse Resolution <10 nsec

Maximum Count Rate 100 MHz

Output Signals
Two fast negative NIM, front panel BNC
Two TTL, one front and one rear panel BNC

GENERAL

Power requirements
+12V @ 180 mA
−12V @ 200 mA
+24V @   70 mA
−24V @ 100 mA

Preamplifier Power Connector
Rear panel, +24V @ 70mA
Amphenol # 17-10090

Dimensions Single width AEC/NIM

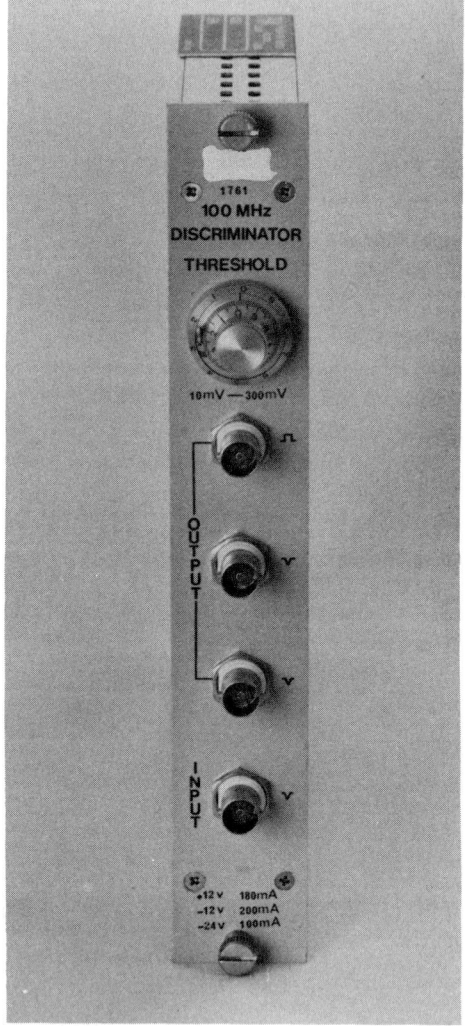

EXHIBIT 4, cont'd
Model 1770 Counter/Timer

The Model 1770 is a dual channel preset counter-timer designed to accept both fast negative and slow positive NIM logic pulses at rates up to 100 MHz and 10 MHz, respectively. Either channel, or the ratio of the count rate in channel A to that in channel B (A/B), can be displayed and read onto an output device in an 8 decade format. In general, this device was designed specifically to be used in photon counting or electron counting applications.

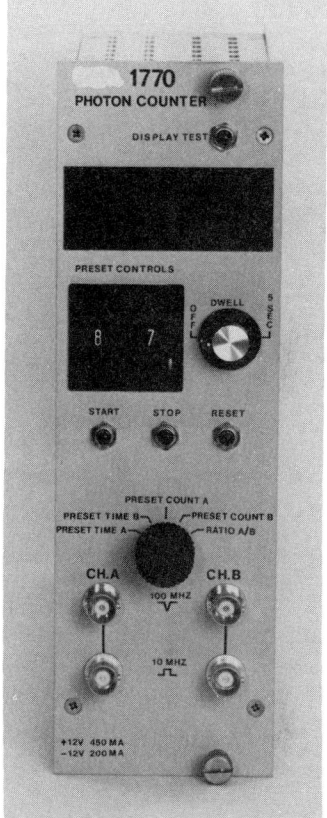

Although results from both channels cannot be displayed simultaneously, or the output presented simultaneously, data can be presented to both independent counters simultaneously. In addition the Counter/Timer can accumulate either the number of events in a Preset Time (1 μsec to 90 sec) or the time necessary to arrive at a Preset Total Count (1 $\times$ 10^0 to 9 $\times$ 10^7 events). In the ratio mode (A/B), the Counter/Timer accumulates the number of events in Channel A which occur during the time necessary to accumulate a preset number of counts in Channel B.

Timing or counting information appears simultaneously in three output formats: an 8 digit LED front panel display; an 8 decade, bit parallel, digit serial, BCD with appropriate timing signals; and a 3 digit resolution, 10V maximum analog output.

Start, Stop, Reset and Gating can be accomplished either internally or externally.

Specifications:

Inputs, Channels A and B
(Front Panel)
Slow NIM Logic: Front panel BNC's, positive TTL, pulse width 50 nsec., 1 kΩ input impedance
Fast NIM Logic: Front panel BNC's, negative fast NIM pulse, requiring −14 mA into 50Ω input impedance, pulse width $\geq$ 4 nsec.
Control (Rear Panel)
External Start, Stop, and Reset: positive TTL

Count Rate
Slow NIM 10 MHz, both channels
Fast NIM 100 MHz, both channels

Pulse Pair Resolution
Slow NIM 100 nsec
Fast NIM 10 nsec

Internal Clock Frequency
10 MHz, crystal controlled
Time base accuracy 5 $\times$ 10^{-6}

Preset Count
1 $\times$ 10^0 to 9 $\times$ 10^7

Preset Time
1μsec to 90 sec.

Count Capacity
8 decades

Dwell Time
100 msec to 5 sec.

Outputs
Parallel BCD: Rear panel, 8 decade, digit valid and external control i/p signals
Analog: Rear panel, 3 digit selectable, full scale 1 to 10V continuously adjustable, 1 kΩ output impedance. Smoothing time constant: 3, 1, 0.3, 0.1 sec.
Display: Front panel, 8 digit LED.
Control: Gate and overflow, both positive TTL.

Dimensions: Standard NIM, double width.

EXHIBIT 5
Sales Forecast 1980-81 (Photon Counter Line)

| | Orders Predicted | | | | | | | | | | | | | | |
| | 1980 | | | | | | | | | | | 1981 | | |
Product	Feb.	Mar.	Apr.	May	June	July	Aug.	Sept.	Oct.	Nov.	Dec.	Jan.	Feb.	Total
1763 North America	8	3	2	3	3	3	3	3	3	3	3	3	3	43
1763 Overseas	7	2	3	3	3	3	3	3	3	3	3	3	3	42
1761 North America	0	2	1	2	1	1	2	1	1	0	0	0	0	11
1761 Overseas	0	0	0	0	0	0	0	0	0	1	1	1	2	5
1770 North America	0	3	0	1	1	1	0	1	1	0	1	1	0	10
1770 Overseas	0	2	0	1	1	1	0	1	1	1	1	1	0	10

EXHIBIT 6
Man-Hours per Month Report (for month ending Dec. 1979)

Personnel	Misc. duties	TX5 optical feedback	510	301	302	303	1204	301S	300 p.p.	Gas hand	301 Mod.
C. Jones	75.5	16.5		3		57.5		7.5			
B. Maclean	38.5										
F. Smith	32.0			60.5				74.			
R. Hall	69.25			35.75		44.75			.25		
P. March	90.75			30.5 + SET UP		SET UP .5 9.		11			.5
M. Mason	39.5			32.75	40.5						
L. Harrison	7.5			37.75				REWORK 4.5			
Total	353	16.5		202.75	40.5	111.75		97.0	.25		.5

Jim Roberts, the project manager and designing technician for the line, estimated the prototype assembly time without further design changes at 40 hours for the 1770. Roberts felt that, given the time, he could redesign the prototype to make the control board easier for the customer to use and the circuitry easier to assemble.

Ross believed that an assembly time of a standard 8 hours per unit could be achieved for the 1770. The 1761 and 1762 even required about 8 hours to assemble in their prototype stage, but were expected to have a standard assembly time of 2 hours each.

Ross believed the assembly operations were producing at 70 percent capacity; however, he was aware that assembly was running short of physical space as new product lines were introduced and production runs were lengthened. Burke submitted her previous month's man-hour report to aid in Ross's planning. (Exhibit 6)

Ross had production progress reports prepared for different products showing their assembly times per successive unit in 1979 and their production history. Four of these reports are presented in Exhibits 7, 8, 9, and 10.

ALH 220	W. P. 1611	Photo detector	610C L	610C P. S.	Q. C.	Eng. C	Medical	Vac.	Stat. hol.	Over-time	Meetings	Sick
									7.5			7.5
					30 l P.S. 3.5				7.5			12.5
							3		7.5			
					6				7.5			7.5
	SET UP .5 14.25		REWORK 7.5					2.5	7.5			
10							4.75		7.5			37.5
					30 l P.S. .5							
10	14.75		7.5		10.0		10.25		45.0			177.5

EXHIBIT 7
Product Progress Report—1611

Description: Monochromator drive unit with precision seven speed stepping motor

History: Product introduction—Jan. 15, 1979
Number shipped—26
Unit assembly time 1979
Estimated rework time of cumulative—21%

(AUGUST)

Count	Hours/Unit	Cumulative	Avg/Unit	Count	Hours/Unit	Cumulative	Avg/Unit
1	77.3	77.3	77.3	14	25.8	540.7	38.6
2	57.9	135.3	67.6	15	25.1	565.9	37.7
3	49.0	184.3	61.4	16	24.4	590.3	36.8
4	43.4	227.8	56.9	17	23.8	614.2	36.1
5	39.6	267.4	53.4	18	23.2	637.5	35.4
6	36.7	304.2	50.7	19	22.7	660.3	34.7
7	34.4	338.6	48.3	20	22.3	682.6	34.1
8	32.6	371.3	46.4	21	21.8	704.4	33.5
9	31.0	402.3	44.7	22	21.4	725.9	32.9
10	29.7	432.1	43.2	23	21.0	746.9	32.4
11	28.5	460.6	41.8	24	20.6	767.6	31.9
12	27.5	488.2	40.6	25	20.3	787.9	31.5
13	26.6	514.9	39.6	26	20.0	807.9	31.0

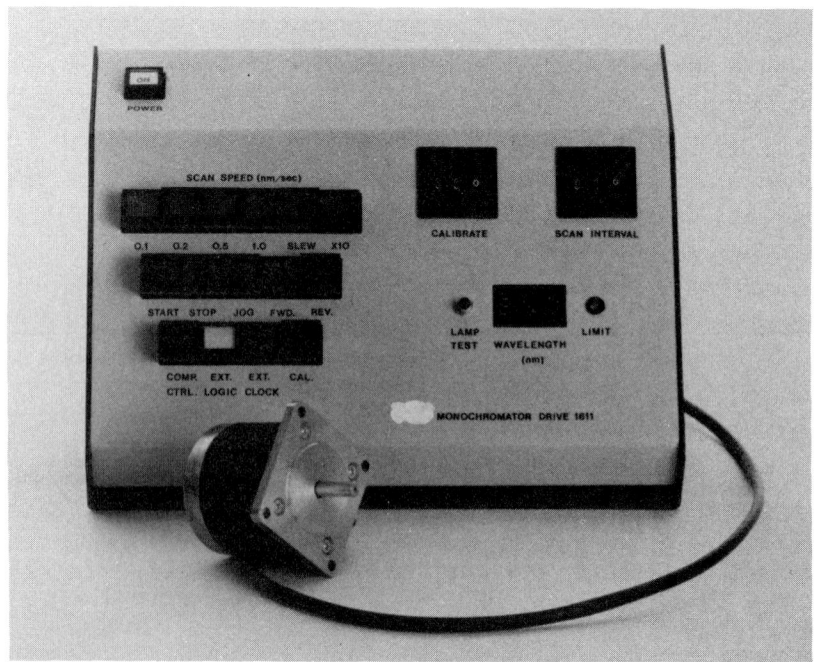

EXHIBIT 8
Product Progress Report B 102—1979

Description: Monochromatic light source

History: Product introduction—Jan. 1979
Number shipped—40 units
Unit assembly times
Estimated rework time of cumulative:
    BATCH 1 22%
    BATCH 2 15%

BATCH 1 (February)				BATCH 2 (March)			
Count	Hours/Unit	Cumulative	Avg/Unit	Count	Hours/Unit	Cumulative	Avg/Unit
1	6.9	6.9	6.9	1	2.0	2.0	2.0
2	5.2	12.1	6.0	2	1.9	3.9	1.9
3	4.3	16.5	5.5	3	1.8	5.7	1.9
4	3.9	20.4	5.1	4	1.8	7.5	1.8
5	3.5	23.9	4.7	5	1.7	9.3	1.8
6	3.2	27.2	4.5	6	1.7	11.0	1.8
7	3.0	30.3	4.3	7	1.7	12.8	1.8
8	2.9	33.3	4.1	8	1.7	14.5	1.8
9	2.7	36.0	4.0	9	1.6	16.2	1.8
10	2.6	38.7	3.8	10	1.6	17.9	1.7
11	2.5	41.3	3.7	11	1.6	19.5	1.7
12	2.4	43.7	3.6	12	1.6	21.2	1.7
13	2.3	46.1	3.5	13	1.6	22.9	1.7
14	2.3	48.4	3.4	14	1.6	24.5	1.7
15	2.2	50.7	3.3	15	1.6	26.1	1.7
16	2.1	52.9	3.3	16	1.6	27.8	1.7
17	2.1	55.0	3.2	17	1.6	29.4	1.7
18	2.0	57.1	3.1	18	1.6	31.0	1.7
19	2.0	59.2	3.1	19	1.6	32.6	1.7
20	2.0	61.2	3.0	20	1.6	34.2	1.7

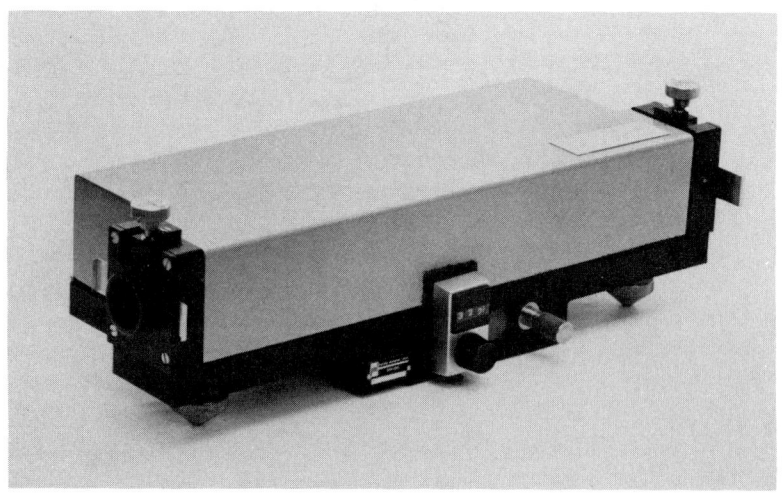

EXHIBIT 9
Product Progress Report 1979—M 301

Description:	Advanced, water cooled power supply for 1000 w light sources

History: Product introduction—Jan. 15, 1977
Number shipped—121 units
Number produced 1979—30 units
Unit assembly times 1979
Estimated rework time of cumulative:
    Batch 1 10%
    Batch 2 10%

BATCH 1 (February)				BATCH 2 (June)			
Count	Hours/Unit	Cumulative	Avg/Unit	Count	Hours/Unit	Cumulative	Avg/Unit
1	10.4	10.4	10.4	1	11.5	11.5	11.5
2	9.9	20.3	10.1	2	10.9	22.5	11.2
3	9.6	30.0	10.0	3	10.6	33.2	11.0
4	9.4	39.4	9.8	4	10.4	43.6	10.9
5	9.2	48.7	9.7	5	10.2	53.9	10.7
6	9.1	57.8	9.6	6	10.1	64.0	10.6
7	9.0	66.9	9.5	7	10.0	74.1	10.5
8	8.9	75.9	9.4	8	9.9	84.0	10.5
9	8.8	84.7	9.4	9	9.8	93.8	10.4
10	8.8	93.6	9.3	10	9.7	103.6	10.3
11	8.7	102.3	9.3	11	9.6	113.3	10.3
12	8.6	111.0	9.2	12	9.6	122.9	10.2
13	8.6	119.7	9.2	13	9.5	132.5	10.1
14	8.5	128.3	9.1	14	9.5	142.0	10.1
15	8.5	136.8	9.1	15	9.4	151.4	10.0

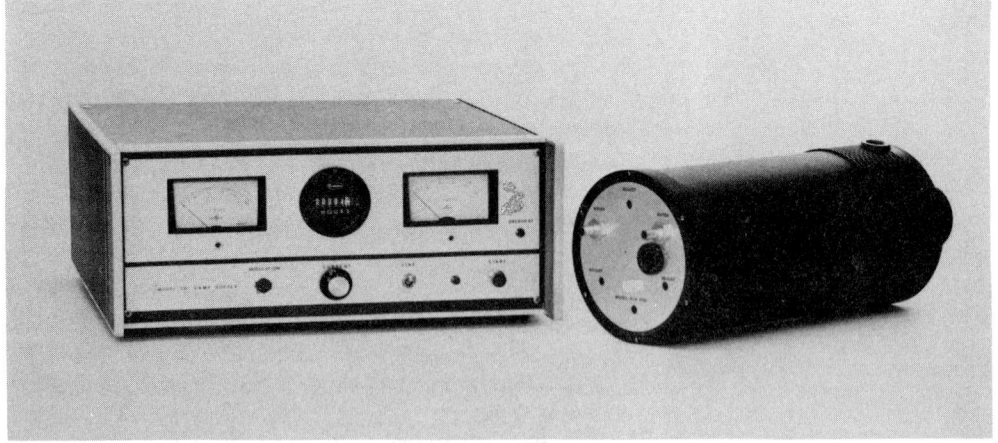

EXHIBIT 10
Product Progress Report—LN 100

Description:	Nitrogen pulse laser
History:	Product introduction—Jan. 15, 1979
	Number shipped—15 units
	Unit assembly times—1979
	Estimated rework time of cumulative:
	Batch 1 23%
	Batch 2 18%
	Batch 3 12%

BATCH 1 (June)

Count	Hours/Unit	Cumulative	Avg/Unit
1	75	75	75
2	53.9	129	64.4
3	44.5	173.5	57.8
4	38.8	212.4	53.1
5	34.9	247.4	49.4

BATCH 2 (July-August)

Count	Hours/Unit	Cumulative	Avg/Unit
1	44.2	44.2	44.2
2	36.2	80.4	40.2
3	32.2	112.7	37.5
4	29.7	142.4	35.6
5	27.8	170.3	34.0

BATCH 3 (September)

Count	Hours/Unit	Cumulative	Avg/Unit
1	29.1	29.1	29.1
2	26.1	55.2	27.6
3	24.6	79.9	26.6
4	23.5	103.4	25.8
5	22.7	126.2	25.2

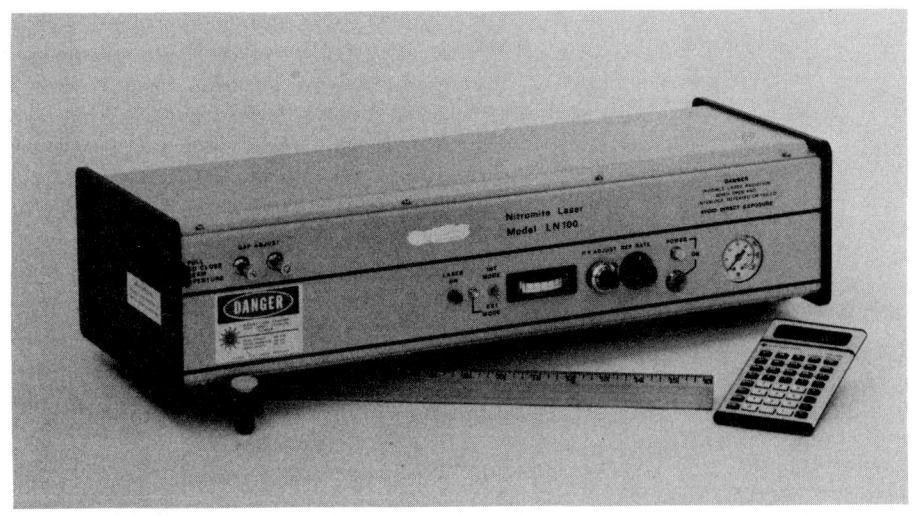

Ross felt that as assembly workers produced more of the units, their assembly time per unit would decrease along a predictable learning or experience curve. He felt that a 72 percent curve, or a 28 percent decrease in assembly time per unit every time the total number of units produced doubled, represented the progress for a new line like the photon counter. Ross was uncertain how closely this predictive model would translate into actual performance given that the product line had never been produced before. Due to the complexity of the new line, especially model 1770, Ross was concerned about possible problems and unrealistic assumptions in scheduling the photon counter line for first deliveries in April.

PART II

PRODUCTION PLANNING, SCHEDULING, AND THE MANAGEMENT OF MATERIALS

MacPherson Refrigeration Limited

In October, Linda Metzler, newly appointed production planning manager of MacPherson Refrigeration, Ltd. (MRL) of Stratford, Ontario was formulating the production plan for the year beginning on January 1. The plan was to be submitted to the plant's general manager by the end of the month.

BACKGROUND

MRL had sales of about $28.5 million. The company had begun in Stratford in 1954 specializing in commercial refrigeration. In 1972, the company opened a new 300,000 square foot plant in Stratford and diversified into the consumer refrigeration market. Subsequently, MRL had added air conditioners to its freezer and refrigerator lines. The company sold its Hercules brand appliances through independent furniture and appliance stores in southern Ontario.

THE STRATFORD PLANT

Since 1962, manufacturing efficiency at the plant had increased dramatically through changes in both process design and assembly technology. Annual output per worker had increased from about 240 appliances in 1963 to the present level of about 450 appliances and was expected to be about 480 appliances next year. The Canadian market was too small to allow the productivity levels of American appliance manufacturers, but MRL was considered to be relatively efficient by Canadian standards.

The Stratford plant had the physical capacity to make only 13,000 appliances per month.

THE PLANNING PROCESS

Each year in September the marketing and sales department produced a forecast of appliances by month for the next year. The production planning department used these forecasts to plan production for the next year. The first step in the planning process was to construct an aggregate production plan which consisted of planned gross production by month for the year. This plan did not indicate

Copyright © 1983, The University of Western Ontario.

Case material of the University of Western Ontario School of Business Administration is prepared as a basis of classroom discussion. This case was prepared by John Haywood-Farmer with the assistance of Bill Rankin.

EXHIBIT 1
Level Production Plan to Meet Peak Demand

	Jan.	Feb.	Mar.	Apr.	May	June	July	Aug.	Sept.	Oct.	Nov.	Dec.
Production plan												
Shipment forecast	4400	4400	6000	8000	6600	11800	13000	11200	10800	7600	6000	5600
Production plan	8440	8440	8440	8440	8440	8440	8440	8440	8440	8440	8440	8440
Shipments	4400	4400	6000	8000	6600	11800	13000	11200	10800	7600	6000	5600
Inventory*	4280	8320	10760	11200	13040	9680	5120	2360	0	840	3280	6120
Extraordinary labour costs												
No. of workers	211	211	211	211	211	211	211	211	211	211	211	211
Hirings	51	—	—	—	—	—	—	—	—	—	—	—
Layoffs	—	—	—	—	—	—	—	—	—	—	—	—
Worker months overtime	—	—	—	—	—	—	—	—	—	—	—	—

Cost of alternative 1			
Hiring costs	51×1800	=	91,800
Layoff costs	0	=	0
Inventory holding costs	$75,000 \times 8$	=	600,000
Labour costs			
Regular	$211 \times 12 \times 2400$ =		6,076,800
Overtime	0	=	0
Total			$6,768,600

*Finished Goods Inventory on December 31 predicted to be 240 units.

numbers of specific appliance types, sizes, or models to be made each month but, as the name indicates, was an aggregate. Linda Metzler's task in October was the construction of this aggregate plan. As the production periods approached later in the year, master production plans would be formulated which would be specific regarding appliance type, model number, etc.

The September forecast is presented in each of Exhibits 1–3. It shows the expected seasonal fluctuations and the aggregate number of appliances to be shipped each month. Linda knew that there would be significant variation of specific appliance types within each month but she also knew that each type of appliance required roughly similar materials and labour resources. For aggregate planning purposes then, the number of appliances to be shipped would be sufficient.

THE AGGREGATE PLAN

In preparation for her decision, Linda gathered the following information:

1. As of October 1, MRL employed 160 hourly paid unionized production workers. Their two-year contract signed in February of last year called for an increase of $0.75 per hour effective next January 1, bringing the average hourly rate to $10.50. With fringe benefits, the monthly cost to MRL would be about $2,400 per worker. Under the agreement, overtime was 1.5 times the regular hourly rate but not all fringes were affected so a worker-month of overtime cost about $3,300. The standard work week was

EXHIBIT 2
Chase Production Plan with Constant Workforce and Overtime

	Jan.	Feb.	Mar.	Apr.	May	June	July	Aug.	Sept.	Oct.	Nov.	Dec.
Production plan												
Shipment forecast	4400	4400	6000	8000	6600	11800	13000	11200	10800	7600	6000	5600
Production plan	4160	4400	6000	8000	6600	11800	13000	11200	10800	7600	6000	5600
Shipments	4400	4400	6000	8000	6600	11800	13000	11200	10800	7600	6000	5600
Inventory*	—	—	—	—	—	—	—	—	—	—	—	—
Extraordinary labour costs												
No. of workers	199	199	199	199	199	199	199	199	199	199	199	199
Hirings	39	—	—	—	—	—	—	—	—	—	—	—
Layoffs	—	—	—	—	—	—	—	—	—	—	—	—
Worker months overtime	—	—	—	1.0	—	96.0	126.0	81.0	71.0	—	—	—

Cost of alternative 2

Hiring costs	39 × 1800	=	70,200
Layoff costs	0	=	0
Inventory holding costs	0	=	0
Labour costs			
Regular	199 × 12 × 2400	=	5,731,200
Overtime	375 × 3300	=	1,237,500
Total			$7,038,900

*Finished goods inventory on December 31 predicted to be 240 units.

EXHIBIT 3
Chase Production Plan with Varying Workforce

	Jan.	Feb.	Mar.	Apr.	May	June	July	Aug.	Sept.	Oct.	Nov.	Dec.
Production plan												
Shipment forecast	4400	4400	6000	8000	6600	11800	13000	11200	10800	7600	6000	5600
Production plan	4160	4400	6000	8000	6600	11800	13000	11200	10800	7600	6000	5600
Shipments	4400	4400	6000	8000	6600	11800	13000	11200	10800	7600	6000	5600
Inventory*	—	—	—	—	—	—	—	—	—	—	—	—
Extraordinary labour costs												
No. of workers	104	110	150	200	165	295	325	280	270	190	150	140
Hirings	—	6	40	50	—	130	30	—	—	—	—	—
Layoffs	56	—	—	—	35	—	—	45	10	80	40	10
Worker months overtime	—	—	—	—	—	—	—	—	—	—	—	—

Cost of alternative 3

Hiring costs	256 × 1800	=	460,800
Layoff costs	276 × 1200	=	331,200
Inventory holding costs	0	=	0
Labour costs			
Regular	2377 × 2400	=	5,704,800
Overtime	0	=	0
Total		=	$6,496,800

*Finished goods inventory on December 31 predicted to be 240 units.

40 hours. The aggregate plan in effect until December 31 called for a total production workforce of 160 at that time.

2. The personnel department estimated that hiring, training, and related expenses amounted to $1,800 per worker. It also estimated a total of $1,200 per worker for severance and other layoff expenses.

3. The accounting department predicted that it would cost about $8 to hold an appliance in inventory for a month during the next year. Raw materials were readily available from regional sources on short notice. The current aggregate plan, supported by marketing's most recent revised forecasts and the master production schedule, predicted an inventory of 240 finished units on December 31.

4. Although MRL manufactured some parts and subassemblies, the plant was primarily a final assembly operation with a throughput time of about three days. The company used an MRP-based planning system. For aggregate planning purposes, management had found that it was adequate to assume that all worker hours scheduled in a particular month would contribute directly to output in the same month. Similarly, experience had shown that no special allowances for learning needed to be considered.

5. There appeared to be three basic tools available to meet demand fluctuations, each of which involved both quantitative and qualitative trade-offs:
a)–building inventory to meet peaks
b)–using overtime
c)–hiring and laying off workers.

THE ALTERNATIVES

Linda identified three alternatives the company could follow in meeting forecasted demand:

1. The production level and the workforce could be held constant throughout the year at a level sufficient to meet the peak demand period. In periods of low demand inventory would be accumulated and would be drawn down during peak demand periods. Linda was attracted by the protection this plan offered against unforeseen demand changes. This plan is shown in Exhibit 1.

2. The production level could vary to meet demand with a constant workforce by the use of overtime in peak months and restricted output in slow months. The workforce would be held at just the number to meet average monthly requirements. MRL would incur no inventory carrying costs with such a scheme. However, Linda wondered if excessive overtime might lead to lower efficiency or if restricted production might promote poor work habits and low morale. This plan is shown in Exhibit 2.

3. Some of these potential problems could be overcome by a strategy that met demand by varying workforce levels. Linda's calculations showed this to be the cheapest of the three alternatives (see Exhibit 3). However, she was well aware that union relations and employee morale could be adversely affected by frequent layoffs. As well, hiring and training new em-

ployees brought their own headaches, especially in a limited labour market such as existed in Stratford.

THE DECISION

Linda knew that these three very different plans were by no means the only feasible ones available. She realized that her decision on an aggregate plan would involve both quantitative and qualitative trade-offs. One nagging thought in the back of her mind was that no matter which plan she chose, she might never know if a better one existed.

Murphy Fabricating Company

The Murphy Fabricating Company was faced once again with a routine, but tough, decision regarding its man power planning. The man-hour load projection for next month and the following six-month period had been revised. Bob Downey, manager of manufacturing, was accustomed to seeing these revisions. The marketing department had issued projections on a rolling basis for the past decade. Only recently, however, had the revised man-hour levels meant much to Bob Downey.

Bob explained his recent interest. "For as long as I can remember, we were able to maintain a relatively smooth employment pattern around here. Corporate headquarters' personnel were so interested in other matters, that any strategy I had for keeping my plant-load rather steady—say allowing for a plus or minus 5% change over a period—went unnoticed. I simply altered my sublet work (to vendors or, in some cases, other plants within the company) up and down to absorb the monthly man-hour variations from marketing's projections. If I did not want to follow that subcontracting cushioning alternative for some reason, I might pull in work and build products ahead of schedule, store it here or maybe even ship it early. Occasionally, I would push out work from requested shipping dates and let the guys in sales worry about keeping the customer happy. These types of adjustments made my man power planning job a lot easier. The foremen were able to keep a relatively stable and experienced workforce, and the union, which was run by senior employees, also liked that. You could say that I never placed much of a load upon the Employee Relations people either!"

Bob continued on. "But now, things are getting changed around here! The sales guys tell me that the name of the game has changed. They say that we have gone from a market where our engineering and quality reputation always sold our product to one of competitive price pressures on almost every job. Now, because of our own cost growth, a lot of the competitors are beating us out. Furthermore, we can't push around schedule dates as easily. Another thing, our replacement parts business has always been treated like a poor stepchild. They say we could make a bundle on this business and we have simply overlooked this market for years.

"The straw that broke my back was the finance department memo stating that all inventory levels over our "normal" targets would be assessed at 18% annual capital carrying cost. That action will cause me to reconsider my build-ahead alternative.

"In examining the options open to us here at Murphy, my understanding of the situation leads me to a choice of these alternatives:

1. Maintain a level employment by replacing all attrition and allow for the build-up of man-hours into work-in-progress product or completed contracts (prior to their normal progress in the shop necessary to meet contract shipping dates). Since most of our work goes to customers who either are (a) not willing to pay progress payments ahead of what they consider to be normal shop progress to meet a contract shipping data, or (b) who do not make progress payments, our manufacturing budget will have to absorb the inventory carrying costs penalty. But then again, that may be cheaper than the hiring/layoff pattern I have seen in some companies that attempt to follow the man-hour requirements that flow from customer shipping dates. The level of employment would have to be set such that over the planning period in question, the shops would be able to meet scheduled shipping dates. We cannot tolerate any slippage in shipping dates.

2. Plan upon perturbations in the workforce which follow the pattern of man-hours requirements. This will keep the build-up of work-in-progress product way down, but it will cost us in other ways when we start altering the workforce by any significant amount.

3. The third alternative would be some best combination of the extremes as in alternatives 1 and 2 above. That is, I could hold down the number of employment level changes in say 2 or 3.

"Maybe you can help me with this planning problem in the sheet/structural shop. Here is the current data:

A. Demand = Firm Order and Forecast (Exhibit 1 is a graph of the required hours per month).

	SEPT.	OCT.	NOV.	DEC.	JAN.	FEB.	MARCH
Days	19	24	18	22	18	20	25
Hours of Load	52,000	45,000	58,000	62,000	69,000	67,000	90,000

	APRIL	MAY	JUNE	JULY	AUGUST
Days	19	20	19	15	20
Hours	75,000	79,000	75,000	55,000	74,000

B. Max regular time capacity = 3,780 hrs/day
C. Employment level forecast at end of August = 435; 6 hr/day/worker
D. Direct labor hours cost = $6.00/hour; 50% overtime premium
E. Variable factory overhead rate = 50% of direct labor, or $3.00/hour
F. G&A, other fixed items overhead rate = 150% of direct labor, or $9.00/hour
G. Hiring cost = $500/new employee (assume 50% turnover on layoff; costs include start-up inefficiencies)
H. Subcontracting cost = $4.00/hour premium
   No difference in material cost

EXHIBIT 1
Demand per Day in Each Month

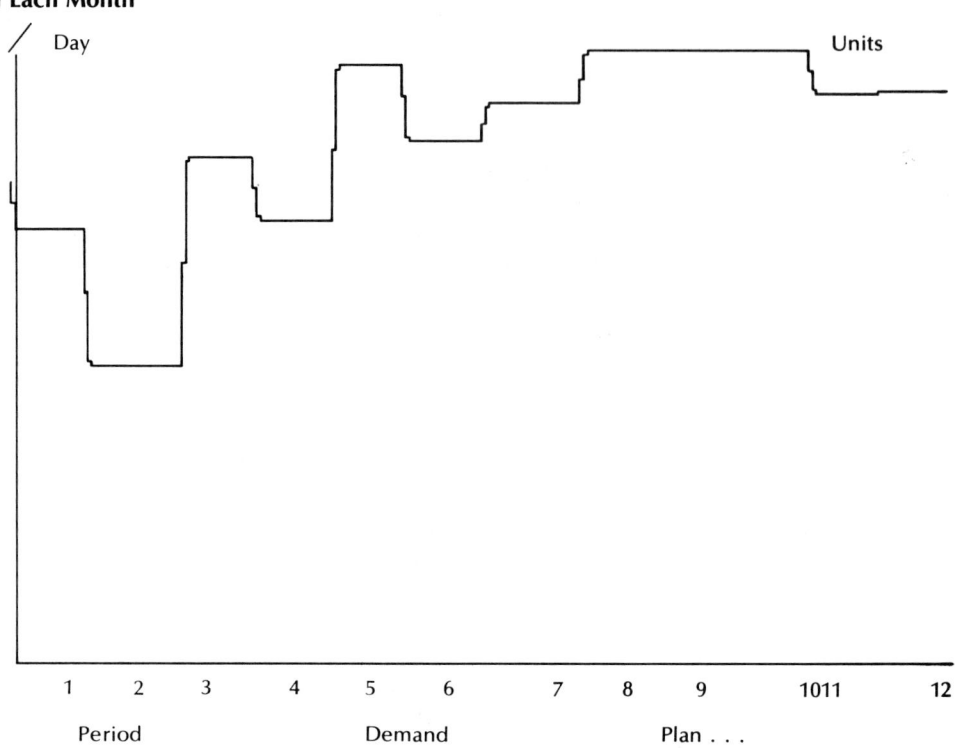

I.   Material as a percentage of Cost of Goods Sold = 70%
     Direct labor as a percentage of Cost of Goods Sold = 20%
     Variable Overhead as a percentage of Cost of Goods Sold = 10%
J.   Layoff cost = $400/worker

"I can use overtime to help out, if you think that is cheaper than adding and subtracting workers from the employment rolls. Although top management wants all the work done in-house, if we can show that it is cheaper to use subletting as an option in man power loading to meet a schedule, then I think we should consider it.

"For every hour of direct labor expended at $6.00/hour, the material is valued at $21.00 per labor hour expended.

"The purchasing people are usually able to schedule materials to conform to the man power plan strategy that is chosen. Therefore, any contract materials put into work prior to the date that would be required on a normal fabricating schedule to meet a shipping target will incur a carrying cost.

"Oh, I just about forgot. Our top management doesn't want us to schedule more than three days per month of overtime, or subcontract more than 5% of any one month's load. Furthermore, Jim Owens in Employee Relations tells me that we should never hire more than 30 employees in any one month."

Lamson Corporation

In this game you will have the chance to try your skill at inventory and operations planning using the information similar in type to that available to Mr. Marino, the operations manager of Lamson Corporation, a large multi-plant manufacturer of sewer pipes. Every two weeks in the summer sales period, Mr. Marino had to decide how many tiles of each type and size should be produced during the coming two weeks. In doing this planning, he took into account sales trends, the time of the year, the capacity of Lamson's tile making machinery, the stock of the various size tiles on hand, the cost of overtime production and the cost of missed deliveries. In this game you will be able to make similar decisions, although the game will be a simplified version of the actual situation. The most important feature of this simplification is that you will be dealing with only two sizes of sewer tile—the 18" diameter size and the 36" diameter size. Mr. Marino, in contrast, had to decide on production levels for 13 different sizes of tile and which plants would produce what mix.

SALES PATTERNS

Company sales, and industry sales in general, were very much influenced by general economic and seasonal factors. Since weather affected tile laying conditions and the number of construction starts, sales of sewer tiles exhibited a yearly sales trend of the following general shape (Figure 1). Sales were low for 6 months, from October 1 to April 1, and rose rapidly in the spring to a summer peak and then tapered off again. About ⅓ of all annual sales were made in the two middle months of the year, while about ¾ were made in the summer sales season. However, there was not necessarily a smooth rise and fall in sales in any particular year. The curve shown is only the average of the experiences of many years. In any given year, biweekly sales might vary ±25% from levels they would assume if a smooth sales curve existed. Last year, the maximum number of 18" tiles sold in any two-week period between April and October was 4,550. The similar figure for 36" tiles was 2,000. Major fluctuations in annual sales and mix levels were caused by economic conditions.

FIGURE 1

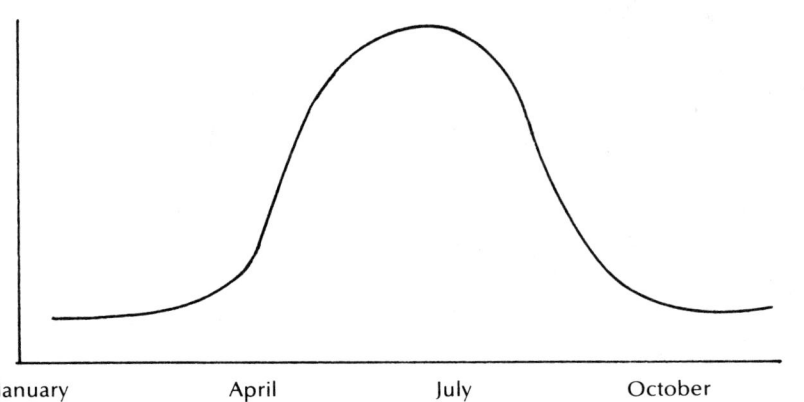

In the game you are about to play, Period 1 refers to the first two weeks in April. Thus, company sales are just leaving the low part of the annual swing. The game culminates in Period 12, the last two weeks in September, when sales are reentering the low winter period. Between Periods 1 and 12, sales follow the general shape of the curve shown in Figure 1.

All sales made by Lamson are booked for delivery within the period being considered. That is, there is no advance ordering. Mr. Marino has no idea what the sales for any coming period will be other than from judgement of the sales level of prior periods and from consideration of the general shape of the sales trend curve.

PRODUCTION CONSTRAINTS

The most popular sizes of concrete tile sold by Lamson were the 18″ diameter and the 36″ diameter sizes. Mr. Marino had found that together, these tiles accounted for a large part of tile sales; in fact, roughly one half of each period's production was devoted to one or other of these sizes. The other half of each period's production was used to manufacture the other sizes of tile produced by Lamson. In order to simplify the game, it has been assumed that Mr. Marino will continue to schedule the production of the less popular eleven tile sizes and that he will use half the production time each period for these sizes. Each participating group will be asked to schedule the number of 18″ and 36″ tiles to be produced during each period. Thus, each group will, in fact, schedule the production of a summer season's supply of 18″ and 36″ diameter tiles.

There were nine possible volume combinations of 18″ and 36″ tiles. Four of these output values were based on the normal capacity output of the plants. The other five values represented the maximum output possible at Lamson, which required 50% overtime.

The nine production levels possible for 18″ and 36″ tiles in each two-week period are shown in Exhibit 1.

EXHIBIT 1
The Nine Possible Production Choices Open to Mr. Marino (each two week period)

	Normal capacity		50% Overtime	
	18″ Tiles	36″ Tiles	18″ Tiles	36″ Tiles
	6,000	0	9,000	0
	4,000	600	7,000	600
	2,000	1,200	5,000	1,200
	0	1,800	3,000	1,800
			1,000	2,400

Please notice that trade-offs are involved in choosing a production level for a period. If the number of 18″ tiles to be produced is increased, the number of 36″ tiles that can be produced will necessarily decrease unless overtime is used.

COST INVOLVED

Inventory Costs

In deciding on production alternatives, Mr. Marino bore in mind several costs which he knew were fairly accurate. For instance, storage costs of an 18″ tile for one period were an average of $2.00. This amount took into account interest on tied-up capital, insurance against breakage and direct handling expense. The inventory carrying costs of each 36″ tile were higher and averaged $6.00 per tile per period. Mr. Marino had found that, over the period of a season, inventory carrying charges could be reasonably calculated on the basis of inventory on hand at the end of each period.

Stockout Costs

Stockout costs also had to be considered by Mr. Marino. A stockout occurred whenever a sale in a particular period could not be filled because there were insufficient tiles of the required diameter on hand or in production during that period. For instance, if 100 tiles were on hand at the beginning of a period, 2,000 tiles were produced during the period, and sales during the period totalled 2,200, then a stockout of 100 tiles would occur. When such a stockout occurred, there was a chance that a future customer of Lamson would be lost. Furthermore, Lamson lost the profit potential on the missed order. Mr. Marino had assessed the risks and costs involved and thought that a stockout cost Lamson $20 for each 18″ tile and $60 for each 36″ tile. These figures took into account the fact that the larger the number of tiles that could not be delivered, the more apt the customer was to take future business elsewhere. Stockouts could not be made up in subsequent periods. If a stockout occurred, the sale was lost forever to the firm and the above costs were incurred.

Overtime Costs

If overtime was used in any period, a fixed charge of $20,000 was incurred, mainly to pay extra wages to the employees. The amount was fixed because the employees had been guaranteed a minimum amount each period overtime was used.

HOW TO PLAY THE GAME

In the actual conduct of this game, teams will make the production decisions normally made by Mr. Marino regarding the 18" and 36" diameter tiles. Before each period, each team will be required to decide on the production level that will be used in the plant. This decision will be made by the team by whatever means it chooses. Thus, a prediction from a plot of past period sales might be used by some teams, a pure guess by others. In making the decision, teams should consider both the possibilities of future sales and the inventories of tiles now on hand.

After each team has decided on the production level it desires for the coming period, the instructor will announce the actual sales levels for this period. Given this information, teams will then be able to calculate inventory on hand, and inventory stockout and overtime costs. These costs will be added to a total period cost which will then be added to a cumulative total of costs.

The objective of the game is to keep the total costs incurred over 12 periods to a minimum. This objective means that teams will have to decide whether it would be cheaper in the long run to incur overtime costs, inventory carrying costs, or stockout costs. It is impossible to avoid all three. At the end of the twelfth period the game will be stopped and final costs calculated. Your team's results will be compared to those of other teams. During subsequent discussions the merits of various inventory and production policies can be evaluated. Teams will probably find it advantageous to split the work of making sales estimates, calculating costs, and keeping records among the various members.

RESULT FORM USED

To make the keeping of results easier for all teams, Exhibit 2 will be used. The exact steps in using this form are:

1. Decide on the production level to be used in the forthcoming period.
2. Enter number of tiles to be produced in Columns A (18") and J (36").
3. Fill in stock on hand at start of period in Columns B (18") and K (36"). These figures come from Columns E (18") and N (36") of the previous period.
4. Enter total stock available for sale in the period in Columns C and L.
   Entry in Column C (18" tiles) = Entry in Column A + Entry in Column B.
   Entry in Column L (36" tiles) = Entry in Column J + Entry in Column K.
5. Obtain actual sales in period from Instructor. Enter in Columns D (18") and M (36").

EXHIBIT 2

NUMBER	MONTH	(A) Number Produced	(B) Stock on Hand at Start of Period	(C) Total Available for Sale C = A + B	(D) Sales in Period	(E) Inventory Remaining at end of Period E = C − D (Minimum = 0)	(F) Inventory Carrying Cost $2 × E	(G) Number of Stock-Outs G = D − C if Greater Than 0	(H) Stock-Out Cost H = $20 × G	(J) Number Produced	(K) Stock on Hand at Start of Period	(L) Total Available for Sale L = J + K	(M) Sales in Period	(N) Inventory Remaining at end of Period N = L − M (Minimum = 0)	(O) Inventory Carrying Cost $6 × N	(P) Number of Stock-Outs P = M − L if Greater Than 0	(Q) Stock-Out Cost Q = $60 × P	(R) Total Inventory Cost R = F + O	(S) Total Stock-Out Cost S = H + Q	(T) Overtime Cost $20,000 (if used)	(U) Total Period Cost U = R + S + T	(V) Cumulative Total to Date
−1	March	7000	400	7400	6000	1400	$2800	0	0	600	100	700	800	0	0	100	$6000	$2800	$6000	20,000	$28,800	(28,800)
0	March	2000	1400	3400	1400	2000	$4000	0	0	1200	0	1200	500	700	4200	0	0	$8200	0	0	$ 8,200	(37,000)
1	April																					
2	April																					
3	May																					
4	May																					
5	June																					
6	June																					
7	July																					
8	July																					
9	August																					
10	August																					
11	September																					
12	September																					
Total																						

6. Compute inventory remaining at the end of the period. Enter in Columns E and N.

    Entry in Column E (18″ tiles) = Entry in Column C − Entry in Column D.

    Entry in Column N (36″ tiles) = Entry in Column L − Entry in Column M.

    Enter zero if any entry is calculated as negative. There can be no negative inventory on hand.

7. Compute inventory carrying costs and enter in Columns F and O.

    Entry in Column F (18″ tiles) = $2.00 × No. in Column E.

    Entry in Column O (36″ tiles) = $6.00 × No. in Column N.

8. Compute stockouts incurred in period, enter in Columns G and P if zero or a positive number. Enter zero if an entry is calculated as negative; there can be no negative stockouts.

    Entry in Column G (18″ tiles) = Entry in Column D − Entry in Column C.

    Entry in Column P (36″ tiles) = Entry in Column M − Entry in Column L.

9. Compute stockout costs, enter in Columns H and Q.

10. Compute total period inventory cost, enter in Column R.

    Entry in Column R = Entry in Column F (18″ tiles) + Entry in Column Q (36″ tiles).

11. Compute total period stockout costs, enter in Column S.

    Entry in Column S = Entry in Column H (18″ tiles) + Entry in Column Q (36″ tiles).

12. If overtime was used, enter $20,000 in Column T. If no overtime was used, enter zero.

13. Compute total period cost and enter in Column U.

    Entry in Column U = Entry in Column R (total period inventory cost) + Entry in Column S (total period stockout cost) + Entry in Column T (overtime cost).

14. Compute cumulative total to date, enter in Column V.

    Entry in Column V = Entry in Column U for current period + Entry in Column V for last period.

EXAMPLE

Each team member should carefully trace the proceedings as outlined in the following example to understand fully all of the steps involved in playing and recording the game.

Mr. Marino has already used the form to record the operating results of the two periods prior to the first period for which you will be required to decide the production level (Period 1). Lamson started Period 1 with four hundred 18″ tiles (Column B) and one hundred 36″ tiles on hand (Column K). Because he knew that a special, large order for 18″ tiles would be placed in Period −1 (a most unusual size of order at this time of year), Mr. Marino decided to go to overtime and to produce seven thousand four hundred 18″ tiles (Column A) and six hundred 36″ tiles (Column J). Thus, seven thousand four hundred 18″ tiles (Column C) and seven hundred 36″ tiles (Column L) were available for sales during Period 1.

In actual fact, the special order was smaller than Mr. Marino had anticipated and total sales turned out to the 6,000 for the 18″ tiles (Column D) and 800 for the 36″ tiles (Column M). Because 18″ inventory available for sale exceeded sales, Mr. Marino entered 1,400 in Column E to show there was inventory remaining at the end of the period, and then entered zero in Column G to show that there had been no stockout of 18″ tiles. Column F then shows the inventory cost incurred by having one thousand four hundred 18″ tiles on hand at the end of the period ($2.00 × 1,400 = $2,800.00). Column H shows that no stockout cost was incurred. Because demand for the 36″ tiles (800) exceeded the total available for sale (700), a stockout of 100 occurred and no tiles were left in inventory at the end of Period −1. To show this occurrence, zero was entered in Column N and 100 was entered in Column O while a stockout cost of $6,000 was entered in Column Q ($60 × 100 = $6,000).

The total inventory carrying cost was entered in Column R ($2,800 + 0 = $2,800) and the total stockout cost in Column S (0 + $6,000 = $6,000). $20,000 was entered in Column T because overtime was used. The total period cost was calculated to be $2,800 + $6,000 + $20,000 = $28,800. This amount was then entered in Column U and also Column V.

Lamson began Period 0 with one thousand four hundred 18″ tiles (Column B) and zero 36″ tiles on hand (Column K). These totals had been brought down from Columns E and N, respectively, of Period −1. At the beginning of Period 0, Mr. Marino elected to produce two thousand 18″ tiles (Column A) and one thousand two hundred 36″ tiles (Column J). No overtime was called for. Thus there were three thousand four hundred 18″ tiles (Column C) and one thousand two hundred 36″ tiles (Column L) available for sale in Period 0.

In Period 0, sales totalled one thousand four hundred 18″ tiles (Column D) and five hundred 36″ tiles (Column M). Thus, the inventory remaining at the end of the period was two thousand 18″ tiles (Column E) and seven hundred 36″ tiles (Column N). There were zero stockouts (Columns G and P). Inventory carrying costs were computed to be $2.00 × 2,000 = $4,000 (Column F) and $6.00 × 70 = $4,200 (Column O). There were no stockout costs (Column H and Q) because stockouts equalled zero in this period.

The total inventory carrying cost for Period 0 was $8,200 ($4,000 + $4,200). This amount was entered in Column R, while zero was entered in Column S since there had been no stockouts in the period. There was no overtime used, consequently a zero was entered in Column T. The Column U entry shows that the total period costs incurred were $8,200. The Column V entry was $28,000 + $8,200 = $37,000. Since your team did not incur these costs we will wipe them off the slate and have you start with a zero cost at the beginning of Period 1 in Column V.

A FEW OPERATING RULES DURING THE GAME

1. The only production combinations your team may choose are those given in Exhibit 1.
2. If your team makes a calculation mistake, a penalty of $25,000 will be assessed and all figures will be corrected.
3. If your team is unable to reach a decision by the end called for by the instructor, it will automatically be decided that you produce 2,000 18″ tiles and 1,200 36″ tiles.
4. Normally, at the beginning of the game, each team will have approximately 10 minutes to make a decision. This time will decrease as the game progresses.

START OF GAME

The game proper starts in Period 1. At the beginning of the game there are two thousand 18″ tiles on hand (brought down from Column E of Period 0) and seven hundred 36″ tiles on hand (brought down from Column N of Period 0). It is now up to each team to pick the production level most appropriate for Period 1 and thus start the playing of the game.

Kameron Mills (J)

Kameron Mills was increasing its production capacity by building a new feed mill. The project consisted of a number of separate tasks, some of which could not be started before others were complete. Exhibit 1 lists the activities along with the times expected for each as "agreed upon" by Kameron Mills' management, and the precedence relationships.

Kameron Mills' management wanted to advance the schedule as much as possible to save valuable time in getting the new mill into operation. Kameron Mills' president commented: "Every week saved is worth \$20,000 in lost contribution if we can get going."

Some of the construction activities could be sped up. For example, the firm's architects, by working overtime, could design the new plant in 10 weeks instead of the 12 weeks originally estimated. This advancement would cost Kameron Mills an additional \$8,000 per week advanced. Exhibit 1 also shows the maximum amount each activity could be crashed as well as the crash cost per week.

Copyright© 1984, The University of Western Ontario.

Case material of the Western School of Business Administration is prepared as a basis for classroom discussion. This case was prepared by Professor J. Britney and Professor R. Britney.

EXHIBIT 1
Activities Involved in Building and Implementing the Feed Mill

Activity	Expected time (wks)	Precedent activities	Minimum time (wks)	Crash cost (\$/wk)
A Design plant	12	None	10	8,000
B Select plant site	8	A	8	—
C Select plant builder	6	A	1	1,000
D Select operating personnel	13	A	13	—
E Prepare the building site	4	B, C	4	—
F Make or buy mill equipment	10	C	8	10,000
G Prepare mill operations manual	6	C	4	500
H Build the plant	10	E, F	6	25,000
I Train plant operators	8	D, G	8	—
J Test the plant	8	H, I	8	—
K Obtain a production license	4	J	4	—

EXHIBIT 2
Gantt Chart for Building and Implementing the Feed Mill

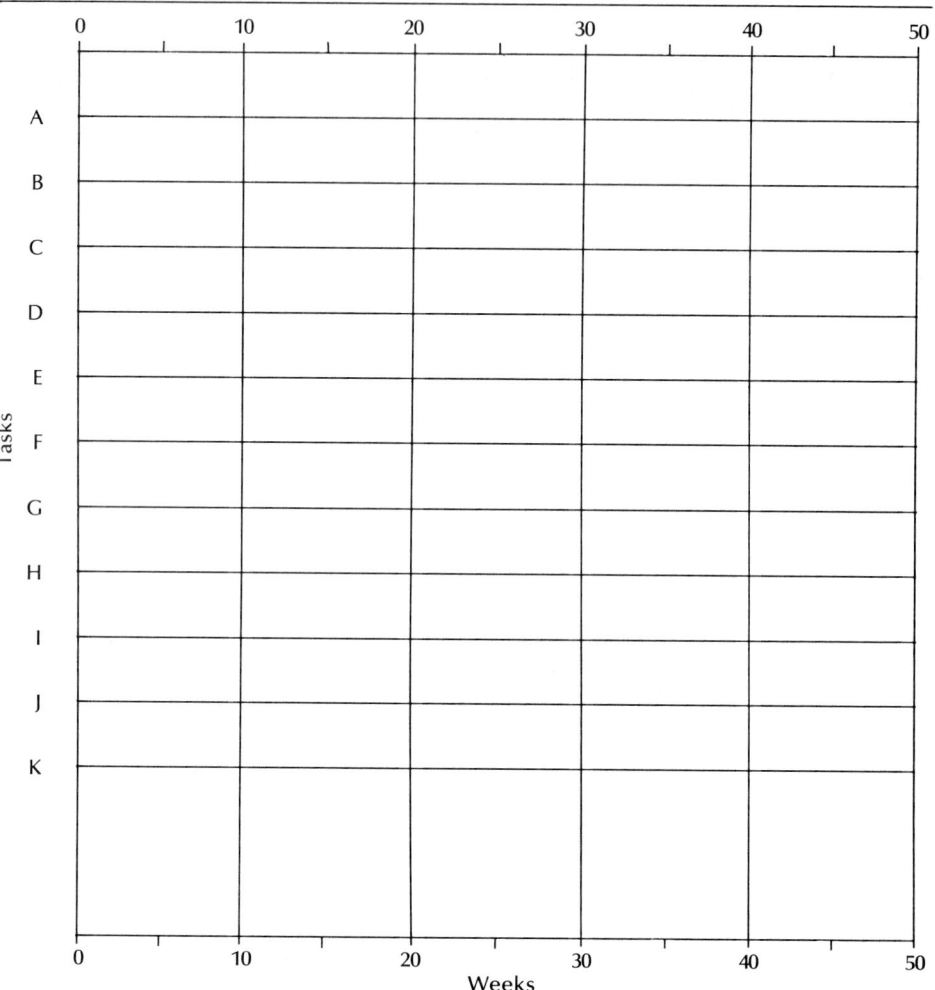

Kameron Mills had already held discussions with Mill Contractors, an independent firm, which was a potential contractor for one of the project's major tasks—building the plant. Kameron Mills intended to do the other tasks either itself or through its agents. During the talks with Mill Contractors, Kameron Mills had explored a number of bonus and penalty clauses. One was that for every week the plant was built ahead of 10 weeks, Kameron Mills would pay Mill Contractors an additional $25,000.

Kameron Mills' management wanted to know which activities it should crash and how it should schedule its workers (Exhibit 2).

Spirit Bottling Company

In early June, 1983, Miles Seabrook, president of Spirit Bottling Company, called in his newly appointed vice-president and manager of the Soft Drink Division, Donald Whitcomb. He wanted to discuss several inventory problems.

Seabrook:

Don, I am concerned about inventory levels throughout the company. Finished goods inventory levels reached $4 million in May, and May was just an average month for the company in terms of production, sales volume, and the accompanying inventory levels.

Whitcomb:

I agree, Miles. Our inventory levels do appear excessive. Besides, they are increasingly expensive to hold and are taking up valuable space.[1] The Rochester plant is a good example. Finished product occupies must of the storage space inside the plant, while empty returnable bottles are stored outside in an open yard.

Seabrook:

I have two questions about our inventory situation. Are our finished goods inventory levels where they should be throughout the company? If not, is it possible to cut these levels, solve our problems in Rochester, and keep the 14 distribution centers supplied with product?

Whitcomb:

I've already done some work to determine whether the company has a problem with excess inventory. I began an analysis of inventory and sales figures for the Mankato distribution center. [See Exhibit 1.] I chose this center because the number of days' supply for each product and package in Mankato was representative of companywide inventory-to-sales levels. So I was able to get a quick idea of the company's inventory situation. It appears we have been operating with excess inventory.

---

[1]In determining the carrying cost of inventory, the company used a carrying cost percentage of 15 percent. This percentage consisted of two elements:

Opportunity cost − Finance charges = 12.5%

Physical costs − Handling storage, obsolescence = 2.5%

EXHIBIT 1
Inventory and Sales Analysis, May 1983 (Spirit Bottling Company, Mankato Distribution Center)

Product and package	Inventory (cases)	Sales (cases)*	Inventory/ sales	Days' supply† (days)
Returnable bottles				
Spirit 6½ oz.	280	2,454	.11	3.5
Spirit 6½ oz. 6-pack	65	1,107	.06	1.8
Spirit 10 oz.	155	2,895	.05	1.6
Spirit 10 oz. 6-pack	100	320	.30	10
Spirit 16 oz.	284	1,418	.20	6.2
Spirit 1 liter	1,208	856	1.41	43
11-Up 10 oz.	138	294	.47	15.3
11-Up 16 oz.	40	10	4.0	125
11-Up 1 liter	50	19	2.63	83
Pep 10 oz.	234	1,168	.20	6.1
Pep 16 oz.	126	178	.70	21
Pep 1 liter	78	68	1.15	35.4
Brite 10 oz.	86	923	.09	2.8
Brite 16 oz.	130	44	2.95	92.8
Brite 1 liter	63	79	.79	25.2
Dr. Spice 10 oz.	98	448	.22	6.8
Dr. Spice 1 liter	33	12	2.75	82.5
Orange Orange SF 10 oz.	102	100	1.02	31.8
One-way bottles (nonreturnable)				
Spirit 10 oz.	248	644	.39	11.9
Spirit 16 oz.	3,206	2,872	1.11	34.6
Spirit 28 oz.	64	97	.66	20.6
Spirit 2 liters Plastic	2,115	4,205	.50	15.59
11-Up 10 oz.	59	36	1.6	49.2
11-Up 16 oz.	75	239	.31	9.7
11-Up 28 oz.	28	22	1.27	40
11-Up 2 liters Plastic	70	170	.41	12.7
11-Up SF 2 liters Plastic	101	63	1.6	50.5
Pep 10 oz.	48	69	.70	21.8
Pep 16 oz.	377	447	.84	26.1
Pep 28 oz.	24	11	2.18	68.5
Pep 2 liters Plastic	188	338	.56	17.24
Brite 10 oz.	74	64	1.16	35.2
Brite 16 oz.	315	619	.51	15.75
Brite 2 liters Plastic	105	286	.37	11.4
Viva GA/CS 28 oz.	61	43	1.42	43.5
Viva 2 liters Plastic	37	106	.35	10.8
Viva T. Water 28 oz.	25	14	1.79	55.5
Dr. Spice 10 oz.	51	16	3.19	102
Dr. Spice 16 oz.	119	680	.17	5.4
Dr. Spice 2 liters Plastic	92	53	1.74	54
Action Ade 10 oz.	127	50	2.54	79.3

*Total case sales for returnables, one-way bottles, and cans amount to 39,603. Total case inventory is 17,003 cases.

†Calculated as inventory divided by average daily sales. Average daily sales were determined by the previous four weeks' sales. This calculation was specific to each product and package combination.

Note: SF = sugar-free; GA/CS = ginger ale/club soda; T. Water = tonic water.

EXHIBIT 1, cont'd

Product and package	Inventory (cases)	Sales (cases)*	Inventory/ sales	Days' supply† (days)
Cans				
Spirit	2,542	7,879	.32	10
11-Up	660	862	.77	23.7
11-Up SF	235	216	1.08	34
Pep	574	1,803	.32	11.2
Lean Green	85	15	5.66	177
Brite	862	2,043	.42	13
Viva	70	125	.56	17.5
Dr. Spice	185	941	.19	6.1
Dr. Spice SF	104	117	.89	28
Action Ade	807	2,115	.38	11.8
Premix (for commercial sales)				
Spirit	147	2,188	.07	2.1
11-Up	27	56	.48	15
Pep	84	176	.48	15
Dr. Spice	13	28	.46	14.4
Syrup (for commercial sales)				
Spirit	270	600	.45	13.9
Pep	105	35	3	95.4
Dr. Spice	70	60	1.16	35
Others	95	150	.63	19.7

Seabrook:

I thought so. I have repeatedly asked our production plant managers to reduce inventory.

Whitcomb:

Miles, in my opinion, the only way to solve the inventory problem is by changing the way we schedule production and transportation. The amount of goods the three plants produce and ship to the 14 distribution centers determines producer inventory levels. I think the solution lies there.

Seabrook:

Have at it then, but I want some results soon.

To answer the questions that Seabrook had raised, Whitcomb knew he had to analyze company inventory levels and scheduling methods in the production plants in Rochester, Minneapolis, and St. Cloud. If the decision was made to reduce inventory levels in these plants substantially, production management would experience the pressures of operating with low inventory levels and could no longer afford low efficiency runs or equipment breakdowns, because stockouts would result.

EXHIBIT 2
Production Assignments by Facility, May 1983

Package and product	Hutchinson	Mankato	Red Wing	Little Falls	Minneapolis	New Ulm
Returnable bottles						
6½ oz. Spirit	R	M	M	R	M	S
10 oz. Spirit	R	M	M	R	M	S
10 oz. 11-Up	R	M	M	R	M	S
10 oz. Pep	R	M	M	R	M	S
10 oz. Brite	R	M	M	R	M	S
10 oz. Orange Orange	R	S	S	R		S
10 oz. Dr. Spice		M			M	
10 oz. SF Orange Orange		S	S		M	S
16 oz. Spirit	R	R	M	R	M	S
16 oz. Brite	R	M	M	R	M	S
16 oz. 11-Up		M			M	
16 oz. Pep		M	M		M	
16 oz. Dr. Spice		M			M	
1 liter All products	R	R	R	R	R	R
One-way bottles (nonreturnable)						
10 oz. All products	R	R	R	R	R	R
16 oz. All products	R	R	R	R	R	R
28 oz. All products	R	R	R	R	R	R
2 liters All products	R	R	R	R	R	R
Cans						
12 oz. All products	R	R	R	R	R	R
Premix						
All products	R	R	R	R	R	R

Note: R = Rochester; M = Minneapolis; S = St. Cloud.

BRIEF HISTORY OF SPIRIT BOTTLING COMPANY

Spirit Bottling Company bottled and marketed soft drinks in a franchise territory covering the southern half of Minnesota and portions of Wisconsin. In 1902, the first bottle of Spirit Cola was sold in Minnesota by a bottling plant in Rochester, which was the predecessor of Spirit's plant in Rochester. Through the years other bottling plants were built or acquired by Spirit and in May 1983, the company consisted of 14 distribution centers and three bottling plants. In 1983, the company bottled and sold 20 national brands for five companies: Spirit, Viva, Action Ade, Blink, Dr. Spice. Total sales in 1982 were 22.3 million cases, consisting of 20 different packages.

Since 1972, the company's stock had been listed on the New York Stock Exchange. During the last two years the stock price ranged from a low of 11¼ to a current high of 25½. The financial condition of the company had remained healthy.

The company was organized into three operating divisions. Individual plants reported to division managers who in turn reported to corporate.

Rush City	St. Cloud	St. Bonifacius	Sauk Center	Princeton	Arkansaw, Wis.	Rochester	Coon Rapids
M	S	R	R	R	S	R	M
M	S	R	R	R	S	R	M
M	S	R	R	R	S	R	M
M	S	R	R	R	S	R	M
M	S	R	R	R	S	R	M
	S		R			R	
M		M		M	M		
	S						M
R	S	R	R	R	M	R	R
M	S	R	R	R	M	R	M
M				M	S		M
M		M		M	M		M
M		M			M		M
R	R	R	R	R	R	R	R
R	R	R	R	R	R	R	R
R	R	R	R	R	R	R	R
R	R	R	R	R	R	R	R
R	R	R	R	R	R	R	R
R	R	R	R	R	R	R	R
R	S	R	R	R	S	R	R

THE PRODUCTION PLANTS

The three production plants (located in Rochester, Minneapolis, and St. Cloud) produced and shipped the company's products to 14 distribution centers, which marketed and sold them in Spirit's franchise territory. Exhibit 2 shows which plants produced and shipped the various products. Exhibit 3 gives data for the cases produced at each of the three plants.

The St. Cloud and Minneapolis plants were similar in size—112,000 square feet and 95,000 square feet, respectively—whereas the newer Rochester plant (built and equipped in 1973 for $9 million) covered 280,000 square feet.

St. Cloud and Minneapolis both had two operating bottling lines. However, they used only one at a time, depending on the size required. Each plant operated with one crew consisting of eight men—one 10-hour shift, four days a week. In contrast, the Rochester plant operated four bottling lines and two canning lines. Bottling line 1 operated two 10-hour shifts per day four days a week. Lines 2 through 6 operated one 10-hour shift four days a week. Each line was operated by an eight-man crew. At all three plants, production runs were made Monday

EXHIBIT 3
Case Production by Facility, May 1983

Plant	Current	Budget	Change	Percent change	Prior year	Change	Percent change
St. Cloud							
Returnable bottles	125,353	131,500	(6,147)	(4.7)%	135,353	(10,000)	(7.4)%
Total	125,353	131,500	(6,147)	(4.7)%	135,353	(10,000)	(7.4)
Minneapolis							
Returnable bottles	164,764	121,300	43,464	35.8	200,226	(35,462)	(17.7)
Total	164,764	121,300	43,464	35.8	200,226	(35,462)	(17.7)
Rochester							
Returnable bottles	185,963	255,300	(69,337)	(27.2)	214,206	(28,243)	(13.2)
One-way bottles	518,707	501,000	17,707	3.5	355,782	162,925	45.8
Cans	381,871	400,400	(18,529)	(4.6)	458,053	(76,182)	(16.6)
Total	1,086,541	1,156,700	(70,159)	6.1	1,028,041	58,500	5.7
Division total	1,376,658	1,409,500	(32,842)	(2.3)	1,363,620	13,038	1.0

through Thursday; Fridays were spent on maintenance and repairs. The capacities and sizes produced by each line at the three plants are shown in Exhibit 4.

The Rochester operation, although generally well managed, had one obvious problem. There was not enough warehouse space for raw materials and finished goods. During May, for example, the plant held 452,785 cases of finished product. Lack of space within the plant cost the company in several ways:

1. The company was forced to store 86,334 cases of used returnable glass in cartons and cases outside in an open yard. The cases covered 24,500 square feet. When it rained the cardboard cartons in a case were ruined. There were four cartons in a case, each carton costing 5 cents.

2. During the winter (December, January, and February), approximately 20 percent of the bottles that had been stored outside would break when they were soaked in the hot caustic solution in the bottle washer. The replacement cost for returnable bottles was $4.30 per case of 24.

3. The space problem forced the Rochester plant to operate an additional 28,000 square-foot warehouse 15 miles from the production plant. The warehouse stored 30,000 cases of finished product in May 1983. Transport drivers were paid $10 per hour to drive a trailer load to the warehouse, unload, and drive back to the Rochester plant. The round trip took an hour and a half. During May, the Rochester transportation department made 33 trips to this warehouse.

THE PRODUCTION PROCESS

The production process began after several pallets of empty bottles were moved by forklift to the back of the bottling line. At this point, an employee loaded the inclined conveyor with cases of empty bottles, which were gravity fed to the

EXHIBIT 4
Line Capacities of Production Plants

Plant	Line number	Package	Line capacity (cases/hour)
Minneapolis	2	6½ oz. R, 10 oz. R	1,000
Minneapolis	2	16 oz. R	1,000
Minneapolis	1	32 oz. R	600
Minneapolis	1	16 oz. R	670
St. Cloud	1	6½ oz. R, 10 oz. R	700
St. Cloud	1	16 oz. R	609
St. Cloud	2	1 liter R	562
St. Cloud	2	10 oz. OWB	500
Rochester	1	2 liters Plastic	960
Rochester	2	1 liter R	1,149
Rochester	2	28 oz. OWB	1,149
Rochester	3	10 oz. OWB	1,463
Rochester	3	16 oz. OWB	1,463
Rochester	4	6½ oz. R, 10 oz. R	1,000
Rochester	4	16 oz. R	938
Rochester	5	Cans	1,875
Rochester	6	Cans	2,000

Note: R = returnable bottles; OWB = one-way bottles.

decaser. The decaser lifted 24 bottles from a case every 2.4 seconds and placed them on an automatic steel conveyor, which fed the bottles into the bottle washer. The washer cleaned and sanitized every bottle by means of a 3.8 percent caustic solution, heated to 140° F. After the bottles rotated through the hot caustic bath, fresh water jets sprayed and rinsed each bottle. The washer then placed each row of 28 bottles onto the bottling line every 3.5 seconds. The steel conveyor carried the clean bottles through two inspection stations. Chipped or cracked bottles were removed by an empty-bottle inspector, and an electronic eye rejected bottles containing foreign particles.

Before the filling process, fresh water was mixed with Spirit Cola syrup or other concentrates in the proper proportions. (A 6½-ounce bottle of Spirit contained 1 ounce of syrup and 5.5 ounces of carbonated water.) The syrup and water mixture flowed through a "carbo cooler," where it was cooled to 34° F., carbonated, and released to the filler.

The washed bottles were engaged, one by one, by the rotating filler, which filled them as they moved through 360 degrees. The fillers contained 60 filling valves and were capable of speeds up to 2,000 cases per hour depending on package type and size. After being filled, the bottles were sealed by the adjacent crowner, which stamped the bottle caps in place. The full bottles then went to the case packer, which dropped the bottles into an empty case every 2.8 seconds. The finished goods traveled along an overhead conveyor to the palletizer, which stacked each pallet. Forklift operators took the full pallets to transports or warehouse storage. The time required for a bottle to flow through the production process was 35 minutes.

THE PRODUCTION SCHEDULING SYSTEM

During Donald Whitcomb's first week as vice-president, he visited the three production plants and discussed production and transportation schedules with the plant managers. After asking these managers a number of questions about their scheduling procedures, Donald believed he had a good idea of what was going on. As a first step in scheduling, each production plant tabulated the previous week's sales and average daily sales by product and by package for their distribution centers. The inventory figures divided by average daily sales gave the number of days' supply "on the floor" for each product and package. Days' supply was the key factor in determining what and when to produce. A product with two days' supply would normally be produced before an item with four days' supply.

Whitcomb recalled a production scheduling meeting where he questioned the production manager from St. Cloud, John Wolfe, and the manager from Rochester, Marcia Fox, on the issue of which product to produce first.

Donald:

If you had a three-day supply of 10-ounce returnable Spirit and a two-day supply of 10-ounce returnable 11-Up, which would you produce first?

Marcia:

I would play it safe and produce 10-ounce returnable Spirit first. Spirit is a high-volume product and I would hate to lose the contribution dollars resulting from a possible stockout.

John:

Well, I would stick to the days' supply calculations and produce 10-ounce returnable 11-Up. I know we have three days of inventory on 10-ounce Spirit. What is there to worry about?

In determining the order of production, the managers also looked at minimizing downtime due to changeovers. There were two kinds of changeovers: product changeovers (e.g., from Spirit to 11-Up) and package changeovers (e.g., from 10-ounce to 16-ounce bottles). A product changeover during producing hours cost the bottler 15 minutes of downtime. A package changeover required approximately 35 minutes. The actual costs involved in these two types of changeovers are shown in Exhibit 5, along with data on fixed costs.

Donald recalled that the changeover issue had surfaced in his conversation with Marcia and John.

Donald:

Suppose the line just finished producing 16-ounce returnable Spirit. There was a two-day supply of 10-ounce returnable Spirit and a three-day supply of 16-ounce returnable Brite on the floor. Which product should be produced first?

John:

16-ounce returnable Brite. Package changeovers require 35 minutes of downtime. That is valuable production time. I believe in maximizing production volume because it reduces case cost.

EXHIBIT 5
Production Cost Information for Spirit Bottling Company

Fixed Costs	St. Cloud	Minneapolis	Rochester
Operating expenses	$30,583	$18,107	$191,185
Indirect labor	16,846	20,960	134,036
Payroll	2,200	2,864	21,553
Depreciation	6,429	3,538	47,640
Total fixed costs	$56,058	$45,469	$394,414

Product Changeover Cost
Washdown expense
24 oz. syrup @ $3.92/gallon = 72¢
Carbon dioxide and water = 6¢
Total = 78¢

Labor cost for mixing concentrate
1 man @ $8/hour
Time required = 15 minutes
Labor cost = $2.00
Total cost = $2.78

Package Changeover Cost
Labor cost for resetting machine
2 men @ $8/hour
Time required = 35 minutes
Total cost = $9.34

Notes: In May 1982 there were 30 product and 15 package changeovers during producing hours in the three production plants.

There was an unwritten policy of guaranteeing production workers 40 hours per week, even though actual production hours were usually fewer than 40.

A 10-hour shift in each producing plant included two 15-minute breaks and a half-hour for lunch.

Marcia:

I disagree. The 10-ounce returnable Spirit should be produced first because (1) 10-ounce Spirit has fewer days' supply on the floor; (2) changeover costs are inexpensive; and (3) large-volume production runs can also mean large inventories.

In deciding how much of each item to produce, the managers studied the following: raw materials inventory, production time required for other products, safety stock levels, warehouse space, sales promotions, product age, and inventory costs. Sales forecasts were occasionally observed but not relied on because they were routinely off by at least 10 percent.

The production manager knew he should not run greater than a 90-day supply of any product and package because of quality control requirements concerning product age. The low-volume items, such as 10-ounce returnable Dr. Spice, were produced every two and one-half to three months. Faster selling items, like 2-liter Spirit, were produced almost daily. A safety stock of two to four days was added to each production run to allow for uncertainties in demand.

Because of present inventory levels, warehouse space was at a premium in all three production plants. This, in addition to the demand for other products to be produced, limited the length of a production run. The actual length of a run really became a judgment call. This was evident to Donald at the scheduling

EXHIBIT 6

SPIRIT BOTTLING CO.—ROCHESTER PLANT
PRODUCTION SCHEDULE

Week of 5/9 - 13/83

Date	Line 1			Line 2			Line 3			Line 4			Canning		
	Item	Hrs	Cases to produce	Item	Hrs	Cases to produce	Item	Hrs	Cases to produce	Item	Hrs	Cases to produce	Item	Hrs	Cases to produce
Monday 5/9	2 liter OWB Spirit	18½	16225	1 liter RET Spirit	9	8055	16 oz. OWB SF Orange orange Spirit	5 3½	4408 3063	6½ oz. RET Spirit	9	1500 6-Pack 5250 regular carton	Spirit	9	2534
Tuesday 5/10	2 liter OWB Pep Spirit	9 9	7854 7893	1 liter RET Spirit	9	8055	16 oz. OWB Pep	9	7812	10 oz. RET Spirit	9	2550 6-Pack 4200 regular carton	SF Dr. Spice	8½	4469
Wednesday 5/11	2 liter OWB Viva Spirit	9 9	8052 7893	1 liter RET Spirit	9	8055	16 oz. OWB Brite	9	7040	10 oz. RET Spirit	9	2550 6-Pack 4200 regular carton	Lean Green Spirit	3 5½	8460 1554
Thursday 5/12	2 liter OWB SF 11-Up Spirit	9 9	7875 7893	28 oz. OWB Viva Spirit	4 4½	3605 4095	10 oz. OWB Pep 11-Up	4½ 4	3806 3264	16 oz. RET Spirit	9	7155	Brite	9	2538
Friday 5/13															

Note: OWB = one-way bottle. RET = returnable

meeting he attended at the Rochester plant. These meetings were held every Thursday to decide the next week's production schedule. The schedule shown in Exhibit 6 was to have been followed the next week.

In the meeting Donald questioned production manager Marcia Fox:

Donald:

Why are we going to produce a five-month supply of Lean Green cans?

Marcia:

The five-month supply requires only a three-hour production run. A run length of less than three hours is not cost justified.

Donald:

Long runs are great—volume is spread over the same fixed costs. But a five-month supply is expensive to hold and product age could be a problem.

EXHIBIT 7
Case Sales by Product for Each Bottling Plant, May 1983

Package and product	Rochester	Minneapolis	St. Cloud
Returnable bottles			
6½ oz. Spirit	31,690	25,695	24,081
10 oz. Spirit	30,439	18,996	24,614
10 oz. 11-Up	3,399	1,735	2,021
10 oz. Pep	8,289	6,439	6,522
10 oz. Brite	7,797	5,570	5,484
10 oz. Orange Orange	3,150	0	7,337
10 oz. Dr. Spice	0	1,946	0
10 oz. SF Orange Orange	0	939	2,423
All 10 oz.	53,074	35,625	48,401
16 oz. Spirit	63,031	53,708	14,200
16 oz. Brite	2,606	5,556	4,036
16 oz. 11-Up	205	3,704	0
16 oz. Pep	366	9,912	1,836
All 16 oz.	66,208	72,880	20,072
All 1 liter	99,494	0	0
One-way bottles			
All 10 oz.	26,978	0	0
All 16 oz.	118,942	0	0
All 28 oz.	18,159	0	0
All 2 liter	123,506	0	0
Cans			
All 12 oz.	406,687	0	0
Premix			
All products	58,472	0	6,980

THE TRANSPORTATION SYSTEM

The company's transport fleet consisted of 17 tractors and 60 trailers. Three tractors and eight trailers were located in St. Cloud. Five tractors and eleven trailers were in Minneapolis, and the remainder were in Rochester.

During Donald Whitcomb's first visits to the production plants, he discussed transportation schedules with each transportation manager. Donald discovered that in setting up a weekly transportation schedule, each manager began by observing a days' supply figure for each product and package in each plant to which they shipped. Products with the lowest days' supply were shipped first.

Each plant had warehouse space assigned for every product and package. For example, in the St. Cloud warehouse, there were three rows of 2-liter plastic Spirit capable of holding 90 pallets of product. The actual amount shipped to a distribution plant was sufficient to bring the plant's inventory level to the maximum level for the shipped products. For example, if there were 1,000 cases of Pep cans on inventory in a distribution plant and the maximum inventory level for Pep cans was 2,500 cases, then 1,500 cases would be shipped to the distribution plant.

EXHIBIT 8
Sales, May 1982

Package and product	Hutchinson	Mankato	Red Wing	Little Falls	Minneapolis	New Ulm
Returnable bottles						
6½ oz. Spirit	3,030	3,561	5,072	3,669	6,510	5,700
10 oz. Spirit	2,870	3,215	3,255	3,922	8,087	5,892
10 oz. 11-Up	168	294		302	781	557
10 oz. Pep	688	1,168	1,133	1,082	2,536	1,484
10 oz. Brite	543	923	748	888	2,213	877
10 oz. Orange Orange	481	405	1,582	321		550
10 oz. Dr. Spice		448			756	
10 oz. SF Orange Orange		100	839			82
16 oz. Spirit	1,026	1,418	6,041	2,894	32,838	3,358
16 oz. Brite	104	44	639	1,370	2,343	926
16 oz. 11-Up		10	363		1,798	
16 oz. Pep		178	771		4,611	
1 liter All products	2,615	1,034	4,728	1,111	10,865	5,151
One-way bottles (nonreturnable)						
10 oz. All products	567	879	394	2,281		1,031
16 oz. All products	1,383	4,857	9,562	2,201	5,624	11,220
28 oz. All products	87	187	959	393	1,889	687
2 liters All products	1,948	5,221	6,201	11,689	8,105	10,569
Cans						
12 oz. All products	9,755	16,116	17,863	16,947	59,070	13,887
Premix						
All products	1,268	2,448	1,948	656	7,804	1,784

CONCLUSION

Donald Whitcomb knew that Miles Seabrook would soon hold a follow-up meeting to the June meeting. Seabrook expected Whitcomb to analyze company inventory levels. If there were problems, Whitcomb would be expected to correct them. Possibly a new scheduling method, which would reduce inventory levels and overall costs, would have to be developed. Donald had compiled company sales and inventory figures for May 1983. (See Exhibits 7, 8, and 9.) This information, along with the other information he had collected would enable him to construct a sample production schedule for each production plant for the first week of June. (See Exhibit 6.)

It appeared that the Rochester plant had outgrown itself. Marcia Fox was convinced the plant should be expanded, at a cost of $21 per square foot. Donald wondered what he should recommend.

Rush City	St. Cloud	St. Bonifacius	Sauk Center	Princeton	Arkansaw, Wis.	Rochester	Coon Rapids
2,690	13,959	4,700	4,910	3,311	4,422	12,070	7,862
829	16,491	4,688	4,150	1,948	2,231	12,861	3,610
98	1,187	451	448	215	277	1,815	562
400	4,360	1,162	1,370	415	678	3,572	1,202
529	4,038	663	1,363	840	569	3,500	1,157
	4,800		578		143	1,770	
124		87		65			466
	2,341						
9,539	10,842	6,241	6,539	3,853	14,829	5,486	26,035
1,005	1,107	280	468	97	2,003	287	1,525
305		177		28			1,228
1,156		208		158	1,836		3,196
640	25,300	8,207	4,680	6,078		25,341	3,747
	2,458	272	336	547	1,188	14,685	2,340
1,183	19,282	2,968	7,358	2,611	9,347	33,275	8,071
87	3,187	340	439	311	745	7,993	855
1,521	9,210	2,255	14,956	6,417	3,821	21,952	19,641
7,027	56,957	16,020	13,112	12,307	9,557	118,456	39,613
260	5,972	4,096	2,064	468	1,008	32,280	3,396

EXHIBIT 9
Inventory, May 1982

Package and product	Hutchinson	Mankato	Red Wing	Little Falls	Minneapolis	New Ulm
Returnable bottles						
6½ oz. Spirit	870	345	731	2,024	7,140	2,561
10 oz. Spirit	1,328	255	924	2,072	3,521	2,355
10 oz. 11-Up	70	138	138	168	204	90
10 oz. Pep	398	234	254	606	298	437
10 oz. Brite	492	86	180	343	265	618
10 oz. Orange Orange	259	168	206	121		218
10 oz. Dr. Spice		98			295	
10 oz. SF Orange Orange		102	425			211
16 oz. Spirit	525	284	1,285	1,013	3,571	1,302
16 oz. Brite	56	130	62	362	1,317	333
16 oz. 11-Up		40			416	
16 oz. Pep		126	201		833	
16 oz. Dr. Spice		53			517	
1 liter All products	1,703	1,432	1,842	1,453	9,178	1,908
One-way bottles (nonreturnable)						
10 oz. All products	623	607	405	660	2,497	448
16 oz. All products	2,773	4,092	4,188	6,283	4,123	8,910
28 oz. All products	609	202	1,176	548	1,820	569
2 liters All products	3,092	2,708	3,475	10,068	13,401	5,864
Cans						
12 oz. All products	4,885	6,124	6,863	8,004	15,801	9,968
Premix						
All products	200	271	159	114	439	213

Rush City	St. Cloud	St. Bonifacius	Sauk Center	Princeton	Arkansaw, Wis.	Rochester	Coon Rapids
995	2,551	2,356	1,480	2,136	2,076	3,064	1,951
383	2,574	1,159	1,111	968	1,568	2,197	603
137	321	346	190	194	127	374	48
140	3,165	164	916	226	378	968	429
164	4,282	87	401	569	281	868	196
	2,686		140			645	
98		157		4	78		97
	939						
913	3,353	2,264	1,509	608	1,492	663	4,047
88	1,180	140	168	97	488	157	190
110		44		44			204
131		94		209	370		299
65		110		88	104		132
646	8,898	5,613	2,191	2,163		4,474	2,229
180	500	821	1,372	147	683	5,743	
1,105	7,875	3,203	2,623	1,295	4,252	8,267	3,357
452	3,641	899	550	580	797	3,054	910
2,911	10,404	6,283	5,259	4,408	4,057	12,015	10,439
5,877	22,748	7,629	6,470	6,116	8,443	25,887	19,573
109	2,070	414	180	111	108	838	498

Kumera Oy (A)

INTRODUCTION

Mr. Vesa Kumpulainen, age 30, managing director of Kumera OY, hung up the telephone and shook his head. "Why is it that our inventory continues to increase and we still can't get the right parts? I just tried to find out the status of the order for Makinen OY and got the same old story. It's been partly assembled but we still lack one part. We are already three weeks late on the order and there's no way I can tell them how long it will be before we can deliver. It looks like I'll have to authorize production to use overtime to make the part."

The problem with the Makinen order was typical of what seemed to be happening at the company. Customer complaints had been increasing, costs were rising and the disputes between departments were becoming more intense. Mr. Kumpulainen knew that something had to be done to get control of the situation. As he reviewed the financial statements for 1975 and 1976 (shown in Exhibit 1) he realized that he must begin soon.

BACKGROUND

The company was founded in Helsinki in 1947 by Mr. Veikko Kumpulainen, father of the current Managing Director, Mr. Vesa Kumpulainen. The mood in Finland in 1947 was very optimistic. There was a considerable backlog of war-indemnity supplies to be delivered to the Soviet Union and the production of these goods would provide a base for industrial development. Finland was to supply products for the heavy metal industry, an industry which had not been very significant for the country before. It was against this background that the firm started manufacturing small bench lathes.

Two years after starting, the company began to produce a new product line, lifting mechanisms for dump trucks. The manufacturing expertise gained by the company in building these mechanisms, enabled them to expand the product line. Over time they added mechanical power transmissions, helical gear boxes, worm gears and clutches. Some of these products brought the company into direct

---

The case was prepared by Professor D. Clay Whybark as a basis for class discussion rather than to illustrate either effective or ineffective handling of an administrative situation. Copyright 1983 by IMEDE (International Management Development Institute), Lausanne, Switzerland. Reproduced by permission.

EXHIBIT 1
Financial Statements

	1976	1975
Income Statements (1,000 Finnish Marks)		
Sales	17,853	16,250
Cost of goods sold		
Direct labor	4,194	3,711
Material	6,227	5,462
Manufacturing overhead	3,043	2,487
Gross margin	4,389	4,590
General and administrative	1,547	1,423
Depreciation	1,503	1,487
Interest	1,249	937
Profit before taxes	90	743
Taxes	20	214
Profit	70	529
Balance Sheets (1,000 Finnish Marks)		
Current assets		
Cash	660	1,803
A/C receivable	3,213	3,462
Inventory	8,756	6,019
Prepayments	303	486
Net plant and equipment	3,897	3,572
Total assets	16,829	15,342
Current liabilities		
A/C payable	4,184	3,573
Notes payable	1,500	1,287
Accruals	2,714	3,206
Long-term debt	6,439	5,354
Capital stock	120	120
Earned surplus	1,872	1,802
Total liabilities	16,829	15,342

competition with a large, well established gear manufacturer, E. Santasalo OY. E. Santasalo had been in operation since 1934 in Finland. Even with this competition, however, the overall growth in the market provided growth for Kumera, and by the middle of the 1950s, the company was firmly established in the new line of products.

During the next few years the company continued to grow. This necessitated acquiring new locations to provide additional space. In 1964 they consolidated all operations into one location about 40 kilometers from Helsinki. By the early 1970s the company was facing another shortage of space. In addition there was an acute shortage of skilled labor in the area near their plant and in Helsinki. To provide more space and better access to skilled labor, they built a facility in Riihimäki, a small town about 60 kilometers north of Helsinki. The experience was so favorable that the company consolidated all their activities in Riihimäki in 1975 and have remained there to date.

EXHIBIT 2
Example Products

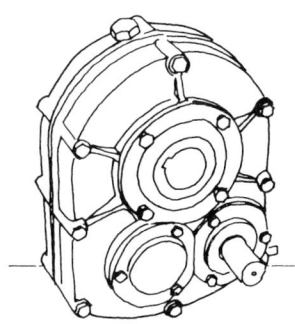

Series 200, double reduction
shaft mounted speed reducers

Series 1000, single reduction
worm gear units

Series C-3000 and C-4000,
triple and four reduction
vertical shaft speed reducers

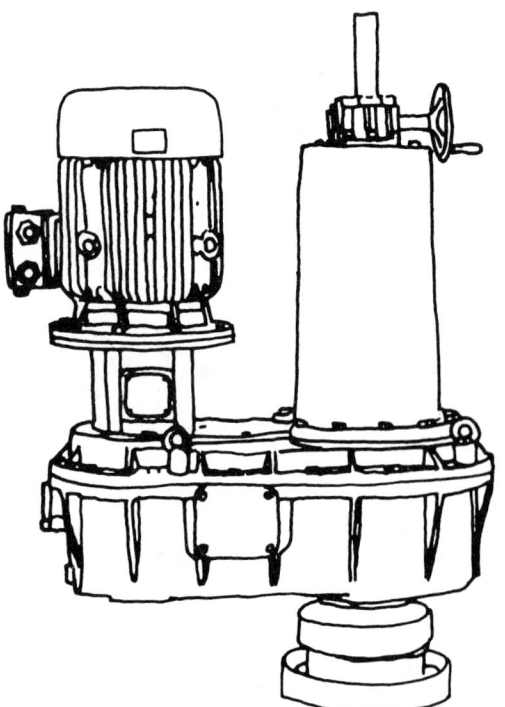

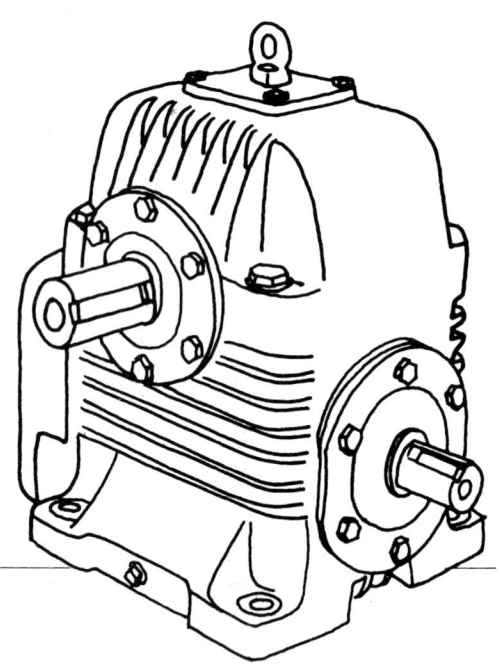

The Kumera product line evolved over this period as well. Under the shadow of the E. Santasalo company, Kumera never attained a leading position in helical speed reducers. They increased the engineering staff and set them to work on developing new products. The result was a series of high quality worm gears and shaft mounted speed reducers that form the basis of their current product line.

As late as 1968, most new products of the company were being created in response to customer requests. There was only a small effort to develop a coordinated line of standard products. In the early 1970s, however, the product line was standardized and a catalog printed. Since then, new products have been added that build upon the gear machining capability of the company. They have produced gears as small as 50 mm. in diameter and as large as 2,200 mm. The gear boxes have ranged in weight from 20 kilograms to 10,000 kilograms. Examples of the company's current products appear in Exhibit 2.

MARKETING ACTIVITIES

The company has an active customer base of 200–300 firms of which 100–150 would place orders in any given year. No single customer is dominating, although just a few customers provide a large part of the company's business. Most customers are engineering oriented manufacturing firms making wood processing equipment, paper machines, plywood equipment, and so on, for the wood products industry. About 50% of Kumera's production is for export: 10% directly and 40% indirectly through their customer's products.

The Soviet Union is a major force in the market. Bilateral trade agreements between Finland and the USSR provide for the export of wood products equipment to the USSR from Finland. Kumera's customers are the manufacturers of this equipment. In order to preserve hard currency there has been minimal participation of Western firms in this trade. Thus, the international competition has been limited for this part of Kumera's business. The greatest domestic competition comes from E. Santasalo, but there are other smaller domestic competitors as well. Kumera faces competition from both international and domestic companies in the Western European and North American markets.

The company's products are sold directly through the catalogs and by sales engineers. In many instances Kumera's sales engineers will work closely with the customer's engineering staff in specifying the Kumera products to be used in the customer's equipment. In some cases this can lead Kumera to design special mechanisms to solve difficult technical problems faced by the customers. The sales engineers have a great deal of discretion in promising delivery dates and quantities while working with the customers.

Much of the competition for business revolves around promising quick delivery of products. No published or "standard" delivery times are available. In many cases, therefore, the company accepts the customer request date as the promised delivery date or simply marks the orders for delivery "as soon as possible." The delivery promises range from immediate for the few stock items to 15 weeks or more for complicated items. The general expectancy is delivery within 2–4 months. For big contracts the competition is keen and quick delivery is often essential. Kumera has not been very successful in participating in these big contracts.

The company has always done well in meeting the technical design aspects of customer service, but the delivery date performance is poor and is getting worse. Actual deliveries for the non-stocked items were taking from 3 to 6 months. Even for the stocked items, requested items were out-of-stock about 30% of the time. This necessitated special runs for stocked items, often using "express" orders to speed them through the factory.

The customer service was a real concern to Vesa Kumpulainen. The historical growth of the business had come from sharing in a growing market, not from improved service and market share. Recently, late deliveries had reached the point where more than 50% were over 3 weeks late. Some of Kumera's competitors were quoting longer delivery times, but were meeting the promises, and this was taking away some of Kumera's business. The situation had reached the point where Kumera was having to pay penalties on some of their late deliveries. The total number of penalties for this year could reach 30 if something was not done to change the situation.

The impact of the difficulties was felt in other parts of the business as well. For example, the spare parts performance had been badly hurt, since spare parts always seemed to have low priority anyway. Many times the service parts were not in inventory. If the request was to meet an urgent customer need, the order was made into an express order to the factory. Even with the express orders, however, many spare parts deliveries were late, creating a loss of good will.

MANUFACTURING ACTIVITIES

The orders come directly from the customer by mail or by phone or from the sales engineers (about half of the orders are from the sales engineers). An internal work order is written for each customer order. It is delivered to the production planning department. After checking the inventory to see if there are any parts in stock, they manually write out individual orders for all the parts that are to be made to satisfy the customer order. These individual orders are released to the shop with due dates derived from the customer order. The production, however, is scheduled for groups of similar parts. Each part has a card with its shop routing indicated and as each operation is finished the completion is marked on the card.

A special shop order, an "express" order, had been designed to speed high priority items through manufacturing. Some express orders are issued directly to the shop from the production planning department. Others are created as conditions warrant. For example, a group of similar parts being produced as a batch might contain one part needed for an urgent order. That part may get pulled from the group and made into an express order. There are several persons that make these changes in priority. In some cases the sales engineers themselves would go into the shop and pull the cards for the parts for some of their customers' orders. In other cases the loudest complaining customer's order would be expedited by the manager that got the angry call from the customer. Finally, the assembly foreman looks to see what parts will be needed for the assembly schedule. He

EXHIBIT 3
Example "Hot-List"

Expedite sheet   Date _____

Assembly shortages

Part number	Customer order	Required	Shortage
1555	3117	14	10
16435	3117	24	24
2064	3221	4	4

Other expedite

2701	5087E *	1	1

*This is an "express" order for a customer

makes a "hot-list" of parts which might be short and tries to get them to the pre-assembly inventory area before the assembly schedule calls for them. He uses one of the two full-time expeditors to help him. An example hot-list is shown in Exhibit 3.

The use of express cards and constant priority changes means that only the urgent orders for important (noisy) customers get produced close to the time they are promised. Regular orders for stock items might be in the shop for half a year. There are hundreds of open production orders in the shop at any time which means that priority changes are difficult to make. First the order must be found and then the express cards or date changes must be manually made. Also, of the hundred or so production orders issued per week, 10 or more are express to begin with. As the priorities are changed and groups of parts are split by making some of the group express, the shop disruption is quite high. Many extra setups can be required for express parts and the grouping of parts doesn't provide as much efficiency when some parts are pulled out and run separately.

Key to much of the shop scheduling is the stock accountant. She tries to maintain sufficient stock on hand of the inventoried parts. She does this by ordering extra whenever an order is needed or by scheduling a stock order whenever a machine center is about to run out of work. She also is responsible for both keeping inventory records and checking inventory balances. The production order in Exhibit 4, for example, is for 50 of the part #16435.

EXHIBIT 4
Order Form for Parts

Work order no. **P 2998**   Due date **ASAP ***

Part no. **16435**   Quantity **50**

Customer order **3097**

                                  Stock Acct. **OK**

                                  Date **MAY 23**

*As soon as possible.

An inventory record for part #16435 is shown in Exhibit 5. There have been both service and assembly disbursements for this part. A physical count was made on May 7 and a 20-unit error was found. The May 23 production order for 50 pieces is shown, even though only four are needed to complete the customer order (customer order number 3097 needs 24 pieces and only 20 are available). On June 3 there was not enough stock for the assembly requirement. This shortage is shown on the "hot-list" in Exhibit 3.

On following up the part needed by assembly to complete the Makinen order Mr. Kumpulainen found it in the lathe department (see Exhibit 6). There were several express orders in the lathe department at the same time. They would need to be finished before the Markinen order part could be started. Some of the express orders were spare parts, some were changes made by sales engineers for a special customer and some were for parts needed by the assembly foreman. Mr. Kumpulainen decided that he would not create an express order for the part but would go back and tell the people at Makinen that their order would be finished in a week—but he knew he was just guessing.

The Makinen order had also been affected by the long lead times for purchasing. The foundry that supplied the gear housing casting for the order promised it to Kumera in 4 months and it was *only* two weeks late. In the last few weeks

EXHIBIT 5
Stock Record for Part #16435

Date	Balance	Receipts	Disbursements	Remarks
Jan 7	33		10	Ord. No. 2067*
Feb 10	23	47		Ord. P2742**
Feb 11	70		24	Ord. No. 2563
March 21	46		1	2953E (spare)
May 5	45	Physical count correction		−20
May 10	25		5	Ord. No. 2892
May 23	20	Ord. No. 3097 requests 24 Ord. P2998 50 pieces		
June 3	0		0	Short for #3117(24)

*Customer order number.
**P signifies production (work order) number (50 pieces were ordered).

EXHIBIT 6
Routing Sheet for Part #16435

Work Order *P2998*   Due date *ASAP*   Quantity requested *50*

Work center #	Description	Quantity complete	Date complete
02	Saw	*50*	*MAY 26*
05	Lathe		
03	Boring		
07	Grinding		
04	Inspection		

lateness was increasing and the foundries had lengthened their lead times significantly. To protect themselves, Kumera increased their purchases of castings for inventory, buying substantially more castings against a forecast instead of for specific customer orders. Special castings, like that required for the Makinen order, were requiring increased lead times, and shortages in the quantities delivered were increasing. Some foundries required a 13-month lead time for special castings. The standard delivery quotation was 4 months.

Even blanket purchased items were creating difficulties for Kumera. Their general rule for blanket contracting is simply "this year plus 15%." This meant significant contracting errors for some items as the product mix changed. The formula worked reasonably well for forgings, steel rods, and much of the hardware, however. Special purchased bearings required 4–6 months lead time for delivery to Kumera.

"We work with several simple principles here," said Vesa Kumpulainen. "One of the first is that the machines should be kept busy. If a machine center is nearly out of work, the stock accountant, or someone, will try to get work to that center even if it means producing parts for inventory. Secondly, we try to take care of the important customers. Unfortunately this really means the noisy ones. We make our quiet customers wait. Finally, we have not been concerned about our inventories until now. The high inflation rate seems to favor high inventories and the Finnish tax law allows inventory adjustments to be used to level tax burdens. Besides our inventory turnovers have been right at the industry average of 2–3 times per year.

"We have been brought up short by the energy crisis, however. All of a sudden it became clear that, even with the inventory, our ability to get the right part at the right time was just about nil. In my present view it seems to me we must get some more people. The people in production planning do both manufacturing and purchasing planning. Compared to other firms, we have too few people. I think we should increase the staff there from 4 to 6 people. In addition, we could add one more purchasing person. It would only raise the total to 3 and we could use the help with the expediting of purchase orders. In addition to these new people, we need another expeditor. With these additions, I think we could cope with the problem."

CASE

16

Midwest Manufacturing Division[1] (Revised)

"Beth, will you please call down to Production Planning and Inventory Control and ask Bob Felice to come to my office? Tell him to bring that inventory information we discussed this morning."

Joe Daily, plant manager of the Breman facility of the Midwest Manufacturing Division (MMD), pondered the telephone call just received from his boss, Mr. Ben Norway, in St. Louis. Mr. Norway had related the division controller's concern about the growing inventory levels at the two MMD plants. Daily was pleased that he had recently made some organizational changes and, in general, placed a considerable amount of emphasis upon good inventory results. Now he would have a chance to explain his inventory control procedures as he and Bob Felice were to go to St. Louis the following day to meet with the other plant manager and members of the divisional staff, including the general manager of MMD, Mr. Norway. Today he wanted to review his plant's inventory position and policies and come to some definite decision regarding future production rates and a possible worker layoff.

THE COMPANY

MMD, a division of Tuttle, Inc., manufactured high-quality electric meter equipment for the utility industry and complex electronic measuring/monitoring systems for both governmental and industrial markets. Its major products were self-contained and transformer-rated metering equipment for residential, commercial, and industrial applications.

In early 1974 the MMD plant in Breman, Oklahoma, was a modern complex devoted to engineering, manufacturing, and distributing watt-hour meter equipment for the utility industry. Its principal manufacturing activity was the production of watt-hour meters for the measurement of electrical power consumption in the residential market. The plant had experienced continuous expansion since

1954, and in 1973 added 200,000 square feet of operational space. An additional 50,000 square feet was scheduled for completion in mid-1974.

The company was organized along functional lines (see Exhibits 1 and 2). Relations between management and labor were considered good. Company executives attributed this to a good employee-relations program, competitive wages, the wage incentive plan, and an active interest by upper-level management, especially the plant manager, Joe Daily.

The plant had never been unionized despite the unionization of nearly every other manufacturer in the area. However, there had been a serious attempt to unionize the plant in the spring of 1973. While the union was defeated, company executives were concerned by the 25% who voted for the union.

George Kelly, industrial relations manager, commented on the local labor situation:

> This is a tight labor market. The unemployment rate in Breman has been less than half the national average. Recently we have been running at about 2%. The type of work we do here doesn't require any formal skills. Most of it is assembly-line operations and is very repetitive. There is no need for a formal training program. Usually the kids who are available to us are the nonaggressive kids; the ones who, if they happen to be on Route 61, might come in to talk to us. In spite of new firms

EXHIBIT 1
Organizational Chart—1974

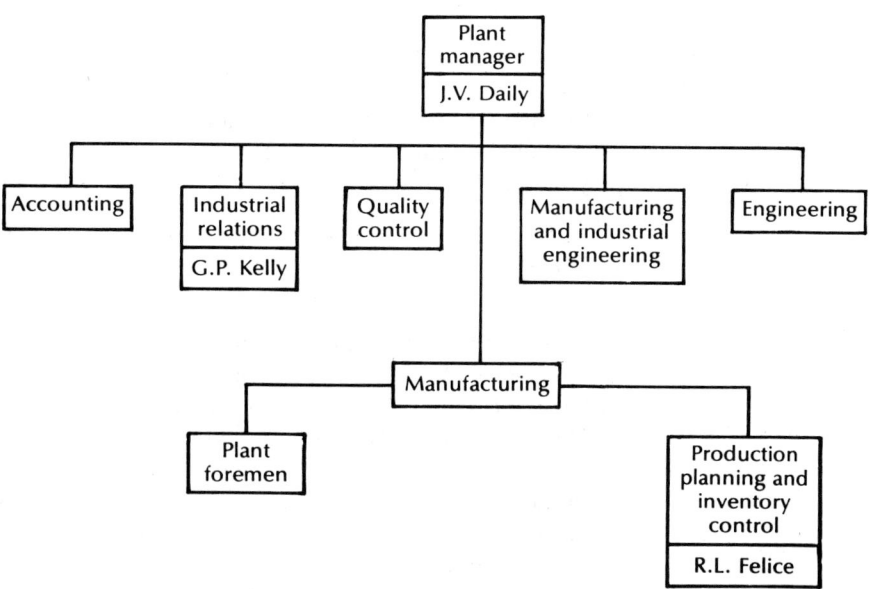

Source: Company records

EXHIBIT 2
Organizational Chart—1974

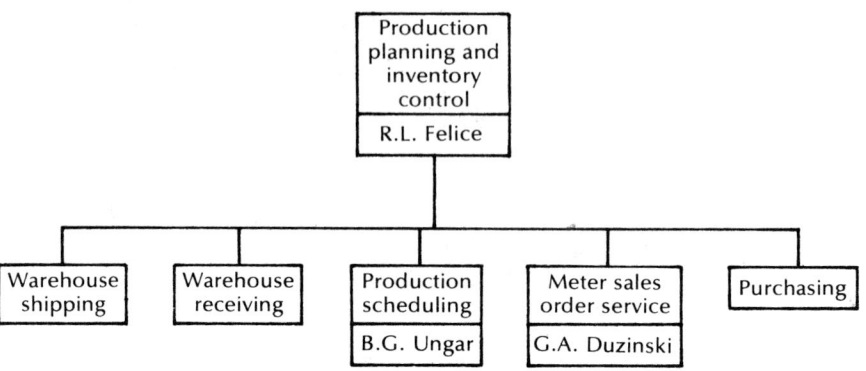

Source: Company records

coming into the area over the years, and some of the older firms expanding, we still have been fortunate enough to get people when necessary. I must admit that we didn't have much of a choice in filling a position though. When we were expanding, we would get maybe six applicants to fill five jobs. The overall population is growing steadily each year, and this is a popular area and not many people leave. We attract people from the rural areas. The rural people are used to work and don't mind the routine. Some of the city kids just don't want to put screws in a meter all day.

THE PRODUCT LINE

MMD-Breman manufactured self-contained and transformer-rated watt-hour meter devices for the utility industry. Two basic meters were produced: single-phase and polyphase.

	PERCENTAGE UNIT VOLUME	AVERAGE STANDARD COST[2]
1. *Single-Phase*	85%	$10.60
2. *Polyphase*	15%	$61.00

A watt-hour meter operates on the principle of electromagnetism. It has a thin metal disk mounted so that it rotates in the field of an electromagnet. This electromagnet is connected to the power lines supplying electricity to the customer. The greater the usage of electricity, the stronger the electromagnetic field becomes; thus, the disk rotational speed varies. A system of gears registers the disk's rotations on four dials on the face of the meter. A permanent magnet keeps the disk from turning when no electricity is being used.

The plant's product line was described by Gerry Duzinski, supervisor of the meter sales order group under Bob Felice:

---

[2]Materials made up 60% of the total cost of the product.

Each meter line has several models. For example, the single-phase and polyphase comes either self-contained or transformer-rated. Within each of these two variations there is a choice of a pointer-type register or the cyclometer-type register. Each line also has variations due to voltage and ampere rating. Furthermore, each meter is available as a socket-connected or bottom-connected device.

Our historical records show a definite, consistent pattern for the mix among different register-type models. The pointer-type/cyclometer-type mix is 55/45.

Approximately 50 percent to 60 percent of the components were common to each category of meters.

In addition to meters, we manufacture electronic measuring/monitoring systems for industrial and governmental contracts. This work is very specialized and we only start production after an order is received. Depending on the complexity of the system order, it could take from one to eight months to complete an order.

FLOW OF MATERIALS THROUGH THE BREMAN PLANT

In 1973 approximately 43 percent of total meter-related inventory was in raw materials and components inventory and 40 percent in work-in-process inventory. The remaining 17 percent was in finished-goods inventory.

Raw materials and components were ordered from independent vendors. On receipt at Breman the materials were stored in a large storage area until requested by a production department. When issued, raw materials, generally metals, were routed to the various fabrication departments. Completed parts were sent to several subassembly areas or directly to final assembly departments. For the average meter, there were five levels of subassemblies in the manufacturing process.

The product mix in production was easily changed merely by changing the schedules of parts into each assembly department. All assembly processes were of similar complexity, and none were considered difficult. Each station in the assembly line and each bench operation required only the simplest skills. In the same building the company maintained a 75,000-square-foot warehouse with a capacity for approximately 380,000 meters. Although there were only two basic types (single-phase and polyphase) of meters carried in finished goods, the variations of register, voltage/ampere ratings, self-contained/transformer type, and socket/bottom connections inflated the finished-goods inventory to 300 different products.

Exhibit 3 illustrates the flow of materials through the plant.

MMD had five sales branches to give it national sales coverage. When an order was received at Breman, an attempt was made to fill it from finished-goods inventory if it was a stock item. The normal time from receipt of an order to shipment of an item in stock was five working days. The average transportation time to deliver the order to the customer was an additional five days. For those orders that could not be filled, or could be only partially filled, the unsatisfied quantity was passed to Production Planning for production scheduling. It was expected that the normal time to shipment of these orders would be three to four weeks, which was competitive with the utility industry standard.

EXHIBIT 3
Simplified Diagram of Flow of Materials—1974

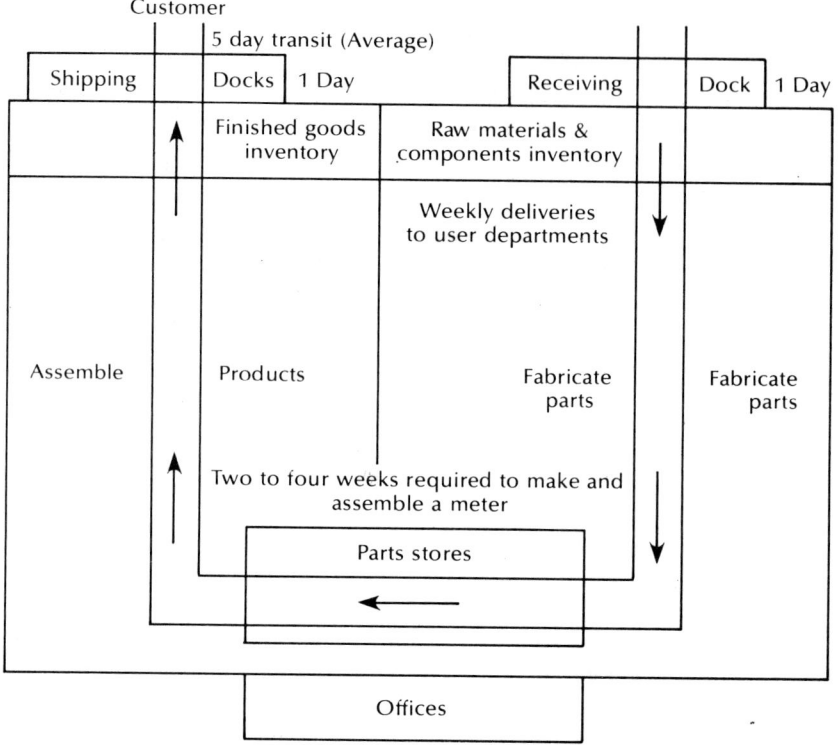

Source: Company records

Production Planning would then schedule models to be produced, filling outstanding orders first and then bringing up finished-goods stock items that were below the optimum inventory level. Once a schedule was made, the scheduler manually wrote a list of parts required to meet the schedule. While the accounting department had a computerized bill of material for determining standard product costs, it was not in a form suitable for use in production control.

Before materials were issued to each of the assembly and fabrication departments, the foreman of each of the 7 production departments was given an opportunity to review the parts and raw material scheduled to come into his department. The foreman had the option to reject or alter the quantity, depending on the material on hand in his department. Frequently, because he was doing other things, he sent the material requirement on for issuance without review or gave it to his parts clerk for review.

Generally, the foremen tried to insure that they did not run out of any needed part that could cause a shutdown of the assembly line. As a result, each foreman carried certain parts as spares within his department. At times these quantities on the production floor became substantial, especially if it were a part common to many models or if the pack quantity was larger than the quantity desired. In an emergency, if a department had a requirement for a part not available on the production floor, the part could be obtained from components/raw material control stock, usually within one hour.

Parts analysts, who worked in production planning and inventory control, determined material and parts requirements from outside vendors. Based on internal reports of inventory and planned production rate schedules that had been exploded into materials and components needs, the analysts identified those items below their reorder point (ROP). Analysts used their judgment in setting order quantities; EOQ were not used. Many of the purchased materials and components could be obtained under a quantity discount pricing schedule. The actual order quantity for each item was then processed through the purchasing department. The time required—from the determination by the parts analyst that an item needed to be ordered to the submission of the order to the vendor by purchasing—was seven working days.

The parts analysts were proud of their performance in ordering raw materials and components. As one analyst put it, "The assembly line has never been closed down once since I've been here, and I've been here seven years now."

DETERMINATION OF INVENTORY LEVELS

In November 1973 Bob Felice was appointed Production Planning and Inventory Control Manager. Shortly thereafter, in December 1973, new inventory guidelines and reordering procedures for raw materials and components, based upon an "ABC" categorization, were established. Exhibit 4 shows the stock levels desired

EXHIBIT 4
Inventory Guidelines and Reordering Procedures—Purchased Materials and Components for 1974

Guidelines

A Items ($15,300+) annual usage
14% total items (738) — 90% total dollars
4 weeks minimum   6 weeks target — 8 weeks maximum

B Items ($4,600–$15,299) annual usage
12% total items (645) — 7% total dollars
8 weeks minimum   12 weeks target — 16 weeks maximum

C Items ($1,530–$4,599) annual usage
27% total items (1,441) — 2% total dollars
8 weeks minimum   17 weeks target — 26 weeks maximum

D Items ($0–$1,529) annual usage
47% total items (2,477) — 1% total dollars
8 weeks minimum   29 weeks target — 52 weeks maximum

Total items = 5,301

Source: Company records, December, 1973.

EXHIBIT 4, cont'd
Reordering Rules from Company Manual–December, 1973

Three employees called Parts Analysts will be responsible for doing the actual ordering of raw materials and components through the Purchasing Department. Using a weekly computer generated Inventory Status Report, analysts will review all of their assigned items and order those that are below their reorder point. Ordering will not be automatic, however. Since these analysts also set the reorder point levels, they are to review the weekly production rates that have been set based on the marketing forecast, to see if the ROP is still valid. Analysts are to consider vendor leadtimes and safety stocks in this evaluation.

The reorder point and reordering rules for each raw material and component item in the computer program will be determined by the following:

1. ROP = Safety stock + Leadtime × Weekly usage rate
   where: Safety stock = Minimum number of weeks' supply of the item stated above for each class of item (e.g., 4 weeks' supply for all A items).
   Weekly usage = Six months marketing forecast exploded into item requirements divided by twenty-six weeks.
   Leadtime = Time in weeks from purchase order placement to delivery by the vendor.

2. When a reorder of an item is required, the established inventory guidelines should be used in determining the amount to be ordered. The exact quantity to be ordered will depend upon the judgment of the analyst, considering current stock status, anticipated usage and quantity discount schedules when appropriate. Every effort should be made to maintain average inventory levels at the target weeks' supply. In no case should levels exceed the maximum weeks' supply.

3. For control purposes each item will be monitored and flagged when its on-hand inventory exceeds the weeks' maximum (e.g., 8 weeks' supply for all A items).

4. For A items, the Purchasing department should attempt to schedule delivery of large orders from vendors over a six-month period rather than all at once.

The target and maximum for each category A, B, C and D have been established by applying the traditional economic order quantity model to a sample of items with a carrying cost of 23% of the item price.

$$EOQ = \sqrt{\frac{2 \text{ (Annual item demand) (Order cost of \$17)}}{\text{(Price per unit) (23\%)}}}$$

EOQ quantities for the sample of items in each category were converted to an equivalent number of weeks' supply. Each maximum was then determined as the sum of the safety stock and the EOQ.

for each category of inventory and explains the reordering procedures under the new inventory management policies at MMD. As Bob Felice explained,

> We don't have anything from the Division that says the target inventory for A items has got to be six weeks. That figure and the others are what we calculated to be a reasonable inventory. Our only guideline on inventory levels from higher authority came down through the budget. They do not tell us that inventories should be a certain percent of sales or what our stockturn should be. I did see a recent trade press article stating that the industry leader has a meter related inventory stockturn of 4.3, based on cost of sales.

Exhibit 5 is a partial copy of the inventory budget made in July 1973. Felice continued:

EXHIBIT 4, cont'd
Survey of Vendor Leadtimes—1973 (in weeks)

Part number	Leadtime	Part number	Leadtime
300000-091	18	202909-285	10
205040-523	30	202909-929	10
200162-479	8	202909-939	10
300979-231	8	202912-738	30
701018-940	25	202922-012	12
700000-910	12	202922-022	10
701018-945	30	202922-355	10
300000-681	16	202933-925	10
703009-393	12	202906-282	16
205040-109	30	202949-515	12
204040-522	30	703030-927	9
205040-223	12	304146-874	16
205040-123	26	202949-505	16
300976-161	8	304145-262	16
202936-065	12	216975-000	8
300001-241	12	202040-514	30
202922-022	10	701018-939	30
202909-865	18	700000-918	14
700000-913	12	300977-181	16
008607-365	22	206013-679	14
008617-242	20	700060-843	12
009803-804	12	300001-271	16
302110-393	12	302108-611	12
700000-913	12	302108-171	10
700000-915	12	703030-437	12
700000-916	12	211865-000	12
700000-918	14	206015-121	12
700000-949	8	300362-203	16
700000-950	10		
083381-068	12		
200953-814	12		
200953-822	12		
202899-248	20		

Total: 61 part numbers
Average leadtime: 14 weeks

Source: Company Records, December 1973

Approximately 35 percent of dollar value of raw materials and components is in material to support the custom ordered systems. We are not able to use the A, B, C analysis for this material because of a number of factors. Right now $5.2 million of our inventory is in electrical components purchased from Japan. This figure is high, because we buy in large quantities due to high transportation costs and long lead times. We made commitments for large quantities in early 1973 when business was strong and the world shortage situation was at its worst. The net result is that I believe we have no control over this type of inventory.

EXHIBIT 5
1974 Budget Inventory Summary Prepared July 27, 1973 (Gross and Net Inventory)

	Actual			Inventory budget				
	1972	7/27/73	12/31/73	Jan.	Feb.	Mar.	Apr.	May
Gross balance-Finished goods	$ 2,159	$ 3,304	$ 3,292	$ 3,951	$ 4,287	$ 4,624	$ 5,267	$ 5,911
Work-in-process	8,677	11,071	11,212	11,487	11,175	10,697	10,599	10,449
Materials	15,837	16,378	16,170	16,534	16,813	17,089	17,134	16,868
Less: Reserves-Shrinkage	589	490	643	667	692	716	741	766
Obsolescence	4,125	3,470	2,857	2,848	2,839	2,824	2,814	2,805
Net inventory	21,958	26,793	27,173	28,456	28,744	28,870	29,446	29,657

Inventory budget

	June	July	Aug.	Sept.	Oct.	Nov.	Dec.
Gross balance-Finished Goods	$ 6,891	$ 6,278	$ 5,971	$ 5,359	$ 4,747	$ 4,134	$ 3,828
Work-in-process	10,020	10,094	10,229	9,640	9,944	10,440	10,174
Materials	16,623	16,491	16,253	16,338	15,833	15,328	15,429
Less: Reserves-Shrinkage	554	566	591	616	640	665	689
Obsolescence	2,790	2,784	2,777	2,762	2,756	2,536	2,324
Net inventory	30,190	29,513	29,085	27,961	27,127	26,702	26,417

Source: Company records. Figures in thousands of dollars and include *meter products and electronic systems.* July 27, 1973.

With regard to our standard meters, our goal in finished goods is a four-week supply for each item. We would like to be able to fill 90 percent of the orders for items carried in finished goods.[3]

We derive our inventory requirement by the marketing forecast, but we often have to modify that by our own feel for what is needed. Marketing is more optimistic, and they want to have all materials on hand to meet all demands. They are not tied to inventory dollar goals. They have a point though: who knows how many sales we lose by being out of stock of an item?

The level of WIP inventory is, of course, determined by the production line rates and the mix of meters that we are producing, so we don't have any specific guidelines here. When walking through the plant, if we notice that there seems to be too much material on the floor, the production supervisor will ask the department foreman to cut back.

MARKETING SALES FORECASTS

Each June the St. Louis office received dollar sales forecasts by meter product line from all of the sales offices. Once approved by headquarters staff, an annual order input for each operating plant was developed. This forecast was a dollar figure only and had to be converted to actual units of each type of meter. This was done by the budgeting section of the accounting department at each plant, based on the previous year's sales figures. If, for example, the sales of the single-phase meter were 80 percent of the total sales dollars in 1973, then 80 percent of the 1974 forecast would be allocated to single-phase models. The number of sales units expected was derived by dividing the dollar figure by the average selling price of each meter. Once this procedure was accomplished, the remainder of the budget was completed and production schedules and manpower planning could be firmed up.

EVENTS LEADING TO THE SITUATION IN FEBRUARY 1974

The company started 1973 with a heavy backlog of sales—209,824 meter units. During the first six months of 1973 meter order input remained strong. To meet demand, MMD-Breman added approximately 200 workers, mostly direct labor employees. Management wanted to be capable of producing enough to meet the fall season demand, which was traditionally the highest of the year. Demand during the first six months of 1973 was 20 percent ahead of the previous year and was the largest increase ever experienced at any MMD plant. With that trend, marketing management expected weekly production needs of about 73,500 meters per week for the remainder of the year.

While July provided a good start for the second half of the year, order inputs from August through December fell below expectations, as weekly meter orders

---

[3]In a random sample by the casewriter of 126 orders during the fall of 1973 for items normally carried in finished-goods inventory, 87 were completely filled and 39 partially filled. There were 320 separate line items ordered, of which 52 could not be filled at all because they were completely out of stock.

for the last half of 1973 averaged only 56,000. During this period, in the fall of 1973, marketing made its usual period forecast, and estimated weekly production needs for the first 6 months of 1974 at 8,800 polyphase and 59,000 single-phase meters. These weekly targets were used for ordering raw materials and component parts from MMD vendors. As the order rate dropped off in late 1973 some workers were utilized to build fabricated parts and subassemblies in anticipation of the higher sales conditions forecast by marketing.

Unlike previous years when MMD-Breman had closed out the year with inventory at it slowest level, the beginning of 1974 saw them starting the slow selling season with a large inventory and a large work force. January's incoming

EXHIBIT 6
Total Inventory by Product Line, 1970—February 1974 (thousands of $)

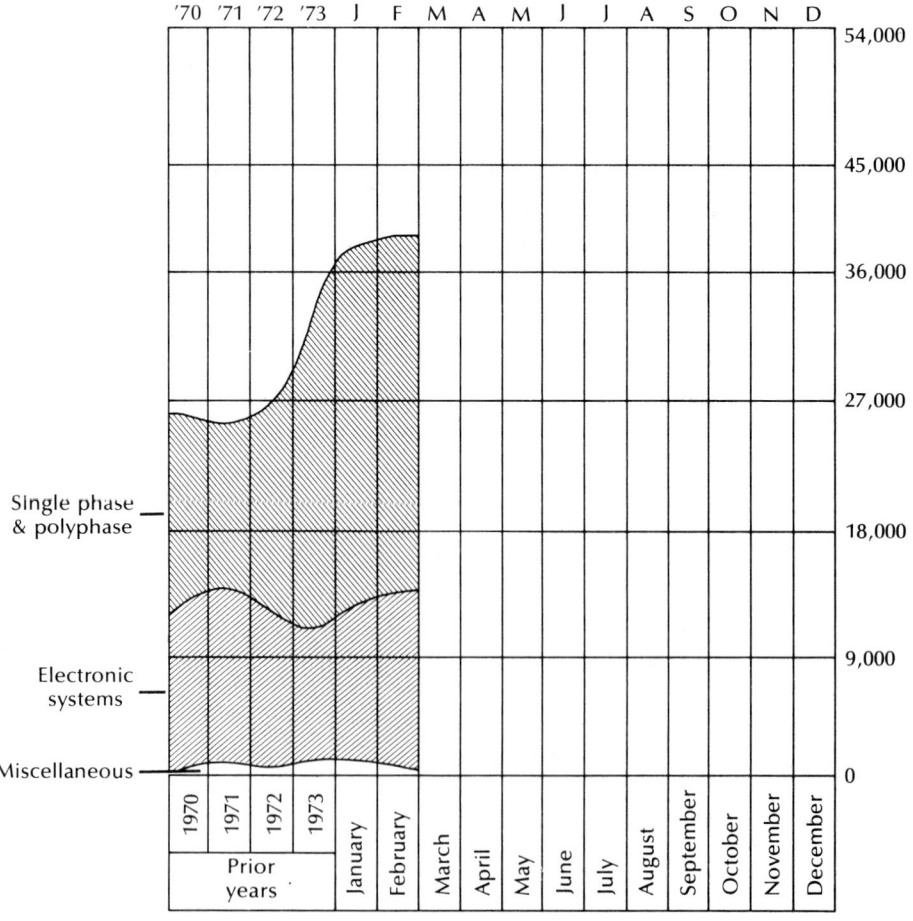

See next page for exact quantities

Source: Company records

orders gave Joe Daily a ray of hope, but February statistics left the situation less than certain.

FEBRUARY	PRODUCTION (Units)	INCOMING ORDERS (Units)
Week Ending 2/1/74	60,021	55,951
Week Ending 2/8/74	61,635	37,821
Week Ending 2/15/74	59,452	34,480
Week Ending 2/22/74	64,493	26,637
Average	61,400	38,722

A key factor in these reduced orders was that in order to fight inflation, the Federal Reserve Board had tightened the money supply. This caused housing starts to decline significantly, which directly affected residential meter installations and thus MMD-Breman's business. As the prime rate reached 12½ percent, inventory carrying cost at the Breman plant was in the neighborhood of 30 percent. Exhibit 11 provides production, shipments and order data for January and February 1974.

EXHIBIT 6, cont'd

Gross Inventory by Product Line—Year End (1970-1974, in thousands of $)

					1974	
	1970	1971	1972	1973	Jan.	Feb.
Meters						
Finished goods	$ 3,804	$ 1,412	$ 1,645	$ 4,269	$ 5,179	$ 5,623
Work-in-process	4,137	4,474	6,404	9,772	9,144	8,799
Raw purchased & components	6,511	5,491	6,194	10,746	11,251	11,043
Total gross	14,152	11,377	14,243	24,787	25,574	25,465
Electronic systems						
Finished Goods	0	0	0	0	0	0
Work-in-process	$ 4,768	$ 1,314	$ 1,648	$ 1,605	$ 2,303	$ 2,921
Raw purchased & components	7,237	10,241	8,204	6,367	7,028	7,163
Total Gross	$12,005	$11,555	$ 9,852	$ 7,972	$ 9,331	$10,084
Miscellanous products						
Finished goods	0	$ 493	$ 514	$ 475	$ 805	$ 879
Work-in-process	$ 61	870	625	680	625	729
Raw purchased & components	361	1,568	1,439	1,844	1,746	946
Total gross	422	2,931	2,578	2,999	3,176	2,554
Summary						
Finished goods	$ 3,804	$ 1,905	$ 2,159	$ 4,744	$ 5,984	$ 6,502
Work-in-process	8,967	6,658	8,677	12,057	12,072	12,449
Raw purchased & components	11,338	11,402	11,406	15,142	15,095	13,989
Japanese purchased	2,771	5,898	4,431	3,815	4,930	5,163
Total raw purchased & components	14,109	17,300	15,837	18,957	20,025	19,152
Total gross	$26,880	$25,863	$26,673	$35,758	$38,081	$38,103

Source: Company records.

EXHIBIT 7

Sales and Cost Data 1971-1974 (in thousands of $)

| | Actual | | | | Forecast |
	1970	1971	1972	1973	1974
Meter sales	$42,137	$51,401	$66,802	$ 79,980	$91,315
Meters direct product costs	$28,845	$34,842	$45,181	$ 51,873	$61,912
Total sales Meters & Systems		$91,201	$92,426	$103,530	Not available

Source: Company records.

EXHIBIT 8

Average Meter Inventory[1] (in thousands of $)

	1969	1970	1971	1972	1973
Finished goods	$ 3,108	$ 3,874	$ 2,483	$ 2,149	$ 3,460
Work-in-process	4,407	4,955	4,429	5,579	8,005
Raw materials & components	6,593	6,618	5,218	5,864	8,195
Total yearly average	$14,108	$15,447	$12,130	$13,592	$19,660

Source: Company records.

[1]Inventory figures are yearly averages of meter products and related materials and components.

EXHIBIT 9

Total Meter Order Inputs (Units-1971 to 1974)[1]

	1971	1972	1973	1974
January	120,365	204,960	157,552	266,924
February	146,207	159,740	178,501	154,883
March	192,577	185,417	269,545	
April	121,667	161,834	221,448	
May	200,177	138,253	236,314	
June	163,651	296,082	315,986	
July	198,385	157,108	259,276	
August	157,360	317,502	278,999	
September	189,932	365,699	242,620	
October	315,553	236,463	236,953	
November	150,692	227,561	291,338	
December	223,994	208,815	145,776	

Source: Company records.

[1]Through 2/22/74

EXHIBIT 10

Employment Data (beginning of year)

Year	Total employees	Total direct labor	Meters direct employees[1]	Electronic systems direct employees
1971	957	700	546	154
1972	1110	845	717	128
1973	1213	950	798	152
1974	1400	1022	840	182

[1]Meter assembly direct labor represented 62% of the meter labor force.

As March 1974 began, Daily's main concern was that the downturn in sales orders might be only temporary, and thus he did not wish to act too hastily. A factor in his thinking was that a price increase implemented in the fall of 1973 had recently been rescinded. Marketing was less optimistic than previously, but still unable to provide a better forecast than the fall 1973 estimates. As a hedge, since the last week in January, Daily had ordered the production level, but not material orders, cut back from these weekly rates, by not replacing any workers leaving the payroll and by using some of the meter employees in the electronic systems work.[4] Any further cutback in the production rate would require direct labor reductions in proportion to the production cut.

MMD-Breman had not had a layoff in ten years. Thus a workforce reduction could hit plant morale hard and thereby affect the productivity of the remaining workers. In addition, with a tight labor market, he was not sure the company would be able to hire people back in the future if sales improved. Overhead was going up with the completion of the new section of the building, and there was still the question of the union. A layoff would be great ammunition for the pro-union people. On the other hand, if current sales rates continued, Daily was not sure how long his storage capacity would carry finished-goods production.

Daily tried to anticipate some of the questions he would be asked in St. Louis. Were Bob Felice's new inventory policies realistic with regard to meter production and sales? He also wondered what help or guidance he could get from the divisional staff and the other plant manager on his production rate decision.

At that moment Bob Felice entered the office. "Please sit down, Bob; let's get started on reviewing our situation. We have a lot to cover before we leave tomorrow." Exhibits 6 through 11 contain some of the information used by Daily and Felice in their review.

---

[4]Raw material and component orders were based upon the six-month production needs forecast which was prepared by Marketing. Generally, forecast quantities for each basic meter model were spread evenly throughout the six-month period for production planning purposes.

EXHIBIT 11
Weekly Status of Meter Instruments—January 1 through February 22, 1974 (units)

Description	Production		Order input		Production budget[3]	Shipments		Inventory[1]	Backlog[1,2]
	Week[1]	Year to date	Week[1]	Year to date	Year to date	Week[1]	Year to date		
Single-phase	57,435	412,826	19,013	367,169	448,375	22,481	318,403	285,549	121,574
Polyphase	7,058	53,133	7,624	54,643	66,905	6,657	45,099	41,160	20,074
TOTAL	64,493	465,959	26,637	421,812	515,280	29,138	363,502	326,709	141,648

Source: Company records: 38 production days.
[1]For week ending 2/22/74 (finished goods only).
[2]Backlog is defined as any orders received, but not yet shipped.
[3]Based on the Marketing Forecast Fall, 1973, and used for ordering materials and components from vendors.

Jones Meter Company

As Frank Klein walked back to his office he knew he would have to make up his mind fairly soon. It was unlikely that he or his team would learn much more about the benefits or costs of an MRP system for Jones Meter Company's Tulsa plant. Frank needed to weigh again in his mind the benefits of an MRP system, particularly IBM's MAPICS software, versus its costs. He knew that MRP installations were often not successful; many observers had stated that most MRP systems had failed to deliver on their promise. The number of so-called "A" users was reputed to be less than 10%. Yet, could the plant really survive with the home-grown system they were now using? Klein's recommendation would be critical for the project and Frank knew that he had to support his decision effectively in order to sell it to his superiors.

COMPANY BACKGROUND

Jones Meter Company made a variety of meters that measured the flow of liquids or gases. These meters were used extensively in oil and gas production, oil and gas pipelines, refineries and petrochemical complexes, and other chemical production facilities. Accurate flow rates were critical to oil and gas producers, royalty owners, regulatory agencies, manufacturing companies, and others. Jones Meter's sales were concentrated in two main types of flow meters: positive displacement (P.D.) meters and turbine meters. The company made other kinds of meters (e.g., rotometers, magnetic meters, Doppler meters) but they were less important. The P.D. and turbine meters were manufactured for a variety of pipe size diameters, (e.g., ½ inch, 1 inch, 4 inch), lengths (e.g., 4 inches, 12 inches), pressures (e.g., 1,000 psi, 7500 psi), and connection types (e.g., flanged, threaded ends, grooved ends) and were applicable for a range of flow rates, viscosities, and liquid purities. Naturally, several of these meters were produced in comparatively high volumes, while most were produced in only modest volumes. Jones Meter also manufactured a number of read-out devices and other electronic gear for displaying and analyzing the liquid or gas flow and its key characteristics. These electronic devices could be matched with different styles and sizes of meters. Jones Meter was willing to customize both its meters and accessories, and a substantial portion of its sales involved such customization.

This case was prepared by Roger W. Schmenner, solely as a basis for class discussion. It is not intended to describe either good or bad management practice.

The company produced all of its meters and accessories at its location in Tulsa, Oklahoma. The plant employed about 1,200 people on two shifts. Meter operations at the plant were highly vertically integrated. There were only a handful of the hundreds of parts comprising a typical meter that were sourced from outside vendors. The company did all of its own stamping, die-casting, machining, plating, painting, and assembly itself. The electronic accessory devices used many more outside vendors for their parts. Plant operations for these devices were largely assembly and test. Everyone tended to divide the plant into three major segments: the fabrication area, the subassembly area, and the final assembly area. The flow of materials naturally moved from fabrication into subassembly and then into final assembly and test. A typical order took about five weeks to progress through the factory, taking about one week in final assembly, two weeks in subassembly, and two weeks in fabrication. There were some parts, however, that could take up to a month in fabrication. These parts were naturally those that required a lot of processing, for example, die-casting, machining, and plating. Screw machining and gear hobbing also tended to take longer than the normal two weeks. Thus, many of the parts from the fabrication area were actually pulled out of inventory to satisfy orders rather than made specifically for that order. In effect, a decoupling inventory existed between fabrication and the subassembly areas. To make matters worse, lead times on some raw materials could stretch up to half a year. Thus, some materials and parts orders had to be made well in advance of any actual end item orders.

Since there was always at least a name plate that differed from one product to another, the company could never really inventory finished goods. Virtually, all production had to be done to order.

PRODUCTION PLANNING AS IT WAS PRACTICED AT THE PLANT

Although each end item was ordered by a customer company, forecasting was still required by the plant. The plant forecasted raw materials to insure itself of their supply. It also built up some work-in-process inventory between fabrication and subassembly so that it could react quickly to selected orders. The sales forecast was done by months for each calendar year. It was not a rolling forecast of every 12 months. This fact limited the usefulness of the forecast at the end of the year when its visibility into the future was next to nonexistent.

Each month there was a load planning meeting that developed the master production schedule for the current month plus the next three months. Only the current month's plan was firm. No one knew precisely whether the master production schedule decided upon at a load planning meeting was actually feasible, that it could be done in the allotted time by the resources then available to the factory. The plant relied on its master scheduler and his associates to determine what would be feasible and what would have to be rescheduled for a later time. These production planners relied on gut feel and various rules of thumb that they had developed. These rules of thumb addressed, for example, how many subassemblies for a particular product group could be put together in a day. These approximate daily rates of production were typically applicable to families of products. For example, there were three distinct families of flow registers for the turbine meter, but each had many variations within its family. The Century I flow register had 75 variations, the Century II had 150, and the Century III had 200 product variations.

The load plan (the master production schedule), as developed each month, indicated what "space" was available in the schedule for production so that, as orders came in, the available capacity could be adjusted. If an order came in that took up all of the available capacity, then it was either put into the next month's production cycle or some negotiation went on to see whether it could be squeezed into the current production schedule. About 200 orders came in every day, some for many meters, but others for only one or two.

The gut feels and rules of thumb that helped plan the master production schedule were adequate in the aggregate, that is, for the product families considered as groups. However, every month about one third of the actual orders were not completely filled. Variations in the actual product mix typically caused imbalances in various departments in the factory and this held up the completion of orders. The rule of thumb that stated, for example, that the Century III family of flow registers needed about twice the assembly time of the Century II family was useful but not detailed enough to account for the fact that many of the 200 variations of the Century III took much longer than twice the time of some of the 150 variations on the Century II.

While the company did develop a master production schedule, the plant's home-grown computer system did not act to explode the master production schedule through the appropriate bills of material to determine what parts were required at every stage and level of production. What the home-grown computer system did was to explode the backlog of orders through the bills of material and not the agreed upon schedule of production. Orders were released to the factory when received and not according to the master production schedule. The requirements for a part for any week were thus subject to continual change as orders for any week were added to the order backlog and run through the computer system. Departments within the factory were sometimes stuck with completed parts they could not use because the order backlog had been changed on them.

In the factory, there was a distinction made between orders and requirements. From the standpoint of the factory floor, what was crucial for any department was what that department was supposed to make for the week—its requirements. While it was of interest to know which orders were the basis for the requirements, what was critical for the department was the requirements number itself.

The requirements placed on different departments differed themselves. Years before, the factory had tried to operate on a lot-for-lot basis, so that the fabrication areas made exactly what the subassembly and final assembly areas needed. Given the extreme vertical integration in the factory and the complexity of the product, the feeder operations had much too little time to react. Too many orders were missed and too much chaos prevailed. To remedy that situation, the decoupling inventory was built up between fabrication and assembly and the demands in the fabrication areas were determined through a modified reorder point system.

The Modified Reorder Point System

This system distinguished between stocked and non-stocked parts. Stocked parts were parts that physically resided in the stockroom and for which perpetual inventory records were kept. They were likely to be made in anticipation of their use which implied that they were not likely to be exotic in nature. Roughly one-quarter of the parts were classified as stocked parts. The remaining three-quarters were classified as non-stocked parts. These parts did not reside in the stockroom but rather got pushed along from one department to another. It was most likely that these non-stocked parts existed for either custom orders or for very high volume orders, the extremes of product demand at the factory. These non-stocked parts were ordered automatically by the home-grown computer system. The stocked parts were subject to the reorder point system while the non-stocked parts were fabricated on a lot-for-lot basis.

The reorder point was calculated using the following formula:

$$ROP = (\text{Forecasted issues from stockroom}) \times \left(\frac{\text{Lead time for production, in days}}{21 \text{ days/month}} \right) + (1.25 \times MAD)$$

Notes:
1. The forecasted issues were the weighted, moving average of what was issued by the stockroom each month.
2. The MAD variable was the mean absolute deviation of actual monthly use of the part from the average monthly use of the part over the previous 12 months.

When the reorder point was struck the economic order quantity was ordered. The economic order quantity was figured in the following way:

$$EOQ = \sqrt{\frac{2 \times 12 \times \text{monthly demand} \times (\text{setup} + \text{order costs})}{\text{unit cost} \times \text{carrying cost percentage}}}$$

The setup costs were the standard costs, not the actual. Order costs were the variable costs associated with an order which, at present, ran $15 for outside purchases and $7.50 for in-house production orders. The unit cost was the standard cost, including variable and overhead costs, and the carrying cost percentage used was 35%.

The economic order quantity was ordered, however, only if it fell within certain bounds. If the economic order quantity was less than two months' or greater than twelve months' supply it was not followed. If it was less than two months, two months' use was ordered; if it was greater than 12 months' supply, only 12 months would be ordered. Currently there was some pressure to reduce the lower limit somewhat as a way of reducing inventory in general. An order could also be placed without the reorder point being struck. This could occur if requirements, as generated from the backlog, exceeded the sum of what was on hand and what was on order. This variation smacked of MRP-type logic.

The Informal System of Production Scheduling

Placing an order on a department for a certain required number of parts did not mean that the department actually produced that number. About half the time, the economic order quantities or other requirements asked of the department were followed, but in the other half of cases, these requirement numbers were ignored. Sometimes more than the requirement was made, and sometimes less than the requirement was made.

Over-runs were encouraged by the way manufacturing was evaluated. Each factory department was evaluated in part on "net allowed hours," that is, the standard hours earned by working on the requirements released. If a department worked hard and beat its standard, it could earn more net allowed hours than it expended in actual hours and thus be favorably reviewed. One way to beat the standard, of course, was not to have many setups. Thus, long runs of few products were embraced by managers needing to earn more net allowed hours.

Under-runs, on the other hand, were due in large part to the mismatch of actual capacity to the planned load for the department. This mismatch had stimulated an informal system that actually ran much of the production of the plant. More than 25% of production was subject to this informal system, and during peak capacity periods more than 50% might be subject. Every department's supervisor had a production coordinator whose job it was to make the informal system work.

What was the informal system? Every day each supervisor received a "tab sheet" which listed each part to be produced, the quantity to be produced (the requirements), the due date, the net allowed hours for the job, and where the part should be routed next. During those times when a department was cramped for capacity, either because overall orders were high or because of a mismatch between the actual product mix and the available capacity, the supervisor would glance down the tab sheet and wonder how he could meet all the production requested of him by the due dates specified. Realizing that much of the quantity demanded (the requirements) was triggered by the reorder point system and not needed immediately for an end item order, the supervisor and his production coordinator would negotiate different production quantities from those specified. The production coordinator would talk to other areas within the factory, perhaps as many as eight or nine, to find out exactly how many units were needed to fulfill orders and how many units were entered into the requirements solely because of the economic order quantity calculation. He could then negotiate to produce only as many units as was required to fulfill the order and hold off on any added production.

With the current home-grown computer system, no supervisor knew exactly what was "hot" on his tab sheet and what was not. Because a supervisor could not be confident that his priorities were shared by all of the other affected departments, without the work of the production coordinator the supervisor would not know when to expect certain materials to be delivered or indeed when he should ship out materials from his own department. In making the determination about what parts should be talked about in the informal system and what should be done with them, the home-grown computer system provided some help:

(1) a bill of materials; (2) a list of where the part was used next in the process; (3) the part's stock status, that is, what was on order, what was on the receiving dock, what was in the storeroom inspected, and an estimate as to what was available on the floor of the factory; and (4) a cost analysis of the standard times for the part and its routing through the process.

Other Problems with the Home-Grown Computer System

In addition to abetting the informal system of production scheduling, the home-grown computer system fostered some other problems.

A. Inventory Control. The plant's auditors had forced it to shut down every year for a physical inventory count. The auditors did not have confidence that the home-grown computer system actually knew what the status of the inventory was at any time. So much inventory was kept in other than storerooms that physical inventories were needed. Individual item cycle counts were not sufficient nor was the ABC inventory scheme used.

The handling of scrap was a case in point. Scrap tended to be collected by supervisors in each department and not disposed of right away. As it bunched up, supervision would lose control over its precise identity. Scrap was linked to parts numbers and not to orders. As so much would be accumulated, supervisors would make an effort to get it identified correctly and back to the loading dock area, but this type of hurried action meant that there were significant "unapplied issues" or variances from what was actually needed to fulfill orders.

B. Engineering Change Orders. The home-grown computer system provided no clear changeover dates for switching from an obsolete part or subassembly to a new part or subassembly. Supervisors would sometimes only see words like "held for tooling" and be confused about when the notice would be effective and when it wouldn't be effective. Changeovers in products, thus, were not as smooth as they could be.

C. Bills of Materials. Because Jones Meter offered so many product variations and custom products, bills of material were very important. About 50% of the orders specified some changes to specific bills of materials. This was handled by what were termed "similar-to" specifications, which stated that the custom product was similar to another one except for some modifications. The bills of material that were adjusted in this way were often informally kept; documentation was sometimes ambiguous, or worse, nonexistent. Orders could be released to the factory without a completely specified bill of materials.

Such similar-to specifications wreaked havoc in the feeder operations, especially when orders were small. Making the subtle modifications required for these customized orders could be costly, but no one knew the precise costs because actual times were not tracked. Not knowing these costs was uncomfortable because management did not know whether the pricing of these custom jobs was appropriate.

EXHIBIT 1
Controlled Interval Schedule (Dept. 15)

Customer order	ITM	SUF	Order no	S T	Part no.	Shp #	PPT #	Del to	Run time	P R	On CIS	Due date	Orig qty	Pieces due	Dlvd today	STS	Family code
TA86506	5	02	593676	x	1234567890	01	F01	R4	.29413		14	840105	5	5			
TA86506	7	02	593683	x	0987654321	01	F01	R4	.29413		13	840105	1	0		1 CP	
TA86506	6	02	593690	x	5432167890	01	F01	R4	.29413		14	840105	3	0		3 CP	
3312246	1A	02	594557	x	6789012345	01	F01	R4	.29413		11	840109	1	1			
AQ23494	1		590398		7890614253	01	F01	Z8	.28647		11	840110	4	0		4 CP	L01000
WI51838	2		594512		1029384756	01	F01	Z8	.28647		6	840117	6	6			L0100
TA86506	8	02	593686		5647382910	01	F01	R4	.29537		16	840105	1	1			
FA82652	1	C1	599318		2910386574	01	F01	R4	.29537		3	840117	10	10			
AP44194	1		596920		5758595056	01	F01	Z8	.28647		5	840118	1	1			L0100
HK23231	1A	01	590154	x	1718191016	01	F01	R4	.39079		15	840109	2	2			
42215421	1	C1	595948	x	2324252627	01	F01	R4	.39079		11	840110	1	1			L0100
CGEM66502	1		595862		0908121363	01	F01	Z8	.28647		4	840118	1	1			
CH77914	A	03	591762	x	8987868584	01	F01	R4	.29422		17	840109	2	2			
CH77914	D	03	592702	x	5916927834	01	F01	R4	.29422		17	840109	4	4			
CH79055	A	01	597652	x	7890634521	01	F01	R4	.29422		6	840116	2	2			
CH79060	A	01	598306	x	7890098712	01	F01	R4	.29545		5	840111	1	1			
CH77963	1	01	592257	x	3456776542	01	F01	R4	.28647		6	840116	1	1			
TL81798	27	03	594184	x	5677659890	01	F01	R4	.29413		12	840109	2	2			
PO17803	1		593273	x	1122334455	01	F01	Z8	.29413		13	840111	6	6			L0100
PG38185	1		594909	x	0099887766	01	F01	Z7	.29537		7	840117	1	1			L0100
CH79047	A	01	596994	x	7982314567	01	F01	R4	.29413		8	840111	1	1			
FATD22897	2A3		520156		3540912387	01	F01	Z2	.28647		40	840113	65	65			L0100
FATD22897	1A2		520170		6767676767	01	F01	Z2	.28647		40	840117	50	50			L0100
FATD22895	2A2		520173		4564789412	01	F01	Z2	.28647		3	840120	20	20			L0100

D. Actual Times. The home-grown computer system did not keep track of actual times spent on a particular order. This being the case, not only did confusion persist but it was difficult to modify production standards over time.

Exhibits 1 and 2 present examples of the Controlled Internal Schedule (the dispatch list or tab sheet available to each department) and of the Stock Order Follow Report (which gave information on parts availability and user expectations).

HOW AN MRP SYSTEM COULD HELP

There were a variety of arguments offered for an MRP system. Many viewed an MRP system as a way to eliminate the problems persisting with the current home-grown system. Chief among the arguments for an MRP system were the following:

1. An MRP system could force the definition of a master production schedule that would be exploded back through the appropriate bills of materials. No longer would the factory's production planning be ruled by an ever changing backlog. Installing an MRP system, however, implied that some part of the schedule would be frozen, say, for two weeks. This type of freeze was naturally welcomed by the supervisors because it would force commitment from production planning and others involved in the current load planning.

2. Under an MRP system every part would get traced to a particular order. No longer would there be any general "unapplied issues." Every part would

Notes to Exhibit 1—Controlled Interval Schedule

This is the Controlled Interval Schedule for Department 15 (flow registers). The full report covers 110 orders, of which only a dozen or so are listed here. The column headings refer to the following:

Customer Order: The company's customer order number
ITM: The item number of the customer order form to which this shop order refers to
SUF: The suffix (further identification), if any, on the item number of the customer order form
Order no: The assigned shop order number for this job
ST: Similar To. If X, then order is similar to the following style number
Part no: Part Number, the identification number for the part or assembly being worked on. Could be a blueprint drawing number.
Ship #: Which shipment the order is part of, usually just 1 shipment
PPT #: Pay Point Number. Refers to the accounting code for labor and/or materials in the department against which this order is going to claim time or materials.
Del to: Deliver To. The department to which this order, once completed, is going to be delivered next. The "DW" after some entries indicates "daywork"—the work done is not associated with particular orders.
Run time: Standard time charged per piece or assembly (in decimal hours)
PR: Field designed for any piece rates. Currently unused.
On CIS: Number of days on Controlled Interval Status (i.e., released to manufacturing)
Due date: Date (year, month, day) the order is due out of the department
Orig pieces qty due: Original Pieces Quantity Due. The quantity due that was released to manufacturing.
Dlvd today: Quantity delivered and updated the night previous to this report.
STS: Order status code (e.g., CP = complete)
Family code: Code indicating groups of homogeneous products. Helpful in determining scheduling constraints. If blank, the order involves a "similar to" designation or an order that was specially negotiated, and thus the family code is overridden.

EXHIBIT 2
Stock Order Follow Report

OFO3 On hand	Unapld issues	C L	US DP	Ident no	Dash	Gross OD & 1st	2nd & 3rd	Future	Order qty	Due date	On CIS	Pay PT	DE PT	PCS due	Pay PT	DE PT	PCS due	Pay PT	DE PT	PCS due
																	BY—USING CODE			
2109	2157	8	6	1234567890	-23	2147	0	0	5500	840315	16	P01	C1	5500	P02	F1	5500			
0	664	8	6	0987654321	-99	1222	0	0	7000	831227	40	P01	A3		N02	F1		N03	D1	
					99				7000	831227	40	B04	A2		N05	F1	3804	N06	D1	3804
					99				7000	831227	40	B07	A2	3804	P08	F1	3840			
0	2896	8	6	5678904321	-19	4119	0	0	5300	840116	40	P01	A1	3315	N02	F1	3315	B03	A1	3315
					19				5300	840116	40	P04	F1							
760	4121	8	6	5432109878	-66	4119	0	0	2500	840116	41	P01	F1	7500						
0	754	8	6	4321456789	-21	1750		0	3500	840104	34	P01	A2	3500	P02	F1	3500			
120	1375	8	6	1213141516	-18	1403	1700	2	5100	840109	32	P01	A3		N02	F1	5284	A03	A2	5284
					18		1		5100	840109	32	N04	F1	5284	N05	F1	5284	B06	F1	5284
0	1682	8	6	6820987596	-33	1600	0	0	5000	840130	13	P01	A3		N02	F1		B03	A2	5654
					33				5000	840130	13	A04	F1	5654	N02	F1	5654	B03	A2	5654
					33				5000	840130	13	P07	F1	5654	N05	F1	5654	B06	A2	5654

get applied somewhere. This, naturally, meant that parts inventories needed to be accurate and remain that way. The production floor would have to be cleaned up and the stockrooms would have to exercise great discipline in disbursements and receipts. Inventory counts and cycle counts would be very important for keeping up accuracy.

3. Bills of material could be changed in an MRP system from the "similar-to" bills provided by the home-grown system to "same-as-except" bills. An MRP system could make it easy to generate formal bills of material without having to develop new engineering drawings or other formal documents. The MRP system would also insist that an order have its own bill of materials before it could be released by the system. This would eliminate much confusion.

4. An MRP system would provide a means of tracking actual times and costs and not simply standards. Thus, under an MRP system, one would know for any work center exactly how much it made during any period of time. Such accounting would be a means by which the real capacities of departments could be kept up-to-date. This, in turn, could lead to the generation of useful shop start dates for orders.

5. With the implementation of an MRP system, the evaluation of managers within the factory would change from a mix of on-time delivery performance and the quantity of net allowed hours earned to a system that simply valued

Notes to Exhibit 2—Stock Order Follow Report

This is the Stock Order Follow Report that is issued to various using departments. In this case, the using department carries the number 6. Only a selection of a half dozen parts or assemblies are copied here. The column headings refer to the following:

On hand: The number of pieces available (on hand)

Unapld issues: Unapplied Issues. The number of stockroom issues of the part that have been released as work-in-process inventory but not tied to particular customer orders.

CL: Item class. 8 = item in stock and unapplied; 4 = item in stock and issued to a customer order; 7 = flow item; 9 = reference item (an organizer item for a department).

Ident no: Identification number for the part or assembly. Could be a blueprint drawing number. Same as Part number in Exhibit 1.

Dash: Current shop order number

Gross requirements, OD & 1st: (Overdue and first week), 2nd & 3rd (second and third weeks), Future (the next 9 weeks)—The demands for the part or assembly, by time period, accounted for by orders other than the current one.

Order qty: The quantity of the current shop order.

Due date: Scheduled due date for the order to where it goes next

On CIS: Number of days on Controlled Interval Status (i.e., released to manufacturing)

The next group of three column headings (PAY PT, DEPT, PCS DUE) are repeated 2 more times as headings. Information under them refer to successive operations for this order. Multiple lines can be included if the successor operations are more than three.

Pay PT: Pay Point. Refers to the accounting code for labor and/or materials in the department against which this order is going to claim time or materials.

Dept: The department where the operation is to be performed

PCS due: Pieces due. The open balance for that operation. If the Pieces due number is less than the Order Quantity some transaction (e.g., yesterday's end-of-day, a partial run) has already been charged against the order. If the two are equal, no transactions have been input. If the pieces due exceeds the order quantity, there is an overrun.

production to schedule. An MRP system would not keep track of net allowed hours and would thus eliminate this tendency for over-runs and the corollary desire to have significant queues of parts in front of each machine.

6. An MRP system held promise for eliminating, if only gradually, the informal system that had sprung up. An MRP system would provide a single data base that could be used by all elements of the factory to indicate actual orders and what the true priorities for any product were. The fabrication area would not be so isolated—it could see farther than before—and thus adjust to what was needed well in advance. Of course, if a capacity requirements planning module were incorporated into the MRP system, the informal system would have even less need to exist. With capacity requirements planning capability, the master production schedule, as finally adopted and frozen, would be more likely to be feasible for the specific product mix contemplated for the factory. This would be particularly useful to the accessories portion of manufacturing that suffered more than meters from mismatches of actual capacity and planned load.

7. An MRP system would provide a clear way for engineering change orders to show their effective dates. This would reduce the confusion prevailing for department supervisors.

8. An MRP system would probably force a change in the management structure at the plant. At present, the production planning function resided within the marketing operation, while purchasing and inventory control reported through a materials department manager to the production manager. With an MRP system, it was likely that production planning would report to the same materials manager as purchasing and inventory control. It was also likely that the materials manager would be at the same level as the marketing and manufacturing managers, reporting directly to the plant manager.

Advantages Foregone by Removing the Home-Grown Computer System

If an MRP system were adopted, some of the special features of the home-grown system would fall by the wayside. For example, some managers liked the distinction between stocked and non-stocked parts and the way the home-grown system was able to treat them differently. An MRP system makes everything a stocked part. Non-stocked parts might be attractive because of the plant's experimentation with just-in-time production methods. In such an innovation, having a stocked part might be a little bit messy and at odds with the just-in-time techniques being followed. Some people had suggested that a phantom stockroom be created so that the just-in-time techniques would not be hindered by the MRP system.

The home-grown system was also good at generating some of the reports for top management, rolling up costs for products and easily, sometimes automatically, cutting purchasing paper for common items that were purchased on the outside. It appeared likely that some of these aspects of the home-grown computer system would have to be sacrificed in a move toward MRP.

THE DECISION

Frank Klein had reviewed several MRP systems including MAPICS, COPICS, AMAPS, HPM3000, and Data 3. Given the Tulsa plant's requirements, the MAPICS choice seemed more complete and safer. Still, the installation was to cost $1.25 million in hardware, software, education, and personnel. This represented 1.3% of the plant's cost of goods sold. He knew that in order to justify such an expenditure, work in process would have to be reduced, the service level to the customers would have to be maintained or improved, the pricing of orders would have to reflect true costs more, and production planning would have to be facilitated. Exhibit 3 documents expected benefits and costs. It was now up to Frank Klein to set this decision in motion.

EXHIBIT 3
Information on the Company and Its MRP Decision

A. Some statistics

Sales volume	$95 million
Cost of goods sold	$52.25 million
Payroll costs (salaries, wages, benefits)	$25 million
Inventory (valued at standard cost)	$13.5 million
Inventory as percent of sales volume, by major product	
—meters	12%
—electronic accessories	30%
Due date performance (percent of sales shipped on time or by mutually renegotiated date)	80%

B. Cost to install the MAPICS MRP system

1. Hardware (2 system 38's, 117 CRTs) + software for MAPICS	$800,000
2. Consulting and user education	250,000
3. Initial systems support, other software, etc.	75,000
4. Additional personnel to assign to installation phase	150,000
TOTAL COST	$1,275,000

C. Estimated benefits expected from MRP system — **Benefits applicable over first 5 years**

1. Tangible, measureable benefits

i. Inventory reduction	$3 M reduction in level of inventory
ii. Reduction in hiring of personnel needed to run informal system, by 20%	$1 M spread over 5 years
iii. Reduction in obsolete and inactive inventory	$70,000 reduction in level of inventory

2. Intangible, Hard-to-Measure Benefits

i. Additional sales attributable to improved customer service and delivery	$0.5 M per year
ii. Premium freight reduction due to less expediting	$90,000 per year spent now on premium freight
iii. Improved equipment operation and maintenance due to improved scheduling	?
iv. Less unplanned overtime and thus improved direct labor productivity	Direct labor overtime for the last week on each month runs between 14-18% of labor expenditures

Parke-Davis Canada Inc.

In September 1980 Warner-Lambert Company approved Warner-Lambert Canada Inc.'s capital expenditure request for an AMAPS MRP package. This request had originated in Warner-Lambert Canada's Parke-Davis division located in Brockville, Ontario, 335 km east of Toronto. Now that 18 months of work in choosing and justifying an MRP system were over, Larry Zylstra, Plant Project Manager of Parke-Davis, had several concerns about implementing AMAPS and wondered what he should do about them. Warner-Lambert had chosen the Brockville plant as the first site in which to install the new MRP system, and Mr. Zylstra knew that the system would be watched with interest. Ward Hagan, Chairman of the Board and Chief Executive Officer of Warner-Lambert, had advised all Warner-Lambert affiliates world-wide that they were not to look at commercial MRP packages nor to develop their own until they had looked at the AMAPS package purchased by Warner-Lambert Canada.

WARNER-LAMBERT CANADA INC.

Parke-Davis Canada Inc. (Parke-Davis) was a division of Warner-Lambert Canada Inc. (Warner-Lambert Canada) which also had five other divisions: Adams Brands Canada Inc. (Adams); Personal Products; Diagnostic Reagents; Capsugel; and Schick Canada Inc. (Schick). The Schick production plant was scheduled to close in June 1981. Each division had different products, production processes, inventory controls and data processing procedures as a result of their separate development before acquisition by Warner-Lambert. Each operated autonomously; communication among them was hindered by different product lines and geographic separation. Exhibit 1 shows a partial organization chart.

Warner-Lambert Canada was itself a subsidiary of the American multinational Warner-Lambert that had many divisions and affiliates, and a varied product line in many businesses including pharmaceuticals, confectionery, sunglasses, contact lenses, and scientific and medical instruments. Warner-Lambert set goals and

Copyright © 1982, The University of Western Ontario.

Case material from the University of Western Ontario School of Business Administration is prepared as a basis of classroom discussion. This case was written by John Haywood-Farmer with the assistance of Elizabeth Martin.

All monetary figures in this case are given in Canadian currency unless otherwise stated. Where appropriate, a conversion factor of Cdn$1.17 = US$1.00 has been used.

EXHIBIT 1
Warner-Lambert Canada Inc.—Partial Organizational Chart

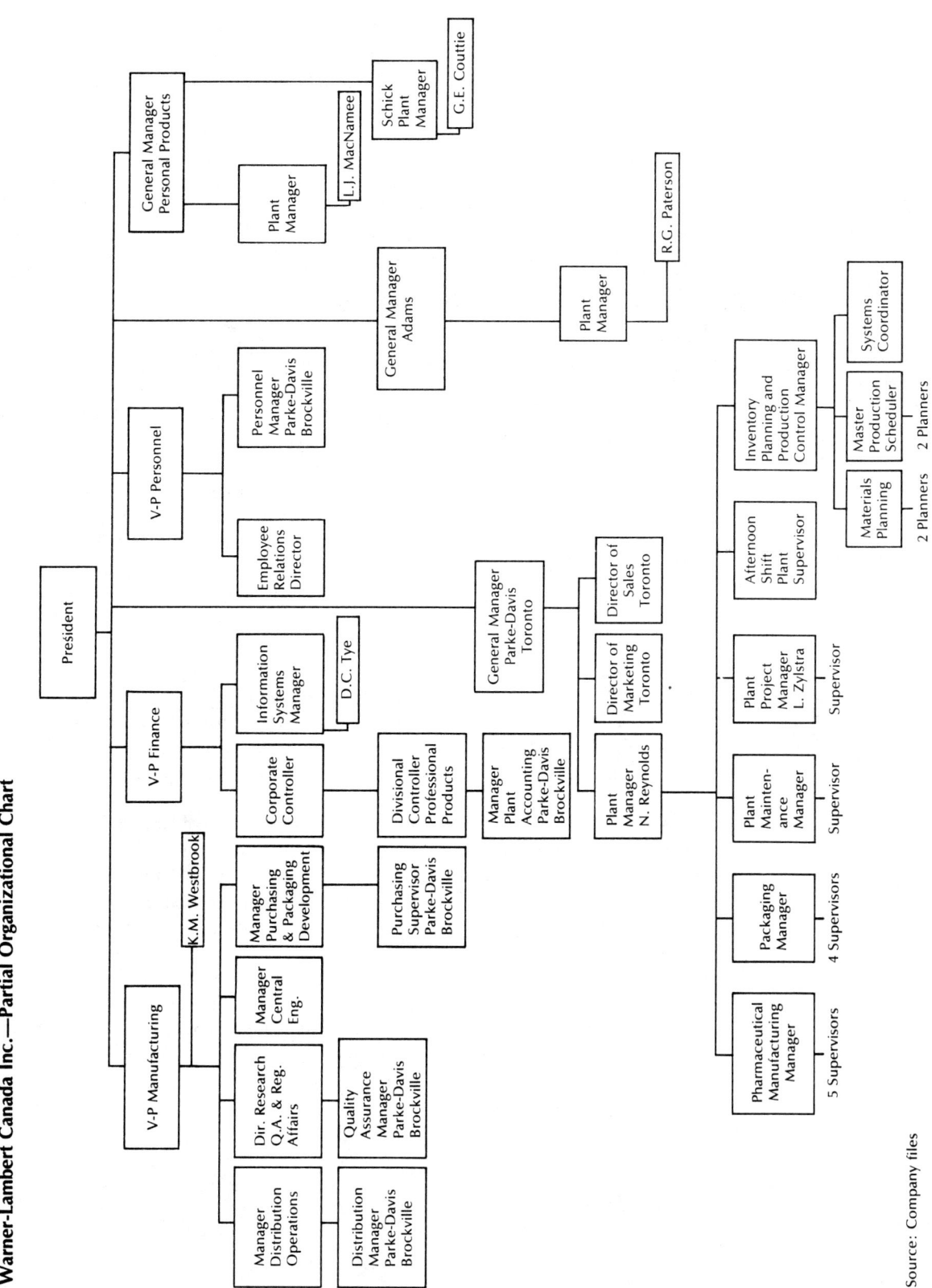

Source: Company files

policies which were followed by Warner-Lambert affiliates in each of the 140 countries in which the company operated.

Major company goals were to grow in sales and earnings world-wide through acquisition, while minimizing the disruption to its employees.

In 1979 Warner-Lambert sales were US$3,217 million. Warner-Lambert Canada's divisional sales were: Adams, $69.1 million; Parke-Davis, $35.2 million; Personal Products, $13.1 million; Schick, $5.9 million; Diagnostic Reagents, $5.7 million; and Capsugel, $0.8 million.

THE PRODUCTION PROCESS AT PARKE-DAVIS

Parke-Davis was responsible for all of Warner-Lambert Canada's pharmaceutical operations from process development through to final sale. The division used about 350 types of chemical raw materials and 800 types of packaging supplies in its production of over 160 different products (about 350 line items) which included vitamins, cough and cold preparations, anti-convulsants, oral contraceptives, and laxatives. Most of the raw materials were used in a number of products.

Parke-Davis' production process involved the mixing of chemicals in bulk lots of liquids, powders, and ointments, and subsequent packaging in small containers as finished units. Management considered two important products to be typical of the production process. Dilantin[1], an anti-epileptic prescription drug sold in two sizes and three forms, and accounting for about 5% of Parke-Davis' sales, was a member of the anti-convulsant group. Benylin[1], which was produced in seven forms and four sizes and made up 15% of sales, was a member of the seasonal cough and cold product group and was sold over the counter. The processes by which the two products were made are described below.

It usually took six to seven weeks to manufacture a product. About 60% of this time was spent wating for the results of laboratory tests or in manufacturing or packaging queues. Quality control also had some queues. About 50 production orders were started each week.

The manufacturing process began with the receipt of raw materials, at which time a sample was taken and checked for identity, purity, and potency. This check usually took about one week (up to four to five weeks for vitamins), during which the material was held in quarantine. When the material was approved, it was moved to the approved raw materials storage area. When production control issued a manufacturing work order, storage room personnel assembled kits of material to make the required batch. This process involved weighing the materials in a purified atmosphere to an accuracy of $\pm$ 0.1% of the specified weight. Weights of up to 6,000 kg were sometimes required. The kits were checked against the material checklist and stored by work order number in wire baskets in a separate room. Some of the very large amounts would be left in the raw materials storage area until production began.

---

[1]Dilantin and Benylin are registered tradenames of Parke-Davis and Company. Parke-Davis Canada is an authorized user of these tradenames.

Dilantin

Dilantin was produced in a two-step process. The five ingredients (one active ingredient, one lubricant, one excipient to give the product the desired bulk or volume, one filler, and one lubricant/filler) were weighed and then sifted. Correct particle sizing had a major impact on the product flow characteristics and evenness of mixing. The ingredients were then vacuum-loaded into a blender where they were mixed. A sample of the resulting powder mixture was then taken for testing and the rest stored in a bulk container. The entire sifting and blending process for a batch of about 500 kg of Dilantin bulk took about 8 hours plus raw material weighing time.

After the laboratory tests for chemical content, and yield reconciliation were completed (about three days) and the bulk approved for filling, the material was placed in about 2.2 million colour-coded gelatin capsules. The capsules were made by Capsugel, another Warner-Lambert Canada division located in Parke-Davis' plant. During the encapsulation process, samples of filled capsules were taken. The laboratory checked the samples to ensure that the weight of the encapsulated material was within acceptable limits. This test took about 0.5 hours. Encapsulation was an automatic process that took about four days to complete (at two shifts per day) for a batch of this size.

Following laboratory approval, the filled capsules were placed on a moving belt in a separate room where two separate operators checked each one visually for split casings, rough cuts, punched ends, and empty capsules, and separated the 1–2% defective capsules. This inspection took about one week for a batch.

The final step in the manufacturing process was an analysis of samples representative of the whole batch for weight variation, chemical identity, purity, and potency. The tests normally took three to four days to schedule and complete, but could be done in two days if advance notice were given.

When the laboratory had reviewed the manufacturing documentation and analytical data, the batch was approved for packaging and the bulk capsules were transferred from the manufacturing department to the packaging department. Plastic bottles were blown out with purified air to remove dust and other particles and placed on a moving line. The capsules were placed in a hopper which fed into a filling machine equipped with a disc with 2,000 holes in it. Each hole took one capsule. One of the three packaging operators checked to make sure each hole was filled. The disc was rotated, allowing the capsules to drop into two bottles, 1,000 in each. A piece of cotton wool was placed in the top of each bottle and the bottles were then capped, labelled, put in trays of six bottles, and wrapped. The labelling machine had a plate unique for each product which was matched optically with a small hole in a unique location in each label. This procedure provided on-line label verification.

A batch of Dilantin capsules took about seven to eight hours to package. Two bottles per hour were checked for proper capsule number and one bottle per thousand for chemical identity. Losses in blending, quality checks, and defectives removed during the processes reduced the original number of capsules to about 2.0 million.

Following completion of the packaging and approval from the laboratory, the packaged Dilantin was transferred to the finished goods storeroom. About 60 such batches were run per year.

Benylin

Benylin was composed of about 15 ingredients including two or three active ones, flavours, colouring materials, sweeteners, other excipients, and water. The manufacturing process began with the weighing of the ingredients. Several of them were then mixed in a processing tank and the resulting solution filtered into another processing tank that could be heated or cooled. Sugars were then added and the mixture heated for about nine hours to ensure dissolution. After the sugars had dissolved, the solution was cooled and alcohol was added. The 10,000 l. batch was then transferred to a storage tank where the final ingredient, colouring matter, was added. The above steps took about two days.

From the storage tank a sample was taken, analysed for specific gravity, evaluated for physical characteristics such as appearance, odour, and taste, and the ingredients reconciled against the job ticket. Following approval by the laboratory, the bulk Benylin was released to the packaging department.

The Benylin was pumped to the packaging department through stainless steel and pyrex pipes into a filling machine when the packaging operation began. The filling machine had a stream of empty, air-blown bottles fed into it. The bottles were automatically filled, capped, and labelled. Each label had a small identifying hole like the Dilantin labels. Each bottle was then weighed on a device set at the expected weight of the contents, bottle, cap, and label. Light bottles were rejected. The accepted bottles were then boxed, cartoned, palletized, and transported to the finished goods warehouse.

The time required for the filling operation depended on bottle size. The line operated at about 102 bottles per minute; the bottles were in 100 ml, 250 ml, 350 ml and 2 l. sizes. The filling operations employed four to five people on a one-shift basis. About 40 batches of Benylin were made per year.

Most of Parke-Davis' equipment handled several products although some were dedicated to only one. Nevertheless, all equipment, rooms, pipes, etc., were thoroughly cleaned following the processing of a batch of material. Cleaning took several hours.

Accompanying each batch of materials was a formula card which listed the ingredients and the steps in the manufacturing process. As each step was completed, operators and their supervisors were required to sign the card to acknowledge that they had carried out the instructions properly.

The plant employed about 300 people. There were small second and occasionally third shifts in some departments.

FORECASTING

The company based its production plans on the demand forecasts produced by brand managers and amended by senior Warner-Lambert Canada financial executives. The brand managers generated forecasts for the next calendar year in three stages with three levels of refinement: a gross annual forecast by product group (or even more aggregated) in July or August; a quarterly forecast by line item in September or October; and a monthly line item forecast in December. The forecasts were based on experience rather than on statistical methods. As the year progressed, brand managers updated their forecasts by producing a rolling forecast for 15 months on a monthly or quarterly basis, depending on the product and with a lead time of at least a month. In addition, unexpected demand changes led to requests by brand managers for last-minute changes to production schedules for two to three line items per week. Turnover among brand managers was fairly high.

Warner-Lambert had considerable sales between affiliates (called Q-9 sales); indeed, the company had a policy of purchasing internally wherever possible, even in the case of products without patent protection. To facilitate such activity, a series of 18-month rolling quarterly forecasts for Q-9 sales was maintained, about half of which was considered firm. Parke-Davis had sales to other affiliates of $109 thousand and bought $2.1 million from other affiliates in 1979. Interdivisional sales within Warner-Lambert Canada were very small.

PRODUCTION PLANNING AT PARKE-DAVIS

Because of regulations of the Health Protection Branch of the federal government, Parke-Davis maintained extremely accurate inventory records of its chemicals. All ingredients were costed to individual work orders and lot numbers were traceable, even on the final product, so that the source could be identified if quality problems arose. Packaging supplies, however, were not highly controlled; the book entries were not made until one to two days or more after a packaging order was issued and completed, but before final quality approval. There was a discrepancy between inventory actually on-hand and available and that listed in the records as being on-hand and available. This situation arose because the packaging inventory records did not account for floor stock already deducted and used but not yet recorded by production planning.

Upon receipt of the annual forecast in October, production planners prepared production plans for each product for the year based on the forecast, on-hand inventory, safety stock levels, standard batch sizes, and other products to be made in conjunction with it. Production plans were firmed six to seven weeks before manufacture was to begin. The batch sizes were based on EOQ's adjusted by equipment size, and were updated irregularly by manufacturing in conjunction with production planning. Based on the production plan and a written list of ingredients (formula card) for each product, materials planners prepared a materials plan, made purchase decisions, and issued purchase requisitions. Purchase quantities were based on an ABC classification system (see Exhibit 2). The production and materials plans were prepared manually and required a lot of clerical work. Clerical procedures were well documented. One person spent at least three hours per day just keeping track of inventory. The plans were adjusted daily. The volume of work required in this procedure, the frequency of adjustments, and human errors meant that the plans were almost never completely up-to-date. This

EXHIBIT 2
Material Classification System

Annual value	Items	Portion total value	Class	Order[1,2,3]
A. Raw materials				
>$10,000	67	89%	A	2
$1,000-$10,000	112	10	B	4
<$1,000	165	1	C	12
B. Packaging materials				
>$8,000	107	66	A	2[4]
$2,000-$8,000	211	25	B	4
$1,000-$2,000	127	5	C	8
<$1,000	395	4	D	12

Source: Company files.
[1]The maximum number of months supply to requisition at a time.
[2]All items except floor stock items to arrive two weeks before expected use.
[3]Floor stock items, such as sugar, mineral oil and glucose, to be requisitioned in full truckloads and to arrive one to two days before expected use.
[4]For labels order 12 months supply for annual requirements less than 20,000 labels and a minimum of 20,000 labels for larger requirements.

fact severely restricted management's ability to control inventory and production cycle times, and to reschedule rapidly.

The planning and control system was an attempt to do a manual MRP. Inventories of raw materials were over 98% accurate and packaging over 90%. About 20% of the time production plans were infeasible, often because materials were either not on hand or unavailable on time. Requests by brand managers for changes were the major cause of these problems.

Six to eight weeks before the item was required as approved finished stock, production planners obtained a formula card from quality control and prepared a packaging order to tell the packaging department what product would be manufactured and what size of package it would require. The formula card was sent to the manufacturing department where the materials were then dispensed. The manufacturing department informed packaging, inventory control, and accounting what had been dispensed and what month manufacture would take place. Inventory control then calculated a product expiry date, put it and the manufacturing date on the packaging order, and then sent the order to the packaging department where the packaging operation was scheduled and labels prepared.

Once the manufacturing department completed the production of the product, it reported the product yield to inventory control and accounting. Inventory control informed packaging that the batch was ready to package (and what the yield had been if it was abnormally low) after it received approval to package from quality control. The packaging department removed the bulk packaging materials from the packaging store room and informed inventory control and accounting. After the packaging operation had been completed, packaging reported the completion and the yield to inventory control, accounting, and distribution. Distribution maintained computer files of finished goods inventory which it updated upon receipt of the packaging report. The final report was the final approval from quality control which was sent to inventory control, distribution, and accounting.

Production planning was responsible for getting orders started on time but once started, orders were not followed closely because it was difficult to keep track of them after they had been released to manufacturing. Attention was drawn to delayed orders only when the finished goods inventory became low enough to affect the ability to service customers. When this happened, production planners examined the orders being processed and expedited the critical ones. About 10–15 orders per week were expedited. However, orders that became less critical were not de-expedited because there was no way to identify them.

The situation was made worse by the independent decisions of production planning, manufacturing, packaging, and quality control. Each department set its own priorities and schedules based on its own convenience and operating efficiency. As a result, order completion time was not easily predictable and buffer inventories tended to build up. Formal meetings between managers of the four departments had been held daily since 1979, but were infrequent prior to that.

The various sources of uncertainty (requests for last-minute changes, inventory inaccuracy, slow response, lack of knowledge of production orders) resulted in orders frequently being completed late. Mr. Zylstra estimated that of the orders, 40% were completed on time, 30% were completed one to five days late, 20% were completed six to ten days late, and 10% were completed 11 to 30 days late. This last category usually consisted of orders which were held up because of problems in production and/or quality control. Such problems could occur at any stage in raw materials receipt and handling, manufacturing, packaging, quality control, or documentation.

In 1979 Parke-Davis had inventories of: raw materials, $0.4 million; finishing supplies, $0.9 million; work-in-process, $1.9 million; and finished goods, $4.8 million. The inventories fluctuated somewhat over the year, reflecting the seasonal nature of many Parke-Davis products and a policy within Warner-Lambert Canada of reducing inventory at year end (November 30). During 1980 inventories reached $9.2 million. Work-in-process varied between 24% and 32% and finished goods 49% and 60% of the total. Despite the high portion of finished goods, poor forecasts and expediting problems had caused stockouts of some items.

Warner-Lambert Canada had had a centralized management information system (MIS) group at the Toronto head office since 1978 to achieve commonality between divisions and get everyone thinking along the same lines. Prior to 1976, Parke-Davis had controlled its own data processing. Parke-Davis plant management felt that the consolidation had resulted in poorer service for the Brockville plant.

Warner-Lambert Canada used inventory turnover as an important evaluative tool. It was calculated as cost of sales divided by the average ending inventory of the November, February, May, August, and November quarters. For Parke-Davis in 1979 the cost of sales had been $18 million, made up of purchases ($11 million), labour ($2 million), and overhead ($5 million), giving an inventory turn of 2.07.

The value had ranged from 2 to 2.25 in recent years and was projected to be 2.2 in 1980. Company officials believed that Parke-Davis' major competitors had inventory turns of 2.25 to 3.5.

PRESSURE FOR AN MRP SYSTEM

In 1975, following a period of reduced profitability, Warner-Lambert had instructed its affiliates to reduce their inventory investments so as to improve profitability and to generate funds for additional acquisitions. Larry Zylstra had been at Parke-Davis for 5.5 years when, in 1975, he was promoted to manager of inventory and production planning and given responsibility for improving inventory turnover at Brockville.

By improving the existing inventory planning system, Mr. Zylstra had realized a 10% annual improvement in inventory turnover up to 1978. These improvements had been achieved by getting better personnel, upgrading existing personnel, giving the planning personnel more responsibility in decision making, and applying known inventory management techniques. However, by 1978 Mr. Zylstra and other senior Parke-Davis managers felt that no additional significant inventory improvements could be made without a substantial investment in staff or general MRP-type manufacturing control software. Warner-Lambert continued to make further improvements part of yearly divisional and personal objectives.

Mr. Zylstra felt that he could not achieve his objectives without a significant improvement in:

1. the approximately six weeks required to generate a material plan once the production plan was established
2. the ability to make projections by answering "what if" questions
3. the ability to replan in reaction to changes in demand, material availability, etc.
4. the ability to highlight exceptions and to be able to predict conditions in the future

Accordingly, in September 1978, he submitted a capital expenditure request for a Hewlett-Packard 3000 minicomputer which he felt would handle material requirements calculations adequately using software to be developed by Parke-Davis personnel. Executives of Warner-Lambert Canada denied this request because the company had centralized data processing in Toronto and a policy of buying only IBM computer hardware. Mr. Zylstra's request, however, highlighted the necessity for Warner-Lambert Canada to take concrete steps to improve inventory control further.

In late 1978 and early 1979 Warner-Lambert engaged Booz-Allen and Hamilton Inc. to study its American operations and to recommend ways to improve inventory control. At the request of its American parent, Warner-Lambert Canada also engaged Booz-Allen and Hamilton as well as Gellman, Hayward and Partners Ltd. Computer Systems Consultants to analyse existing computer systems and to recommend an effective computer strategy for each division. Booz-Allen and Hamilton concluded that Warner-Lambert Canada could reduce its average inventory by $3.4 million from a forecasted 1980 level of $23.3 million (up from $22.3 million in 1979) by changing forecasting techniques ($1.3 million), inventory procedures ($1.0 million), material planning ($0.7 million), and shop floor controls ($0.4 million) in all divisions. Expected savings by division were: Adams, $1.4 million; Parke-Davis, $0.8 million; Schick, $0.4 million; and Personal Products, $0.8 million. Gellman, Hayward and Partners suggested that a suitable system would cost about $4,500 per month.

THE SOFTWARE EVALUATION TEAM

In May 1979 Warner-Lambert Canada created the Software Evaluation Team to determine how Warner-Lambert Canada should acquire MRP capability to satisfy each of its three continuing manufacturing sites. (At this time no decision had been made to acquire an MRP system.) The team was composed of:

Mr. K.M. Westbrook	Inventory Manager, Head Office (Project Leader)
Mr. G.E. Couttie	Industrial Engineer, Schick
Mrs. L.J. McNamee	Production Control Manager, Personal Products
Mr. R.G. Paterson	Material Control Manager, Adams
Mr. D.C. Tye	Systems Manager, Manufacturing, MIS, Head Office
Mr. G.L. Zylstra	Plant Project Manager, Parke-Davis

The team investigated three possibilities: (1) adopting existing Warner-Lambert programs, (2) developing software in-house, and (3) purchasing a commercial package. The team concluded that the computer-based systems in Warner-Lambert affiliates in France, the United Kingdom, and New Jersey were haphazardly developed and insufficiently integrated to be of use. The team also ruled out in-house development because it would take too long and would require the hiring of a large number of programmers for a relatively short time. Warner-Lambert had a practice of maintaining a stable workforce.

The team members then focused on searching for a commercial MRP software package. They wanted a package that could use Warner-Lambert Canada's IBM 370/148 mainframe computer and DL/1 data base manager, and that would deal adequately with the features of each of Warner-Lambert Canada's divisions. Despite the differences between its divisions, Warner-Lambert Canada considered common software desirable to reduce costs, to achieve as much commonality as possible in data files, to allow units to learn from each other, and to allow easier communication between operating units and centralized functions (see Exhibit 1).

The team developed a checklist of selection criteria (Exhibit 3) which was a composite of the requirements of each division and the head office and represented an unattainable ideal system. During their study the team members attended conferences and seminars, talked to system vendors, studied written material, and contacted numerous companies using or evaluating MRP systems. They identified about 150 available packages, only about 12 of which were fully integrated, and finally selected a short list of eight.

The team members recognized that all MRP packages had a common structure and, consequently, that calculations were generated in the same way. They rec-

EXHIBIT 3
Manufacturing Systems Software Evaluations Consolidated Checklist

These listings are in no particular order.

General requirements/Questions
  i) System must be IBM 370/148 and DL/1 compatible
  ii) Must be able to customize four ways and use from remote locations
  iii) Cost?
  iv) What training and education services are offered?
  v) What ongoing service is provided and from where?
  vi) How long to install and when available?
  vii) Names of successful pharmaceutical/confectionery users must be provided

Modules required
Terminology may differ from package to package and some modules may be combined in some packages.
  i) Purchasing
  ii) Forecasting
  iii) Production Planning/Master Scheduling
  iv) MRP
  v) Inventory Control
  vi) Capacity Planning
  vii) Shop Floor Control
  viii) Bill of Materials

Requirements by module
  i) *Purchasing*
    a) Linked to MRP, Master Schedule and Inventory Control
    b) Generates orders
    c) Monitors lead time
    d) Monitors vendor performance
    e) Records receipts, reports daily
    f) Tracks overdue orders, reports daily
    g) Reports weekly on pending receipts
    h) Valuation of orders and receipts
    i) Link to Cost System/or Purchase Price Variance
    j) Separate sorts for Purchasing and Inventory Control departments
    k) Purchasing and Inventory Unit of Measure conversion
    l) Change order capability
    m) Contract Purchase Order capability
    n) Partial receipt capability
    o) Projection of value of receipts and purchase price variance
    p) Min/Max and economic order quantity
  ii) *Forecasting*
    a) Generate forecasts from history as marketing tool
    b) Track actual *vs.* forecast
    c) Calculate mean absolute deviations
    d) Manual over-ride into MPS
    e) Signal when outside set parameter
  iii) *Production Planning/Master Scheduling*
    a) Capability to split bulk batches between different package sizes
    b) Buckets as per MRP
    c) Discrete lot sizes
    d) Lead time offset

EXHIBIT 3, cont'd

Requirements by module—cont'd

iv) *MRP*
   a) Capable of regenerative and net change (Brockville)
   b) Run weekly
   c) Closed loop, i.e., all materials, work-in-process, etc., considered
   d) Output grouped by family
   e) Multiple level explosion with manual override facility at bulk level
   f) Lead time offset
   g) Pegging
   h) Bucketless or—min. weekly for 3 months) 15 months
      —min. monthly for 15 months)
   i) Material kitting/availability/trial allocation/simulation
   j) Valuation of explosions
   k) Lot sizing
   l) Link to all other modules
   m) "What if" feature

v) *Inventory Control*
   a) Link to Purchasing and MRP
   b) Includes all inventory except finished goods
   c) On-line enquiry as minimum
   d) Records by lot number
   e) Lot number reconciliation
   f) Hard copy history
   g) Multiple location buckets
   h) Multiple inventory buckets, e.g., quarantine, available, committed, etc.
   i) Shortage reports by supply and by product
   j) Pegging
   k) Cycle counts
   l) Valuation
   m) Transaction records
   n) Pre-allocation to Rx by lot number
   o) Grouping by product capability
   p) ABC analyses

vi) *Capacity Planning*

vii) *Shop Floor Control*
   a) Cycle time monitoring *vs.* standard
   b) Daily reports by work step/cost centre, showing current, next and queued jobs
   c) Work order tracking
   d) Automatic and manual release of orders
   e) Past due report
   f) Input on-line
   g) Priorities by work centre
   h) Work centre input/output analysis *vs.* standard
   i) Link to payroll

viii) *Bill of Materials*
   a) Field sizes, descriptive and quantitative?
   b) Print Rx cards?
   c) How engineering changes handled?
   d) Include non-materials
   e) Routings if current DL/1 not sufficient

Source: Company files.

ognized that Parke-Davis' requirements, unique in the process industries, would necessitate changes in any commercial package to include the ability to:
1. trace and control products by lot number
2. keep inventory records in fractional units (Parke-Davis kept its records in kg but needed an accuracy of 1 g for some products)
3. integrate the data and activities at more than one plant
4. possibly increase the size of the data storage fields

None of the systems studied had a high rating when measured against the checklist and there were other important considerations, particularly involving potential vendor support. The team wanted a vendor that would provide good support services and, in particular, would not render the package obsolete by producing a new one. The team agreed that the best chance for successful implementation and most vendor support would come from the system requiring the least change. When all factors were considered, the team decided that the Advanced Manufacturing, Accounting and Production System (AMAPS) sold by COMSERV Corporation was the most attractive.

THE DECISION TO BUY

COMSERV was asked to issue a quote for an AMAPS system for Warner-Lambert Canada. Its proposal called for the purchase of seven of the nine modules of AMAPS, all on-line where available. It recommended that installation begin at Parke-Davis and take place over a period of 24 months in two phases with acceptance by Warner-Lambert Canada being mandatory after each phase. Exhibits 4 and 5 describe the associated costs and the proposed implementation schedule. The proposal offered a 33% discount off the software price to the first additional Warner-Lambert affiliate that adopted AMAPS and a 67% discount to subsequent affiliate adopters.

Following feedback from Warner-Lambert Canada, COMSERV issued a revised quote for a five module (two on-line) system (see Exhibit 4).

COMSERV recommended that Parke-Davis be the first site within Warner-Lambert Canada for installation because its inventory records were more accurate, its bills of material were better structured, its management was more enthusiastic and more oriented towards a disciplined approach, and its personnel had more computer expertise. Installation at the other divisions would begin within three months of the start at Parke-Davis and would follow a similar schedule.

Mr. Zylstra made his own estimates of the costs and benefits to the Brockville plant of acquiring three AMAPS modules (see Exhibit 4). The Software Evaluation Team, supported by the data in Exhibit 4 and similar data for the other divisions, recommended that Warner-Lambert Canada buy the three AMAPS modules and install them first at Parke-Davis. Warner-Lambert Canada accepted the proposal and forwarded it to Warner-Lambert. Warner-Lambert subsequently approved the purchase of five AMAPS modules, at the insistence of Mr. Hagan, and advised all affiliates to postpone any MRP development plans until AMAPS had had a chance to prove itself in Warner-Lambert Canada.

EXHIBIT 4
Cost and Benefit Estimates of AMAPS

	COMSERV Quote 1	COMSERV Quote 2	Larry Zylstra's estimate[1]
Costs			
Software			
Bill of materials	$52.65 thousand	$52.65 thousand	$18.43 thousand
Material control	64.35	64.35	22.52
Material requirements planning	35.10	35.10	12.29
Process and routing	52.65	35.10[2]	—
Master production scheduling	64.35	46.80[2]	—
Shop floor control	64.35[2]	—	—
Capacity requirements planning	35.10[2]	—	—
Total	368.55	234.00	53.24
Less 20% discount	(73.71)	(46.80)	—
Total soft ware	294.84	187.20	53.24
Management services			
Definition review[3]	11.23	11.23	3.93
	2.81[2]		
Specification review[4]	9.36	—	3.28
Modifications[5]	24.57	—	11.88
Account manager[6]	91.96	91.96	32.19
	40.72[2]		
Installation[7]	22.70	22.70	7.94
	6.78[2]		
Education[8]	15.91	20.04	35.0
Consultation	146.72	103.19	70.0[9]
Total	372.76	249.12	164.22
In house costs			
Evaluation and visits			11.0
Temporary staffing requirements			40.0
Project team			122.0
Support staff			50.0
Total			223.0
GRAND TOTAL	667.60	436.32	370-440
Annual benefits			
25-50% inventory turnover improvement at 25% carrying cost[10]			393-665
5% saving on purchases			305
4-7% saving in direct and indirect labour			97-170
15-25% reduction in overtime premiums			3-6
25% reduction in obsolescence			50

Source: Company files.

[1]The COMSERV Quotes are for Warner-Lambert Canada as a whole, Mr. Zylstra's are for Parke-Davis only. Mr. Zylstra allocated some costs to Parke-Davis based on the division's share of total Warner-Lambert Canada inventory (35%).

[2]In the second phase of installation.

[3]The definition review's goal would be to ensure that AMAPS would meet all the user's needs. The end result would be an integrated system design which would provide the necessary information to solve problems and allow for future module integration.

[4]Once the conclusions resulting from the definition review had been approved by the user, the AMAPS documentation would be updated to reflect the changes made.

[5]These were the specific modifications required by Parke-Davis to allow for lot-number traceability and fractional on-hand inventory record keeping. The revised COMSERV quote assumes that the modification will be made at a later date.

[6]A COMSERV supplied manager responsible for leading the installation of AMAPS, developing and maintaining schedules of installation and client activities, coordination of all COMSERV resources relative to client needs, performing user education, identifying and solving implementation problems, and many other duties. Not a decision maker but a resource person and advisor.

[7]Included loading, testing and debugging the modules.

[8]Included attendance by Warner-Lambert Canada personnel at courses and seminars developed by COMSERV and other organizations as well as in house training.

[9]Considered to be optional.

[10]The saving was expected to come 55% from raw materials reductions and 45% from work-in-process reduction.

EXHIBIT 5
Implementation Schedule Proposed by COMSERV

General Project Plan

-MONTHS-

ACTIVITY	1	2	3	4	5	6	7	8	9	10	11	12	13	14	15	16	17	18	19	20	21	22	23	24
I. Client-Account manager—Technical manager familiarization	───																							
II. Project organization		────																						
III. Project review meetings																								
A. Project team/Account manager																								
B. CEO/Account manager	─ ─ ─ ─ ─ ─ ─ ─ ─ ─ ─ ─ ─ ─																							
C. Quarterly COMSERV/Client Steering committee review																								
D. Account manager status reports			‐					‐			‐				‐				‐		‐			‐
IV. Standard system installation																								
A. Technical manager preparatory visit				─																				
B. Installation schedule				───	─																			
V. Education																								
A. AMAPS overview				─																				
B. In-house training				─																				
C. Formal education schedule				─									─											
VI. Definition review																								
Bill of material system	x																							
Material control system		x																						
Material requirements planning			x																					
Process and routing system							x																	
Shop floor control system							x																	
Capacity requirements planning								x																
Master production scheduling									x															
VII. Specification review																								
Bill of material system						x																		
Material control system							x																	

VIII. Modification, coding testing
- Material requirements planning
- Process and routing system
- Shop floor control system
- Capacity requirements planning
- Master production scheduling

IX. Module installation
- Bill of material system
- Material control system
- Material requirements planning
- Process and routing system
- Shop floor control system
- Capacity requirements planning
- Master production scheduling

X. Pilot start-up
- Bill of material system
- Material control system
- Material requirements planning
- Process and routing system
- Shop floor control system
- Capacity requirements planning
- Master production scheduling

XI. Live start-up
- Bill of material system
- Material control system
- Material requirements planning
- Process and routing system
- Shop floor control system
- Capacity requirements planning
- Master-production scheduling

Source: Company files

EXHIBIT 6
The Organization AMAPS Modules and Data Files

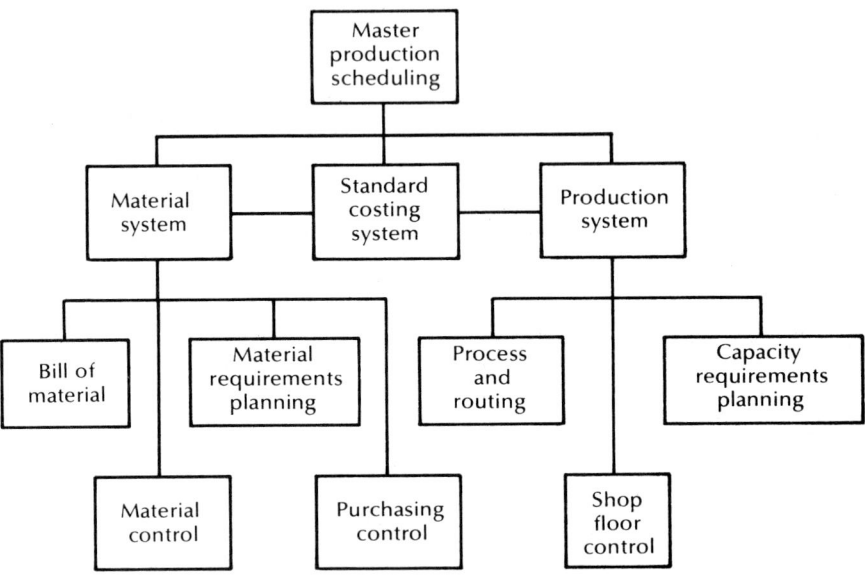

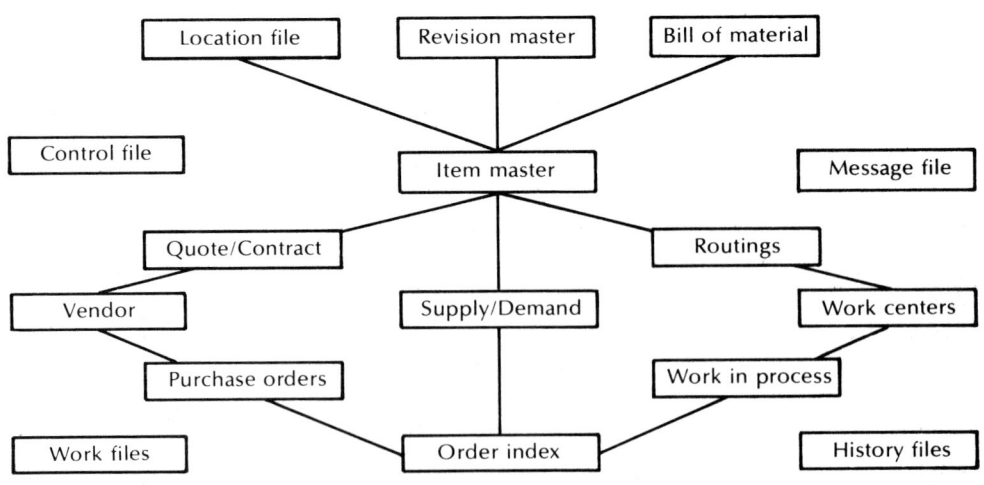

Source: Company files

The Software Evaluation Team chose the Master Production Scheduling System and the Purchasing Control System in addition to the three modules chosen by Mr. Zylstra (Exhibit 4). The decision was made on the basis of the module hierarchy (Exhibit 6) despite the fact that Parke-Davis preferred Process and Routing to Purchasing Control strongly favoured by Adams. Master Production Scheduling would give a rough cut at a capacity plan, whereas COMSERV advised that the Purchasing Control System would be required to get the lot traceability feature.

Upon approval of the AMAPS purchase, Warner-Lambert Canada established an eight-man steering committee composed of the three plant managers and head office representatives from manufacturing, inventory, finance, auditing, and information systems. The committee was to oversee the installation of the system in the three plants, resolve disputes between the plants, and approve plant requests for extra funds or staff. A five-man project team was appointed in each plant composed of a project leader, the plant manager, and representatives from production planning, finance/accounting, and one other area. Mr. Zylstra was the project leader in Brockville. His duties included setting task lists and timetables, critical path scheduling, and educating Parke-Davis personnel.

AMAPS

COMSERV Corporation was headquartered in Minneapolis, Minnesota with regional offices in Pennsylvania, Georgia, Illinois, California (2), Texas, and Massachusetts. It employed about 200 people, had annual sales of software and services totalling about $6.5 million, and was growing rapidly. AMAPS was about five years old and had about 100 users.

AMAPS consisted of numerous data files and program modules which were completely integrated (see Exhibit 6). Its file organization was compatible with DL/1 and other data base managers. The data base approach minimized file duplication and thus saved on data entry, processing, and storage. It was a dynamic information system that enabled managers simultaneously to plan, schedule, allocate resources, control, and account for activities. The enhanced ability to carry out these functions increased managerial knowledge, control and performance, and allowed a reduction in inventory. The system operated on an exception basis so that when conditions varied from a plan pre-established by the user, management would be alerted by an appropriate report. Examples might include late receipts from suppliers, materials not picked on time, production orders finished late, and orders not firmed on time. Exception reports kept report volume down and allowed easier identification of problems.

The package consisted of nine modules:
1. Bill of Materials System
2. Material Control System
3. Material Requirements Planning System
4. Process and Routing System
5. Master Production Scheduling System
6. Shop Floor Control System

7. Capacity Requirements Planning System
8. Purchasing Control System
9. Standard Costing System

The Material Requirements Planning and Capacity Requirements Planning modules were available only in batch mode but the others were available in either batch or on-line mode. Additional descriptions of each module's functions are given in Exhibit 7. The modules sold for $35,000–$47,000 each, plus a $17,500 premium per module for on-line access. A 20% discount on the total software price was offered if five or more modules were purchased. The modifications to AMAPS required by Warner-Lambert Canada could be performed either by Warner-Lambert Canada or by COMSERV on a fixed-price basis. COMSERV was considering providing the modifications as options to the standard package rather than as individual changes. If it became an AMAPS user with a maintenance contract, Warner-Lambert Canada could obtain consultation services and new or updated modules that might be developed in the future. The ideas for such enhancements often resulted from the semi-annual meetings of AMAPS users. The AMAPS maintenance agreement had an annual cost of 10% of the current selling price of the modules purchased and was adjusted yearly.

EXHIBIT 7
Description of AMAPS Modules

1. **Bill of Materials System (BMS)**
   The function of BMS is to create, maintain and retrieve the product structure data base. It provides engineering, manufacturing, and accounting personnel with a single source of information to help:
   —design products, assemblies, and parts
   —determine manufacturing processes
   —generate material and labour requirements
   —issue material
   —develop item and product costs

2. **Material Control System (MCS)**
   MCS maintains extensive data base files of inventory status and material planning information. It exercises control by measuring events that occur against the pre-determined plan (master production schedule) as determined by the Material Requirements Planning System. Its goals are to reduce lead times, to improve on-time delivery, and to reduce operating costs by reducing inventory levels. To do so, MCS provides planners with timely information in a continuously changing environment. It allows planners to answer such questions as:
   —what materials are short
   —where is each order in the plant
   —when will each order be completed
   —which orders have been scrapped
   —when are operations out of control

   MCS is bucketless with an unlimited planning horizon and allows pegging. Its time-phased allocation feature allows redirection, if necessary, of components or subassemblies by identifying the specific requirement date of each detailed demand for an item. It also allows an ABC parts classification, order tracking and control, engineering change effectivity, automatic preparation of release and purchase orders, and, in conjunction with the Process and Routing System, calculation of manufacturing lead times based on order quantity. Finally, MCS identifies exceptions to the operating plan which require replanning by the Material Requirements Planning System.

EXHIBIT 7, cont'd

3. **Material Requirements Planning System (MRP)**

   Assuming accurate inventory and bill of material data and a valid master production schedule, MRP allows a projection of what will happen. MRP allows bucketless replanning on either a regenerative or a net change basis. It operates with BMS and MCS which control the necessary data files and direct the planning activities of MRP.

   Like MCS, MRP permits an unlimited planning horizon, pegging, calculation of manufacturing lead times based on order quantity, time-phased allocation, and engineering change effectivity. MRP permits the insertion of dampeners so that minor data changes will not trigger an update. These dampeners include ones based on order status, rescheduling, order quantity, and priority of exception conditions. MRP can be used to project inventory balances, to plan orders based on lot sizing rules, and to carry out a level-by-level explosion. Runs often take hours so on-line access is impractical.

4. **Process and Routing System (PRS)**

   PRS creates and maintains the data bases for controlling the implementation and execution of the manufacturing plan. The files describe the sequence of operations required to produce a part of assembly, the number of machines, labour grade and capacity of each work centre, and information on tooling, processes and routings. The PRS data base is used for scheduling, costing, capacity planning, work centre loading, inventory accounting, identifying exceptions to plan, measuring resource utilization, calculating inter-operation time, and calculating lead times.

5. **Master Production Scheduling System (MPS)**

   MPS provides the tools to create a feasible production plan and feed this plan to MRP. It maintains the master schedule and compares customer orders, the master schedule, the forecast and the production plan. MPS allows identification of overloaded points in the production system and integration of master schedule assemblies and independent service parts demand.

6. **Shop Floor Control System (SFC)**

   SFC implements and measures the effectiveness of the manufacturing plan at the shop floor level. It detects and reports exceptions to the plan and keeps managers posted on what is happening on the shop floor. This information can be used by managers to plan and schedule production operations, to pinpoint problem areas, and to improve efficiency. SFC also creates shop-floor documentation such as production orders, move/send tickets, inspection tickets, labour use tickets, machine use tickets, and setup tickets.

7. **Capacity Requirements Planning System (CRP)**

   CRP is a tool to support manufacturing planning. It projects the capability of the manufacturing facility to meet production needs on an infinite loading basis, i.e., without regard to available capacity. CRP provides the information necessary for managers to resolve the overloading problem created by this approach by scheduling, work centre, plant and equipment, master schedule lot sizes, or other changes. CRP allows determination of factory loading in the short, medium or long term at the discretion of the user. It also allows the load to be pro-rated to different time periods and to be identified by order. Runs often take hours so on-line access is impractical.

8. **Purchasing Control System (PCS)**

   PCS' goal is to allow acquisition of high quality products on time at the lowest possible cost by reducing paperwork and expediting so that managers have more time to manage. It links supply requisitions generated by MRP or MCS to contracts or purchase orders. The module helps identify orders that will be late and notifies buyers of critical follow-up points during the order life cycle. PCS accepts free form text so that qualitative factors can be dealt with. It aids in quality analysis of purchased goods and projects future cash needs. Finally, PCS allows an analysis of vendor and buyer performance regarding quality, delivery, price, and lead times.

9. **Standard Costing System (SCS)**

   Using data base files maintained by other modules, particularly BMS and PRS, SCS develops product costs. Users are allowed to over-ride the data files and enter labour, outside vendor, or system generated costs directly. SCS is flexible in the types of costs that are maintained, labour rates, overhead allocations, cost element identification, cost calculations, cost generation, and which components are included in the cost calculations. It allows cost analysis and budget re-calculation.

Sources: Company files and a COMSERV catalogue describing AMAPS.

PLANNING AND CONTROL WITH AMAPS

Mr. Zylstra felt that with AMAPS, the production process would not change, although there would be some changes in the ways information was handled and plans and schedules were prepared. The system would significantly reduce the flow of paper within and between departments and would allow much more rapid data file updating which would be done on-line from Brockville; however, report generation could be initiated only by MIS in Toronto. The exception reports would help planners and schedulers identify what had to be done that day. Although this would remove some discretion from managers, it would also free them from routine clerical tasks so they could devote more time to more important managerial duties. The system would thus enhance managers' abilities to do their tasks and enrich their jobs.

LARRY ZYLSTRA'S CONCERNS

Mr. Zylstra approached his new job with mixed feelings. His assessment had given him confidence that AMAPS would work well and that COMSERV would provide continuing good service. On the other hand, there were some things he was not so sure of.

Mr. Zylstra knew that at least some Parke-Davis departments would have to change their procedures. In packaging, for example, production floor requirements were usually filled with full cartons even if the number of items thus sent greatly exceeded demand. The MRP system would necessitate up to one extra person in packaging, either breaking bulk cartons or documenting returned items. The packaging department manager was more responsible for staffing levels than for inventory accuracy. To achieve the benefits projected from AMAPS, operating departments would have to coordinate their activities much more closely. In addition, brand managers would have to meet minimum lead times more often, and the accounting department would have to interact with AMAPS. Indeed, if AMAPS were successful, it was likely that the accounting department would use the Standard Costing System in the future. Information would have to be kept up-to-date and reports produced at the right time.

The problems associated with obtaining the required cooperation and coordination were compounded by the general feeling throughout Warner-Lambert Canada that Parke-Davis had its production in good order, and by Mr. Zylstra's staff position. He would have to rely heavily on other people for both information and implementation within operating departments. Errors in either would likely be attributed to the project team. Mr. Zylstra wondered what type of person it would take to do this job.

Mr. Zylstra also wondered how he should approach making actual production decisions with AMAPS. The most abrupt way would be simply to install the system and switch the whole factory over to AMAPS-based decisions on a certain day. Mr. Zylstra considered this "cold turkey" approach to be suicidal. An alternative would be to run the existing manual system in parallel with AMAPS for a while before switching over. A third alternative would be to run a test operation using artificial data to simulate the operation before basing actual production decisions on the MRP system. Both of these alternatives offered the additional option of using just part of the product line (but which part?) or all of it.

Finally, Mr. Zylstra was uncertain how performance in the installation should be measured, how frequently it should be measured, and how long it should take to achieve corporate goals. He had heard many anecdotal horror stories of MRP implementation failures. He hoped to be able to complete implementation at Parke-Davis within 18 months. With attention in Warner-Lambert focused on the Brockville plant and the benefits he had identified for AMAPS, Mr. Zylstra did not want to fail.

G.T. Conner Company, Inc.

Garry Conner angrily pushed the salesmen's reports to the back of his desk. As owner and president of G.T. Conner Company, he knew he could not avoid studying the salesmen's reports. But, for the moment, he needed to cool off in the brisk March air. Walking outside, he remembered that for two years, since early 1974, his salesmen had complained about increasing customer dissatisfaction with the company's parts and repair service. He needed to find the problem and solve it.

After sales, service had always been emphasized by the Conner Company, and Mr. Conner attributed much of his company's success to an efficient parts department and shop. However, rapid sales growth during the 1960s and early 1970s had overburdened these departments. (See Exhibit 1.) Company salesmen had recently reported customers complaining about the deteriorating quality of service they received. Particularly irritating to Mr. Conner was the increase in back orders for spare and repair parts. He felt he maintained an ample parts inventory, yet more and more frequently, a back ordered part would delay repair work or alienate a customer. The parts department manager, with 15 years of experience in ordering parts, was nearing retirement, and no one was qualified to replace him. Mr. Conner knew he must solve the dilemma of his parts inventory in order for his company to satisfy its existing customers and to continue to attract new ones.

THE INDUSTRY

The commercial turf equipment industry in the United States is almost completely dominated by two firms: Bryce (a subsidiary of Wentworth Industries) and Stevens. A third domestic firm, Hahn, is currently undergoing bankruptcy proceedings. Although there are several manufacturers of consumer lawnmowers, including Burton, Snapper and Simplicity, only Bryce and Stevens provide a full line of mowers, tractors and accessories to commercial customers. These customers included golf courses, airports, park departments and other facilities with large areas of tended grass.

This case was prepared by George L. Cornell, Jr., under the supervision of Professor Curtis J. Tompkins, Professor of Business Administration. Revised by Susan Overholt and Professor John L. Colley, Jr., 1976.

EXHIBIT 1
Comparative Income Statements

	1961	1966	1971	1972	1973	1974	1975
Income							
Net income from sales	1,023,232	1,450,418	2,320,411	2,449,958	2,557,902	2,665,974	2,753,534
Cost of sales							
Inventory-Beginning	68,433	115,998	234,449	248,059	311,541	245,276	432,668
Purchases	778,351	1,092,441	1,596,874	1,704,202	1,630,777	1,986,403	1,720,184
Total	846,784	1,208,439	1,831,323	1,952,261	1,942,318	2,231,679	2,152,852
Inventory-Ending	97,609	142,884	248,059	311,541	245,276	432,668	304,497
Cost of merchandise	749,175	1,065,555	1,583,264	1,640,720	1,697,042	1,799,011	1,848,355
General ship expense	4,291	6,787	11,728	16,972	14,382	16,947	16,317
Depreciation-Shop and carts	847	718	43,274*	68,286	67,384	51,981	2,738
Cost of sales	754,323	1,073,060	1,638,266	1,725,978	1,778,808	1,867,939	1,867,410
Gross profit	268,909	377,358	682,145	623,980	779,094	798,035	886,124
Selling expenses							
Selling salaries	72,016	105,776	173,273	180,202	192,184	191,608	213,188
Advertising	14,917	5,776	6,720	9,403	4,812	9,578	7,475
Sales promotion	13,640	12,293	30,290	29,629	26,618	34,766	35,235
Service & delivery	16,967	25,687	35,859	47,198	44,137	45,678	54,343
Depreciation-Service equip.	5,014	7,262	21,966	20,613	25,277	24,988	15,397
Richmond expenses	3,902	3,777	7,181	7,893	7,445	7,774	8,279
Wholesale	10,716	3,262					
Total selling expenses	137,172	163,833	275,289	294,938	300,473	314,392	333,917
Administration expenses							
Rentals	19,047	35,064	40,427	41,231	41,221	41,209	43,862
Admin. salaries	30,773	60,880	82,492	84,781	83,468	89,702	109,049
General office expense	6,494	13,630	18,455	22,277	27,225	24,791	29,245
Heat, light, power	2,633	5,695	7,547	8,246	9,101	9,643	11,001
Communications	3,378	7,748	11,104	13,099	13,896	12,777	13,175
Interest	1,403	4,736	11,293	17,545	20,455	21,458	17,567
Insurance	5,083	11,329	29,998	28,765	34,974	32,857	35,664
Taxes	7,124	12,287	28,280	38,872	35,907	45,510	37,837
Depreciation—furn. & fix.	778	1,340	2,223	2,270	2,625	2,672	407
Bad debts	7,479	5,625	4,500	7,500	7,500	7,500	11,250
Building repair & main.	764	2,153	4,304	5,828	10,993	6,628	6,843
Profit sharing contrib.	5,404	16,154	36,028	34,067	33,551	36,049	44,207
Total administration	90,360	176,641	276,651	304,481	320,916	330,796	360,107
Total expenses	227,532	340,474	551,940	599,419	621,389	645,188	694,024
Operating profit	41,377	36,884	130,204	124,561	157,705	152,847	192,100
Other income-net	1,240	6,280	15,625	17,583	23,491	40,200	38,477
Net income for period	42,617	43,164	145,830	142,144	181,196	193,047	230,577

*First year of golf cart sales.

Competition between Bryce and Stevens is intense, and product innovation very important in the fight for market share. Bryce first developed a riding greens-mower in the early sixties, and although Stevens developed a similar machine, it was three years late in marketing it. As a result, Bryce gained a significant part of Stevens' market share. More recently, Stevens had developed a riding trap rake and had won back part of its lost share.

Both Stevens and Bryce have a network of distributors and dealers. Bryce traditionally selects different dealers for its commercial line than for its consumer line. Most Stevens' dealers carry both its commercial and consumer line, and it is likely that commercial sales suffer as a result. The consumer line is high volume and requires minimal after-sales service.

In commercial turf equipment sales, after-sales service by the dealer is a necessity. Much of the equipment has to be rebuilt periodically by the dealer or distributor. Gangmowers, for example, need to have cutting blades sharpened, repositioned or replaced and their motors tuned at regular intervals. Repairs the customer could make himself depend upon efficient spare parts ordering by the dealer. The ability of a dealer to provide good service is reflected directly by his sales, because the competing lines of equipment differ only slightly in quality or price.

COMPANY HISTORY

In 1936, Steven Richardson, a golf course superintendent in Fairfax, Virginia, founded the S.G. Richardson Company, a one-man dealership housed in his garage, to sell Worthington gangmowers. Until that time, Worthington had relied entirely on its factory salesforce and had shipped all equipment directly to customers from its New Jersey plant. Mr. Richardson was able to expand his business rapidly, and by 1945, annual sales volume had reached $100,000. At that time, Richardson maintained two offices: the main office, in Bethesda, Maryland, with seven employees and a four-person sales office in Philadelphia.

In 1946, Bryce Manufacturing Company, one of the two leading turf equipment manufacturers, bought Worthington in order to broaden its product line. Bryce had established dealers in the Philadelphia area, but offered Mr. Richardson distribution rights for the commercial products in Virginia, Maryland and Washington, D.C. Mr. Richardson accepted the territory, then sold his company to his brother-in-law, Garry Conner, in May, 1946.

Under Mr. Conner's direction, the G.T. Conner Company (as it was renamed) increased sales and profits every year. Population growth in the Washington area, construction of new golf courses and the favorable economic environment during the late 1940s and 1950s spurred the demand for turf care products. Mr. Conner gradually added products of other manufacturers to his product base until, by 1960, the Conner Company provided a full product line and after-sale service to its commercial mower customers. From 1961 through 1967, the Conner Company ventured into the consumer mower market as a wholesale distributor for Bryce consumer lawnmowers. Although sales increased significantly, profits did not, and the wholesale line was dropped. Growth strategy was redirected toward better serving the commercial equipment customer, and earnings were reinvested to upgrade facilities, expand spare parts inventory, and provide financial security for the company. In 1966, the company moved from its cramped Bethesda office to a new building on a 3.5 acre lot in Gaithersburg. The company building contained a warehouse, shop parts department, showroom and offices.

Distribution rights for Carter golf carts in the Washington area were acquired in 1967. This addition proved much more profitable than the consumer lawnmower wholesaling, and, by 1975, golf cart sales and leases accounted for over $450,000 of total sales. In that year, gross sales were $2,896,772 resulting in net profits of $230,577, nearly 20% over the previous year. Corresponding balance sheets are shown in Exhibit 2. The business was handled by a staff of 37: seven salesmen, seven parts department personnel, three bookkeepers, two secretaries, nine mechanics, two truck drivers, five golf cart servicemen and two officers.

EXHIBIT 2
Comparative Balance Sheets

	1973	1974	1975
Assets			
Current			
Cash in bank	$ 116,946	$ 68,720	$ 172,048
Accounts receivable	389,384	267,043	238,142
Reserve for bad debts	(9,092)	(6,379)	(7,802)
Inventories	245,276	432,668	304,497
Prepaid insurance	8,469	9,429	10,030
Other prepaid items	1,202	1,202	
Total current assets	$ 752,185	$ 772,683	$ 716,915
Fixed			
Golf carts	$ 486,023	$ 536,220	$ 550,230
Furniture & fixtures	31,441	31,441	31,441
Machinery & equipment	20,717	20,717	35,775
Service equipment	98,037	114,563	102,827
Less reserve for depreciation	(343,232)	(409,042)	(402,628)
Total fixed assets	$ 292,986	$ 293,899	$ 317,645
Total other assets*	26,058	46,217	63,637
Total assets	$1,071,229	$1,112,799	$1,098,197
Liabilities and capital			
Current			
Accounts payable	$ 64,437	$ 40,324	$ 85,820
Notes payable—bank	245,896	199,630	3,394
Dividends payable	20,633	41,265	41,265
Accrued taxes payable	19,556	3,838	17,688
Other accrued items	79,799	86,450	88,838
Total current liabilities	$ 430,321	$ 371,507	$ 237,005
Capital			
Capital stock issued	$ 51,581	$ 51,581	$ 51,581
Earned surplus	495,105	589,327	689,711
Profit for period	94,222	100,384	119,900
Total capital	$ 640,908	$ 741,292	$ 861,192
Total capital and liabilities	$1,071,229	$1,112,799	$1,098,197

*Includes cash value life insurance, contra items and leasehold improvements.

THE CUSTOMERS

Mr. Conner estimated that, in the 30 years he had owned the distributorship, sales to golf courses had averaged 55% of total sales. Currently, that percentage was nearer 45%. The second largest groups, all government facilities, including regional parks and military installations, accounted for 25% of sales. Remaining sales were to schools, turf farms, airports, cemeteries, lawn maintenance firms and apartment complexes.

EXHIBIT 3
Breakdown of Annual Sales by Product Line

	'74-'75	%	'73-'74	%	'72-'73	%	'71-'72	%	'70-'71	%
Bryce equipment	746,750	26.6	770,216	28.3	785,940	30.3	819,144	32.9	747,269	31.3
Bryce parts	452,597	16.1	371,870	13.6	338,078	13.0	305,493	12.2	316,069	13.2
Kut-Kwik equip.	34,526	1.2	46,085	1.7	37,418	1.4	34,757	1.4	28,108	1.2
Kut-Kwik parts	29,025	1.0	25,584	.9	14,409	.6	13,567	.5	15,223	.6
West Point equip.	18,578	.6	10,602	.4	12,156	.5	19,757	.8	20,531	.9
West Point parts	9,140	.3	11,756	.4	7,411	.3	9,513	.4	12,070	.5
Carter	191,421	6.8	186,084	6.8	103,237	4.0	166,555	6.7	197,730	8.2
Repair parts	159,152	5.7	132,171	4.8	116,342	4.5	113,312	4.5	88,349	3.7
Repair labor	67,113	2.4	74,593	2.7	60,184	2.3	66,284	2.7	57,117	2.4
Cushman	110,650	3.9	144,962	5.3	141,100	5.4	102,071	4.1	66,693	2.8
John Bean	100,037	3.6	72,893	2.7	58,877	2.3	105,654	4.2	65,814	2.7
Misc. equipment	189,332	6.7	171,821	6.3	224,392	8.7	135,157	5.4	70,018	2.9
Bunton	14,585	.5	13,403	.5	19,076	.7	18,128	.7	16,680	.7
National	17,302	.6	,11,805	.4	23,335	.9	20,176	.8	23,071	1.0
Royer	16,256	.6	14,420	.5	22,102	.9	6,191	.2	23,317	1.0
Miscellaneous golf	64,518	2.3	70,046	2.6	63,292	2.4	64,169	2.6	67,811	2.8
Fert. & chem.	168,788	6.0	204,034	7.5	178,222	6.9	181,529	7.4	205,226	8.6
Massey	44,382	1.6	32,244	1.2	36,697	1.4	62,606	2.5	132,891	5.5
Giant vac	25,670	.9	33,075	1.2	29,896	1.2	6,103	.2		
Used equipment	17,548	.6	16,815	.6	23,315	.9	13,403	.5	34,518	1.4
Golf car rental	290,535	10.4	268,794	9.8	246,631	9.5	188,354	7.5	130,082	5.4
Service & delivery	3,294	.1	5,767	.2	5,760	.2	9,267	.4	6,695	.3
Purchase used equip.	24,938	.9	27,107	1.0	27,521	1.1	23,518	.9	36,859	1.5
Discount	16,651	.6	17,544	.6	16,562	.6	13,342	.5	17,688	.7
Rainy/Skinner							856		16,997	.7
	2,812,788	100	2,733,691	100	2,591,853	100	2,498,906	100	2,396,826	100

Bryce equipment: Tractors, greensmowers, gangmowers, handmowers, riding rotary mowers, utility vehicles
Bryce parts: Repair and replacement parts for Bryce equipment
Kut-Kwik equipment: Large riding rotary mowers (36″–60″ cut)
West Point equipment: Vertifiers, power drags
Cushman: Full line of turf utility vehicles (3- and 4-wheel models)
Repair parts: Tecumseh, Kohler, Briggs & Stratton, Wisconsin component parts
Carter: Gasoline and battery-powered golf carts
Miscellaneous equipment: Sod cutters, aerators, chippers, sprinklers, etc.
Bunton: Rotary mowers, trimmers
National: Riding reel-type mowers
Royer: Mobile, high-capacity processing plants
Miscellaneous golf: Golf cups, flags, tee-markers, benches, hole-cutters, ball washers
Fertilizers & chemicals: Herbicides, fungicides, wetting agents, fertilizers
Massey: All-purpose tractors, rotary cutting units
Giant vac: Various sizes of commercial blowers and vacuums

Sales efforts were still focused on golf courses. Mr. Conner visualized his company as a supply house for golf courses, and the addition of golf carts in 1967 reflected his interest in broadening the services he could supply courses. Greens-mowers and gangmowers, necessities at a golf course, required replacement parts for years after the initial sale, making the sale valuable in terms of future parts orders. Exhibit 3 shows the growing importance of parts sales in volume, and Exhibit 4 indicates the strength of Bryce parts in monthly sales. Most factory parts were sold to customers at 45% above wholesale prices, so parts sales were very profitable.

The purchaser of turf equipment at a golf club was usually the greens super-intendent, although the club's Board had financial control. The superintendent's job depended partly upon the reliability of the equipment he recommended and of the dealer who sold the equipment. Greensmowers needed to be replaced or repaired quickly to ensure the good condition of the course. Members were sensitive to poor course upkeep and blamed the superintendent for mowing delays. Reflecting on the company's success in attracting golf course superintendents as customers, Mr. Conner stated, "We built the business on service, no question about it."

THE PARTS DEPARTMENT AND PARTS INVENTORY

Although parts sales had grown rapidly since 1970, the total number of employees in the parts department had not increased in 10 years. The turnover rate among these employees was very high: three had been working for the company less than one year. A listing of parts department employees and their responsibilities is given in Exhibit 5.

EXHIBIT 4
Monthly Sales of Repair Parts* and Bryce Parts

	'70–'71		'71–'72		'72–'73		'73–'74		'74–'75	
	Repair Parts	Bryce Parts	Repair Parts	Bryce Parts	Repair Parts	Bryce Parts	Repair Parts	Bryce Parts	Repair Parts	Bryce Parts
October	$ 8,039	$ 18,924	$ 10,851	$ 19,970	$ 7,229	$ 17,683	$ 12,127	$ 21,548	$ 9,806	$ 29,177
November	3,464	16,774	8,211	14,881	4,435	23,464	6,824	35,155	7,546	39,177
December	3,576	16,523	4,005	24,028	9,003	37,694	5,922	24,870	7,546	36,592
January	5,885	52,784	7,829	41,308	8,372	43,580	7,926	45,280	10,158	59,592
February	5,582	30,124	9,518	32,451	5,565	36,383	5,730	36,057	10,795	44,618
March	7,874	37,116	10,330	38,684	11,573	42,902	12,520	38,390	11,573	33,917
April	8,227	19,916	10,055	18,869	10,949	18,769	12,943	24,239	14,990	36,798
May	8,936	17,671	13,913	27,612	11,982	24,686	15,291	28,674	23,123	35,795
June	9,586	26,765	12,552	23,981	12,521	29,716	14,039	27,106	19,136	38,872
July	8,366	31,544	10,063	20,120	13,745	26,453	16,423	34,823	19,131	39,543
August	9,285	26,881	9,005	22,254	11,646	20,810	12,596	26,914	12,494	30,719
September	9,529	31,047	6,980	21,335	9,322	25,938	9,830	28,814	12,854	27,797
	$88,349	$316,069	$113,312	$305,493	$116,342	$338,078	$132,171	$371,870	$159,152	$452,597

*Includes Wisconsin, Briggs & Stratton and Kohler component parts.

EXHIBIT 5
Parts Department Personnel

No. of workers	Age	Job title	Description of duties
1	59	Department manager	Responsible for overall efficiency of dept., manages parts inventory
1	30	Secretary	Takes phoned orders, types invoices, files
2	27,48	Sales clerks	Sells parts at front counter, takes phoned orders and removes items from stock to aid shipper
1	22	Shipper	Packages parts for UPS or truck shipment
1	24	Receiver	Unloads incoming freight, places parts in stock or warehouse
1	20	Helper (summer only)	Aids receiver or shipper as needed

Approximately 7,000 different items were stocked in the parts room. The items were arranged on shelves by part number within manufacturer. The smallest parts were kept in drawers, and larger parts were kept in labeled boxes on the shelves. Parts too large for the shelves were placed on racks at the back of the room. Empty boxes located on the shelves indicated that the parts were on the back racks.

Physical inventory of the parts stock was taken at the end of each fiscal year. There was no perpetual inventory system, and the consensus was that to set one up would create more problems than it would solve. Nor was there a consistent reordering procedure. Mr. Smith, the parts department manager, ordered all Bryce parts. These accounted for almost 45% of the parts and 75% of the parts sales. (See Exhibit 4.) All other parts were ordered by the secretary and the sales clerk. Although Mr. Smith provided general supervision, the secretary and sales clerk were responsible for maintaining proper inventory levels for these other parts.

Weekly stock orders were prepared by Mr. Smith from the "Want List," which was a clipboard hung near the shelves. When anyone who took a part out of stock to fill an order noticed that the supply of that part was low or gone, he would write the part number, description and manufacturer on the Want List for reorder. Several problems plagued this system. One was that it was very possible for two reorders to be made on a certain part in the same week if two different people wrote the same part on the list, and Mr. Smith didn't notice the duplication. Often a part would not be written on the list until it was stocked out, rather than low. "Low" was a relative term that varied by part and had not been quantified. Most customer back orders and all orders for parts to be used in the shop for equipment repair were phoned into the factory the same day.

Mr. Smith made three large stock orders a year for Bryce parts. Bryce sent a computer printout each year that showed the number of each part purchased the year before and the times each part was ordered. From this printout, one page of which is shown in Exhibit 6, and the annual physical inventories, Mr.

EXHIBIT 6

1975 Service Parts Pre-Season Stock Order (08/26/75)

Net purchases in 1974	75% of net purchases	On hand	Pre-season order	T U R F	Part Number	Description	N R	# of times ordered	Net dollar amount
6	5			T	107803	KIT	#	1	12.06
1	1			T	107811	BREAKER	#	1	1.83
6	5			T	107917	AMMETER		3	17.19
13	10			T	107927	REGULATOR		4	269.29
1	1			T	107998	PINION		1	14.05
15	11			T	108029	SPROCKET		1	166.65
30	23			T	108077	ROLLER	#	1	977.70
NO LONGER AVAILABLE				T	108090	N. L. A.		1	862.75
12	9			T	108093	WHEEL		2	220.80
30	23			T	108096	AXLE		1	735.90
14	11			T	108100	REEL		2	883.26
14	11			T	108111	BRACKET	#	1	87.78
20	15			T	108125	REEL		2	925.60
10	8			T	108126	AXLE		1	187.30
190	143			T	108127	REEL		1	9,023.10
4	3			T	108208	CUSHION	#	1	42.76
4	3			T	108332	HUB	#	1	96.24
NO LONGER AVAILABLE				T	108341	N. L. A		1	32.40
120	90			T	108346	REEL		1	5,023.20
130	98			T	108347	REEL		1	6,036.05
35	26			T	108484	ADAPTER		1	206.50
2	2			T	108491	HOSE	#	1	11.32
1	1			T	108495	CABLE	#	1	8.29
2	2			T	108542	DEFLECTOR	×	1	28.28
130	98			T	108557	VALVE		2	143.00
20	15			T	108563	SHACKLE		1	38.60
2	2			T	108573	COUPLING		1	22.50
1	1			T	108828	SHAFT	#	1	144.29
1	1			T	108959	CHAIN	#	1	65.07
7	5			T	109365	KNUCKLE		2	274.56
2	2			T	109366	KNUCKLE		1	81.08
NO LONGER AVAILABLE				T	109605	N. L. A.	×	1	557.86
5	4			T	109866	SHIELD	#	1	24.05
1	1			T	109878	CABLE	#	1	4.07
40	30			T	110022	SHACKLE		3	49.60
30	23			T	110024	SPRING		3	335.10
31	23			T	110029	HINGE		2	479.26
55	41			T	110031	TUBE		3	270.60
8	6			T	110032	ROD		3	341.92
40	30			T	110033	HITCH		2	504.00
4	3			T	110041	BRACKET		1	16.28
10	8			T	110042	BRACKET		1	40.70
56	42			T	110466	BALL	×	4	94.08
50	38			T	110469	YOKE		1	687.50
16	12			T	110480	STEM		6	263.64
1	1			T	110615	TUBE		1	3.53
2	2			T	110623	SPROCKET	×	2	214.28
5	4			T	110651	CABLE	#	2	26.45
1	1			T	110678	CROSS	#	1	20.29

EXHIBIT 7
Yearly Service Parts Order Schedule

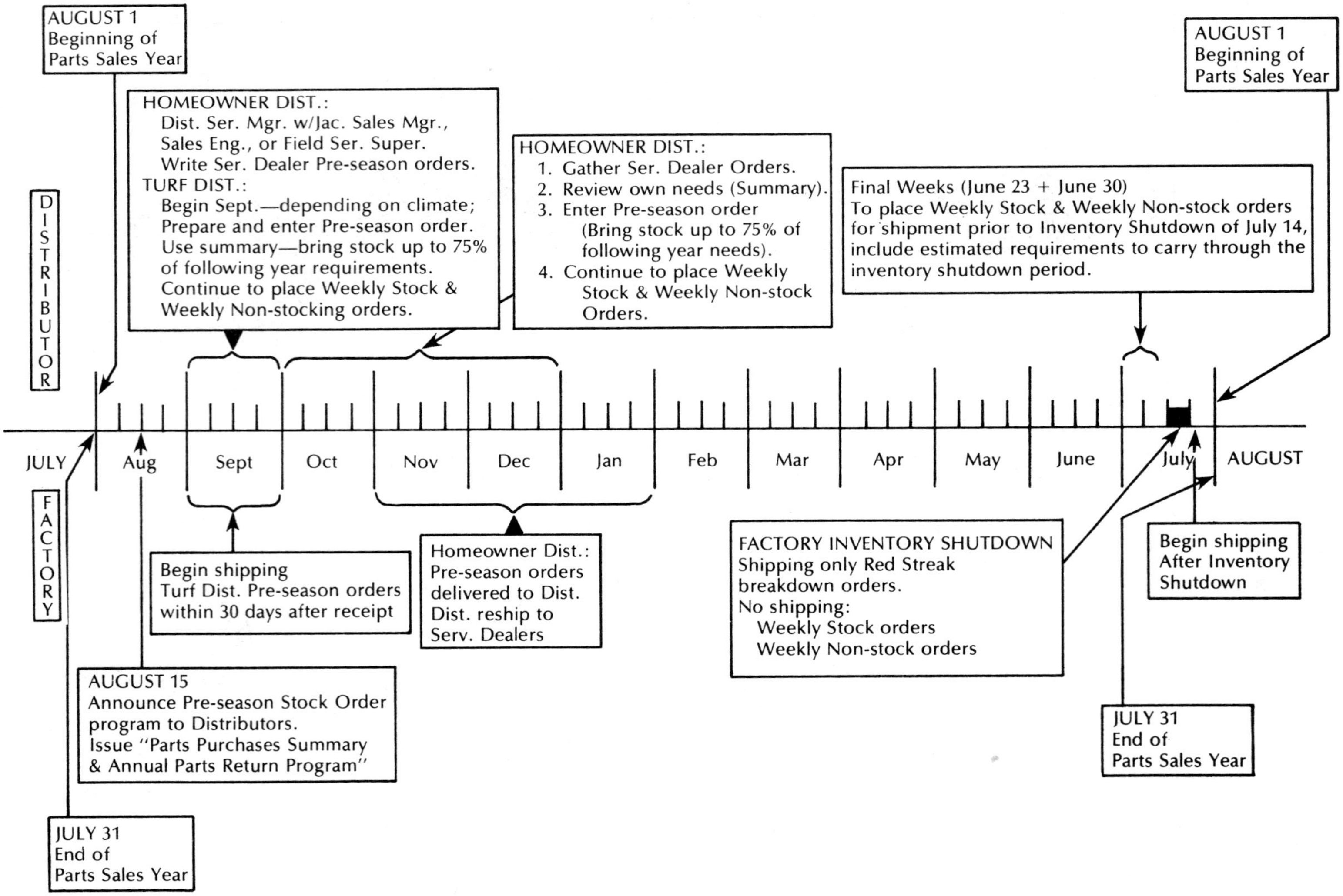

AUGUST 1
Beginning of
Parts Sales Year

AUGUST 1
Beginning of
Parts Sales Year

Final Weeks (June 23 + June 30)
To place Weekly Stock & Weekly Non-stock orders
for shipment prior to Inventory Shutdown of July 14,
include estimated requirements to carry through the
inventory shutdown period.

Begin shipping
After Inventory
Shutdown

JULY 31
End of
Parts Sales Year

FACTORY INVENTORY SHUTDOWN
Shipping only Red Streak
breakdown orders.
No shipping:
  Weekly Stock orders
  Weekly Non-stock orders

HOMEOWNER DIST.:
1. Gather Ser. Dealer Orders.
2. Review own needs (Summary).
3. Enter Pre-season order
   (Bring stock up to 75% of
   following year needs).
4. Continue to place Weekly
   Stock & Weekly Non-stock
   Orders.

HOMEOWNER DIST.:
Dist. Ser. Mgr. w/Jac. Sales Mgr.,
Sales Eng., or Field Ser. Super.
Write Ser. Dealer Pre-season orders.
TURF DIST.:
Begin Sept.—depending on climate;
Prepare and enter Pre-season order.
Use summary—bring stock up to 75%
of following year requirements.
Continue to place Weekly Stock &
Weekly Non-stocking orders.

Homeowner Dist.:
Pre-season orders
delivered to Dist.
Dist. reship to
Serv. Dealers

Begin shipping
Turf Dist. Pre-season orders
within 30 days after receipt

AUGUST 15
Announce Pre-season Stock Order
program to Distributors.
Issue "Parts Purchases Summary
& Annual Parts Return Program"

JULY 31
End of
Parts Sales Year

JULY   Aug   Sept   Oct   Nov   Dec   Jan   Feb   Mar   Apr   May   June   July   AUGUST

DISTRIBUTOR

FACTORY

Smith prepared these large stock orders. Exhibit 7 shows Bryce's recommended order schedule. The large stock orders were intended to satisfy the definite seasonal trends in repair part sales and Bryce part sales. Some compliance with the Bryce schedule was required because many parts were stocked out at the factory during peak demand, and only the early orders were quickly filled.

When a new product was added to an existing line, or a new line was taken on, back-up parts inventory was especially hard to determine. Recently, the company had taken on the distribution of Sutherland mowers and had sold several already, but had no idea of what parts would be needed to provide sufficient service.

Mr. Conner knew that in most retail operations, a small percentage of inventory accounted for a very large percentage of dollar sales. He asked Mr. Smith to test this by separating Bryce parts purchased in the last year into three classes according to purchase volume: over $500, $151–$500, and $0–$150. Mr. Smith's findings are below.

	# OF PARTS	% OF BRYCE PARTS PURCHASED	PURCHASE VALUE	% OF TOTAL PURCHASE VALUE
Over $500	107	6.0	$178,738	66.3
$151–$500	192	10.8	38,400	14.2
0–$150	1,477	83.2	52,648	19.5
	1,776	100.0	$269,786	100.0

Mr. Conner saw his suspicion was correct but wondered how he could use this information to help solve his inventory management difficulties.

Mr. Conner considered one control method, the economic order quantity, for use in managing the Bryce parts inventory. He estimated that the average cost of placing and receiving an order was $8, and that the carrying cost was 20% of inventory value. Although there was some variation, he figured three weeks was the average lead time for a Bryce parts order. Mr. Conner believed the Bryce parts purchase summary (Exhibit 6) would yield a good approximation of the annual rate of demand. But, Mr. Conner hesitated to implement an EOQ system with the 3,000 different Bryce parts stocked. He also worried that the seasonality evident in parts sales would undermine the system's effectivenss. An EOQ system would also conflict with Bryce's suggested ordering timetable (Exhibit 7). Mr. Conner was intrigued by the system's potential, especially when supplemented by a reorder point model, but he was unconvinced of its feasibility in this case.

The parts inventory was recognized as being very important to the company's sales growth. But, the system that had worked satisfactorily with $100,000 volume had not been updated as sales had grown to $2,700,000.

PARTS ROOM SERVICE PROBLEMS

Nearly as important as maintaining an adequate inventory of parts was the fast processing of customer orders. Roughly 65% of parts orders were received by phone. It was not uncommon during the busier weeks of spring and early summer for three or four phone extensions to be busy most of the day with incoming orders. Mr. Smith, the two sales clerks, and the secretary handled phone orders. Familiarity with the voluminous parts catalogues and some mechanical knowledge were required because customers often could not order by part number and had to describe a part by its function and location on a machine.

Another 30% of parts sales were made across the counter. During spring and summer, a repair part might be needed so critically by a Washington area customer that he would drive to the office to save the time required by UPS or mail shipment. The two sales clerks served the counter customers, although when the counter was very busy, Mr. Smith, the shipper or the receiver would also help. The counter was particularly busy during the morning and early in the week.

The remaining 5% of orders were received by mail. These orders and the majority of the phone orders were shipped daily by UPS. The sales clerks pulled the ordered parts and placed them in brown paper bags identified by writing the customer name and the date on the bag. The bags were placed in a large upright wooden bin which was separated into 18 numbered compartments. The bin location of each order was written on the order form (later copied on the invoice) so the shipper could easily locate each order when it was to be shipped. Order forms that had been filled (with back orders noted) were returned to Mr. Smith's office. He ordered the parts that had been back ordered by the clerks, then cleared each order for shipment. The secretary typed invoices for the cleared orders and sent the finished invoices to the shipper. The shipper boxed each invoiced order, sending one copy of the invoice as a packing slip and returning the other copy to the secretary for billing. The secretary usually typed the invoices in batches, and the shipper often would not receive any completed invoices until late afternoon. He would then receive 20 or more for packaging before the 4:30 UPS pick-up. Given normal interruptions, the shipper could package approximately 60 packages in a day. His log book of shipments showed great variation in the number actually shipped each day, even though the wooden bin remained full of unpackaged orders. During July and August, an average of 34 packages were shipped per day. On several days, however, only 20 or fewer were packaged and sent out. When not packaging parts for shipment, the shipper helped the receiver or sales clerks, although Mr. Conner suspected he also spent some time "looking busy."

Parts and some equipment received from suppliers were checked in by the receiver. This often included unloading trailer trucks with a forklift and stocking larger items in the warehouse. Smaller parts were put into stock in the parts room. Often back ordered parts would be received as part of a larger weekly parts order. These were bagged and identified by customer name and placed in the wooden bin for shipment.

Although there was considerable variation, Mr. Smith estimated that a typical phone order was shipped within three days. Ideally most would be shipped the same day, but several bottlenecks were possible. When the front counter was busy, the sales clerks didn't have time to pull the ordered parts. This delayed invoicing the orders. The secretary often waited to type invoices until several orders had accumulated, creating another delay. Back ordered parts could be held

EXHIBIT 8
Parts Department Layout

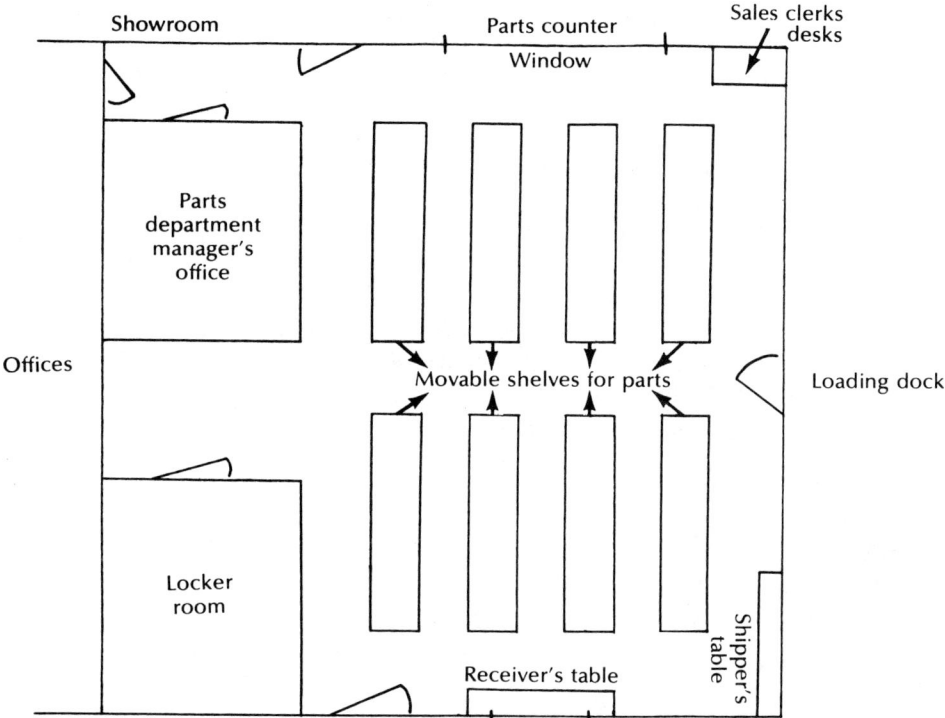

up when the receiver was overburdened by a particularly heavy rush of incoming shipments. Mr. Smith viewed the delays as unavoidable consequences of spring and summer business, but Mr. Conner wondered if some more efficient system might speed service.

Mr. Hardy, general manager and vice-president, added a concern about the parts room layout (Exhibit 8). From his office Mr. Smith couldn't spot bottlenecks to shift personnel to where they were needed most. The shipper and the receiver were especially isolated, and Mr. Hardy shared Mr. Conner's suspicion that idleness and low morale resulted. Although there was some teamwork when one group became particularly busy, each worker felt he had only one area of responsibility, not that he was expected to do whatever was needed to speed service.

AN ASSISTANT FOR MR. SMITH

Dave, the receiver, was a junior college graduate and had been hired as a potential assistant to Mr. Smith. Mr. Smith had been responsible for his training. After two months as shipper, Dave had been made the receiver. At the time of the case, he had been in the job nearly a year, without receiving any training on handling phone orders, counter work or parts ordering. He was able to learn something of the other jobs by offering his help when his own duties were completed, but his morale deteriorated under Mr. Smith's neglect. Mr. Conner was aware of this situation but was undecided about what action he should take. He knew Mr. Smith could be defensive about his job, and Mr. Conner wondered if Mr. Smith viewed Dave as a threat. There were some other problems involved, however. If Dave were moved to one of the sales clerk positions, Mike, the younger sales clerk, would have to become the receiver, a far more strenuous job. Mike, who had been with the company for six years, would view this as a demotion and undoubtedly would resent the change. Mr. Conner knew Mike was unusually moody because he had once counseled him on his attitude toward customers.

The shipper and the secretary would probably sympathize with Mike if he were moved because they had been angered when Dave was hired as the likely assistant to Mr. Smith. And Mr. Smith's reaction was questionable, for Mr. Conner knew either he or Mr. Hardy would have to be very much involved to insure Mr. Smith changed the status quo. Despite the probable repercussions, Mr. Conner wanted to develop an assistant to Mr. Smith, and Dave seemed like a capable prospect. Mr. Conner pondered the best way to make changes and preserve morale.

MARKET DEVELOPMENTS AND THE COMPANY'S FUTURE

Mr. Conner had attended a golf course superintendents convention in Minneapolis in mid-February. This was an annual meeting attended by over 300 superintendents and representatives from all the major turf equipment manufacturers. Many turf equipment distributors also attended, because the convention offered a chance to entertain customers and to meet with factory personnel. Mr. Conner had anticipated seeing Bryce's president, Steve Lunn, but found out when he arrived in Minneapolis that Mr. Lunn had been reassigned by the parent company. This was a shock to all Bryce distributors, who agreed the timing of the change couldn't have been worse. The change, in addition to the recent firing of Bryce's marketing vice-president, pointed to Wentworth's dissatisfaction with Bryce's recent performance. To Mr. Conner, this reawakened a continuing concern that his company was too dependent upon Bryce parts and equipment sales. What if Wentworth sold Bryce to a company with a complementary product line, such as International Harvester? The acquiring company would naturally combine the distributorships and favor its own. Mr. Conner wondered if his company could survive this loss in sales or whether he should attempt further diversification in product line.

Of growing concern to Bryce and its distributors was the proliferation of "will-fit" parts sales. "Will-fit" parts, manufactured by independent companies, fit Bryce or Stevens equipment. One eastern company had manufactured copies of Bryce and Stevens replacement parts for several years in an attempt to capture the lucrative replacement parts business. Quality control was not as strict nor the materials used as reliable but this company had been able to rapidly increase sales by price cutting. A new parts manufacturer had recently entered the midwest market, and the volume of sales of "will-fit" parts had become a definite threat to Stevens, Bryce and turf equipment distributors. Mr. Conner guessed he had lost 5% of his parts sales to these companies. To prevent further loss, he determined to provide quicker service and sufficient inventory while keeping his margins intact.

Mr. Conner was well satisfied with the past performance of his company. Partly due to his closeness to the business, he had never set formal sales or profit targets nor articulated definite growth strategy. The general economic downturn of the early 1970s was being felt by the company, and Mr. Conner thought it was time to examine closely the company's position to see where improvements could be made. The first problem he needed to solve was the parts ordering and inventory system, so that changes could be implemented when Mr. Smith retired. He also needed to solve the personnel and strategy problems. His walk completed, Mr. Conner returned to his office to begin looking at alternative solutions.

The Chap Stick Company
The Warehouse Consolidation Decision

Mr. Dan French, President of the Chap Stick Company, was reviewing possible actions to improve the company's profit performance. It was June, 1978 and his annual Management Report to the parent company was due in two months. Since its acquisition in 1963, the Chap Stick Company had operated as an independent subsidiary of the A.H. Robins Company. A change in Robins' top management early in 1978 created some uncertainty at Chap Stick about the degree of independence Robins would permit in the future. The corporate office made clear Chap Stick's need to define and implement specific operating plans to achieve higher profit performance goals. (See Exhibits 1 and 2 for financial statements.)

A.H. Robins had requested a detailed strategy which would reduce costs and increase profits. French was also concerned with developing a plan to increase his company's return on assets. Lynn Wilburn, a student at the Darden School of Business Administration at the University of Virginia and a summer employee of Chap Stick, had spent four weeks collecting information on Chap Stick's distribution systems. It was now up to French to develop specific recommendations based on Lynn's research. In particular, he wondered if Chap Stick's distribution system, with warehouses in Lynchburg, Virginia and Memphis, Tennessee, was the least costly and most efficient system possible. Any strategies included in his Management Report had to be substantiated with projected savings.

HISTORY OF THE COMPANY

The Morton Manufacturing Company of Lynchburg, Virginia, was founded in 1919 by Mr. John T. Morton and Dr. J.B. Whitehouse to manufacture and market the now famous "Chap Stick" lip balm. The original base company gradually expanded by purchasing additional businesses and relocating them in Lynchburg. In 1963, the A.H. Robins Company of Richmond, Virginia, purchased 100% of

Copyright © 1985 by the Colgate Darden Graduate Business School Sponsors, University of Virginia, Charlottesville, Virginia. Reproduced by permission.

This case was originally prepared by Elizabeth Phillips, and rewritten for classroom use by Lisa Norford, under the supervision of Robert D. Landel, Professor of Business Administration.

the stock of Morton Manufacturing. A.H. Robins was an international company which manufactured and distributed pharmaceutical and consumer products. In 1966, the Morton Manufacturing Company was renamed the Chap Stick Company after its best known product.

1978 ORGANIZATION

The Chap Stick Company had eight divisions in 1978. Company executives had functional, not divisional, responsibilities (Exhibit 3). The Chap Stick Division manufactured Chap Stick® Lip Balm, Blistr-Klear®, and other skin care and beauty aid products developed for over-the-counter retail sales. Most of these products were manufactured and packaged in Lynchburg, Virginia, although some were shipped in bulk form to the Miller-Morton Company in Richmond for packaging. The Miller-Morton Company, also a subsidiary of A.H. Robins, marketed and distributed all Chap Stick Division products to retail outlets. All Chap Stick

EXHIBIT 1
A.H. Robins: Comparative Income Statement

Year ended December 31		1977	1976
Net sales		$306,713,000	$284,925,000
Interest and other income		2,776,000	3,586,000
	Total income	309,489,000	288,511,000
Cost of sales		122,374,000	108,519,000
Research and development		16,107,000	12,729,000
Marketing, administrative and general		117,908,000	105,509,000
Interest		2,106,000	1,719,000
Litigation settlements and related expenses		3,331,000	1,146,000
	Total costs and expenses	261,826,000	229,622,000
	Earnings before income taxes	47,663,000	58,889,000
Provision for income taxes		20,862,000	27,534,000
	Net earnings	$ 26,801,000	$ 31,355,000
Earnings per common share		$1.03	$1.20

Statements of Consolidated Stockholder's Equity

	Common stock ($1 par value)	Additional paid-in capital	Retained earnings	Total
Balance—January 1, 1976	$26,127,000	$693,000	$150,465,000	$177,285,000
Net earnings			31,355,000	31,355,000
Cash dividends—$.30 per share			(7,838,000)	(7,838,000)
Balance—December 31, 1976	26,127,000	693,000	173,982,000	200,802,000
Net earnings			26,801,000	26,801,000
Cash dividends—$.32 per share			(8,361,000)	(8,361,000)
Balance—December 31, 1977	$26,127,000	$693,000	$192,422,000	$219,242,000

Source: A.H. Robins Annual Report.

A.H. Robins: Comparative Balance Sheets

December 31		1977	1976
ASSETS			
Current Assets			
Cash		$ 8,474,000	$ 12,097,000
Certificates of deposit and time deposits		29,992,000	22,110,000
Marketable securities—at cost which approximates market		5,145,000	16,562,000
Accounts and notes receivable—less allowance for doubtful accounts $1,069,000 (1976—$817,000)		62,246,000	51,045,000
Inventories		66,924,000	60,854,000
Prepaid expenses and taxes		7,142,000	5,690,000
	Total current assets	179,923,000	168,358,000
Property, Plant and Equipment			
Land		4,105,000	3,324,000
Buildings and leasehold improvements		45,350,000	36,238,000
Machinery and equipment		37,749,000	29,936,000
		87,204,000	69,498,000
Less: Accumulated depreciation and amortization		37,453,000	30,432,000
		49,751,000	39,066,000
Intangible and Other Assets			
Excess of cost over net assets of subsidiaries acquired		49,715,000	48,721,000
Patents, trademarks and goodwill		3,929,000	4,238,000
Deferred charges		606,000	913,000
Other assets		3,121,000	1,372,000
		57,371,000	55,244,000
		$287,045,000	$262,668,000
LIABILITIES AND STOCKHOLDERS' EQUITY			
Current Liabilities			
Notes payable		$ 7,015,000	$ 2,795,000
Long-term debt payable within one year		5,750,000	5,750,000
Accounts payable		18,203,000	14,657,000
Federal, foreign and state income taxes		8,458,000	7,658,000
Accrued liabilities		11,659,000	10,594,000
	Total current liabilities	51,085,000	41,454,000
Long-Term Debt		15,000,000	18,750,000
Deferred Income Taxes		1,431,000	622,000
Minority Interests in Foreign Subsidiaries		287,000	1,040,000
Stockholders' Equity			
Capital stock			
Preferred, $1 par—authorized 10,000,000 shares, none issued			
Common, $1 par—authorized 40,000,000 shares		26,127,000	26,127,000
Additional paid-in capital		693,000	693,000
Retained earnings		192,422,000	173,982,000
		192,242,000	200,802,000
		$287,045,000	$262,668,000

Division sales were to the Miller-Morton Company at a pre-determined percentage-above-manufactured cost transfer price. These sales amounted to less than thirty percent of total Chap Stick Company sales revenue.

The Blair Division, acquired in 1919, had a product line of over 300 items, including cosmetics, toiletries, fragrances, personal care and health aids, food products, home helpers, popular gifts and fashion jewelry. This division accounted for about half of the company's sales in 1977. Some of the products were manufactured by Chap Stick and others were purchased. Sales were through independent direct-selling dealers recruited through various advertising media. A typical dealer was a housewife who sold Blair products in her spare time to her neighbors, family and friends. During 1977, approximately 50,000 dealers submitted a total of 250,000 orders to the Blair Division. This method of direct selling and distribution was similar in some respects to that used by the Avon Company.

The Wade Division, originally the Anna Elizabeth Wade Company of Orange, New Jersey, was acquired in 1953 and relocated in Lynchburg. This division's product line included flavorings, napkins, greeting cards, religious items, specialty cooking supplies and lamps (Exhibit 4). Company emphasis in 1978 was to sell Wade products only to such fund-raising organizations as churches and schools. In 1977, approximately 38,000 orders at an average value of $118 per order were shipped by the Wade Division.

The Shelby Division (acquired in 1969 as the Shelby Specialty Company) had the same general product line as the Wade Division, and followed the same marketing policy. In 1977, the combined Wade and Shelby Division sales were approximately equal to the sales of the Chap Stick Division.

EXHIBIT 2
Comparative Income Statement* January 1, 1977–December 31, 1977

	1977 Budget	1977 Actual	1976 Actual
Net sales	$16,347,973	$16,976,139	$15,120,801
Cost of goods sold	8,665,731	9,336,876	8,226,956
Gross profit	7,682,242	7,639,263	6,893,845
Expenses			
Selling	1,187,789	1,188,330	1,051,775
Advertising	2,936,469	2,885,944	2,608,482
Administrative	1,968,882	2,206,898	1,821,646
Research and development	185,941	169,761	177,913
Total expenses	6,279,081	6,450,933	5,659,816
Earnings before tax (operating profit)	1,403,161	1,188,330	1,234,029
Provision for income tax	701,580	594,165	617,014
Net earnings	$ 701,581	$ 594,165	$ 617,015

Source: Chap Stick Company Statement.
*All financial data from Chap Stick Company Operations have been disguised and altered to protect the interests of the Company.

EXHIBIT 2, cont'd
Comparative Balance Sheet* December 31, 1977

		December 31, 1977		December 31, 1976
Assets				
Current				
Cash		$ 362,412		$ 203,900
Accounts receivable		1,806,585		1,682,369
Finished stock	3,018,839		2,762,377	
Raw materials, bulk stock, packaging materials	1,849,989		1,587,208	
Work-in-process	21,751		—	
Total inventory		4,890,579		4,349,585
Samples		85,110		78,130
Insurance		28,051		25,200
Other		855,358		856,834
Total current assets		8,028,095		7,196,018
Plant, property and equipment		2,852,174		2,608,841
Less: Accumulated depreciation		1,544,189		1,353,912
Net PPE		1,307,985		1,254,929
Other assets		653,142		664,943
Total assets		$9,989,222		$9,115,890
Liabilities				
Current				
Accounts payable		$ 462,551		$ 426,760
Salaries and commissions		64,919		—
Royalties		1,205		9,680
Provision for income tax		342,020		446,639
Other		267,044		231,865
Total current liabilities		1,137,739		1,114,944
Other liabilities				
Due to parent		366,909		101,817
Deferred liabilities		12,435		21,135
Total other liabilities		379,344		122,952
Stockholders' equity				
Capital stock—common		365,400		365,400
Capital in excess of par value		60,159		60,159
Retained earnings—beginning	7,452,435		7,452,435	
Net earnings for year	594,145		—	
Ending retained earnings		8,046,580		7,452,435
Total stockholder's equity		8,472,139		7,877,994
Total liabilities and equity		$9,989,222		$9,115,890

Source: Chap Stick Company Statements.
*All data have been disguised to protect the Company.

The other four divisions were much smaller than Chap Stick, Blair, Wade or Shelby. The Kenneth Division, established in 1975, offered a famous beauty advisor's advice via mail and a mail-order catalogue line of beauty products. The Chap Stick Company through the Caron Division manufactured Caron Colognes and toilet waters and distributed all of the A.H. Robins Caron Perfumes Division's products in the U.S.A. The University Food Supplement Division (UFS) was established to take advantage of the growing health food market. By 1978, this

EXHIBIT 3
Organization Chart

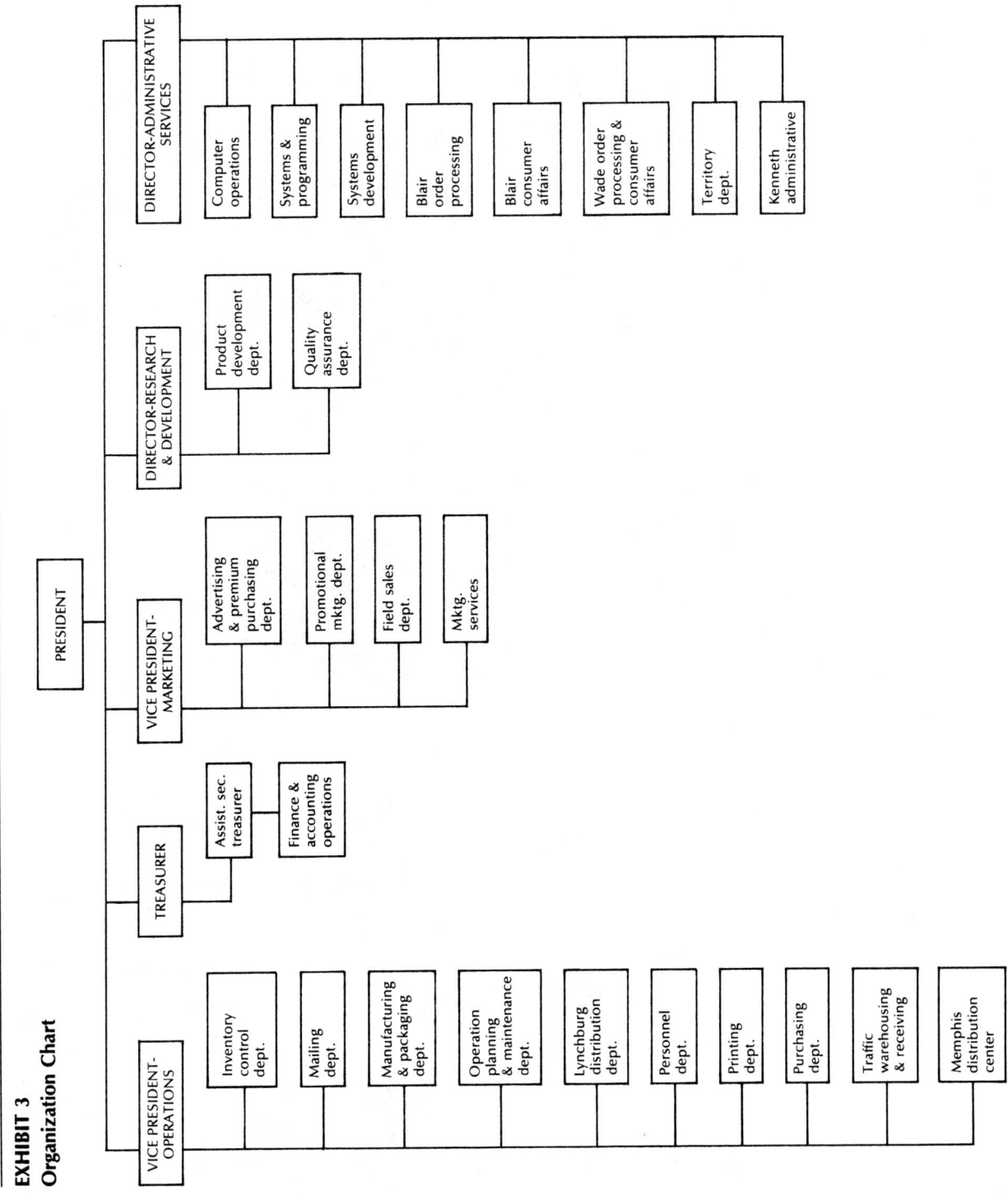

PRESIDENT

VICE PRESIDENT-OPERATIONS
- Inventory control dept.
- Mailing dept.
- Manufacturing & packaging dept.
- Operation planning & maintenance dept.
- Lynchburg distribution dept.
- Personnel dept.
- Printing dept.
- Purchasing dept.
- Traffic warehousing & receiving
- Memphis distribution center

TREASURER
- Assist. sec. treasurer
- Finance & accounting operations

VICE PRESIDENT-MARKETING
- Advertising & premium purchasing dept.
- Promotional mktg. dept.
- Field sales dept.
- Mktg. services

DIRECTOR-RESEARCH & DEVELOPMENT
- Product development dept.
- Quality assurance dept.

DIRECTOR-ADMINISTRATIVE SERVICES
- Computer operations
- Systems & programming
- Systems development
- Blair order processing
- Blair consumer affairs
- Wade order processing & consumer affairs
- Territory dept.
- Kenneth administrative

EXHIBIT 4

division was being phased out, due to its limited success. The Mid-State Division sold specialized cosmetics and was generally considered a part of the Blair Division. The Kenneth, Caron (U.S.A. Shipments), UFS and Mid-State Divisions' 1977 combined sales were less than one million dollars.

SALES OF THE BLAIR, WADE AND SHELBY DIVISIONS

Sales of the Blair, Wade and Shelby Divisions were highly seasonal, with peaks occurring from March to May and September to November. Blair Division dealers and fund-raising organizations selling Wade or Shelby Division products purchased the goods from the appropriate division and then resold them to the ultimate consumer. Advertisements run in such nationally known magazines as *Reader's Digest* and *Good Housekeeping* were used to recruit Blair dealers. Purchased mailing lists provided names of fund-raising organizations.

The sales price of any one product sold by these divisions varied, depending on quantity discounts earned and special sales promotions. Often a product was designated as a "free good." If a Blair dealer ordered less than a specified dollar amount, he was required to pay the freight charges from either the Lynchburg or Memphis warehouse. A free goods voucher, for goods whose resale value was equal to the dollar amount of the freight charges, was sent to the dealer to be redeemed with a second order. In the past, only 34% of these vouchers were actually redeemed.

There was a great deal of intentional overlap between the product lines of these three divisions. Although the Shelby division's product line was more limited than that of the Wade Division, it consisted of the same types of products. Nearly all of the Wade Division products were also sold by the Blair Division.

Total annual dollar sales for each division were forecast with reasonable accuracy, but it had been very difficult to accurately predict demand for any one product.

THE MANUFACTURING AND PACKAGING DEPARTMENT

Some Chap Stick Company products were manufactured in Lynchburg, while others were purchased, both in the United States and abroad, for resale. All of the products of the Chap Stick Division were manufactured in Lynchburg and transferred immediately to the Miller-Morton warehouse in Richmond. Because this division had such a stable product line, specialized automated filling and packaging equipment had been designed for its products. The processes used to manufacture products for the other divisions were only partially automated. General purpose filling equipment was used, and the loading and unloading, labelling and packaging operations were done with both manual and automated equipment. Products were mixed in batch sizes and then placed into the appropriate containers. A wide variety of products, such as pie mixes, flavorings, household cleaners, fragrances, beauty creams and medicines, were manufactured in this manner for the Blair, Wade and Shelby Divisions.

Ed Thaxton, head of the Manufacturing and Packaging Department, scheduled production. He received annual gross sales projections and notification of special sales promotions by product from the Marketing Department. Whenever Mr. Thaxton saw that the inventory level of a manufactured item was low, he scheduled a batch of that product to be mixed and filled. This visual control system was simple, yet often ineffective in coping with highly variable sales. Unit sales of most products were often sporadic and stockouts occurred regularly.

Mr. French knew that Mr. Thaxton's department and the Inventory Control department did not always coordinate their activities, and that this lack of coordination also resulted in stockouts. Once, when the filling machines were set up to place vanilla flavoring into number 3 bottles, Mr. Thaxton decided to fill 1,000 extra bottles of flavoring thus avoiding additional setup costs in the future. The following week, red food coloring in number 3 bottles stocked out. Mrs. Lipscomb, Manager of the Inventory Control Department, was not aware that the 1,000 extra number 3 bottles had been used and planned to use them for the red food coloring. Consequently, she had to place a rush order for the number 3 bottles. Production of the red food coloring was delayed. When the bottles arrived, the scheduled production flow had to be interrupted to allow the immediate production of the food coloring. This caused other orders to be pushed behind schedule.

DISTRIBUTION DEPARTMENT

The Distribution Department in Lynchburg received orders, selected the goods out of inventory, packaged the orders and metered the appropriate postage on the packages. When an order from a Blair dealer was received it was keypunched for computer processing. A computer-prepared order invoice and order cart were passed down a packing line which consisted of several filling stations, each manned by one person. Each person would check the invoice to see if any of the requested items were in his section. If the item was there, the filler put the item into a cart and passed the cart and the invoice on down the line. After the order was filled, it was sent to the packaging area and then to the postage area. The same order filling process was used in Memphis.

Blair sample kits, sent to prospective dealers, contained 4 to 6 items. They were the only prepackaged goods. Some of the kits were assembled at the company, while others were filled at a sheltered workshop (a state-run workshop employing handicapped people) in the Lynchburg area. The workshop was used to offset capacity constraints and to reduce overtime work. Only certain kits could be assembled by the workshop because the workshop employees could not successfully handle some of the products. Sample kits were also assembled in Memphis.

Sales orders from Blair dealers and Wade fund-raising organizations were shipped either by United Parcel Service (UPS) or the United States Postal Service (USPS). The computer at the Lynchburg plant printed the invoices, indicating whether to ship the order by UPS or USPS and whether to send it from the Lynchburg or Memphis warehouse. The computer compared the shipping costs from each warehouse and then selected the least-cost alternative. At times it was not possible to ship by UPS due to stringent address and zone regulations and/or customer preference.

LABOR

Employees in the Manufacturing and Packaging and the Distribution Departments were not unionized and, with the exception of the foremen, were paid hourly. There was no incentive system. Because most jobs were of a low-skill content, employees could be easily moved from one job to another whenever necessary. Each job was graded and annual reviews determined whether an employee moved up to the next job grade.

INVENTORY CONTROL DEPARTMENT

Inventory records were kept manually in Lynchburg on all 3,900 stockkeeping units (raw materials, supplies, containers or finished goods). Since many of the finished goods were sold by more than one division, each item's inventory record card indicated the sales history by division. Separate records were maintained for inventory stored in the Memphis warehouse. Periodically, Mrs. Lipscomb reviewed all *purchased* finished goods and determined if replenishment orders should be placed with vendors and for what amount. Each item's historical usage rate was considered to be an indication of future demand. Any past or projected special promotions or sales of an item also had to be taken into consideration. By comparing historical usage data with forecasts from the marketing department, Mrs. Lipscomb determined future demand and ordered accordingly. If her projected future demand exceeded the on-hand quantity of an item, she reordered. The quantity ordered depended on any minimum order requirements imposed by suppliers, volume discounts, order lead time, and the historical order quantity. Sometimes large quantities were ordered in anticipation of future price increases.

Mrs. Lipscomb also reviewed stocks of raw materials, containers, labels and packaging supplies. She had to predict the sales rate of each manufactured item and then determine if Mr. Thaxton would be scheduling a batch run sometime in the near future. If Mrs. Lipscomb saw that Mr. Thaxton would be making a run, she had to determine if on-hand stocks of ingredients, containers and labels were sufficient to meet production needs. A bill of material record, specifying the raw materials required for a batch run of a manufactured good, was maintained for each product that the Chap Stick Company manufactured.

All stockkeeping units were classified as either a raw material or a finished good. These classifications were then broken down into more specific categories. All inventoried items were reviewed on a periodic basis. Exhibit 5 gives the review period and order quantity for each category of goods.

Mr. Gene Angel, Director-Administrative Services, was in the process of defining how the computer could be used in the inventory management activity and hoped to have that project completed sometime in 1979. Automation of the inventory system had been attempted before by computer system personnel from the Corporate office but had failed. The current project was viewed with much skepticism, especially by Mrs. Lipscomb. Since 1966, Mrs. Lipscomb had been responsible for the inventory control of all 3,900 items. Mr. Thaxton decided when to run replenishment batches of the 650 products manufactured by Chap Stick for the Blair, Wade and Shelby Divisions. The Marketing Department decided

EXHIBIT 5
Stock Keeping Units Inventory Items by Categories

Category	Review period	Order quantity	# of items in category	Additional information
Raw Materials				
Ingredients	2 weeks	2-3 months supply; large minimum orders	30	Received within 2-3 weeks
Containers	2 months	Large orders; Volume discounts	550	
Labels	2 months	Large orders; Volume discounts	500	
Packing cases to order dept. supplies	2-3 months	5-6 months supply; Volume discounts	150	
Finished goods				
Manufactured goods	6 weeks	Thaxton's decision	650	
Purchased goods	1–1½ months	4 months supply	900	Variable demand
Premiums	Weekly	3-4 months supply	900	Limited time only specials—Purchased items Demand difficult to predict Premiums were managed by the Marketing Department
Memphis stock	1–1½ months	1 month supply	200	

when and how much to order for all premium items (special one-time sales items). The flow of goods through the company is depicted in Exhibit 6.

FINANCE

All financing was done through the A. H. Robins Company. Excess cash was loaned to Robins for investment at the same interest rate the Chap Stick Company was charged when it borrowed from Robins, about 10%. A limited amount of capital was available from Robins, precluding major investments in the near future.

HISTORY OF THE MEMPHIS DISTRIBUTION CENTER

The Memphis branch of the Chap Stick Company (then Morton Manufacturing) opened in February, 1946. The intention was to increase Blair Division sales in areas west of the Mississippi and in Alabama, Louisiana, Tennessee and part of Kentucky through an increased ability to service customer demands. The use of the Memphis Distribution Center was also supposed to reduce total transportation expenses. All administrative functions were still handled in Lynchburg. The appropriate processed orders were sent to Memphis for filling, packaging and mailing.

In June, 1949, the Memphis operation expanded into a separate profit center, handling all operations except for payroll and manufacturing. Blair dealers could mail orders directly to Memphis and receive their shipments from there. It was thought that this would reduce order processing time, provide better customer

EXHIBIT 6
Flow of Goods

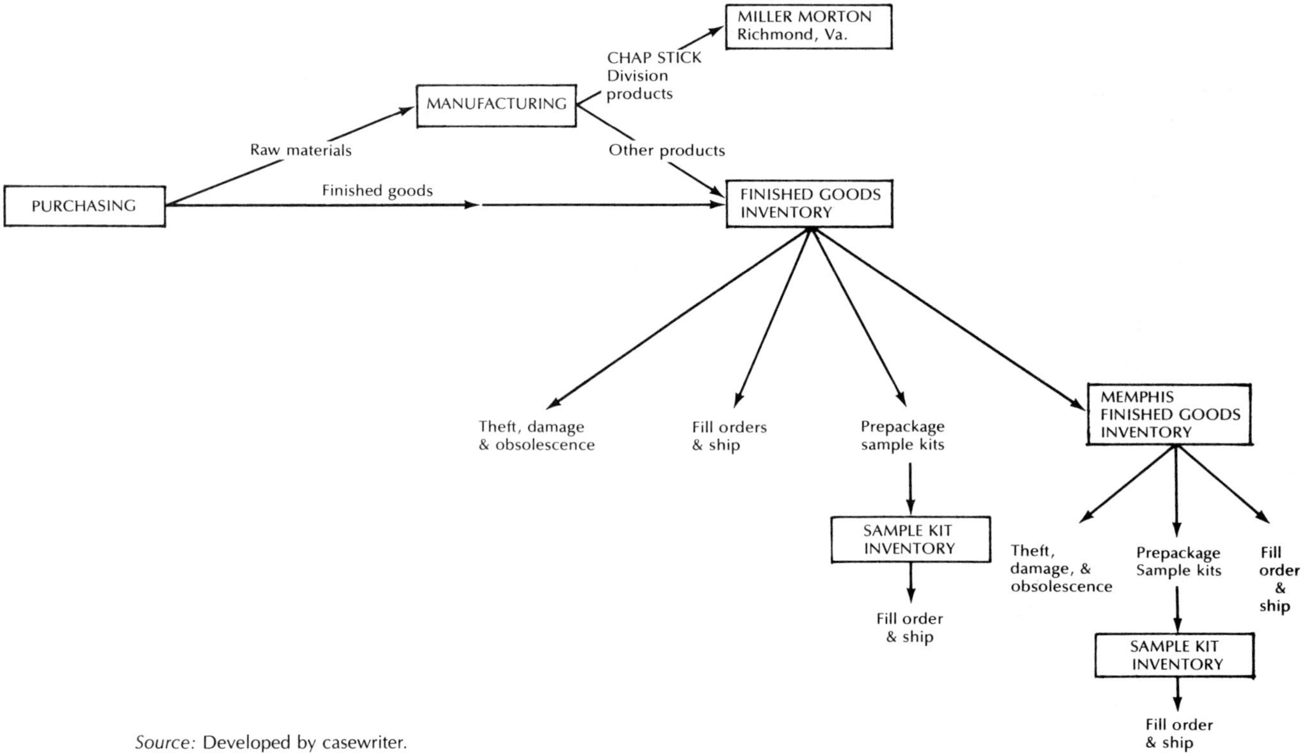

Source: Developed by casewriter.

service and decrease administrative pressures on the Lynchburg operation. Then in May, 1965, the Memphis setup was converted back to a simple distribution center, with all orders again processed in Lynchburg. It was felt that the need for additional control and the installation of a computer in Lynchburg necessitated this move. The Memphis center had remained as a distribution center for Blair and Wade products since that time.

MEMPHIS OPERATION IN 1978

The Memphis building was leased through 1981 at an annual cost of $23,000. It was felt that the rent would be raised substantially if the lease were renewed. Charlie Leys, Vice President of Operations, suspected that the cost of renting another suitable building in the Memphis area would also be quite high.

Because the Memphis building was six stories high with only one elevator and because of the haphazard way shipments were received and stored, physical control of the inventory was a constant problem. It was frequently necessary to call Mrs. Lipscomb in Lynchburg for assistance in locating stock in the Memphis warehouse. Although she was over 600 miles away, she was often able to determine which floor the stock was on and how many units should be there.

Mrs. Lipscomb spent at least one day a week compiling Memphis inventory movement information and an assistant worked two days weekly on Memphis inventory control. One day a month, an assistant compiled month-end data on the Memphis operation. Every item stocked in both Memphis and Lynchburg required two separate inventory records. The Accounting Department had to keep separate records on the Lynchburg and Memphis operations so as to evaluate their performances separately. It took at least one-half day per month to compile separate data on Memphis.

Weekly rail car shipments were made from Lynchburg to Memphis. Four man-hours were required to write up the shipment and check the stock, and another 12 man-hours to gather the stock and strap it to pallets. Two men spent four hours each per week loading the car. It took at least 17 days for an order to reach Memphis after order receipt in Lynchburg—7 days to process the order and 10 shipping days. Because of occasional late deliveries and the difficulty in predicting demand, it was not uncommon for stock needed in Memphis to be in Lynchburg and vice versa. The distance between the two locations made stockouts more difficult to deal with.

If a Blair or Wade order could not be completely filled, there were two options: (1) hold the order until all ordered goods were in stock, or (2) ship a partial order and ship the remaining items later. The second option was most often chosen. Splitting a shipment, however, could result in higher postage costs and it certainly aggravated customers. This partially negated the prime advantage of using the Memphis Distribution center—a cheaper way to ship to some parts of the country. 1977 dollar sales by state are shown in Exhibit 7.

Seasonal sales made it difficult at times to meet demand with a relatively stable work force. It was often necessary to both hire temporary employees and work overtime to fill orders.

The Memphis warehouse had 23 full-time employees, only three more than in 1975, although there had been a 32% sales increase and a 51% increase in sample kits shipped during the same time period. In Memphis, the same employees received, filled and shipped orders, while separate departments in Lynchburg handled these duties.

Stock pilferage was a problem in both locations, although worse in Memphis. Almost all of the company's products were small, easy to conceal and easy to resell.

POSSIBLE CONSOLIDATION OF DISTRIBUTION CENTERS

If all warehousing operations were centralized in Lynchburg, it would be necessary to add a second shift at the plant. Twenty-two additional people would be needed for the positions indicated in Exhibit 8. It would also be necessary to redesign the filling and packing lines. The Lynchburg warehouse foreman felt that centralizing operations and redesigning the lines would create an opportunity to improve the overall operations. Adding a second shift would increase flexibility

EXHIBIT 7
Dollar Sales by State—1977

Top 24.2%

Source: Developed by casewriter.

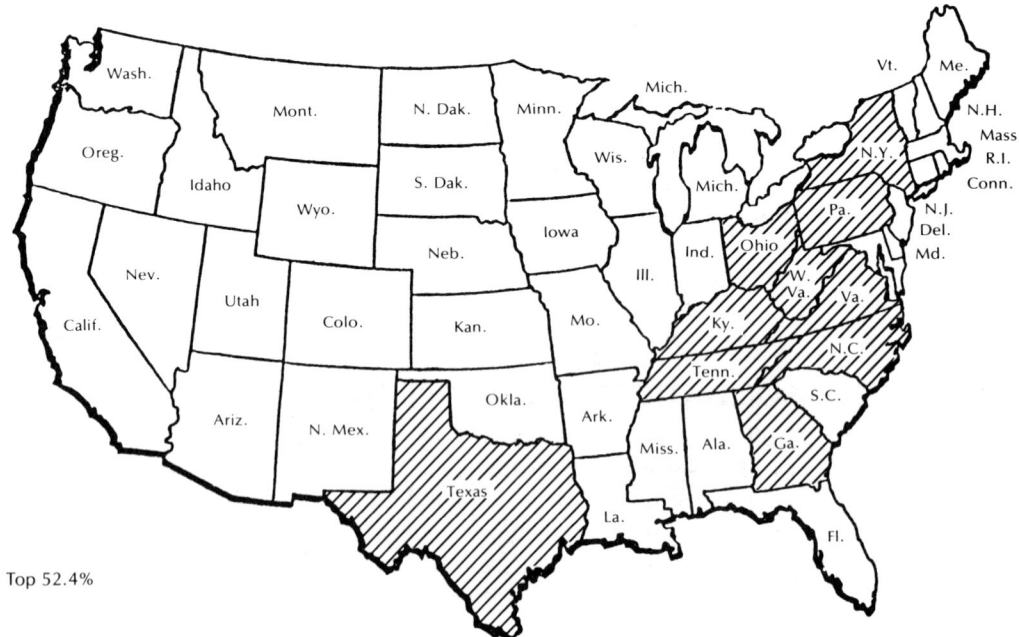

Top 52.4%

EXHIBIT 7, cont'd

Top 79.9%

EXHIBIT 8
Additional Employees Needed—Positions and Expected Wage Costs

Blair Division		Wade Division	
Position	**# Needed**	**Position**	**# Needed**
Supervisor	1	Stockman	1
Filler	5	Packer	1
Packer	6		
Stockman	2	**Administrative**	
Stapler	1	Order processing	1
Scale operator	2	Reshipments and replacements	1
Post Office man	1		
Total employees needed = 22			
Estimated			
wages:			
First year:	$145,000		

Source: Developed by casewriter.

EXHIBIT 9
Estimated Postage Costs

Zone	Orders	Postage amount
Memphis Postage by Zone		
1	73	$ 139.88
2	862	2,145.11
3	2,696	7,658.41
4	2,911	9,666.02
5	1,129	4,207.62
6	97	480.01
7	1	6.02
8	45	320.18
TOTAL	7,814	TOTAL $24,623.25

Avg. $3.15

Zone	Orders	Postage amount
Lynchburg Postage by Zone		
1	0	0.00
2	1	1.61
3	4	8.53
4	2,230	7,626.21
5	3,959	16,080.23
6	1,354	6,282.18
7	208	1,243.83
8	58	407.98
TOTAL	7,814	TOTAL $31,650.57

Avg. $4.05

EXHIBIT 10
Cost of Operating Memphis (1,000s)

	1978	1979	1980	1981
Salaries	$181.8	$192.7	$204.3	$216.5
Salaries—Lynchburg	11.0	11.7	12.4	13.1
Sick allowance	3.6	3.8	4.0	4.3
Depreciation	2.2	2.2	2.1	.7
Drayage + Freight in Memphis	13.0	14.0	15.2	16.4
Rent	23.3	23.3	23.3	23.3
Repairs & maintenance	3.6	4.0	4.4	4.8
Operating supplies	93.0	111.6	133.9	160.7
Taxes	10.3	12.4	14.8	17.8
Travel & entertainment	.4	.4	.4	.4
Utilities	6.2	6.8	7.5	8.2
Telephone	4.8	5.7	6.7	7.9
Miscellaneous	5.0	5.0	5.0	5.0
Insurance	9.8	11.8	14.1	16.9
Personnel relations	.2	.2	.2	.2
Taxes—Social Security	13.4	14.8	15.6	17.6
Retirement	7.4	7.4	7.4	7.4
Telephone: Computer hook-up	3.6	4.1	4.7	5.4
	$392.6	$431.9	$476.0	$526.6
Freight to Memphis		$ 50.2	$ 57.2	$ 65.2

Source: Developed by casewriter.

EXHIBIT 10, cont'd

Assumptions

Salaries	6% increase per year
Sick allowance	6% increase per year
Depreciation	No new equipment
Drayage & freight	8% increase per year based on Blair operating expense in Memphis

1978–1977 budgeted to actual	10.9%	Avg. 8.7%
1977–1976	6.5%	

Rent	Same as 1978 budget
Repairs & maintenance	10% increase per year

1978–1977 budgeted to actual	10.6%	Avg. 19.9%
1977–1976	29.2%	

10% used rather than 20% since 20% is too high and 10% is more recent

Supplies operating	20% increase per year

1978–1977 budgeted to actual	26.3%	Avg. 21.6%
1977–1976	17.0%	

Taxes	20% increase per year

1978–1977 budgeted to actual	34.0%	Avg. 22.8%
1977–1976	11.5%	

Travel & entertainment	Same as 1978 budget
Utilities	10% increase per year

1978–1977 budgeted to actual	2.2%	Avg. 32.0%
1977–1976	61.9%	

Telephone	18% increase per year

1978–1977 budgeted to actual	17.0%	Avg. 18.4%
1977–1976	19.7%	

Miscellaneous	Same as 1978 budget
Retirement	Same as 1978 budget
Personnel relations	Same as 1978 budget
Taxes	Social Security Taxes

	1978	6.05% on 1st $17,700
	1979	6.13% on 1st $17,700
	1980	6.13% on 1st $17,700
	1981	6.65% on 1st $17,700

Unemployment taxes
Federal .7% on 1st $6,000
Tenn.—State 1.0% on 1st $6,000
Va.—State .4% on 1st $6,000

Insurance	1978 $6.26/$100 payroll

Total dollar cost has been increasing at a rate of 20% per year

Freight Lynchburg to Memphis	Mr. French's estimates

in meeting customer demands. Some of the current overtime work could then be done on the second shift. For example, during the slack order period of June to August, the second shift could be used to prepackage sample kits for fall sales.

It was not known if the Memphis lease agreement could be broken before 1981 or if there would be a penalty cost. The lease required that the company return the building to its original state before vacating. It would cost an estimated $3,373 to restore the building. About six months of storage in an outside warehouse in Lynchburg would be required for the Memphis inventory. This storage would

EXHIBIT 11
Cost of adding a shift at Lynchburg to fill, pack, and mail Memphis volume (1,000s)

	1979	1980	1981
Second shift salaries	$145.0	$153.7	$162.9
Employee in Lynchburg	11.7	12.4	13.1
Sick allowance	3.8	4.0	4.3
Depreciation	2.2	2.1	.7
Drayage & Freight			
Operating supplies	111.6	133.9	160.7
Taxes	12.4	14.8	17.8
Travel & entertainment			
Utilities			
Telephone			
Miscellaneous	5.0	5.0	5.0
Insurance	11.3	13.5	16.2
Personnel relations			
Taxes-Social Security	11.1	11.7	13.2
Retirement	5.0	5.0	5.0
	$319.1	$356.1	$398.9
Freight and postage increases due to shipping from Lynchburg instead of Memphis			
West Coast regular orders freight	$ 14.1	$ 15.6	$ 17.1
Regular orders previously mailed from Memphis warehouse	43.8	50.3	58.0
Replacement orders previously mailed from Memphis warehouse	12.0	16.3	22.2

Assumptions

Salaries	6% increase per year
Sick allowance	Same as at Memphis now since approximately the same # of employees
Depreciation	Same as Memphis operation—will move the equipment to Lynchburg
Drayage & Freight	No change in this expense at Lynchburg
Repairs & Maintenance	No change in this expense at Lynchburg
Supplies Operating	Same as Memphis operation—same volume of orders
Taxes	Although this expense in Memphis is made up of some types of tax which are not applicable in Virginia—i.e., the Tennessee Franchise and Exercise Tax—there will be other types of taxes particular to Virginia. Assumption: Same expense as Memphis operation.
Travel & Entertainment	No increase in these expenses at Lynchburg
Utilities	No increase in these expenses at Lynchburg
Telephone	No increase in these expenses at Lynchburg
Personnel Relations	No increase in these expenses at Lynchburg
Miscellaneous	Same as at Memphis
Retirement	Same as at Memphis
Taxes	Social Security Taxes
	1978 6.05% on 1st $17,700
	1979 6.13% on 1st $17,700
	1980 6.13% on 1st $17,700
	1981 6.65% on 1st $17,700
	Unemployment taxes
	Federal .7% on 1st $6,000
	Va. State .4% on 1st $6,000
Insurance	22/23 = 95.6% of Memphis Expense

Source: Developed by casewriter.

cost $1.50/skid (a storage platform) to move the inventory in, $1.00/skid to remove it and $.75/month/skid for storage. About 1,000 skids of inventory were involved. It would cost about $10,000 to ship that inventory back to Lynchburg.

If the Chap Stick Company continued to operate the Memphis warehouse, no additional repairs of equipment would be necessary, despite a projected 10% annual increase in regular sales and a 20% annual increase in shipments of Blair sample kits. Exhibit 9 shows the postage expense for the March, 1978 orders that were shipped from Memphis ($24,623.25) and it shows the estimated postage expense if those same 7,814 orders had been shipped directly from Lynchburg ($31,650.57) instead of Memphis.

Mr. Leys, Vice President of Operations estimated that, in 1978, it cost $392,600 to operate the Memphis warehouse and these charges would increase steadily (Exhibit 10). It would probably cost around $319,000 in 1979 to operate a second shift at the Lynchburg warehouse (Exhibit 11). Severance pay for the Memphis employees could range from $36,900 to $42,300, but about $12,600 in overtime expense could be saved in 1979.[1]

Mr. French estimated that if he kept the Memphis operation, it would cost $50,200 in 1979 to ship goods from Lynchburg to the Memphis warehouse. Furthermore, he expected that annual shipping costs would rise about 4% annually due to increases in shipping rates alone.

Mr. French, confident about real growth possibilities in the Blair and Wade orders, was anxious to study the data in Lynn's study. He recalled an earlier conversation with Lynn just after she had completed the sample postage study in Exhibit 9. They estimated, based on those results, that the Chap Stick Company would incur additional postage expenses of $43,800 if the 1979 Memphis based business was to be served from Lynchburg. This estimate incorporated the Marketing Department's forecast of an annual 10% increase in regular orders and a 20% increase in Blair sample kits over the next three years—1979, 1980 and 1981.

Mr. French knew that he would have to estimate the net savings from closing the Memphis warehouse and also consider any less tangible benefits before he could make a decision. He also wondered if any other steps could be taken to improve Chap Stick's profit performance. Any potential benefits or disadvantages resulting from a change in operations needed to be made explicit in his Management Report.

---

[1]Overtime savings would occur due to a reduction in overtime hours in inventory control, accounting and shipping departments and due to increased flexibility in meeting demand at Lynchburg.

PART III

QUALITY MANAGEMENT

Noram Foods

On August 20, 1982, Leo Marsden, plant manager for Noram Foods of Toronto, Ontario, was considering the impact of changing Noram's policy on package weight. He knew this was a matter of overall corporate concern. Before raising the possibility of a change in policy with the company's executive committee, he wished to have a clearer picture of the options available and the implications of any change in policy. He was particularly concerned about the capability of the plant to hold tolerances on weights.

NORAM FOODS

Noram Foods was a major producer of a variety of consumer food products, including baby foods, cereals, and a variety of canned products. Noram Canada was part of Noram International which had plants in 12 different countries. The head office of Noram International was located in New York. Head office control was primarily financial, as part of Noram's success was based on giving its international units a large amount of local autonomy. Moreover, food tended to be subject to specific and different governmental legislation in each country in which Noram produced its products. Noram Foods had existed in Canada for over 80 years and its brands were extensively advertised. Even though management had frequently been pressured to do custom packaging or produce "no-name" products, it had steadfastly refused to get involved in either. Management believed that exclusive concentration on the production of high-quality branded products was in the corporation's best interest.

Noram Foods in Canada had an enviable record of sound financial performance, although the 1981–1982 period had seen declining profits as the Canadian economy as a whole was suffering under conditions of high unemployment, high interest rates, and high inflation. In July, 1982, the president had called for special vigilance by all managers to look for opportunities to increase revenues or reduce costs. Leo Marsden believed the weight control issue represented a major opportunity for re-evaluation and increased performance.

Copyright © 1982, School of Business Administration, The University of Western Ontario.

This case was prepared by Professor M.R. Leenders and John Walsh, based on research by Professors Forsyth and Wood.

NORAM FOOD'S POLICY ON WEIGHT CONTROL

Leo Marsden's concern was with the company's current policy on weight control which read:

"At least 95% of all packaged net weights shipped will be above the stated net weight."

Leo believed this policy could result in too high a proportion of overweight packages at substantial cost to Noram. He had therefore requested a meeting with Noram's packaging engineer, Joe Turner, who was the recognized expert in the company on statistical quality control and filling and weighing equipment. In discussing the current policy with Joe, Leo said:

I know that Noram has had this policy for about 20 years now and that during this period Noram has never been cited for putting out underweight products. A lot of things have happened over the past 20 years, however. For example, today's weighing technology is a heck of a lot better than what it used to be. We've also gone metric in the meantime and I think we could save a bundle if we took a more realistic look at our policy. The last time I brought this issue up at an executive meeting, was about 10 years ago. At that time, the vice president of marketing was completely opposed to any changes. I can still remember how upset he was. He said:

'The consequences of underweight product reaching the public could be disastrous for this company. We have a fantastic reputation to protect and I don't want to run any risk that we will lose something that took decades to build and on which we have spent tens of millions of advertising and promotion dollars. If you're proposing that we start playing statistical games with the government and the consumer, I don't want any part of it.'

Leo continued:

Nevertheless, especially in today's economic climate, we would be remiss if we didn't at least look at any major opportunity at cost reduction. Before I propose anything to the executive committee, however, I want to be sure I'm on safe ground. I want to be absolutely sure, for example, that I do not propose anything we're not capable of doing in this plant.

Joe Turner replied:

Leo, I think I know what you're saying, but it is more than just a matter of statistics and technology in filling and weighing. From time to time, I've had discussions with our marketing guys about this whole area. They keep insisting that if we ever get caught with underweight packages, it will be seen by consumers as just as serious as a citation for unsanitary conditions. It is a topic where a lot of corporate psychology is involved. We see ourselves as real corporate winners in the food field. Our current policies on sanitation, weight control, package design, and a host of other areas all reflect that winning attitude. In that kind of an environment, how much of a risk should this company take? Also, as you can well appreciate, our wide product diversity makes it difficult to apply the same weight policy to everything we do. Even now, on some products, we have substantially less than 5% of our packages underweight, just to make sure we run no chance of running below the government permitted tolerances.

Both Joe and Leo agreed that raising the issue of weight control without getting down to specifics was going to be meaningless. They, therefore, agreed to concentrate on a specific product line, pre-cooked baby cereals, to see what options might be available and what impact any change in policy might possibly have. Leo and Joe decided they would go and have a good look at the pre-cooked baby cereal package line.

FILLING OPERATIONS

Noram used a variety of filling equipment in its plant. For some less popular products, or products with unusual physical characteristics, some older equipment was used. Almost all of the larger-volume product lines were produced on sophisticated modern, high-speed filling equipment of recent vintage. Designed and made in the United States, this equipment was developed especially for the types of products Noram manufactured. An interesting design trade-off on filling equipment involved speed of fill versus tolerance holding ability on weight or volume. Obviously, a greater filling speed resulted in a higher capacity of the equipment and a lower labour cost per unit produced. On the other hand, a lower filling speed afforded better weight and volume control, resulting in a package weight and volume closer to specifications. Overweight packages resulted in higher material costs for Noram, underweight packages might result in adverse consumer reactions or government citation. For many products, Noram not only had weight standards, but also volume standards. "Settling" of product in a package after filling was always a concern, as Noram managers believed consumers might be upset if on opening a box or bag they found a substantial empty space at the top of the package. Special vibrators were attached to the filling equipment to encourage settling before package closure. Particle size and weight also affected filling rates and weight and volume control. For example, a granola-type cereal with particles ranging in weight from ½ gram to 7 grams and particle size up to about a cubic centimetre was much more difficult to control than pre-cooked baby rice cereal in which unit size and weight were small and uniform.

For pre-cooked baby cereals, the filling operation was performed on a double line consisting of 9 pieces of equipment (see Exhibit 1). The parallel lines were designed to optimize staffing, since one operator could attend to two pieces of equipment at the same time. The first unit in each line, a bottom maker, formed the pre-made carton and sealed the carton bottom. The sacker, second in line, formed the wax-paper liner and inserted it into the carton completing the package. From the sacker, the carton was moved to the Wair filler, which measured out by weight the cereal content and inserted it into the waiting carton. From the filler, the carton was moved to the top sealer for final closure and then to the

EXHIBIT 1
The Pre-Cooked Baby Cereal Line, Overhead View

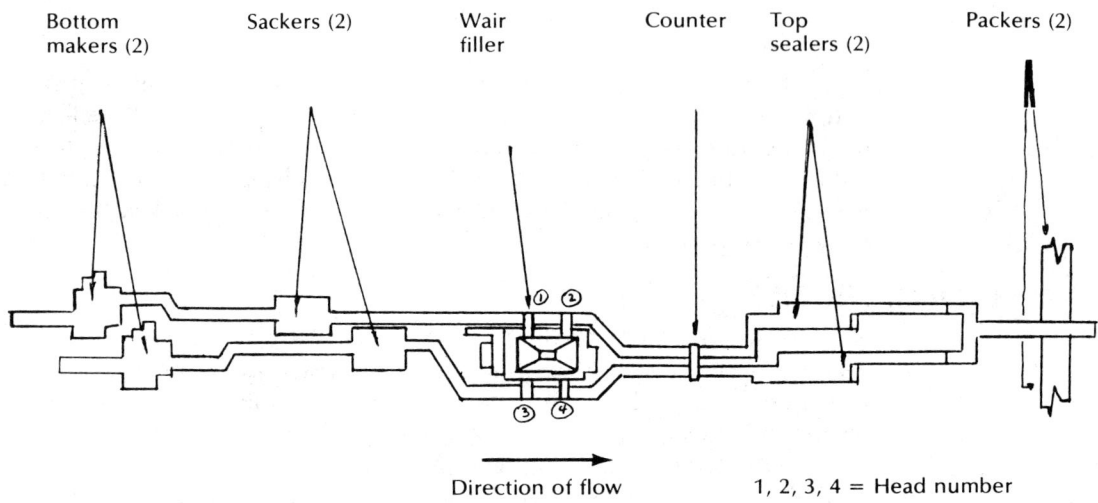

Bottom makers (2) Sackers (2) Wair filler Counter Top sealers (2) Packers (2)

Direction of flow   1, 2, 3, 4 = Head number

packer. The crew consisted of five operators. Three operators looked after the following tasks. One tended the bottom makers and sackers, making sure that each unit was kept supplied with raw materials like flat cartons and wax paper. The second operator looked after the Wair filler, while the third operator packed the completed cartons into cases at the end of the line. One operator, trained in line machine operation and minor maintenance, was responsible for effective operation of the whole line. Another acted as a spare operator who could temporarily relieve any of the other operators and also assist in maintenance. The top sealer glue supply tended to be touchy and had to be watched carefully. A considerable amount of the spare operator's time was spent on the two top sealers. This operator also rotated with the other line personnel and assisted on cut-ups. Often the cartons had to be removed from the packing line because of bad package seals. These packages were cut up for scrap and the food salvaged and repacked. Also, the work arrangement allowed for job rotation each half hour, although, in some lines, this was hampered because the packing job was critical and many of the operators were incapable of keeping up with the line. Apparently, partial rotation, where it occurred, caused little concern.

THE WAIR FILLER OPERATION

The net weight filler consisted of four separately-operated filler heads fed from a food bin located on the floor above the filler room. The capacity of the Wair filler was placed at about 100 cartons of 454-gram pre-cooked baby cereal per minute by the machine's manufacturer. This amounted to a filling speed of about 25 cartons per filling head per minute. The capacity of the other machines on the lines was in balance with the filler capacity. Actual experience with the equipment showed that daily effective capacity ran at about 85% for the 7½ hour shift the equipment operated.

The Wair filler operator was primarily concerned with package weight control. This job consisted of taking full cartons from each head (four cartons from one of the four heads every 10 minutes), pouring their contents into a plastic container, and check weighing the pre-cooked cereal to determine the actual net weight. The operator recorded the weight for each head on a control chart (X and R chart) and noted its position between the control limits. If the point fell outside of the specified limits, the operator adjusted the questionable filler head. If the filler head continued out of control after the adjustment, the operator summoned the operator in charge of the line who decided on further action. Typically, the machine was allowed to continue if the condition was one of overweight. However, an underweight situation was cause for the discontinuation of the operation.

The filler machine operator, during the normal course of the line operation, had control over the in-feed of cereal weight (variable high–low adjustment), food agitators (used to maintain cereal consistency, prevent lumping and make room in the carton for the required net weight), vibrators (to make the food settle in the carton), and the stop-start controls for the line. Each of the four heads on the Wair operated independently of the others and could be adjusted without affecting the operation of the other heads. By operating the Wair with split heads setup, at least part of the line could continue to operate at all times except under severe breakdown conditions.

When Joe Turner and Leo Marsden observed the filling operation, they noted everything was running smoothly on August 20, 1982. The line was running pre-cooked baby cereal and seemed to be meeting its daily production goal of about 38,000 cartons. Since the rice cereal was the most popular of the pre-cooked baby cereals, and since the 454-gram size was the most popular package weight, approximately 60 days a year were scheduled for this package size and cereal alone. The remainder of the year, the machine produced a variety of package sizes in rice, soya, barley, oats, and mixed pre-cooked baby cereals. Leo Marsden believed that the cost of 454 grams of pre-cooked baby cereal ranged from about 40 to 60 cents. This cost was a fully allocated one, including an appropriate share of overheads in the various processing departments, prior to filling as well as a share of general plant overhead.

The equipment in the baby cereal area was about three years old and had operated well since its original installation. When Leo Marsden asked Joe Turner what new technology was coming along on the horizon, to replace it, Joe replied:

> As you well know, Leo, the technology in measuring and weighing and packing equipment is changing all the time. They are always trying to increase speed and accuracy. However, the costs are going up substantially as well. I'm not aware of anything at the moment that would make it worthwhile for us to pull out this line

EXHIBIT 2
Wair Filler Plot, Head No. 3

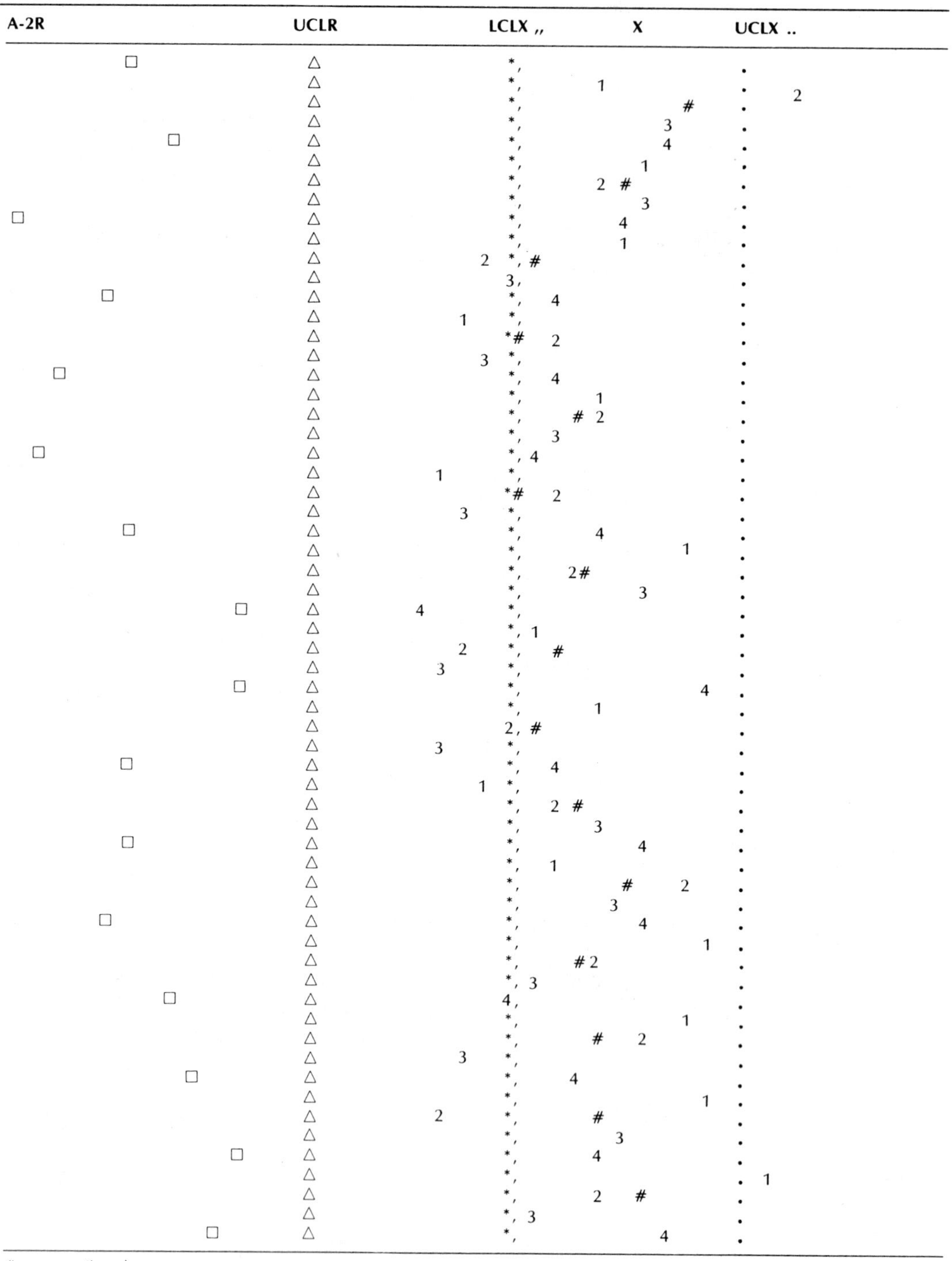

A-2R	UCLR	LCLX ,,	X	UCLX ..

= Sample means
1. 2. 3. 4 = Individual sample weights

now and substitute it with something better. It may well be that in another year or so, somebody may have some new equipment that's attractive enough for us to take a good look at. Frankly, compared to some of the older equipment in other parts of our plant, the performance of these two lines and this particular filler is quite astounding. We really have no problem staying within a plus or minus one percent range on weight control in this department, which, considering the speeds we're running at, is outstanding performance.

Joe Turner moved to the Wair filler operator and asked her to show Leo her weight control charts. Leo noted that the equipment was consistently running within the control limits specified. (See Exhibit 2 for a typical Wair filler plot.) Joe also selected at random one of the sheets summarizing the previous day's operation (see Exhibit 3). It summarized both the day's performance for one of the filling heads, as well as the month's to-date statistics for the same head. Leo asked Joe to make a copy of this and also to bring him the latest government regulations on weight control. Leo knew that with the introduction of the metric system, the government had issued new regulations on acceptable tolerances. He wanted to be absolutely sure that he had the latest information available on consumer packaged goods.

EXHIBIT 3
Wair Filler Operating Results

Date:	August 19, 1982
Product:	Pre-Cooked Baby Food
Package weight:	454 g
Head:	#3
Capability:	1.65 g

	Month to date	Day
A-2R	2.281 g	2.829 g
Std. dev.	1.517 g	1.882 g
Mean range	3.124 g	3.876 g
UCL (range)	7.123 g	8.837 g
LCL (range)	0 g	0 g
5% control	2.497 g	3.096 g
UCL (mean)	4.778 g	5.925 g
LCL (mean)	0.214 g	0.267 g
Sample size (R)	630	45
Sample size (A)	622	45
# light	119	8
Total lightweight	257.516 g	20.52 g
% light	4.783 %	4.444 %
Total overweight	6749.944 g	572.040 g
Mean overweight	2.713 g	3.178 g
Mean % overweight	0.598 %	0.700 %
Percentage variability	8.061 %	−14.061 %

EXHIBIT 3, cont'd
A Note on Control Chart and Control Chart Summary Calculations

Date, product, package weight, head: Each day summary tables of operations for the Wair Filler were prepared. On any given day there might be several summaries for each head as package weights or products changed. This summary refers to the previous day's run, Thursday August 19th 1982, of 454 gram Pre-Cooked Baby Cereal through #3 head.

Capability: This is the standard deviation determined by NORAM management which under the filling conditions relevant to this product, speed, particle size, Wair manufacturer specifications etc., should be achieved in meeting the "95% of all packages shipped should be over stated net weight" policy.

A-2R: This is a factor calculated using Table C. For n = 4, A-2 is .73 and R is the mean range of a number of samples. Thus, for the Month to Date figure,

$$A\text{-}2R = 0.73 \times 3.124 = 2.281$$

Std. dev.: This is the sample standard deviation. Theoretically it is calculated as the square root of the sum of the squared deviations of n observations from the mean divided by n − 1. The bigger the standard deviation the more 'spread out' the distribution about the mean.

$$S = \sqrt{\frac{\Sigma\,(y_i - \bar{y})^2}{n - 1}}$$

If MEAN RANGE is divided by D2 (a factor taken from Table B equal to 2.059 for n = 4), we have a very close approximation of the population standard deviation. Thus, for the Month to Date figure,

$$\text{Std. dev.} = 3.124/2.059 = 1.517$$

Mean Range: This is the average of the ranges in the samples taken for the day.

UCL (Range): This is the Upper Control Limit on the Range. It is calculated as D4 × MEAN RANGE where D4 is a factor equal to 2.28 for a sample of n = 4 (see Table C for D4 factors). Thus, for the Month to Date figure,

$$\text{UCL (Range)} = 2.28 \times 3.124 = 7.123$$

LCL (Range): This is the Lower Control Limit on the Range. It is calculated as D3 × MEAN RANGE where D3 is a factor equal to Zero for a sample of n = 4. The Lower Control Limit on the Range is therefore Zero (see Table C for D3 factors).

Operators use the upper and lower control limits on the range to monitor the filling operation.

5% control: This is the mean setting to ensure that not more than 5% of the packages filled will be below 454 grams. At this setting 90% of observations will be between some upper and lower bound on a normal distribution, where the lower bound is 454 (there will be 5% observations in each tail).

We can calculate this 5% control level in the following way. Table A shows the percentage of observations which will be within a given number of standard deviations from the mean. If we want to find how many standard deviations on either side of the mean will contain 90% of observations (NORAM policy), find .4500 in the body of Table A and read off 1.645. We can interpret this as 45% of observations will be between the mean and minus 1.645 standard deviations and 50% above the mean. Table A is a 'one tail' table. Thus, for the Month to Date figure,

$$5\% \text{ control} = 1.645 \times 1.517 = 2.497$$

UCL (Mean): This is the Upper Control Limit on the Mean. It is calculated as 5% CONTROL LEVEL + A-2R. Thus, for the Month to Date figure,

EXHIBIT 3, cont'd

$$UCL \ (mean) \ = \ 2.497 \ + \ 2.281 \ = \ 4.778$$

LCL (Mean): This is the Lower Control Limit on the Mean. It is calculated as 5% CONTROL LEVEL − A-2R. Thus, for the Month to Date figure,

$$LCL \ (mean) \ = \ 2.497 \ - \ 2.281 \ = \ 0.214$$

Sample size (R): This is the unadjusted sample size. Each sample consists of four packages. The 630 samples reported for the Month to Date represents 2520 individual packages.

Sample size (A): This is the adjusted sample size. 'Wild' samples are disregarded in calculations. The 622 samples reported for the Month to Date represent 2488 packages. In this regard we can think of two kinds of 'causes' for package weight variation. There are statistical variations which we can regard as normal fluctuations around a mean and which arise from the acceptable operating characteristics of the equipment, and there are assignable variations where the variation from target is a result of some malfunction. If a blockage occurs, for example, and produces a half filled package in a sample this would be termed 'wild' by Noram and the whole sample discarded for computational purposes. The reasoning here is that Noram wishes to track statistical variation and not malfunctions. In the event of a 'wild' sample being detected operators would take the appropriate action to ensure that affected packages were removed from production. A total of 8 such samples have been omitted for the Month to Date SAMPLE SIZE (A).

 # light: This is the number of packages in the samples under the net weight of 454 grams. For example if, in one of the samples of four packages, one of the packages was less than 454 grams this would count as one light package. For the Month to Date figure 119 such packages have been recorded in the samples.

Total lightweight: This is the total amount in grams of underweight in the light packages. For example, if a light package has been detected in a sample, weighing in at say 451 grams, this would be recorded as 3 grams of lightweight. The TOTAL LIGHTWEIGHT associated with the 119 # LIGHT for the Month to Date figure is 257.516.

% light: This is the percentage of packages in the adjusted sample under the net weight. It is calculated as # LIGHT divided by the number of packages in SAMPLE SIZE (A) and expressed as a percentage. Thus, for the Month to Date figure,

$$\% \ light \ = \ 119/2488 \ = \ 4.873\%$$

Total overweight: This is the total weight in grams in excess of the net weight requirements. Each package that weighed in excess of 454 grams would contribute to the TOTAL OVERWEIGHT.

Mean overweight: This is the TOTAL OVERWEIGHT divided by the number of packages in SAMPLE SIZE (A). Noram does not deduct the number of light packages from SAMPLE SIZE (A) in computing MEAN OVERWEIGHT. Thus, for the Month to Date figure,

$$Mean \ overweight \ = \ 6749.944/2488 \ = \ 2.713$$

Mean % overweight: This is the MEAN OVERWEIGHT divided by the PACKAGE WEIGHT and expressed as a percentage. Thus, for the Month to Date figure,

$$Mean \ \% \ overweight \ = \ 2.713/454 \ = \ 0.598\%$$

Percentage variability: This can be interpreted as a measure of Wair Filler performance against 'standard'. It is calculated as CAPABILITY minus STD. DEV. and expressed as a percentage of CAPABILITY. A positive figure indicates performance better than standard, while a negative result suggests worse. Thus, for the Month to Date figure,

$$Percentage \ variability \ = \ 1.650 \ - \ 1.517/1.650 \ = \ 8.061\%$$

EXHIBIT 3, cont'd
Table A.   Areas Under the Normal Curve

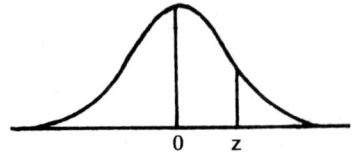

z	.00	.01	.02	.03	.04	.05	.06	.07	.08	.09
0.0	.0000	.0040	.0080	.0120	.0160	.0199	.0239	.0279	.0319	.0359
0.1	.0398	.0438	.0478	.0517	.0557	.0596	.0636	.0675	.0714	.0753
0.2	.0793	.0832	.0871	.0910	.0948	.0987	.1026	.1064	.1103	.1141
0.3	.1179	.1217	.1255	.1293	.1331	.1368	.1406	.1443	.1480	.1517
0.4	.1554	.1591	.1628	.1664	.1700	.1736	.1772	.1808	.1844	.1879
0.5	.1915	.1950	.1985	.2019	.2054	.2088	.2123	.2157	.2190	.2224
0.6	.2257	.2291	.2324	.2357	.2389	.2422	.2454	.2486	.2517	.2549
0.7	.2580	.2611	.2642	.2673	.2704	.2734	.2764	.2794	.2823	.2852
0.8	.2881	.2910	.2939	.2967	.2995	.3023	.3051	.3078	.3106	.3133
0.9	.3159	.3186	.3212	.3238	.3264	.3289	.3315	.3340	.3365	.3389
1.0	.3413	.3438	.3461	.3485	.3508	.3531	.3554	.3577	.3599	.3621
1.1	.3643	.3665	.3686	.3708	.3729	.3749	.3770	.3790	.3810	.3830
1.2	.3849	.3869	.3888	.3907	.3925	.3944	.3962	.3980	.3997	.4015
1.3	.4032	.4049	.4066	.4082	.4099	.4115	.4131	.4147	.4162	.4177
1.4	.4192	.4207	.4222	.4236	.4251	.4265	.4279	.4292	.4306	.4319
1.5	.4332	.4345	.4357	.4370	.4382	.4394	.4406	.4418	.4429	.4441
1.6	.4452	.4463	.4474	.4484	.4495	.4505	.4515	.4525	.4535	.4545
1.7	.4554	.4564	.4573	.4582	.4591	.4599	.4608	.4616	.4625	.4633
1.8	.4641	.4649	.4656	.4664	.4671	.4678	.4686	.4693	.4699	.4706
1.9	.4713	.4719	.4726	.4732	.4738	.4744	.4750	.4756	.4761	.4767
2.0	.4772	.4778	.4783	.4788	.4793	.4798	.4803	.4808	.4812	.4817
2.1	.4821	.4826	.4830	.4834	.4838	.4842	.4846	.4850	.4854	.4857
2.2	.4861	.4864	.4868	.4871	.4875	.4878	.4881	.4884	.4887	.4890
2.3	.4893	.4896	.4898	.4901	.4904	.4906	.4909	.4911	.4913	.4916
2.4	.4918	.4920	.4922	.4925	.4927	.4929	.4931	.4932	.4934	.4936
2.5	.4938	.4940	.4941	.4943	.4945	.4946	.4948	.4949	.4951	.4952
2.6	.4953	.4955	.4956	.4957	.4959	.4960	.4961	.4962	.4963	.4964
2.7	.4965	.4966	.4967	.4968	.4969	.4970	.4971	.4972	.4973	.4974
2.8	.4974	.4975	.4976	.4977	.4977	.4978	.4979	.4979	.4980	.4981
2.9	.4981	.4982	.4982	.4983	.4984	.4984	.4985	.4985	.4986	.4986
3.0	.4987	.4987	.4987	.4988	.4988	.4989	.4989	.4989	.4990	.4990

Source: W. Mendenhall and L. Ott, "Understanding Statistics"
Duxbury Press, 3rd edition, 1980.

EXHIBIT 3, cont'd

Table B. Factors for Estimating s from $\bar{R}$

Number of observations in subgroup	Factor for estimate from R D2
2	1.128
3	1.693
4	2.059
5	2.326
6	2.534
7	2.704
8	2.847
9	2.970
10	3.078

Table C. Factors for Determining from $\bar{R}$ the 3-Sigma Control Limits for $\bar{X}$ and R Charts

Number of observations in subgroup n	Factor for $\bar{X}$ chart A2	Factors for R chart	
		Lower control limit D3	Upper control limit D4
2	1.88	0	3.27
3	1.02	0	2.57
4	0.73	0	2.28
5	0.58	0	2.11
6	0.48	0	2.00
7	0.42	0.08	1.92
8	0.37	0.14	1.86
9	0.34	0.18	1.82
10	0.31	0.22	1.78

Source: Adapted from E.L. Grant and R.S. Leavenworth, "Statistical Quality Control," 5th edition, McGraw-Hill, 1980.

GOVERNMENT LEGISLATION

Joe Turner returned to Leo Marsden's office later on the same day. He brought with him, not only a copy of the Wair filler chart that Leo had requested, but also copies of the consumer packaging and labelling act and various amendments and information brochures provided by the Department of Consumer and Corporate Affairs of Canada.

Joe said:

Leo, I've gone through all of this governmental material. As you can well appreciate, the primary reason for its existence is to protect the consumer from misrepresentation by the manufacturer of consumer packaged products. Therefore, there are all kinds of packaging and labelling regulations which we must conform to. For example, we are required to label everything in French and English. Where we state weights, we can only do so in the prescribed form and with the appropriate spacing. For example, it is correct to state that a package weighs 454 grams and we are supposed to represent it as 454 g. It is incorrect to say it contains 453.592 grams. Moreover, there can only be one typed space between the weight measure, in this case grams, and the number preceding it. Neither is it correct to put a period like we normally do for Mr. or Mrs. as for an abbreviation. All the symbols with the exception of the litre symbol "L", must be shown in lower case and cannot have a period or the letter "s" behind it. It is also not necessary to use phrases such as "net" or "net weight" as part of the net quantity declaration. If we choose to use such terms, they have to be shown in French as well. I'm sure I'm just repeating things you already know. However, I have underlined here a few specific points which deal with the net weight issue you're trying to raise. For example, here in the consumer packaging and labelling act: 7(3): where a declaration of net quantity shows the purported net quantity of the pre-packaged product to which it is applied, that declaration shall be deemed not to be a false or misleading representation of the net quantity of the pre-packaged product if it is, subject to the prescribed tolerance, not less than the declared net quantity of the pre-packaged product and the declaration otherwise meets the requirements of this Act and the regulations.

Joe Turner continued:

As I understand it, in March, 1975, a further amendment was made to the consumer packaging and labelling regulations. The sections of greatest pertinence for us are 39, dealing with tolerances and 40, dealing with inspection; Schedule 1, part 3 dealing with the permitted tolerances.

Here they are:

Tolerances

39. (1) For the purposes of Schedule 1, *catch weight product* means a product that because of its nature cannot normally be portioned to a predetermined quantity and is, as a result, usually sold in packages of varying quantity.

(2) Subject to subsection (3), the amount set out in column II of an item of the appropriate Part of Schedule I is the tolerance prescribed for the purposes of subsection 7(3) of the Act for the net quantity set out in column 1 of that item.

(3) Where the net quantity of a prepackaged product referred to in Part I, II, III, IV, V, or VI of Schedule I is declared by weight or volume and that net quantity is not set out in column I of that Part, the tolerance prescribed for the purposes of subsection 7(3) of the Act for that net quantity is an amount based upon linear interpolation between the appropriate tolerances appearing in column II of that Part.[1]

Inspection

40. (1) Where an inspector wishes to inspect any lot, shipment, proposed shipment or identifiable quantity of prepackaged products all purporting to contain the same net quantity of product (hereinafter referred to as a *lot*) to determine whether the

---

[1]Excerpt from CONSUMER PACKAGING AND LABELLING ACT, Consumer Packaging and Labelling Regulations amendment, P.C. 1975-479 4 March, 1975, see Exhibit 4.

EXHIBIT 4
Declaration of Net Quantity by Metric Units of Weight on Products Other than Catch Weight Products

Item	Column I Declared weight	Column II Tolerances
1	1 g*	0.16 g
2	1.5 g	0.20 g
3	2 g	0.25 g
4	3 g	0.32 g
5	4 g	0.38 g
6	5 g	0.44 g
7	6 g	0.50 g
8	8 g	0.59 g
9	10 g	0.68 g
10	15 g	0.88 g
11	20 g	1.05 g
12	30 g	1.36 g
13	40 g	1.63 g
14	50 g	1.87 g
15	60 g	2.1 g
16	80 g	2.5 g
17	100 g	2.9 g
18	150 g	3.8 g
19	200 g	4.5 g
20	300 g	5.8 g
21	400 g	7.0 g
22	500 g	8.0 g
23	600 g	9.0 g
24	800 g	11.0 g
25	1 kg**	12.5 g
26	1.5 kg	16.0 g
27	2 kg	19.4 g
28	3 kg	25.0 g
29	4 kg	30.0 g
30	5 kg	34.0 g
31	6 kg	39.0 g
32	8 kg	46.0 g
33	10 kg	53.0 g
34	15 kg	68.0 g
35	20 kg	80.0 g
36	Over 20 kg	0.4% of declared weight

*g = grams
**kg = kilograms
Excerpt from CONSUMER PACKAGING AND LABELLING ACT, Consumer Packaging and Labelling Regulations amendment, Schedule 1, Part III, P.C. 1975-479 4 March, 1975

lot meets the requirements of the Act and these Regulations respecting the declaration of net quantity and where, in his opinion, it is impractical or undesirable to inspect all the separate prepackaged products in the lot, he may inspect the lot by selecting and examining a sample of the lot.[1]

Leo Marsden thanked Joe Turner for his work. He concluded:

Joe, why don't both of us think this whole situation out for a week or so and then get together on it again. I want to be thoroughly familiar with this whole situation before I look at any options or propose any changes. I like the idea of concentrating first at the pre-cooked cereal line, because it is a steady seller and it is an area we appear to have under reasonable control. I know we can't stop there, but it is a good place to start.

---

[1]Excerpt from CONSUMER PACKAGING AND LABELLING ACT, Consumer Packaging and Labelling Regulations amendment, P.C. 1975-479 4 March, 1975, see Exhibit 4.

The Problem with Kathy (A)

"John, I've had it with Kathy! When this meeting is over she's getting a written reprimand. And if she doesn't straighten up I'll keep writing reprimands till we've gone through the whole union procedure and she's out on the street and out of my hair!"

"Calm down Ann; I know you're mad after all the trouble she's caused, but remember, the way to get rid of a bad worker is to follow the procedures and get plenty of facts. You have to be able to show she can't do the work. If she can't, it really is to her advantage to go somewhere else. It's not right, though, to fire someone who *could* do the work if we just helped a little more."

"John, I've helped her. I've had the other calibrators help her. She seems to know how to do the job but just look at this Q.C. report (Exhibit 1). Last week our rejects were 17% of production. I can't live with that; the standard allows for only 8%. Anyway, Charlene and the others will be here in a few minutes. The data they've got should solve my problem. While we wait let me buy you coffee."

BACKGROUND: GAUGE FABRICATION AND CALIBRATION

Ann Pitts was the foreman of the mechanical gauge department of Special Components Corporation (SCC), a leading manufacturer of small components and subassemblies for many motor vehicle manufacturers. By generally concentrating on high-volume jobs, such as filters, pumps, and gauges, SCC had been able to remain a low-cost producer in a highly cost-competitive market.

As a foreman Ann was rated primarily on 3 key goals:
1. No grievances from the union (official complaints about contract violations),
2. Quantity of products shipped on time,
3. Meeting budgeted costs for her department.

While not explicitly included in the foreman's rating, quality of production was also an important consideration. Attention to quality over the years had provided SCC with a reputation as a high quality supplier.

The mechanical gauge department produced various gauges for measuring pressure, temperature, and vacuum. While SCC had many proprietary design

·Copyright © 1985 by the Colgate Darden Graduate Business School Sponsors University of Virginia, Charlottesville, Virginia. Reproduced by permission.

This case was prepared by Dennis Harbin under the supervision of Professor Edward W. Davis, The Colgate Darden Graduate School of Business Administration, University of Virginia.

EXHIBIT 1

Data on Gauge Rejects (% Trays Rejected)

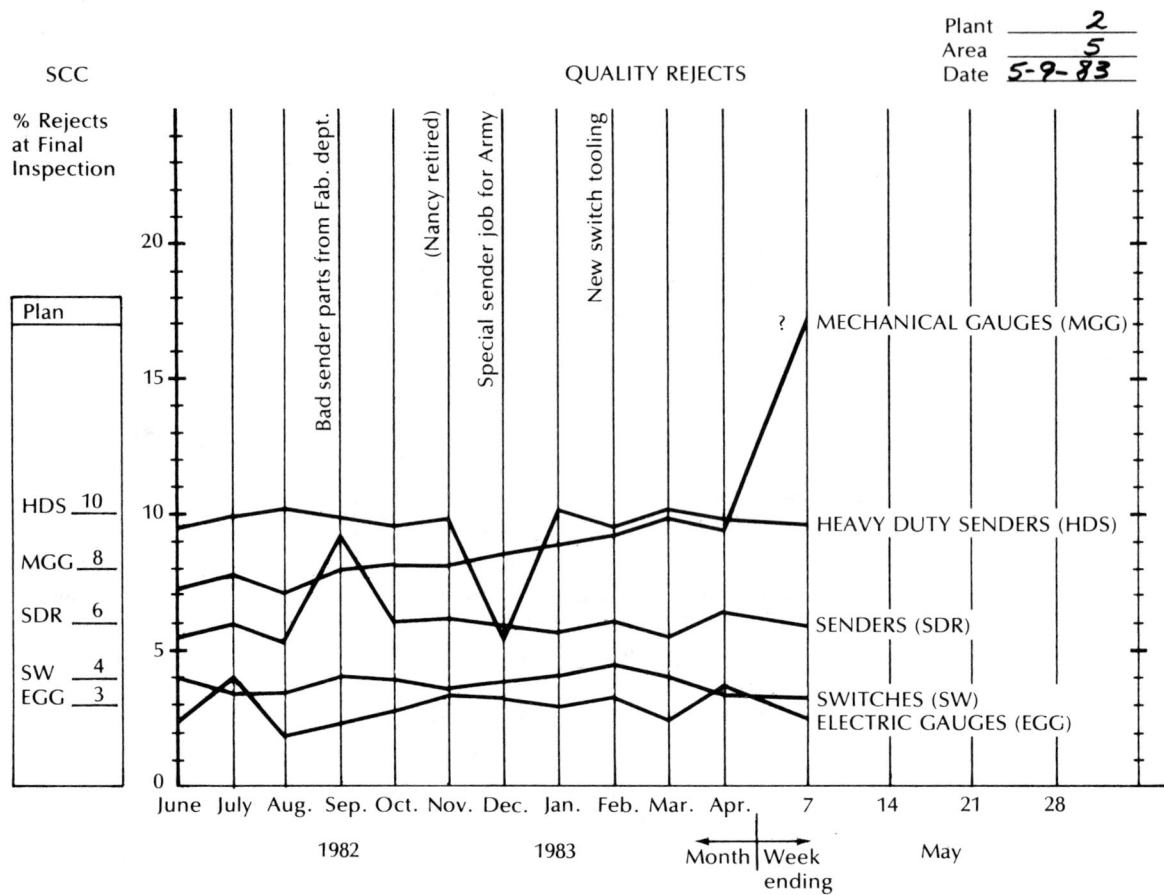

Plant _____ **2**
Area _____ **5**
Date **5-9-83**

SCC   QUALITY REJECTS

% Rejects at Final Inspection

Chart annotations (top, vertical): Bad sender parts from Fab. dept. | (Nancy retired) | Special sender job for Army | New switch tooling

? MECHANICAL GAUGES (MGG)
HEAVY DUTY SENDERS (HDS)
SENDERS (SDR)
SWITCHES (SW)
ELECTRIC GAUGES (EGG)

Plan

	SCC
HDS	10
MGG	8
SDR	6
SW	4
EGG	3

Y-axis: 0, 5, 10, 15, 20

X-axis: June July Aug. Sep. Oct. Nov. Dec. Jan. Feb. Mar. Apr. 7 14 21 28

1982   1983   Month | Week ending   May

features in their gauges and their manufacturing process, the gauges used the Bourdon tube type mechanism patented by Eugene Bourdon, in 1849. Exhibit 2 shows a schematic diagram of how the gauge works. The Bourdon tube was an oval piece of tubing bent in a circular arc and sealed at one end. Applying pressure to the tube, through the fitting attached to the open end, caused the tube to try to straighten. This movement caused the closed end of the tube to move outward pulling the calibration link which moved the quadrant gear. As the quadrant gear moved it turned the pinion gear on the pointer shaft. By adjusting the length of the link the gauge could be calibrated (adjusted) so the pointer would indicate the correct pressure, within the given limits required by the customer. Because the distance the end of the tube moved was very small, the material in the tube and its shape, i.e., thickness, oval, and arc, had to be closely controlled or calibration became difficult if not impossible.

EXHIBIT 2
Operation of Bourdon Tube Gauge

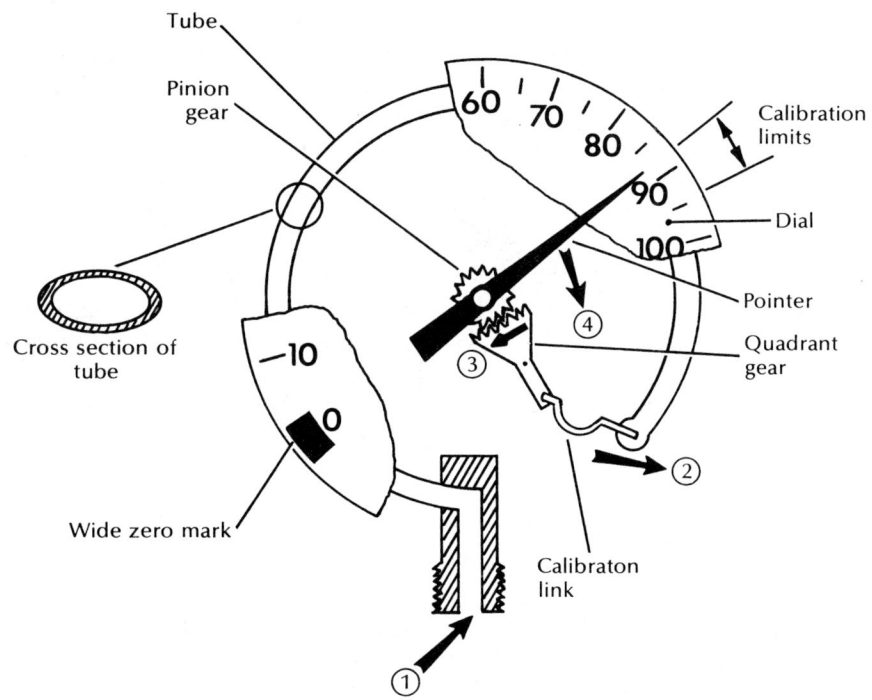

① Pressure is applied to inlet fitting.

② Pressure causes tube to try to straighten moving
   free end out and pulling on link.

③ Link pulls on quadrant gear causing quadrant
   gear to rotate.

④ Quadrant gear rotates pinion gear and pointer.

Ann's department was divided into 5 areas based on the type work done. The first area was tube forming. In this area the tube of the correct material and size was formed from round tubing into the proper oval shape for the specific gauge to be made. The oval tube was then formed to the proper circular arc, cut to length, and the one end was sealed. The last operation in this area was to solder a connection fitting to the open end of the tube and pressure test it for leaks.

The second area was mechanism assembly. Here the tube and other parts were assembled to form the basic mechanism for the gauge. While each type was technically different, the basic mechanisms were so nearly identical this one area made them for all the gauges: pressure, vacuum, and temperature.

The last three areas were quite similar. They were the calibration areas for: (1) low-pressure gauges, (2) vacuum and high-pressure gauges, and (3) temperature gauges. Ann's current problem was in the calibration of low-pressure gauges, which represented the majority of the production in her department. Calibration was the last step in the assembly process and required skill and practice to do it quickly. Because of the importance of calibration, this work was considered to be the best job in the department; it was also the highest-paying. Kathy Clark, Donna Norville, and Lonny Veach were the workers assigned to calibrate gauges at the time of case-writing. Kathy was the youngest calibrator, with only 2 years seniority, while Donna and Lonny had been with the company over ten years, with most of that time spent in gauge calibration.

The calibration process involved several steps to ensure meeting the specification limits. The basic process started by placing the gauge to be calibrated in the calibration stand, which automatically held the gauge in place when the stand was operated. Next the pointer was loosely installed, pointing at the mark for zero, and pressure was applied. The specification for most of the gauges required the pointer to indicate 87 to 93 psi (pounds per square inch), as shown in Exhibit 2. If the gauge did not read within these limits the reading could be adjusted by bending the calibration link with a special pair of pliers. This would also change the zero position of the pointer, which had to be positioned such that the pointer at least touched the wide zero mark. By combinations of adjusting the link and repositioning the pointer is was possible to calibrate a correctly-made mechanism within the specified limits. When the calibration was correct, the pointer was tapped with a small hammer to lock it in position on the shaft. The gauge was then placed in a tray of good gauges for shipment.

Each calibrator was responsible for the quality of the gauges he or she produced. This meant they had to inspect the gauge for obvious physical defects, such as scratches on the dial or incorrect fittings. It also meant they had to ensure the calibration stand was applying the correct pressure to the gauge during calibration. Each calibrator was assigned to work on a particular stand: Kathy used Stand #1, Donna, Stand #2, and Lonny, Stand#3. To ensure correct stand pressure they used a "master gauge" with a larger, more accurate dial to check the stand after every tray of 12 gauges was calibrated. Because the master gauges were very sensitive and subject to damage, they were not permanently installed on the stands. Master gauges could be shared if the master assigned to a particular stand was being repaired. If a stand was discovered to be applying an incorrect pressure the calibrator could readjust it using a master gauge. If it was off very far the calibrator might recheck the last tray of gauges and fix any that were out of limits. The calibrators also adjusted their stands at the start of every day, and the adjustment was checked by the Inspection Department, using their own master gauge. If inspection found the pressure below 87 psi or above 93 psi the cause was found and fixed. To assure the accuracy of the master gauges used by the calibrators, they were checked weekly by the Inspection Department. They were also checked and readjusted every 90 days in SCC's central standards laboratory. The central standards lab maintained all the measurement equipment for SCC and provided special measurement services when needed.

Because each calibrator was responsible for the quality of his/her own work, only a small random sample of finished gauges from all calibrators was normally taken for quality control inspection. This inspection was done in a separate, small area near the gauge production department. Depending upon the results of this inspection the gauges completed since the last inspection were either accepted for shipment or rejected. Any rejected gauges were tagged and sent back to the department for repair by one of the more skilled workers in the group. A separate stand, which was always kept in top-notch condition, was used for repair work.

THE MEETING TO DISCUSS THE PROBLEM

In the conversation recorded earlier, Ann Pitts had been speaking with John Condon, General Foreman for Instruments at SCC. They were waiting for the arrival of three other supervisory personnel to discuss the problem of rejects in gauge calibration. The meeting had been called at Ann's request. The following dialogue occurred as two of the expected individuals arrived in quick succession:

Ann:

Hi, Ken, glad you could make it. John, this is Ken Willens; he was with the pump plant until this Monday. He's replacing Chris Covert as our labor relations person. Ken, I don't know who you've met this week so let me introduce these people. This is John Condon, the general foreman for instruments and all the miscellaneous departments in this end of the plant, and Charlene Hazen here is our Q.C. foreman. Gary Stevens said he would be a little late; he's our product engineer.

As you know, the reason we're here is because of the quality problems we've been having, especially the problem with Kathy Clark.

Ken:

Are you sure there is a problem with Kathy?

Ann:

You bet there is! The purpose of this meeting is to make sure we have the proof needed to write a reprimand without getting a grievance!

John:

Calm down, Ann. We know you're upset. Why don't you fill us in on the background a little, then we can go through the data to make sure we have all the facts we need to cover you.

Ann:

OK. As you know, Kathy started with SCC, in my department, about 2 years ago. She was a good worker and moved through all the jobs. When Nancy Smedley retired last year I put Kathy into the calibration job. She was a little slow learning it but she made it through the probation period and now the job is hers. It's a higher job classification so I can't move her back on the line. She's pretty chummy with the shop committeeman so I can't get the union to approve a transfer.

She's been on that job now about 6 months. Right after she got reclassified she started complaining about how hard the job was. She said the machine was no good, but the tool room checked it and said it was OK. Then she complained about the assembly people not doing their jobs right. When we moved into our spring rush she just went nuts. She complains about everything and keeps making bad gauges. I've talked to her, the other calibrators have talked to her but she just complains. I could live with her complaints if she just made good parts, so I could stay on schedule.

One last thing, with the quality problems she's caused, we've added more people to inspect and repair rejected gauges. They're not in my budget, so I'm getting killed on the cost reports. Something has got to be done!

John:

Charlene, why don't you explain what you've found.

Charlene:

OK. Well . . .

The conference room door opened at this point as Gary Stevens, senior product engineer for gauges, arrived.

Ann:

Hi Gary, glad you could make it.

Gary:

Glad to help. Sorry I'm late. We just finished measuring the last gauges in the lab.

Ann:

I think you know everyone except Ken. He's our new labor relations man. Ken Willens, Gary Stevens.

John:

Charlene was just explaining what she's found. When she's done we'll take a look at what you've got. Charlene, go ahead, please.

Charlene:

Thanks John. First the Q.C. report (Exhibit 1) for this month in John's area shows when the problem started. We plot a full year on the report, so you can see trends in problems and see if solutions we've implemented really worked. You can see the steady increase in rejects over the past 6 months, with a large jump last week. I marked on the report the month Nancy retired. That was the last month Ann's department was ahead of plan on rejects. This report reflects the percentage of trays we accept or reject. With the sampling plan we use, if we reject one tray we generally reject everything Ann's people made during the last hour or so. In the

EXHIBIT 3
Pareto Analysis of Reject Causes

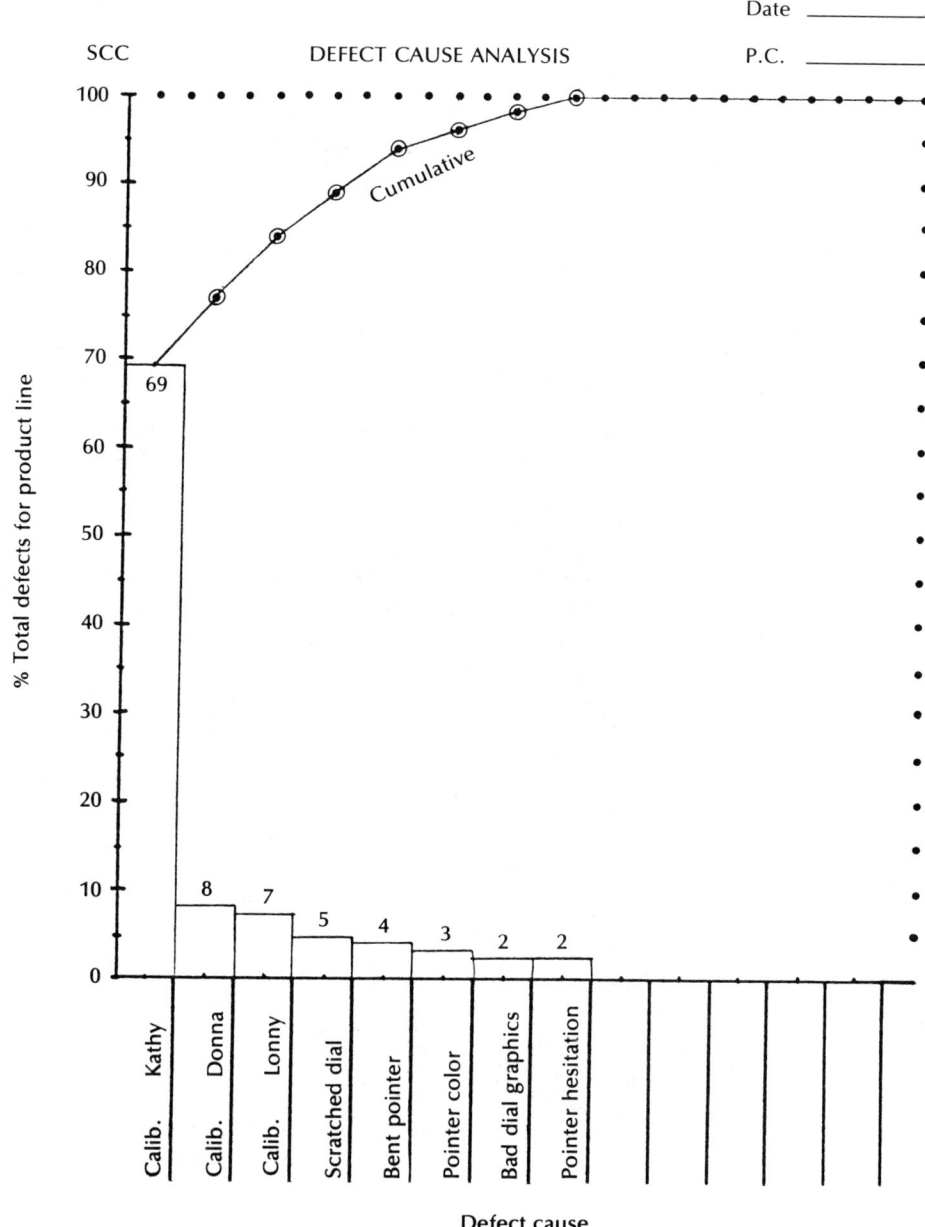

end I think the average is pretty close to the percentage of bad gauges Ann's people find when they check the rejected trays.

These are just department totals so I made a Pareto chart of the problem causes (Exhibit 3). As you can see from the chart, Kathy is clearly the major cause of rejects.

Ken:

I talked with Kathy. She claims it's the equipment and the poorly assembled gauges.

Ann:

We've already checked the equipment! The other calibrators don't have any problems, so I'm not wasting any time with the assemblers. Besides, she used to be an assembler; she knows they're doing it right.

Charlene:

But Al, the data we collect really can't answer whether the mechanism, the stand, or the calibrator caused the calibration to be off. I believe the data Gary has collected will answer that. But, I do have some data on the calibration stands which may help us understand this situation better. We check each stand at the start of every day with a master gauge and record the reading. To do this we have the calibrator set the stand using the master gauge and check to be sure it reads within 87–93 psi. If it's beyond the limits we have the machine repaired or adjusted. We also check our inspection master gauge and the masters for each stand once a week with a dead weight tester (slowest but most accurate way to check the accuracy of a pressure gauge) and record the results. The stand masters are also used to check the stand after every tray of gauges (12 per tray). If needed, the stand is readjusted to read correctly using the stand master. We keep a log of the readings we get when we check the 3 calibration stands and the repair stand each morning. We also record the readings we get when we check the master gauges on the dead weight tester each week. Here are the log sheets for the past 2½ months (Exhibit 4). After a problem is fixed with a stand or when a master comes back from the lab, we note the new reading in the comments column. I've circled the times each machine was out enough to need work. Hers (Stand #1) is no worse than the other two.

Ann:

Like I said, the machine is not the problem; she is.

Ken:

It does look like you've got a case. But, there's another small problem before we look at what Gary has. Kathy tells me you don't fix all the bad gauges, that some get shipped.

John:

Everybody knows we don't fix everything; it just isn't economical. If they're close and we're behind, we may ship them.

EXHIBIT 4

YEAR 1983
MONTH MARCH

Calibration Stand-Daily Log

GAUGE INSPECTION

S.C.C.

DAY	STAND*				DEPARTMENT MASTERS					INSP. INIT.	COMMENTS
	1	2	3	REP.	INSP.	1	2	3	REP.		
1	87¾	90	90¼	90¼						PAC	
2	91	92	88¾	90¼						PAC	
3	90½	90½	89½	90						PAC	
4	90	89	94½	90¼						PAC	BAD REGULATOR STAND #3 (89½)
7	90	90¾	91½	90	90¼	90	89½	89	90	PAC	90 DAY LAB CHECK MASTER #3 (90½)
8	89½	90¾	89¾	90½						PAC	
9	93	89¾	88½	89¾						PAC	
10	89¼	92	88¾	89½						PAC	
11	87¾	91½	89½	90						PAC	
12	92	88¾	88½	89½						PAC	
14	89¼	91½	91¼	91	90	90	89½	90¼	89¾	PAC	
15	91¾	91½	89¾	90¼						PAC	
16	90¾	89¾	89¾	90¼						PAC	
17	91	89¾	90¾	89½						PAC	
18	90¾	90½	85½	90						PAC	BAD SEAL STAND #3 (89¼)
19	88½	86	89	89¾						PAC	BAD SEAL STAND #2 (90½)
21	91¾	90¼	89½	90½	90	89¾	89¾	90	89¾	PAC	90 DAY LAB CHECK MASTER-INSP (90)
22	86¾	90½	88¼	89¼						PAC	BAD SEAL STAND #1 (88¾)
23	88¼	89	90¼	89¾						PAC	
24	87¼	90¼	89¾	90½						PAC	
25	91	86¼	91	90½						PAC	BAD SEAL STAND #2 (89¾)
26	93¼	90½	92	89½						PAC	REPEATED ADJUSTMENT STAND #1 (91¼)
28	93¾	89	87¼	90¾	90	89¾	89	90	90	PAC	REPEATED ADJUSTMENT STAND #1 (92), 90 DAY LAB CHECK MASTER #2 (89¾)
29	90	88¾	89¼	90½						PAC	
30	88¾	91	88½	89½						PAC	
31	89¼	90¾	90	86¼						PAC	BAD SEAL REPAIR STAND (89¾)

*Note: Production had 4 stands; 3 used for calibration and one used only for repair work. Inspection also had one stand but kept no log of its readings.

EXHIBIT 4, cont'd

YEAR 1983
MONTH APRIL

Calibration Stand-Daily Log

GAUGE INSPECTION

S.C.C.

DAY	STAND*				DEPARTMENT MASTERS					INSP. INIT.	COMMENTS
	1	2	3	REP.	INSP.	1	2	3	REP.		
4	90	(86½)	(86)	89¾	89¾	89¾	89½	90	90	PAC	BAD SEAL STAND #2 (89½) & #3 (91) 90 DAY LAB CHECK
5	89¾	90¼	89¼	89½						PAC	SEALS TRASHED MASTER #1 (90)
6	92¼	90¾	89¼	90½						PAC	
7	91½	90¾	90	89½						PAC	
8	90	90¼	89	90¾						PAC	
9	92½	90	88¼	90¾						PAC	
11	88	90¼	90	90	90	90	89½	89¾	90	PAC	
12	91¼	90	90¾	90¾						PAC	
13	91½	89¾	91	91						PAC	
14	88	88¾	89½	91¼						PAC	
15	90½	90	91	90¼						PAC	
16	89¾	90¼	90	89¾						PAC	
18	(93¼)	90¼	92¾	90½	89¾	90	89	89½	90	PAC	READJUSTED MASTER #2 IN LAB (90½), REPEATED ADJUSTMENT
19	90¼	89¼	91¼	90¾						PAC	STAND #1 (91)
20	89¼	89½	91	90¼						PAC	
21	89¼	90½	90½	91						PAC	
22	89	89¼	90½	90½						PAC	
23	91¼	91	90½	90½						PAC	
25	91¼	91	88¾	89½	90	90	90¼	89¼	89½	PAC	
26	88	90	90½	90½						PAC	
27	90	91	92¼	89¼						PAC	
28	89¼	88¼	90¾	90½						PAC	
29	90	88¼	92½	89¾						PAC	
30	90	91	90½	89½						PAC	

GAUGE INSPECTION S.C.C.

YEAR 1963
MONTH MAY

Calibration Stand-Daily Log

DAY	STAND*				DEPARTMENT MASTERS					INSP. INIT.	COMMENTS
	1	2	3	REP.	INSP.	1	2	3	REP.		
2	92 3/4	88 1/4	89 3/4	89 3/4	89 3/4	89 3/4	90	89 1/2	89 1/2	PAC	90 Day Lab Check Repair Master (89 3/4)
3	91 1/4	90 1/2	90	89 3/4						PAC	
4	87	91	92 3/4	90						PAC	
5	89	91 1/4	92	89 3/4						PAC	
6	90	90 1/2	90 1/4	90 1/4						PAC	
7	90 1/4	91 3/4	89 1/2	90 1/4						PAC	
9	91	88 1/4	88 3/4	89 3/4	89 3/4	89 3/4	89 3/4	89 1/4	90 1/2	PAC	
10	91	91	89 1/2	90 1/4						PAC	
11	88 1/4	90 1/2	89 1/4	90 1/2						PAC	

Ann:

We fix the bad ones. If people would do their job right, I wouldn't have to risk shipping some that are close. Besides, the customer uses a wider spec to check them and we always stay within that limit.

Gary:

That wider spec is to allow for variation between their test equipment and our stands, not for you guys to dump your rejects. Anyway, I don't see it as a big issue; warranty costs are low on these parts, only about 3½% of sales. If that answers your question Ken, I'll explain what I've got.

Ken:

It may be a problem, but let's go on. I'll figure a way to deal with it if I need to.

Gary:

Like I said when I got here, we just finished taking the measurements so I haven't had any time to do much with the data (Exhibit 5). What I can say is, she makes a lot more bad gauges than the other calibrators. She also doesn't seem to get parts that are more difficult to calibrate than the other operators.

Ann:

I think this meeting is over.

Gary:

Like I said, Ann: I haven't had much time with the data. Let me explain what we did while you all look over the data. Then you can decide what to do.

John:

Sounds good. Let's take a look.

Gary:

It's taken quite an effort to get this data; Ann and Charlene have helped a great deal. We took the first three trays of gauges calibrated by each calibrator on Tuesday morning and made three tests. The last test caused all the gauges to need recalibration, so Ann is absorbing some extra costs to get this done.

Our objective was to gather enough information to see whether the problem was with the mechanisms, the stand, or the calibrator. We also wanted to see if the inspection stand was making the problem look better or worse than it really was.

To start with, we had the calibrators write the reading they set the gauge at, at the high check point, on the back of the gauge and number them in the order they were calibrated. Each person used a different color grease pencil, so the data is organized by color. Kathy used red, Lonny used green, and Donna used blue. The data for each calibrator was kept separate to allow us to look at differences between calibrators. If you look at the data sheets (Exhibit 5) the readings are listed down the columns in the order in which the gauges were calibrated. The horizontal lines divide the trays. Recording the data in the order in which the gauges were

EXHIBIT 5

Test Data on Gauges Produced 5/10/83

Production Sequence No.	Reading Found By			Tube Free-End Travel @ 90 PSi (inches)	Reading Error Caused By		
	Calibrator (PSi)	Inspection (PSi)***	Engineering Lab (PSi)		Calib. & Travel (Lab-90) (PSi)	Travel (PSi)**	Calibrator & Stand (PSi)
1	*91	90	90	.158½	0	+1	-1
2	90	87	88	.153½	-2	-1	-1
3	90	89	90	.154½	0	0	0
4	91	89	89	.156½	-1	+1	-2
5	92	91	90	.159½	0	+2	-2
6	90	90	89	.156	-1	0	-1
7	91	89	89	.158½	-1	+1	-2
8	92	91	91	(160½)	+1	+2	-1
9	92	92	91	.169½	+1	+2	-1
10	91	91	92	.157½	+2	+1	+1
11	90	92	92	.156	+2	0	+2
12	91	89	90	.157	0	+1	-1
13	91	(96)	(95)	.158½	(+5)	+1	(+4)
14	90	(86)	(86)	.154	(-4)	0	(-4)
15	90	91	90	.154½	0	0	0
16	91	92	93	.167½	+2	+1	+1
17	91	92	92	.157	+2	+1	+1
18	91	89	89	.157	-1	+1	-2
19	91	92	91	.157	+1	+1	0
20	91	92	92	.159	+2	+1	+1
21	91	90	90	.158½	0	+1	-1
22	90	91	89	.154½	-1	0	-1
23	90	(90)	88	.156	-2	0	-2
24	91	(94)	93	.157	+3	+1	+2
25	91	*89	88	.157	-2	+1	-3
26	90	91	89	.156	-1	0	-1
27	91	91	91	.158	+1	+1	0
28	91	87	91	.157	+1	+1	0
29	91	92	91	.158½	+1	+1	0
30	91	88	87	.158	-3	+1	(-4)
31	92	92	92	.159½	+2	+2	0
32	90	88	88	.154	-2	0	-2
33	91	90	89	.158½	-1	+1	-2
34	91	92	91	.158½	+1	+1	0
35	90	89	89	.155½	-1	0	-1
36	92	92	92	.160	+2	+2	0

MEAN

VARIANCE

STD. DEV.

90 PSi GAUGES PRODUCED
5-10-83

COLOR: RED   STAND: 1 KATHY
DATE: 5-11-83   PAGE: 1 OF 3
ENGR: GRS

HISTOGRAM
CALIBRATOR AND STAND ERROR

ERROR (PSi)

* FIRST GAUGE AFTER READJUSTING STAND
** FROM GRAPH IN TR-G00516
*** TRAYS CHECKED IN INSPECTION IN ORDER:
RED (1-12), GREEN (1-12), BLUE (1-12), RED (13-24), GREEN (13-24), ETC.

280 *Quality Management*

EXHIBIT 5, cont'd

Production Sequence No.	Reading Found By			Tube Free-End Travel @ 90 PSI (inches)	Reading Error Caused By		
	Calibrator (PSI)	Inspection (PSI)	Engineering Lab (PSI)		Calib. (Travel Lab-90) (PSI)	Travel ** (PSI)	Calibrator + Stand (PSI)
1	*91	92	92	.157	+2	+1	+1
2	91	92	91	.159	+1	+1	0
3	90	91	89	.156	-1	0	-1
4	90	90	90	.155½	0	0	0
5	91	90	90	.158½	0	+1	-1
6	91	90	90	.157	0	+1	-1
7	91	89	89	.157½	-1	+1	-2
8	92	92	92	.159½	+2	+2	0
9	91	92	92	.159	+2	+1	+1
10	91	92	91	.156½	+1	+1	0
11	90	90	90	.155½	0	0	0
12	90	91	90	.155	0	0	0
13	90	90	90	.155	0	0	0
14	91	91	89	.156	-1	0	-1
15	92	93	92	.160	+2	+2	0
16	90	92	90	.155½	0	0	0
17	90	91	89	.155½	-1	0	-1
18	90	89	88	.155	-2	0	-2
19	91	90	90	.156½	0	+1	-1
20	91	91	90	.158	0	+1	-1
21	91	91	90	.158½	0	+1	-1
22	90	92	90	.155½	0	0	0
23	91	91	90	.156½	0	+1	-1
24	91	92	90	.155½	0	0	0
25	91	89	89	.158	-1	+1	-2
26	91	90	90	.157	0	+1	-1
27	91	90	90	.157½	0	+1	-1
28	91	91	91	.158½	+1	+1	0
29	91	92	91	.158½	+1	+1	0
30	91	91	90	.157½	0	+1	-1
31	91	93	91	.157½	+1	+1	0
32	91	89	89	.157	-1	+1	-2
33	91	88	89	.158	-1	+1	-2
34	91	90	90	.157½	0	+1	-1
35	92	91	90	(161)	0	+2	-2
36	91	90	89	.158½	-1	+1	-2

MEAN
VARIANCE
STD. DEV.

90 PSI GAUGES PRODUCED
5/10/83

COLOR: GREEN   STAND: 2 DONNA
DATE: 5-11-83   PAGE: 2 OF 3
ENGR: GRS

HISTOGRAM
CALIBRATOR AND STAND ERROR

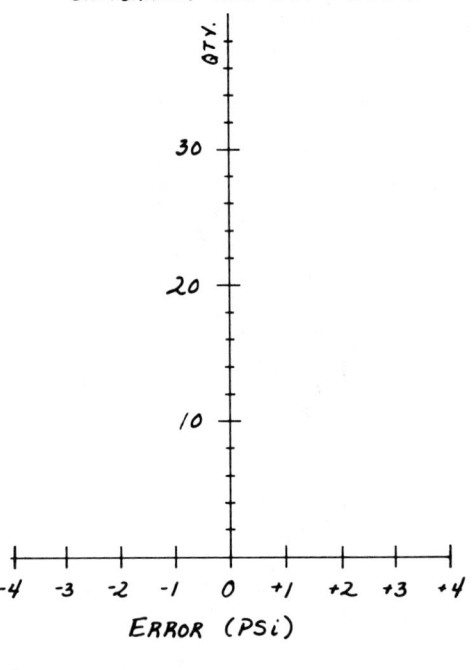

ERROR (PSI)

* FIRST GAUGE AFTER READJUSTING
  STAND
** FROM GRAPH IN TR-G00516

EXHIBIT 5, cont'd

Production Sequence No.	Reading Found By			Tube Free-End Travel @ 90 PSI (inches)	Reading Error Caused By		
	Calibrator (PSI)	Inspection (PSI)	Engineering Lab (PSI)		Calib. & Travel (Lab-90) (PSI)	Travel ** (PSI)	Calibrator & Stand (PSI)
1	*91	92	91	.157	+1	+1	0
2	91	90	89	.157½	-1	+1	-2
3	90	90	90	.156	0	0	0
4	92	(94)	92	(160½)	+2	+2	0
5	91	90	90	.158½	0	+1	-1
6	92	91	91	.160	+1	+2	-1
7	91	92	91	.158½	+1	+1	0
8	90	91	90	.155	0	0	0
9	91	92	91	.157	+1	+1	0
10	91	90	90	.158½	0	+1	-1
11	90	88	88	.154	-2	0	-2
12	90	89	88	.155½	-2	0	-2
13	92	91	90	.159½	0	+2	-2
14	91	89	88	.157½	-2	+1	-3
15	90	92	90	.155	0	0	0
16	91	91	90	.158½	0	+1	-1
17	91	90	89	.156½	-1	+1	-2
18	91	91	91	.158	+1	+1	0
19	90	89	88	.154	-2	0	-2
20	91	92	90	.159	0	+1	-1
21	91	91	90	.158½	0	+1	-1
22	90	90	89	.155	-1	0	-1
23	91	90	88	.157½	-2	+1	-3
24	90	90	88	.155	-2	0	-2
25	90	*90	89	.153½	-1	-1	0
26	90	89	89	.156	-1	0	-1
27	91	92	90	.158	0	+1	-1
28	90	91	90	.154	0	0	0
29	90	88	88	.155	-2	0	-2
30	91	91	91	.158	+1	+1	0
31	91	89	89	.156½	-1	+1	-2
32	91	90	90	.158	0	+1	-1
33	92	91	90	.159½	0	+2	-2
34	90	90	89	.156	-1	0	-1
35	90	89	88	.154	-2	0	-2
36	92	90	90	.160	0	+2	-2
MEAN							
VARIANCE							
STD. DEV.							

90 PSI GAUGES PRODUCED
5/10/83

COLOR: BLUE   STAND: 3 LONNY
DATE: 5-11-83   PAGE: 3 OF 3
ENGR: GRS

HISTOGRAM
CALIBRATOR AND STAND ERROR

* FIRST GAUGE AFTER READJUSTING STAND
** FROM GRAPH IN TR-G00516

calibrated allows us to look for trends in the readings. Trends are usually caused by tool wear or in this case by the calibration stand pressure drifting; either from the master gauge "drifting" or from the stand pressure regulator drifting. That's why they check the pressure after every tray. We know the stand pressure drifts some during use so they check to make sure the pressure hasn't drifted enough to cause the gauges to be calibrated wrong even though they read right on the stand. The column labeled "reading found by calibrator" is the reading the calibrator wrote on the back of the gauge.

We then had Charlene's inspector recheck each gauge on the inspection stand and record the reading. These readings are listed in the "reading found by inspection" column. By comparing them with the readings found in our engineering lab you can see how often inspection would have rejected a gauge engineering would have accepted. Of the 108 gauges we checked there were only 2 which inspection would have rejected but engineering would have accepted and none the other way around. That's about 2%, so while it is a factor it's not significant. One last thing on this, the inspection stand is readjusted when it is off by more than 1.0 psi not the 3.0 psi used in production.

I then took the gauges to the engineering lab and had Don Kennedy, the instrument technician, check each gauge with the dead weight tester at 90 psi and record the readings. We also checked the master gauges in the standards lab and found they were all OK. It was slow work but it eliminated any measurable error from our readings. I've circled the out-of-print readings. You can see Kathy has a lot more bad gauges.

The last thing we did was to cut the calibration link and measure the travel of the tube. Ken, the tube is the part that really makes the gauge work. Our objective was to see not only whether the gauges Kathy was getting were worse than those the other calibrators got but also how much, if any, of the calibration problem was being caused by tubes having too much or too little travel. While there were several out-of-print, Kathy's were no worse than the other calibrators and they seem to be able to make them work.

The "tube free-end travel" column (Exhibit 5) shows the actual amount of travel in inches. The distance the free end of the tube moves at any pressure determines the pressure the gauge will read. Here's a copy of a page from a test we ran in the lab a few years ago (Exhibit 6). Basically, this graph shows that for every one-thousandth of an inch (.001) the tube travel is off the nominal, .155 inch at 90 psi for these gauges, the pressure indicated will be wrong by .36 psi. As an example, go back to the data sheets with the gauge readings (Exhibit 5). The first gauge calibrated by Kathy (red) had a travel of .158½ inches. That's .003½ above the nominal, that's about the thickness of a piece of paper; not much distance, but it causes the gauge to read high by 1 psi (column "reading error caused by travel"). Because of variations in the tube material and in the forming operation there will always be some error in the gauge reading even if the stand applied the correct pressure. The calibrator normally allows for this by cycling the gauge a couple of times to see how high or low it reads. If the gauge will be within limits they do not move the pointer or adjust the link to compensate. Kathy cycles the gauge 3 times to get the error; the other calibrators use 2 cycles. She says her stand jumps around

EXHIBIT 6
Lab Data on Tube Stiffness

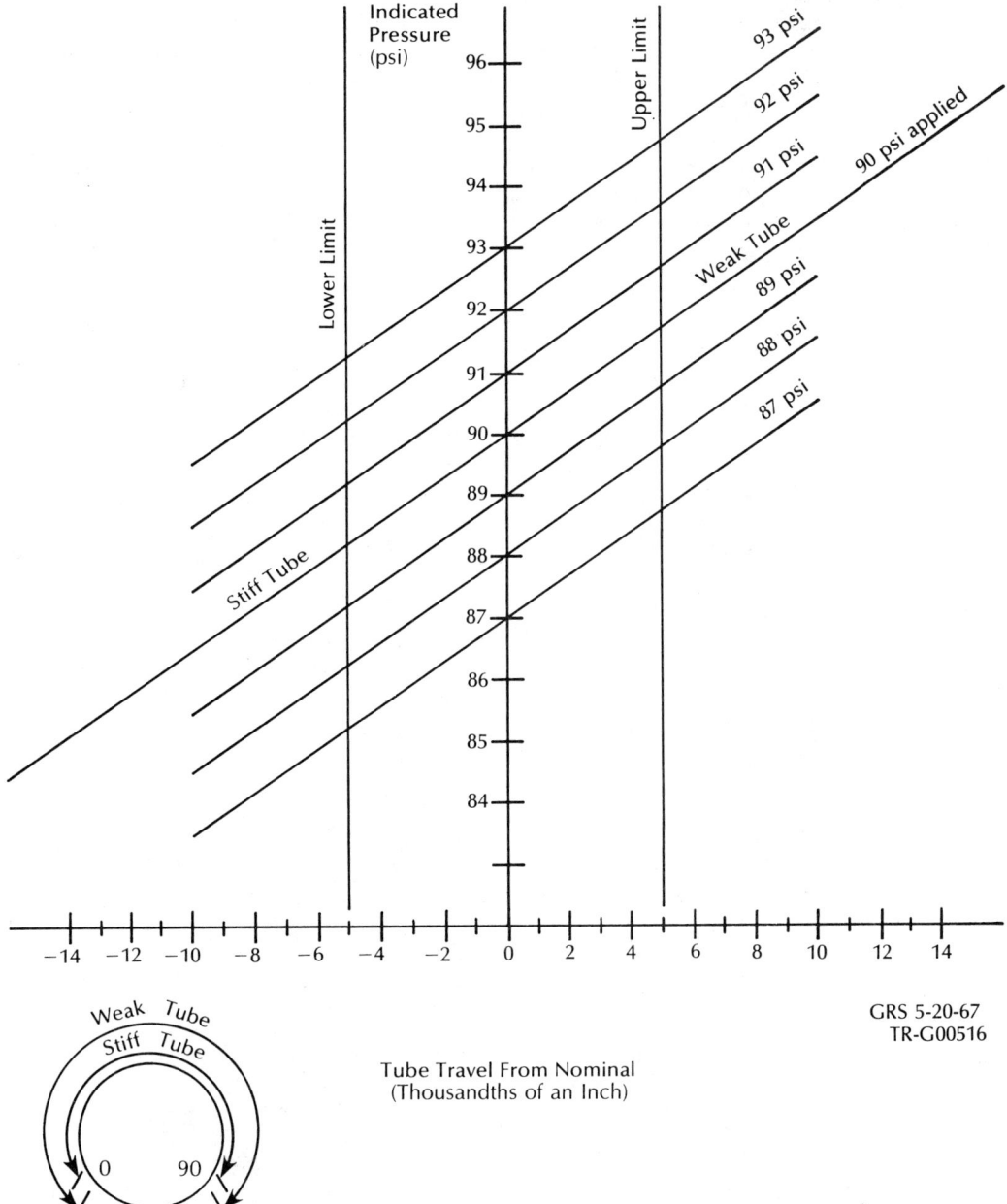

Effect of Weak or Stiff Tubes on Gauge Reading
90 Psi Tubes

GRS 5-20-67
TR-G00516

a lot, so she uses 3 even though it is a little slower. When we see a gauge that reads incorrectly we have to remember the stand caused part of the error by applying a little too much or too little pressure, the gauge caused part of the error because the tube is too weak or too stiff, and the calibrator caused part of the error positioning the pointer and part of the error adjusting the link.

While Don was measuring the gauges I started some of the analysis. The last three columns on the data sheets (Exhibit 5) show the reading error caused by calibration and by the tube travel. The column labeled "calib. & travel" is just the error from 90 psi when we tested the gauge in the lab. It's the total of the travel error, and the error caused by the calibrator and the stand. The column "travel" was calculated from the graph I gave you (Exhibit 6) and the travel measured for that gauge. The last column "calibrator & stand" was obtained by subtracting the travel error from the total "calib. & travel." This is the error caused by the combination of the calibrator and the stand. Comparing this last column with the data Charlene has on the stand alone would show us how much of the problem is the equipment and how much is the calibrator.

That's all the data. Normally, I would have plotted some histograms and probability graphs of the data in the "calibrator & stand" column, and of the data from the daily stand check data Charlene has (Exhibit 4). I would also have plotted some control charts for the stands and their master gauges. The histograms and probability plots would allow us to see how the stands and calibrators compare in terms of their capability to produce within limits. The control charts would allow us to see if any of the stands or master gauges tend to drift enough to cause a problem. I'm not sure you need them in this case. I could do them this afternoon if you would like, just to be sure we didn't miss something.

Ann:

Thanks Gary, I don't think you need to spend the time. We have the data if anyone ever wants to look at it. Ken, do you see any problem with a written reprimand?

"Hello, Charlene? This is Gary Stevens. I've run into some problems with some other work I was doing in the lab so I'm not quite done analyzing the data for Ann's meeting this morning. Could you help me finish the last few things? Thanks, I'll be right over."

BACKGROUND ON ANN'S MEETING

Ann Pitts was the foreman of the mechanical gauge department of Special Components Corporation (SCC). A meeting had been held the day before the upcoming meeting (see *The Problem with Kathy (A)* for details of the previous meeting and the data discussed there). At that meeting several pieces of data had been discussed concerning a problem Ann was having with a high reject rate on one line of gauges. Because no analysis of the data had been completed, John Condon, the general foreman Ann reported to, had asked for a follow-up meeting the next morning. Gary Stevens, product engineer for gauges, had been assigned to analyze the data he and Charlene Hazen, quality control foreman for gauges, had gathered.

Because the problem appeared to be caused by one worker, Kathy Clark, the plant labor relations representative, Ken Willens, was also present. If the data supported Ann's belief that Kathy was causing the problem, a reprimand would be written against Kathy. If the problem continued, eventually Kathy would be fired. The goal of the meetings was to ensure that the facts would support a reprimand without the union filing a grievance (formal complaint of contract violation).

THE WORK REMAINING

"Hi Charlene. Thanks for the help. I think I've got some good information to help Ann with her problem. Let me quickly explain what I've done.

"First I plotted (Exhibit 1) your data from the weekly checks of the master gauges (A case, Exhibit 4). Kathy's master (stand #1) looks OK but there are some problems with two of the other masters. I also plotted the data for the calibrator stand daily log (A case, Exhibit 4) in Exhibit 2. *Text continued on p. 296.*

EXHIBIT 1
Plots of Weekly Check of Master Gauges

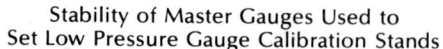

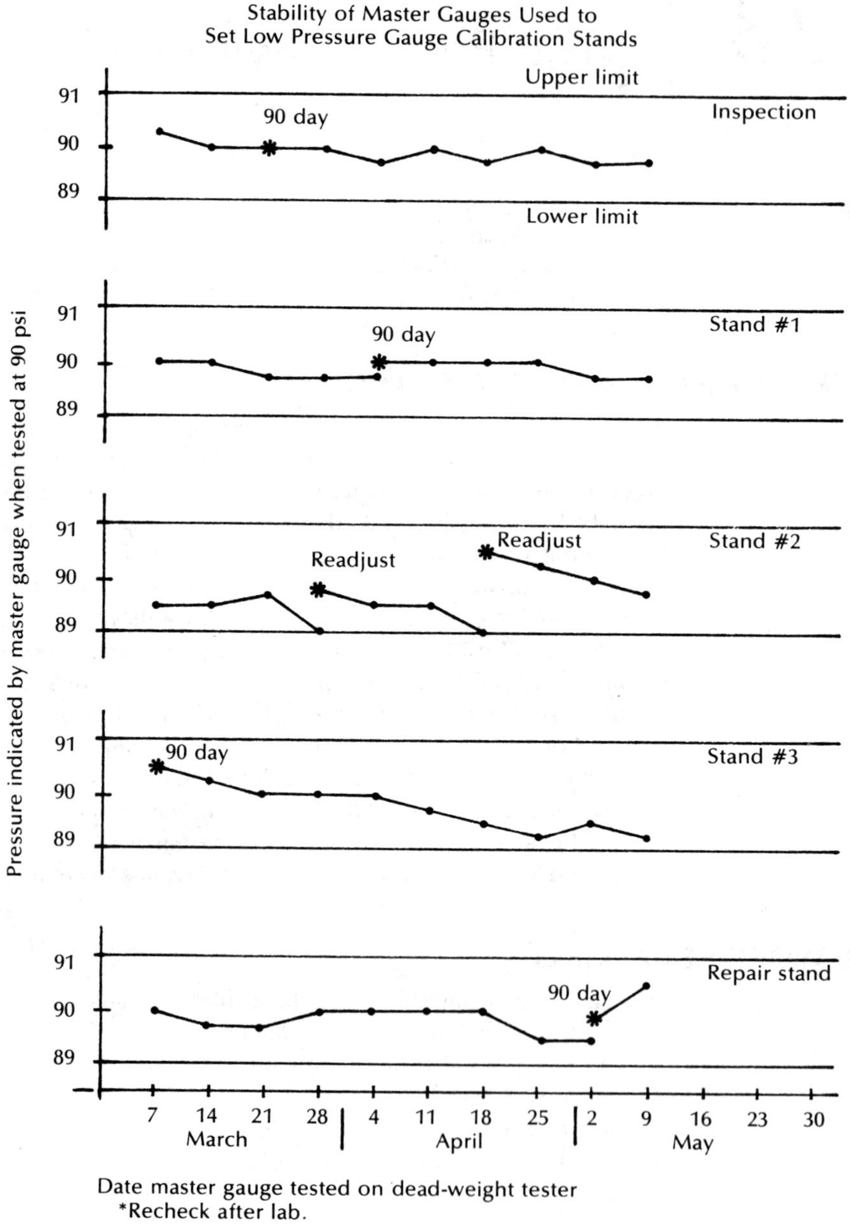
Stability of Master Gauges Used to
Set Low Pressure Gauge Calibration Stands
Upper limit
Lower limit
Inspection
Stand #1
Stand #2
Stand #3
Repair stand
90 day
Readjust
91
90
89
Pressure indicated by master gauge when tested at 90 psi
7
14
21
28
4
11
18
25
2
9
16
23
30
March
April
May
Date master gauge tested on dead-weight tester
*Recheck after lab.

EXHIBIT 2
Plots of Calibrator Stand—Daily Log

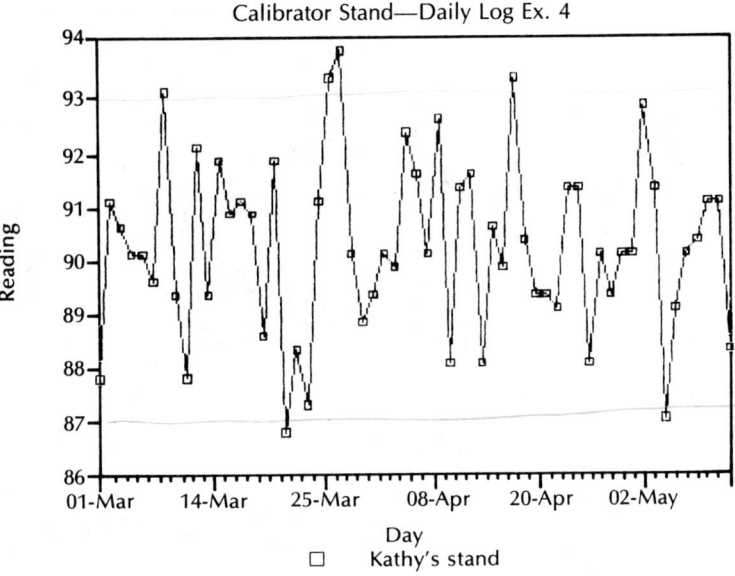

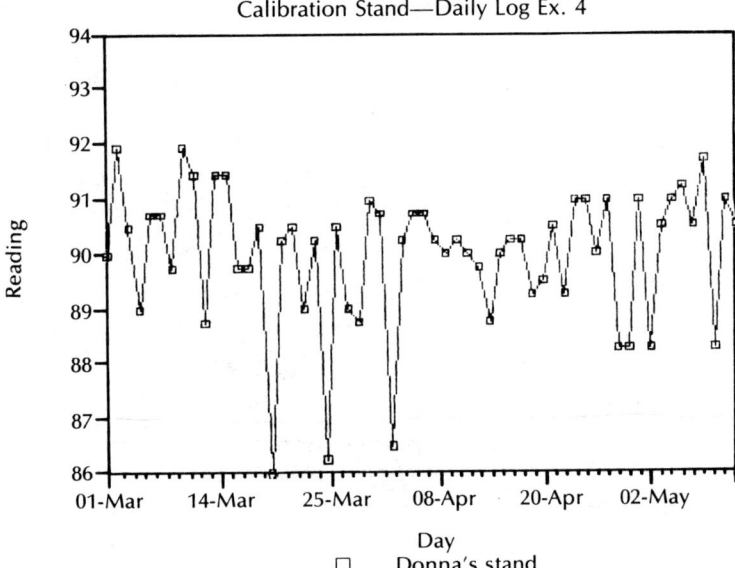

EXHIBIT 2, cont'd

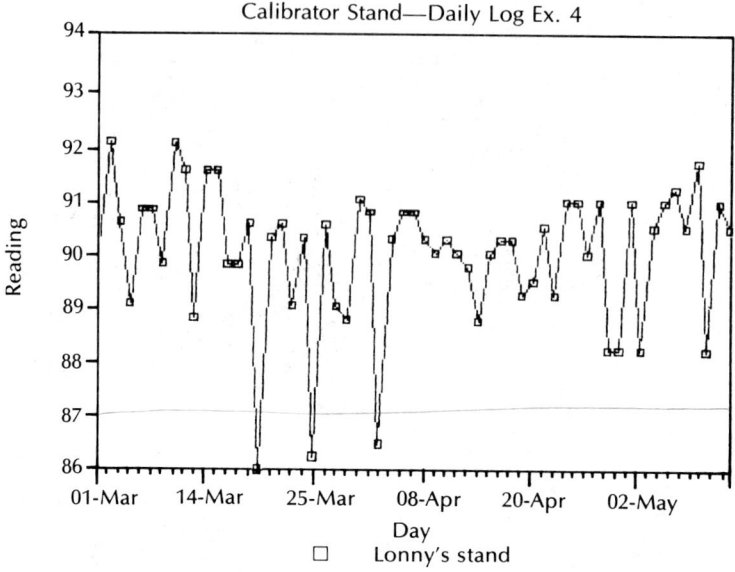

Calibrator Stand—Daily Log Ex. 4
□ Lonny's stand

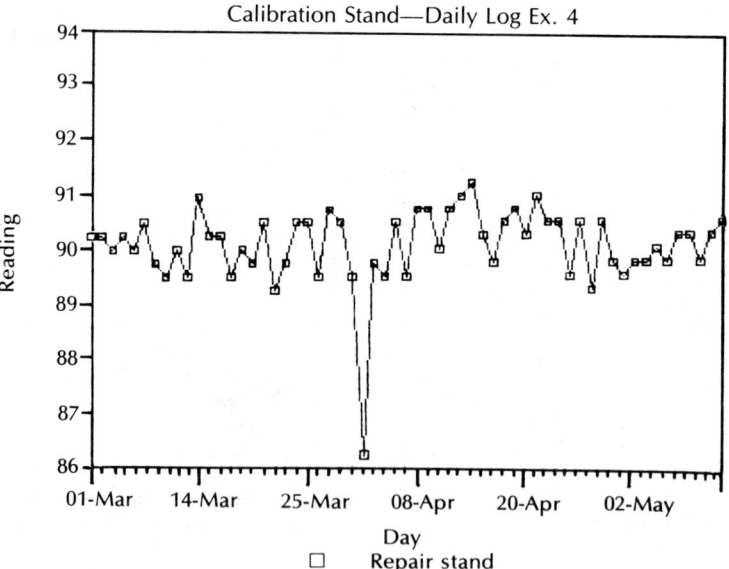

Calibration Stand—Daily Log Ex. 4
□ Repair stand

EXHIBIT 3
Histograms of CDFs of Calibration Stand—Daily Log

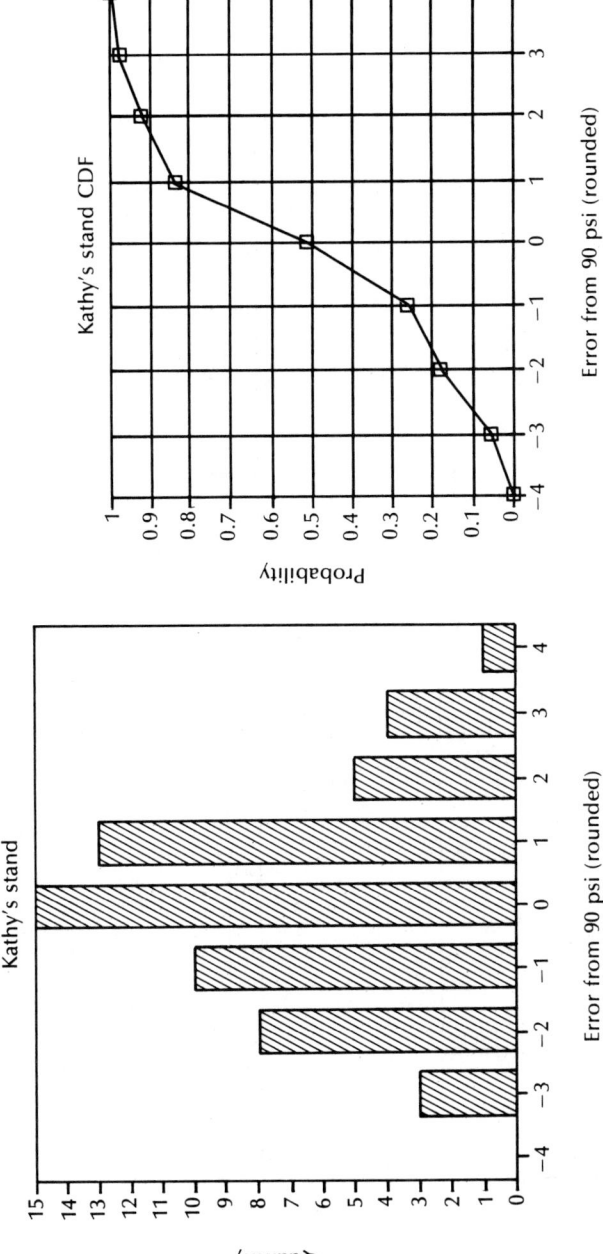

Data for probability plot (Stand #1)

Error (psi)	−4	−3	−2	−1	0	+1	+2	+3	+4
Quantity		3	8	10	15	13	5	4	1
Cum. quantity		3	11	21	36	49	54	58	59
Cum/(36 + 1)		.050	.183	.350	.600	.817	.900	.967	.983

Avg = .15
Var = 2.61
St Dev = 1.62

EXHIBIT 3, cont'd

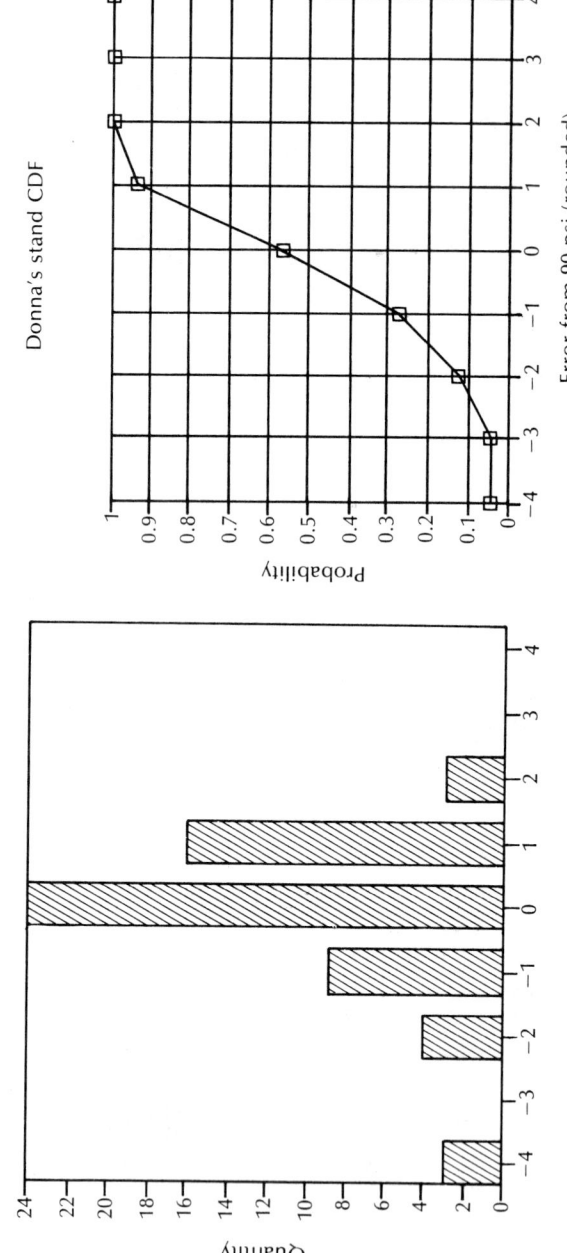

Donna's Stand

Donna's stand CDF

Data for probability plot (Stand #2)

Error (psi)	−4	−3	−2	−1	0	+1	+2	+3	+4
Quantity	3	0	4	9	24	16	3		
Cum. quantity	3	3	7	16	40	56	59		
Cum/(36 + 1)	.05	.05	.117	.267	.677	.933	.983		

Avg = 0
Var = 1.62
St Dev = 1.27

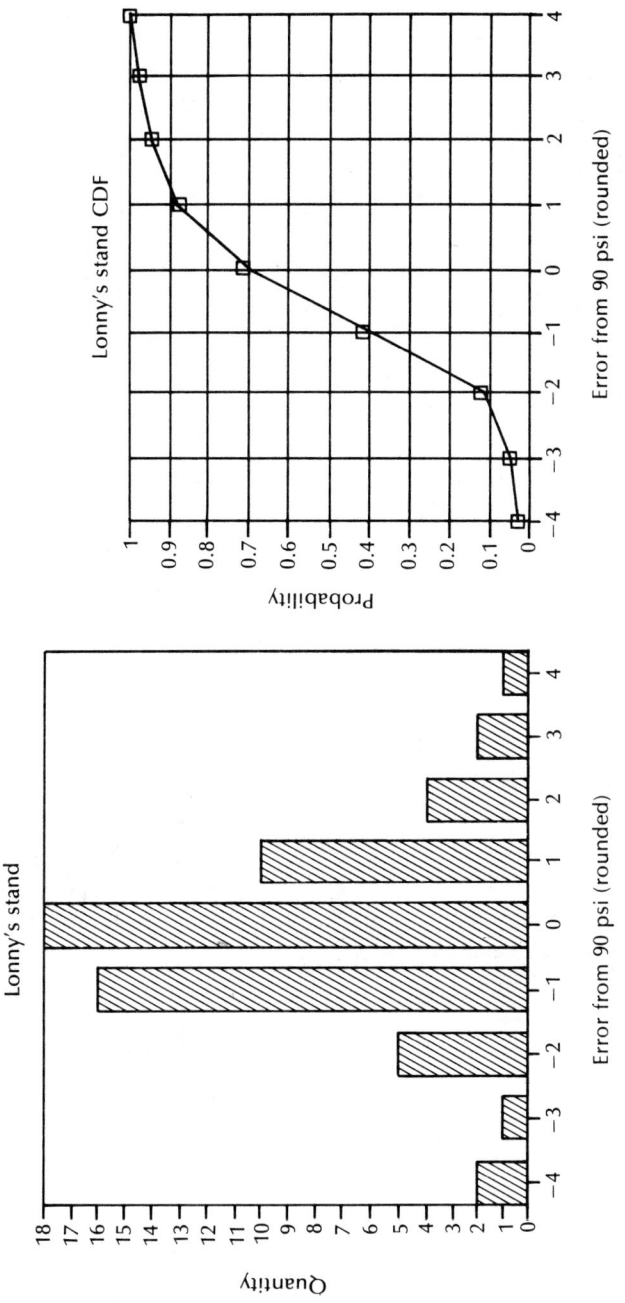

Data for probability plot (Stand #3)

Error (psi)	−4	−3	−2	−1	0	+1	+2	+3	+4
Quantity	2	1	5	16	18	10	4	2	1
Cum. quantity	2	3	8	24	42	32	56	58	59
Cum/(36 + 1)	.033	.050	.133	.400	.700	.867	.933	.967	.983

Avg = .02
Var = 2.31
St Dev = 1.52

EXHIBIT 3, cont'd

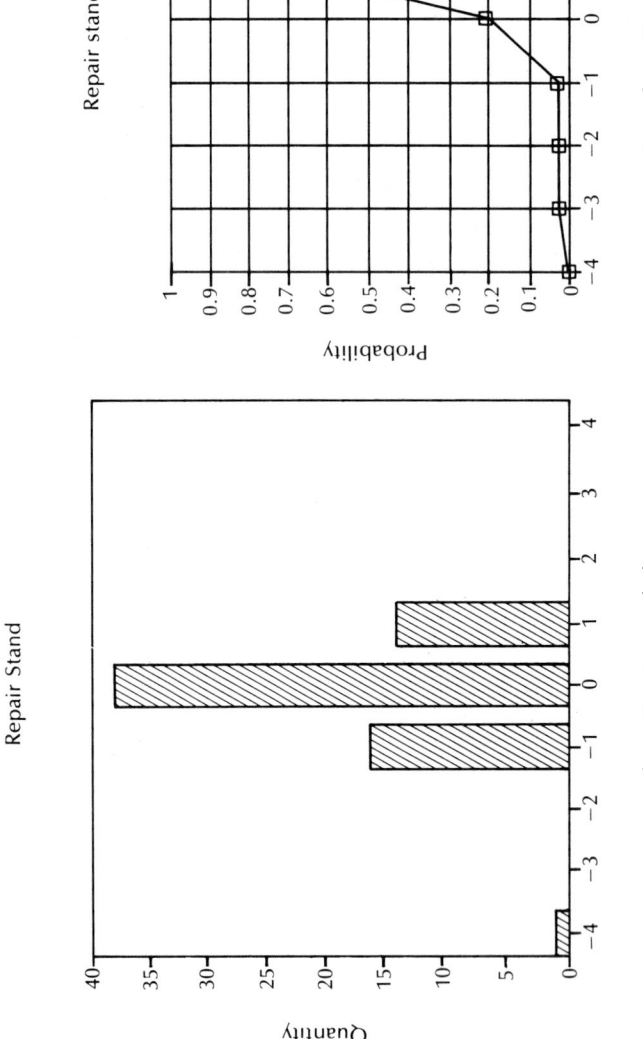

Repair Stand

Error from 90 psi (rounded)

Repair stand CDF

Error from 90 psi (rounded)

Data for Probability Plot (Repair Stand)

Error (psi)	-4	-3	-2	-1	0	+1	+2	+3	+4
Quantity				1	20	15			
Cum. quantity				1	21	36			
Cum./(36 + 1)				.027	.568	.973			

Avg = .07
Var = .49
St Dev = .7

EXHIBIT 4
Histograms of "Reading Error Caused by Calibrator and Stand"

Production Sequence No.	Reading Found By – Calibrator (PSi)	Reading Found By – Inspection (PSi)	Reading Found By – Engineering Lab (PSi)	Tube Free-End Travel @ 90 PSi (Inches)	Reading Error Caused By – Calib. ↑ Travel (Lab-90) (PSi)	Reading Error Caused By – ↑ Travel *** (PSi)	Reading Error Caused By – Calibrator & Stand (PSi)
1	*91	90	90	.158½	0	+1	-1
2	90	87	88	.153½	-2	-1	-1
3	90	89	90	.154½	0	0	0
4	91	89	89	.156½	-1	+1	-2
5	92	91	90	.159½	0	+2	-2
6	90	90	89	.156	-1	0	-1
7	91	89	89	.158½	-1	+1	-2
8	92	91	91	(.160½)	+1	+2	-1
9	92	92	91	.159½	+1	+2	-1
10	91	91	92	.157½	+2	+1	+1
11	90	92	92	.156	+2	0	+2
12	91	89	90	.157	0	+1	-1
13	91	(96)	(95)	.158½	(+5)	+1	(+4)
14	90	(86)	(86)	.154	(-4)	0	(-4)
15	90	91	90	.154½	0	0	0
16	91	92	92	.157½	+2	+1	+1
17	91	92	92	.157	+2	+1	+1
18	91	89	89	.157	-1	+1	-2
19	91	92	91	.157	+1	+1	0
20	91	92	91	.159	+2	+1	+1
21	91	90	90	.158½	0	+1	-1
22	90	91	89	.154½	-1	0	-1
23	90	90	88	.156	-2	0	-2
24	91	(94)	93	.157	+3	+1	+2
25	91	*89	88	.157	-2	+1	-3
26	90	91	89	.156	-1	0	-1
27	91	91	91	.158	+1	+1	0
28	91	87	91	.157	+1	+1	0
29	91	92	91	.158½	+1	+1	0
30	91	88	87	.158	-3	+1	(-4)
31	92	92	92	.159½	+2	+2	0
32	90	88	88	.154	-2	0	-2
33	91	90	89	.158½	-1	+1	-2
34	91	92	91	.158½	+1	+1	0
35	90	89	89	.155½	-1	0	-1
36	92	92	92	.160	+2	+2	0
MEAN	90.83	90.44	90.17	157.18	.17	.81	-.64
VARIANCE	.42	3.92	3.24	3.24	3.24	.49	2.56
STD. DEV.	.65	1.98	1.80	1.80	1.80	.70	1.60

90 PSi GAUGES PRODUCED
5/10/83

COLOR: RED   STAND: 1   Kathy
DATE: 5-11-83   PAGE: 1 OF 3
ENGR: CRS

HISTOGRAM
CALIBRATOR AND STAND ERROR

QTY.
CUM.
CUM/(36+1)

30
20
10

-4 -3 -2 -1 0 +1 +2 +3 +4
ERROR (PSi)

* FIRST GAUGE AFTER READJUSTIG
   STAND
** FROM GRAPH IN TR-G00516

EXHIBIT 4, cont'd

Production Sequence No.	Reading Found By			Tube Free-End Travel @ 90 PSI (inches)	Reading Error Caused By		
	Calibrator (PSI)	Inspection (PSI)	Engineering Lab (PSI)		Calib. & Travel (Lab-90) (PSI)	Travel ** (PSI)	Calibrator & Stand (PSI)
1	*91	92	92	.157	+2	+1	+1
2	91	92	91	.159	+1	+1	0
3	90	91	89	.156	-1	0	-1
4	90	90	90	.155½	0	0	0
5	91	90	90	.158½	0	+1	-1
6	91	90	90	.157	0	+1	-1
7	91	89	89	.157½	-1	+1	-2
8	92	92	92	.159½	+2	+2	0
9	91	92	92	.159	+2	+1	+1
10	91	92	91	.156½	+1	+1	0
11	90	90	90	.155½	0	0	0
12	90	91	91	.155	0	0	0
13	90	90	90	.155	0	0	0
14	91	91	89	.156	-1	0	-1
15	92	93	92	.160	+2	+2	0
16	90	92	90	.155½	0	0	0
17	90	91	89	.155½	-1	0	-1
18	90	89	88	.155	-2	0	-2
19	91	90	90	.156½	0	+1	-1
20	91	91	90	.158	0	+1	-1
21	91	91	90	.158½	0	+1	-1
22	90	92	90	.155½	0	0	0
23	91	91	90	.156½	0	+1	-1
24	91	92	90	.155½	0	0	0
25	91	89	89	.158	-1	+1	-2
26	91	90	90	.157	0	+1	-1
27	91	90	90	.157½	0	+1	-1
28	91	91	91	.158½	+1	+1	0
29	91	92	91	.158½	+1	+1	0
30	91	91	90	.157½	0	+1	-1
31	91	93	91	.157½	+1	+1	0
32	91	89	89	.157	-1	+1	-2
33	91	88	89	.158	-1	+1	-2
34	91	90	90	.157½	0	+1	-1
35	92	91	90	(.161)	0	+2	-2
36	91	90	89	.158½	-1	+1	-2
MEAN	90.83	90.78	90.08	157.22	.08	.78	-.69
VARIANCE	.30	1.39	.90	2.25	.90	.34	.71
STD. DEV.	.55	1.18	.95	1.50	.95	.58	.84

90 PSI GAUGES PRODUCED
5/10/83

COLOR: GREEN   STAND: 2 (Donna)
DATE: 5-11-83   PAGE: 2 OF 3
ENGR: GRS

HISTOGRAM
CALIBRATOR AND STAND ERROR

QTY	7	13	14	2
CUM	7	20	34	36
Cum ÷ 37	.189	.541	.919	.973

ERROR (PSI)

* FIRST GAUGE AFTER READJUSTING STAND
** FROM GRAPH IN TR-G00516

EXHIBIT 4, cont'd

PRODUCTION SEQUENCE NO.	READING FOUND BY			TUBE FREE-END TRAVEL @ 90 PSi (INCHES)	READING ERROR CAUSED BY		
	CALIBRATOR (PSi)	INSPECTION (PSi)	ENGINEERING LAB (PSi)		CALIB. ↑ TRAVEL (LAB-90) (PSi)	TRAVEL ** (PSi)	CALIBRATOR ↑ STAND (PSi)
1	*91	92	91	.157	+1	+1	0
2	91	90	89	.157½	-1	+1	-2
3	90	90	90	.156	0	0	0
4	92	(94)	92	(160½)	+2	+2	0
5	91	90	90	.158½	0	+1	-1
6	92	91	91	.160	+1	+2	-1
7	91	92	91	.158½	+1	+1	0
8	90	91	90	.155	0	0	0
9	91	92	91	.157	+1	+1	0
10	91	90	90	.158½	0	+1	-1
11	90	88	88	.154	-2	0	-2
12	90	89	88	.155½	-2	0	-2
13	92	91	90	.159½	0	+2	-2
14	91	89	88	.157½	-2	+1	-3
15	90	92	90	.155	0	0	0
16	91	91	90	.158½	0	+1	-1
17	91	90	89	.156½	-1	+1	-2
18	91	91	91	.158	+1	+1	0
19	90	89	88	.154	-2	0	-2
20	91	92	90	.159	0	+1	-1
21	91	91	90	.158½	0	+1	-1
22	90	90	89	.155	-1	0	-1
23	91	90	88	.157½	-2	+1	-3
24	90	90	88	.155	-2	0	-2
25	90	*90	89	.153½	-1	-1	0
26	90	89	89	.156	-1	0	-1
27	91	92	90	.158	0	+1	-1
28	90	91	90	.154	0	0	0
29	90	88	88	.155	-2	0	-2
30	91	91	91	.158	+1	+1	0
31	91	89	89	.156½	-1	+1	-2
32	91	90	90	.158	0	+1	-1
33	92	91	90	.159½	0	+2	-2
34	90	90	89	.156	-1	0	-1
35	90	89	88	.154	-2	0	-2
36	92	90	90	.160	0	+2	-2
MEAN	90.75	90.42	89.58	156.96	-.42	.72	-1.14
VARIANCE	.46	1.59	1.18	3.80	1.19	.53	.85
STD. DEV.	.68	1.26	1.09	1.95	1.09	.73	.92

90 PSi GAUGES PRODUCED
5/10/83

COLOR: **BLUE**   STAND: **3** Lonny
DATE: **5-11-83**   PAGE: **3** OF **3**
ENGR: **GRS**

HISTOGRAM
CALIBRATOR AND STAND ERROR

QTY.	2	12	11	11
CUM.	2	14	25	36
Cum ÷ 36	.054	.375	.675	.973

ERROR (PSi)

* FIRST GAUGE AFTER READJUSTING STAND
** FROM GRAPH IN TR-G00516

Next I plotted the histograms and cumulative distribution functions (Exhibit 3) for your daily checks of the stands (A case, Exhibit 4).

The last thing I did, and what I need your help with, was to fill in the histograms for the gauge data (A case, Exhibit 5). Using the histograms of the stands alone (Exhibit 3) versus the histograms of the combination calibrator (the person) and the stand (Exhibit 4) ought to allow us to say something about the calibrator's performance. After we finish these, we should be in a position to draw some conclusions.

Gould Inc. (A)

Jim Woods sat at his desk thinking of the alternate ways in which he could push his plant's productivity beyond the levels he had already achieved since his arrival in Westport. In his two years as Plant Manager, he had persuaded Division Management to invest over $1 million on plant equipment changes. New equipment had been installed, old equipment had been scrapped and renewable equipment had been overhauled. Operational procedures had also been improved upon. The positive effect on productivity was already beginning to show through the increases in the plant's overall performance figures. Satisfied with these results, Woods turned his attention to the labor element of his plant's productivity.

There were two alternate methods by which Jim Woods thought he might improve labor's productivity. One involved an employee incentive program (the Share Plan) and the other an employee problem-solving participation program (Quality Circles). Woods was aware that the Battery Division's management team wanted to implement the new Share Plan Incentive Program in one of its ten battery plants, and that the Westport plant was a likely candidate for the pilot run of this program. Westport was second in performance to the new Ames plant, but it already had another type of incentive program in operation. Any encouragement from Woods would pretty well assure that Westport would be the first to test the Share Plan in operation.

Woods had also developed an interest in quality circles over the past year. Quality circles were groups of employee volunteers who gathered together regularly to solve job-related problems and to develop new methods to improve productivity in the workplace. Many American companies were beginning to pay closer attention to this phenomenon which was credited with turning Japanese manufacturers from "Junk Merchants of the World" to "Market Threats of the Decade." Every good businessman was cognizant of the threat imposed by Japanese high-grade, low-cost producers. A recent television special, "If Japan Can, Why Can't We?" had only fueled Jim's interest in adapting Japan's successful managerial technique to his own needs in Westport. Division management's positive response to quality circles only strengthened his desire to get them started.

    Case prepared by Nicole L. Grondin, 1981, under the supervision of Professor Alexander B. Horniman. The cooperation of Gould, Inc. is gratefully acknowledged. Certain data, locations, and names have been disguised for proprietary purposes.

Perhaps as a third alternative, he thought, a program could be developed where both the Share Plan and quality circles could be implemented together as an integrated system. Quality circles could be used to bring out any improvements or changes in the plant that could be made to increase productivity and quality. The Share Plan, in turn, could reward all employees by sharing productivity gains 50/50 with them. Positive quality circle results would translate into extra earnings through the Share Plan, which in turn would encourage even greater participation in quality circles.

The implications of accomplishing such a feat successfully were staggering. Not only could the Automotive Battery Division benefit from the productivity and operational gains to be achieved, but the entire corporate structure could also gain from the benefits of being on the leading edge of a developing managerial philosophy.

CORPORATE BACKGROUND

Until 1967, Gould had been known as a "battery company." The company's growth had occurred through the consolidation of several small battery manufacturers acquired by Gould over the years. With an annually compounded growth rate of 4% in the replacement market and 2% in the original equipment market, the battery industry was categorized as a mature industry. Sales volume and profits were limited by what could be realistically called a semi-fixed market demand. As a result, the market developed into a hotbed of competition for the sale of what was essentially an industrial commodity.

Gould's strategic direction changed when, in late 1967, William T. Ylvisaker took command as CEO of the company. Under Ylvisaker's charge, Gould redirected its corporate objectives and began to develop a new plan aimed at improving the company's growth prospects. Product development was heavily emphasized. Above average opportunities and compensation packages were provided to attract highly motivated managerial talent. Emphasis was placed on building a group of profitable businesses through internal development which, in turn, were complemented by the acquisition of compatible operations offering the potential of high growth markets. The older parts of the Gould structure contributed resources and traditions, while the newer parts provided the strategy for growth.

Ylvisaker's expansion strategy through the use of integrated technologies proved to be extremely successful. It had since become the basis for Gould's 18-

EXHIBIT 1
Percent Sales and Earnings by Business Segment (1979)

	Sales by segment	Earnings by segment
Electronics	25.9%	35.6%
Electrical	24.9%	12.2%
Battery	23.2%	21.0%
Industrial	26.0%	31.2%

Source: 1979 Corporate Fact Book, Gould Inc., page 3.

fold sales growth from a small battery manufacturer in 1967 to a major electrical/
electronics firm with sales of over $2 billion in 1980. Gould's organizational struc-
ture consisted of several product groups, supported by divisions organized into
product and market related operating groups. The company's current objective
in all of the markets it served was the attainment of a large share, and, whenever
possible, market leadership with technical leadership in the products serving these
markets. In those markets where leadership had been attained, Gould's objective
was to achieve above average profit margins (see Exhibit 1).

AUTOMOTIVE BATTERY DIVISION (ABD)

The Automotive Battery Division, one of five divisions in Gould's Battery Group,
was the major supplier to the U.S. motor vehicle market. The division also produced a full range of sizes of lead-acid batteries for off-highway applications in
agriculture, construction and watercraft.

During the 1970s, the division's technological leadership enabled it to grow
at a rate faster than the overall industry. Its success has been marked by important
product developments that have included plastic battery cases, the Gould Dry-
namic® process and the first maintenance-free battery introduced into the replacement market. The industry, however, was now in a major transition from a
mature, rather standardized product featuring a lead-antimony alloy to one uti-
lizing a more sophisticated lead-calcium maintenance-free construction. The ABD
was working diligently to stay on the leading edge of this technological transition
in the product's development.

From 20 to 25 percent of the industry's total annual unit sales were made to
original equipment manufacturers. The balance was made to the replacement
market which was dominated by a relatively wide base of large national retailers
made up of mass merchandisers, oil companies, vehicle dealers, battery specialists
and parts distributors. These retailers purchase and resell batteries under their
own private label brand names. More than 80 percent of the industry's total
replacement sales reached the battery user under names owned and controlled
by the marketer rather than the manufacturer.

COMPETITION

Competition was exceedingly sharp in the automotive battery industry in the late
1970s. As a result of increased foreign auto competition, sales revenues from the
original equipment market had declined due to the drop in U.S. automobile
production. Many of the larger battery manufacturers such as Delco, Globe Union
and Gould were left with excess production capacity. As an alternative to shutting
down costly manufacturing facilities, price competition became a tool to maintain
high-volume production. With declining prices, diminishing sales volume and
rising raw material costs, profit margins were continually squeezed.

The replacement market was also seriously affected by the economic downturn
in 1979. Compounded by an exceedingly mild winter and normal market cycli-
cality, replacement sales had dropped below last year's sales. Sales orders in the

replacement market consisted of ranging quantities of different battery types. Low-volume, high-variety production required frequent assembly line changes for each new type of battery ordered. This was accomplished through the use of general-purpose production equipment and fluctuating levels of semiskilled labor. The flexibility built into the replacement battery production process enabled manufacturers to react more quickly and efficiently to fluctuations in market demand.

In either OEM or replacement battery manufacturing plants, divisional pressure was high on Gould's line managers to maintain profit margins by cutting production costs and increasing production yields. To achieve these objectives, management's focus in the Automotive Battery Division turned to improving productivity in the workplace.

THE SHARE PLAN

In an effort to find new ways to increase productivity in the workplace, Will Vanheat and Jeff Harmon from ABD staff attended a seminar on worker motivation and its affect on productivity in 1979. (See Exhibit 2 for job titles and company position.) The seminar was led by an industrial engineering consultant who felt that job enrichment programs were not the answer to a manager's motivational problems. The consultant asserted that pay, job security and the rules of the workplace were the three basic elements of primary concern to the blue collar worker. In order to increase productivity, the worker had to believe that his job would not be jeopardized by any increased output, that management was "playing fair," and that he would share in the gains earned by increasing his productivity. Through this sharing process, the workers and management could strive for a common goal from which both groups could benefit. The consultant's answer to this delicate issue was his development of the Share Plan, an incentive program for direct and indirect production workers.

In the Share Plan, a labor unit cost base was established for each product type, based on past labor performance experience. When labor costs per unit were then reduced from the old base, the gains were shared 50/50 by employees and management. The *entire* group of plant workers shared in any productivity gains no matter who was specifically responsible for them. As a result, employee interest would refocus its attention on how many units were completed in a specific number of input hours. They would not only be rewarded for beating the overall base standard, but would also be motivated to work together to minimize production problems. (See Appendix A for some of the main features of the Share Plan.)

At the end of the seminar, Vanheat and Harmon returned to Gould ABD excited by the possibility of the productivity improvements offered by the Share Plan. The division had used other types of incentive systems before, but this plan seemed to resolve many of the problems encountered by previous incentive systems. The consultant was soon commissioned to adapt this motivational program to the needs of the battery division. Minor revisions were made and division

EXHIBIT 2
Organizational Chart—Automotive Battery Division

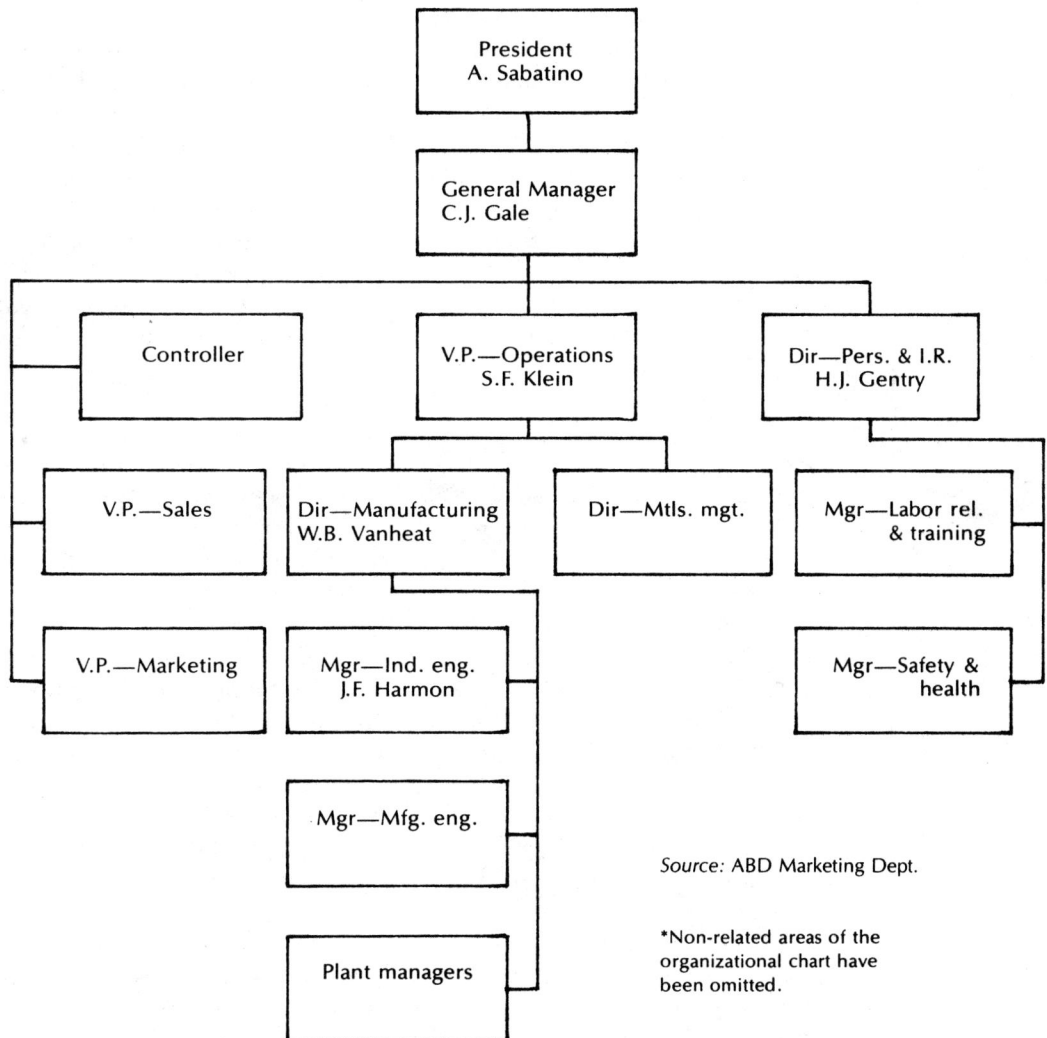

Source: ABD Marketing Dept.

*Non-related areas of the organizational chart have been omitted.

management accepted the Share Plan as one possible motivational program that could be used in its plants. Copies of the plan were distributed to plant managers. They were asked to comment on what type of response they would expect from the labor force if such a program were offered. They were also asked to suggest ideas on how the Share Plan could possibly be implemented in their respective locations if no incentive program was already in operation in their plant.

QUALITY CIRCLES

While Jim Woods was giving careful consideration to the possibility of implementing the Share Plan in the Westport plant, he was also considering the possibility of implementing quality circles. Woods was first introduced to quality circles from journal articles he had read in a variety of business periodicals. The frequency with which quality circle articles appeared increased directly with the mounting concern for continuing slow growth in U.S. productivity compared to most of its trading partners. In the midst of the 1979 economic recession, it had become a hot topic of conversation in academic as well as in business circles.

Quality circles were started in Japan in 1962 in an effort to reintroduce quality in the Japanese manufacturing process. Japan had a critical need to overcome its reputation as a source of cheap, poorly made goods; therefore, a participatory system was created where employees could voluntarily become involved in the problem-solving mechanism for improving product quality as well as production processes.

Japan's quality circles were made up of small groups of people who did similar work and who reported to the same supervisor. The people in each group normally worked together and faced the same kinds of production problems. Each group met together voluntarily on a weekly basis to discuss, analyze and propose solutions to problems they encountered in their respective work. It was management's responsibility to train each individual to use special problem-solving, analytical tools and to provide the resources and technical personnel to help them solve the problems on which they were working.

The quality circle process involved identifying a problem, setting priorities for working on it, finding causes, proposing solutions and where possible, implementing solutions. Its purpose was to improve quality and cost awareness through a participatory vehicle for production employees. It required little or no change in the organizational structure and was educational as well as work-oriented. Its ultimate goal was to improve communication and reduce conflicts, which in turn linked all levels and functions of the organization into an integrated unit and improved the efficiency of the entire production process. (Appendix B includes some of the elements of quality circles.)

Woods knew that the successful implementation of either the Share Plan or quality circles would be dependent upon an accurate assessment of the company structure and organizational climate in which the Westport plant operated. Only then could an appropriate plan of action be developed. The following information describes the Westport operation and its people.

WESTPORT PLANT MANAGEMENT

Management at the Westport plant was considered a well-qualified, hard-charging group of individuals. (See Exhibits 3 and 4.) Jim Woods, an MBA, was hired into Gould's new Management Development Program (MDP), and both corporate and division management had high hopes for Woods' future with the company. Involvement was a key characteristic with Woods. He was 100% involved in the management of the Westport plant, which was indicative of his "hands-on" man-

EXHIBIT 3
Organizational Chart—Westport Plant

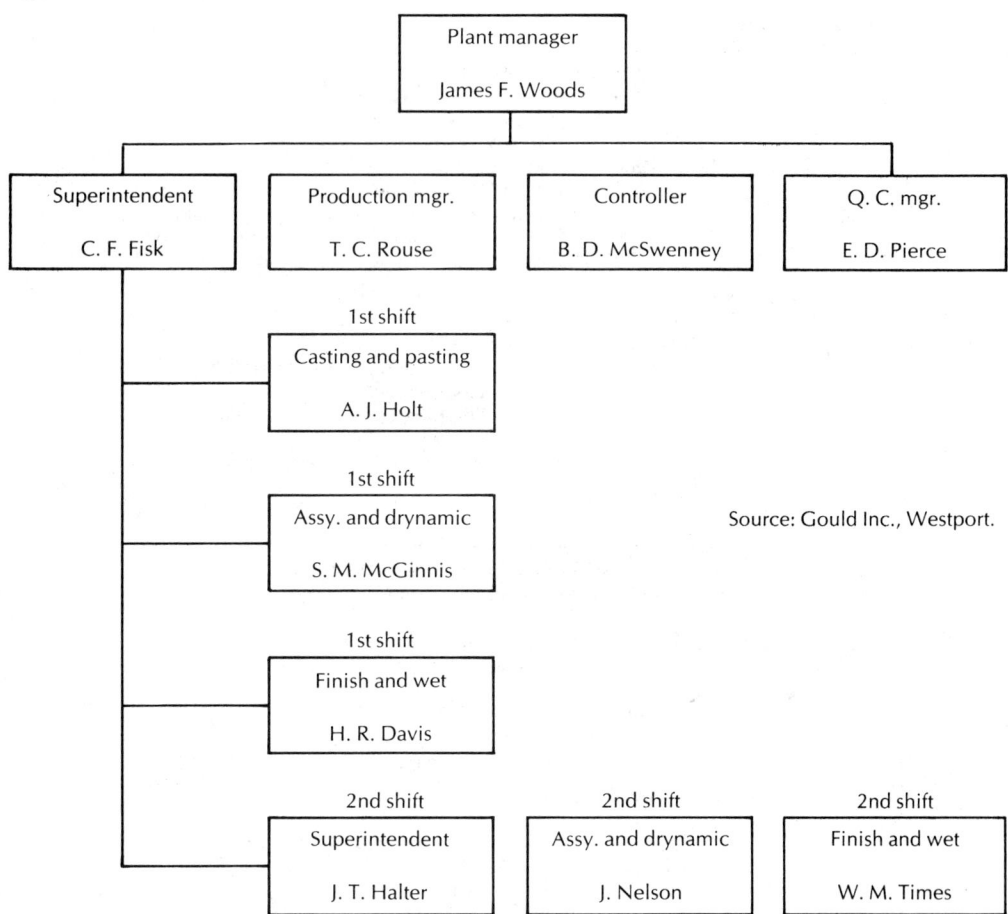

Source: Gould Inc., Westport.

agerial style. It was also the cause of resentment on the part of some plant employees. They resented the fact that Woods got directly involved in their respective production areas. Many resented his youth and felt that he did not have sufficient battery production experience to be issuing orders to people who had years of experience behind them. Aside from this issue, Woods was extremely strong in the areas of administrative and financial responsibilities. As an MBA student, he had developed special skills in assessing operational problems and in formulating the best solutions for maximizing available capital. The appointment as Plant Manager was Woods' first experience in a line-management position although it was his second assignment as an MDP. In his first assignment, Woods was special assistant to the President of the Automotive Battery Division.

EXHIBIT 4
Management Team Histories

Jim Woods, Plant Manager
  Age: 30
    1967–1971   University of Michigan, B.S.E.
    1971–1974   Ford Motor Company
                 Production Design Engineer
    1974–1976   University of Michigan, MBA
    1976–1980   Gould Inc., ABD
                 Hired into Gould's new
                 Management Development Program (MDP)
                 76–77   Assistant to ABD President
                 77–80   Plant Manager, Westport

  · Chuck Fisk, Plant Superintendent
  Age: 28
    1970–1980   Gould Inc., ABD
                 70–72   Wafer Clerk, North Bergen, N.J.
                          Floor Supervisor
                 72–73   Shipping Supervisor, Westport
                 73–78   Night Superintendent
                 78–80   Plant Superintendent

Tom Rouse, Production Manager
  Age: 47
    1965–1970   Gould Inc., ABD
                 Production Manager, Westport
    1970-1971   American Cyanamid
                 Cost Accountant
    1971–1975   General Battery Corporation
                 Production Manager
                 Controller
    1975–1980   Gould Inc., ABD
                 Plant Accountant, Westport
                 Production Manager

Bill McSweeney, Controller
  Age:42
    1959–1963   Virginia Technological Institute, B.S.
    1963–1965   Armed Services
    1965–1966   General Electric
                 Billing Clerk
    1966–1970   Burlington Industries
                 66–67   Cost Accounting Trainee
                 67–70   Plant Accountant
    1970–1980   Gould Inc., ABD
                 Controller, Westport

Ed Pierce, Quality Control Manager
  Age: 33
    1972–1980   Gould Inc., ABD
                 Quality Control Technician, Westport
                 Quality Control Manager

Chuck Fisk, Plant Superintendent, had worked for Gould since age 18. Fisk's father had also been a lifelong Gould employee and Chuck prided himself on the 58 years the Fisk name had been associated with Gould. Fisk had transferred to the Westport plant when he was first promoted to department supervisor. In his next promotions, Fisk assumed the positions of Night Shift Superintendent and then finally Plant Superintendent. As superintendent, Fisk was in contact with the largest number of plant employees. He was well-liked by his subordinates and when referred to by employees, was typically considered "one of them" because of his prior work affiliation. Fisk was criticized by the workers for his slowness to follow through on employee requests, suggestions, problems, etc. Situations were often brought to his attention several times before any remedial action was taken.

Tom Rouse, Production Manager, was responsible for all customer contact and for the areas of order arrivals, production scheduling, inventory management and shipment scheduling. Rouse was directly responsible for some clerical staff and for company truck drivers who transported all plant shipments. Tom was a very easy-going, pleasant individual who was respected by everyone. When the occasion called for it, he was reputed to stand firmly behind what he thought to be correct or fair.

Bill McSweeney, Plant Controller, had been with Gould for ten years at the Westport plant. He was a quiet, conservative person who did not become very involved in the daily operation of the plant. He had direct responsibility for the office staff and handled all of the plant's financial operations.

Ed Pierce, Quality Control Manager, had also been with the Westport plant for eight years. He was responsible for all component and unit testing to ensure the levels of quality mandated through Gould policy. Pierce was viewed as an excellent battery technician although his interpersonal skills were not so highly respected.

MANAGEMENT PERFORMANCE

The evaluation of each battery plant was based on overall plant performance against budget. Component factors considered in this performance were customer service, quality, labor productivity and cost performance compared to budget. Westport's top five managers participated in a bonus plan measured against overall plant performance. In a well-performing plant, managers could earn up to approximately 25 percent more than their base salaries. Westport managers had earned such a bonus over the past few years.

LABOR FORCE

The labor force at the Westport plant could be characterized by one word—stable. Average seniority in the plant was 8.5 years, and turnover in a bad month might double from a level of 1% to 2% total.

As in most Gould plants, the Westport plant was unionized through the International Brotherhood of Electrical Workers (I.B.E.W.); therefore, wage rates were the same throughout the division. In comparison to the rest of the area's manufacturing workforce, Gould employees were the highest paid employees. The lowest wage rate in the plant was $7.17 per hour. Overtime, when necessary, was available on a voluntary basis by employee seniority. Employees were often known to refuse to work overtime. The reason given was that they ended up paying more out in taxes than they earned for the extra effort.

With the development of government activity concerning Equal Employment Opportunity and Affirmative Action programs, Gould's Westport plant had complied by integrating its workforce. The number of black employees had grown to 20 percent of the labor force over the last five years. Due to the labor contract's job bidding procedure, which gives highest seniority employees the first choice on job bids, most first shift jobs were filled by white employees. The majority of the black employees worked in less desirable second shift jobs because of their lower ranking seniority. Since plant layoffs are also determined by seniority, the larger number of employees laid off in the February, 1980 cutback were black.

LABOR PERFORMANCE MEASUREMENT

Each employee's performance was measured against a production standard established for each job. Any employee on a new job had one month to qualify for the job at 100% standard performance. Consistent failure to maintain a reasonably high level of standard performance was determined as sufficient cause for dismissal.

The Westport Plant had not always used standards as a measure of performance. Standards had originated in 1973 at the time of the establishment of an old incentive program that had been used by the division. Before the old incentive program, performance was measured on an individual basis subject to management's opinion of what each employee should be able to produce in each job function. When the old incentive program was implemented into the plant's wage compensation structure, standards were established against which each employee earned a weekly bonus based upon his individual performance in excess of 100% standard. Bonus payments were measured against unit output, machine downtime and material scrap levels. Under the old incentive system, downtime credit relied heavily upon the supervisor's judgment. In some jobs, employees earned up to 50 percent more than their base salaries. In other jobs, employees could not seem to get above 10 percent of their base wages.

Because of some of the perceived inequities in the old incentive system and because the incentive plan became a political issue during the 1977 contract negotiations, the I.B.E.W. union leaders (EM 2 Council) rescinded the old incentive program in 1977. Without an incentive bonus to work for, the plant employees attempted to return to their old production patterns prior to the incentive program, but management continued to enforce the standards established at the time the incentive program was implemented. Neither the workers nor the union had any control over management's decision to continue the standards, but many felt that the old incentive system had been established as a managerial ploy to get the standards into operation regardless of what happened to the incentive program. Even though the old incentive system had been removed by the EM

2 Council, management's reputation as a trustworthy group had been considerably damaged.

UNION LEADERSHIP AND UNION–MANAGEMENT RELATIONS

Union leadership over much of 1979 had been unstable due to the fact that no member really wanted to run for the position of union president. Dick French, a plant maintenance man, finally accepted the position in early 1980. He attended the I.B.E.W. meetings and all sessions of the I.B.E.W.–Gould contract negotiation.

The Union's Executive Committee acted as liaison between the management team and the union membership. The Committee worked closely with management to resolve union grievances and to communicate policy changes to the union members. The Executive Committee, excluding French, was made up of three senior Gould employees. Paul Johns, a warehouseman, had been with Gould for 27 years. Johns was a strong force in the union, but did not want the responsibility or the headaches that came with being its leader. Johns was respected by both employees and management alike. Susan Amis, a group stacker, had been with Gould for 25 years. She, too, was a strong force in the union, especially in the assembly area of the plant. She was viewed by management as being somewhat "vocal." Bill Chancey, a warehouseman, was the least senior member on the Committee. He had been with Gould for 17 years. Chancey was the least outspoken of the three.

Union-Management meetings could be characterized as adversarial in a friendly sort of way. Chuck Fisk usually came to meetings prepared with counterarguments to grievances previously submitted by the union. Fisk was a key force at meetings because of the insights he had developed over the years regarding the people that worked in the plant. He knew how they thought and he knew how they reacted. He was often at an advantage in fighting grievances. Resolutions, however, were usually met at the first or second step of the grievance procedure. Rarely did a grievance ever reach a fourth-step hearing.

At one union–management meeting, management made a preliminary presentation to the Executive Committee to discuss the possibility of implementing the Share Plan in the plant. Division management had already taken steps to introduce the Plan to I.B.E.W. national officials at a prior meeting. With very little effort to discuss it, Dick French stated flatly that the Plan was unacceptable to the union. Upon further questioning, he explained that a union official at a recent chapter meeting had told him the Plan was no good. When asked what objections the union had to the Plan, he replied that he could not remember, but he knew that it was a plan by management to "screw" the people like the old incentive system had done. Management asked the Executive Committee to continue to think about it and then let the subject drop.

In July, 1980, French resigned as President of the union after six months in the position and after all of the out-of-town union negotiation meetings were over. Shortly after his resignation, union leaders found several unsettled grievances in

French's files that were way past due for any type of procedural processing, which left many of the grievants upset at French's opportunistic behavior and irresponsible performance.

Les Whellan, then Vice President, assumed French's duties as President of the union. Whellan, a truck driver, worked mostly out of Gould's warehouse located a mile away from the main plant. During a busy week, Whellan spent most of his time on the road and was often absent or late for union–management meetings. He frequently had to be briefed on labor problems occurring in the plant and was often confused about the text of the labor contract. As a truck driver, he was part of the regular bargaining unit but also was covered by a separate set of operating procedures established specifically for truck drivers.

THE WESTPORT ENVIRONMENT

Over the past two and a half years, plant staff and facilities engineering had worked hard to improve the manufacturing process at the Westport plant. Old worn-out equipment was replaced with new machinery that provided technological advances in the production process. Over $1 million was spent on lead-oxide pasting machines, an automated Plastic Line, new casting machines, new burning machines, new boost circuits, and corrosion-resistant conveyors. Additional non-productive equipment was also installed to comply with OSHA's newest lead standards. The new regulation required that maximum exposure to lead-in-air be reduced to 50 micrograms of lead per cubic meter of air, down from 200 micrograms, averaged over eight hours. Expensive ventilation systems were installed to reduce lead-in-air levels in lead-exposed areas.

As a result of these expenditures, production results immediately began to substantiate the worth of Woods' investment decisions. Since no new capital investments would be in sight for the near future, managers and supervisors strove hard to get top-quality performance from the employees and the new equipment. The demands of the results-oriented management team were occasionally met with resistance from members of the labor force. Many employees still resented the strict enforcement of production standards and a few plant employees made it a practice to use the union contract to foil management plans whenever possible. There were many occasions when Chuck Fisk attempted to second-guess union members' future actions to allow him to accurately estimate his potential production capacity.

Westport produced lead–antimony batteries for the replacement market. The year 1979–1980 had been a poor year for the replacement market. A continuous drop in battery sales initiated orders from corporate and division executives to cut back on manpower and to hold inventories as low as possible. All efforts were centered on maintaining divisional flexibility to allow quick reaction to changes in market conditions. As a result of top-management demands, the Westport plant was forced to lay off its entire second shift of 30 employees on February 1, 1980.

The entire Westport city area was affected by manpower cutbacks. One major area employer, Middleton Steel, had laid off hundreds of employees in September and November of 1979. By mid-summer, 1980, many were still unemployed with little hope of returning to work in the near future. Gould's second shift experienced one of the shortest layoffs in the area. In spite of this, employees were not recalled to work until July 15, 1980. Westport management initiated the recall to build up inventory stock in anticipation of fall sales and a promising forecast of an increase in demand in the near future.

A call came booming over the loudspeaker as Jim laid down the Share Plan folder.

"Jim Woods, in-house phone!"

He quickly picked up the line, "Yeah, Jim Woods here. . . . The pasting line is down again? I'll be right out."

Woods threw the folder in his desk as he put on his safety glasses. He knew that the Share Plan and quality circles could be useful in their own right, but were they right for Westport? Could he pull either one of them off, given the nature of the Westport operation and the characteristics of its employees? Should he implement one program and then the other, or should both be implemented together? What would he need to change in Westport's operation before any motivational plan could be successful? And finally, were the plant employees ready to become involved in a program where they would participate directly in working with management to solve job-related problems?

Managing change, Jim decided, was no simple matter.

APPENDIX A—THE SHARE PLAN

Main Features:

- —Increased productivity is shared by all employees in the group.
- —The past average productivity level is used as the measurement base. The average man-hours required during a base period to produce a unit of product is established as standard.
- —The value of the output of the group is the total unit produced multiplied by the past average man-hours standard.
- —Everyone in the plant or department is included in the plan. The input is the total man-hours worked by the group.
- —Productivity improvement is shared 50/50 between employees and management.
- —Gains are calculated weekly, with a moving average to span several weeks to create a stable output level. Losses are absorbed into the moving average.
- —Man-hour standards are frozen at the past average. Standards will not be changed by either management or the employees, except for capital equipment and technology changes, which are specifically defined. Increased productivity will be shared with no attempt to pinpoint whether employees or management created the savings.
- —An agreed ceiling is established on productivity sharing earnings. The excess

Source: Mitchell Fein, "Improving Productivity by Improved Productivity Sharing," *Record*, July, 1976.

over the ceiling will be carried forward to future weeks and eventually "bought back" from the workers by cash payments.

Main Constraints:

—Total unit man-hour costs under the plan cannot exceed unit costs in the past. Costs must decrease as productivity is raised.

—Management rights are not changed. All changes in methods and quality must be approved by management. Production levels, schedules, assignment of employees, etc, are vested in management, as they were before.

Note:

—Union contractual agreements are not altered.

APPENDIX B—QUALITY CIRCLES

I. Quality circles are groups of people from the same work area, who voluntarily meet together on a regular basis to identify, analyze, and solve quality, production and other problems in their area.

II. All employees of the plant are free to:

1. Join, or not join, to drop out or return to an established circle in their work area. However, membership may be delayed pending space availability and scheduled new member training.

2. Suggest problems to circles as potentials for investigation and resolution.

III. Management will:

1. Be supportive of circles by:
   a) Allowing company time for circles to meet.
   b) Encouraging circle members to attend scheduled circles to conduct effective meetings.
   c) Providing adequate meeting areas for circle activities.

2. Be participative in circle actions by:
   a) Replying in a reasonable time to circle requests and when necessary, to give detailed explanations to denied requests.
   b) Implementing circle solutions expeditiously, upon approval by appropriate authority.
   c) Respecting the autonomy of the circles, e.g., not independently resolving a problem that a circle is solving.

3. Have the right to suggest problems to circles and/or departments where new circles may be formed.

IV. Circles will:

1. Be totally voluntary.
2. Assume that each member has one vote.
3. Set up schedules for meetings and presentations within the framework of known plant work loads.
4. Collaborate on any work related problem in their areas pertaining to:

Source: Quality Circles, J.F. Beardsley and Associates.

   a) Quality of product.
   b) Production of product.
   c) Working conditions.
5. Not address the following subjects:*
   a) Benefits and wages.
   b) Items covered by the union contract.
   c) Hiring, firing policies.
   d) Personalities.
   e) Shift schedules.
   f) Elimination of job positions.
   g) Matters being handled in the grievance procedure.
6. Have the right to accept/refuse problems submitted from any source.
7. Identify, analyze and implement solutions to problems. If implementation requires management approval, the circle will present the problems and their requested solutions to management for acceptance.
8. Present periodic reviews to management on the progress of the circle.
9. Improve communications between all employees.

V. Organization:
   1. *Quality Circles* are small groups of employees usually 3 to 10 in number, who do similar work, voluntarily meet regularly to identify and analyze causes of problems in their work area, recommend their solutions to management, and where possible, implement the solutions themselves.
   2. *Quality Circle Leader* is normally the immediate supervisor of the circle members. He/she is responsible for the operation of the circle and trains circle members in the quality circle techniques. He/she works closely with the facilitator.
   3. *Quality Circle Facilitator* is responsible for the overall quality circle program. The facilitator:
      a) Is appointed by management.
      b) Works closely with the steering committee.
      c) Trains circle leaders and assists in training circle members.
      d) Maintains records.
      e) Coordinates circle operations.
      f) Interfaces between circles and company organizations and departments.
   4. *Steering committee* is responsible for establishing quality circle program policies, procedures, objectives, and resources. It is composed of managerial members representing various plant functions (cost, quality control, etc.) and two members of the bargaining unit. The committee publicizes circle activities within and outside of the plant. They also show their visibility by meeting regularly with the facilitator and by attending management presentations.

---

*All changes to the production process must be approved by Division Engineering.

5. *Quality Circle Members* are responsible for learning and applying the following techniques:
   a) Brainstorming.
   b) Cause and effect analysis.
   c) Data gathering.
   d) Pareto analysis.
   e) Histograms.
   f) Presentation techniques.
   g) Control charts.
   h) Decision making.
   Members are also expected to regularly attend and actively participate in scheduled circle meetings.

Centel of Virginia

Dan Martin sat in his office considering the alternatives before him. He had just made a presentation to the division vice-president and his department heads of the Central Telephone Company of Virginia on Quality Circles, a form of participative problem solving being used by an increasing number of American companies. In his presentation Dan had also recommended the specific implementation plan Centel should use. Daryl Ferguson, the Division Vice-President, and Don Roberton, the Customer Services Manager, believed Centel would make better use of Quality Circles by changing the concept to fit the structure and work flow at Centel. They were basing their beliefs primarily on the Fall Rush Program. Dan Martin had studied the concept of Quality Circles and was not sure how successful the program would be if changed. Mr. Ferguson asked him to reanalyze the situation taking into account the differences in a service company like Centel and a manufacturing company (where Quality Circles first originated). Dan knew he had to either come up with a new plan or better defend his old plan and soon. Mr. Ferguson wanted his new recommendations within one week.

COMPANY BACKGROUND

The Central Telephone Company of Virginia is one of seventeen divisions of the Central Telephone & Utilities Corporation (Centel). With corporate headquarters in Chicago, Centel has eleven divisions offering phone service throughout the country. Together, these divisions constitute the fifth largest telephone system in the U.S. Centel also owns and operates electric utilities in Colorado and Kansas. Through its subsidiary Centel Communications Company, the company is involved in other communications-related businesses including cable television, the sale of business communication systems, and the design and marketing of acoustic enclosures for public telephones. Telephone revenues comprise over 70% of total sales for the corporation.

CENTRAL TELEPHONE COMPANY OF VIRGINIA

Centel of Virginia is the third largest subsidiary of the Central Telephone & Utilities Corporation. Covering a service area of 6,070 square miles, Centel serves

Copyright © 1985 by The Colgate Darden Graduate Business School Sponsors, University of Virginia, Charlottesville, Virginia. Reproduced by permission.

This case was prepared by Dennis Harbin under the supervision of Professor Edward Davis, The Colgate Darden Graduate School of Business Administration, University of Virginia.

142,600 customers in 29 counties throughout the State. For organizational purposes the service areas are broken down into geographic territories. Charlottesville is the location of the division offices and the customer services offices for the surrounding area. Other customer services offices serve the Martinsville/Lexington area and the remaining Centel service area in Virginia. Centel employs 1,460 employees in Virginia of which 77% are hourly. Most of the hourly workers are represented by the International Brotherhood of Electrical Workers (IBEW). In 1980 Centel's management had a good working relationship with the Union. Centel had rarely had to lay off workers in the past, except for the '73–'74 recession, but with the rapid gains in telecommunications technology over the past few years, the practice could change. Turnover was very low and the average worker had been with Centel approximately seven years.

An organization chart of the division management is shown in Exhibit 1. Mr. Ferguson has been the head of the Virginia division for almost two years. Mr.

EXHIBIT 1
Division Organization Chart

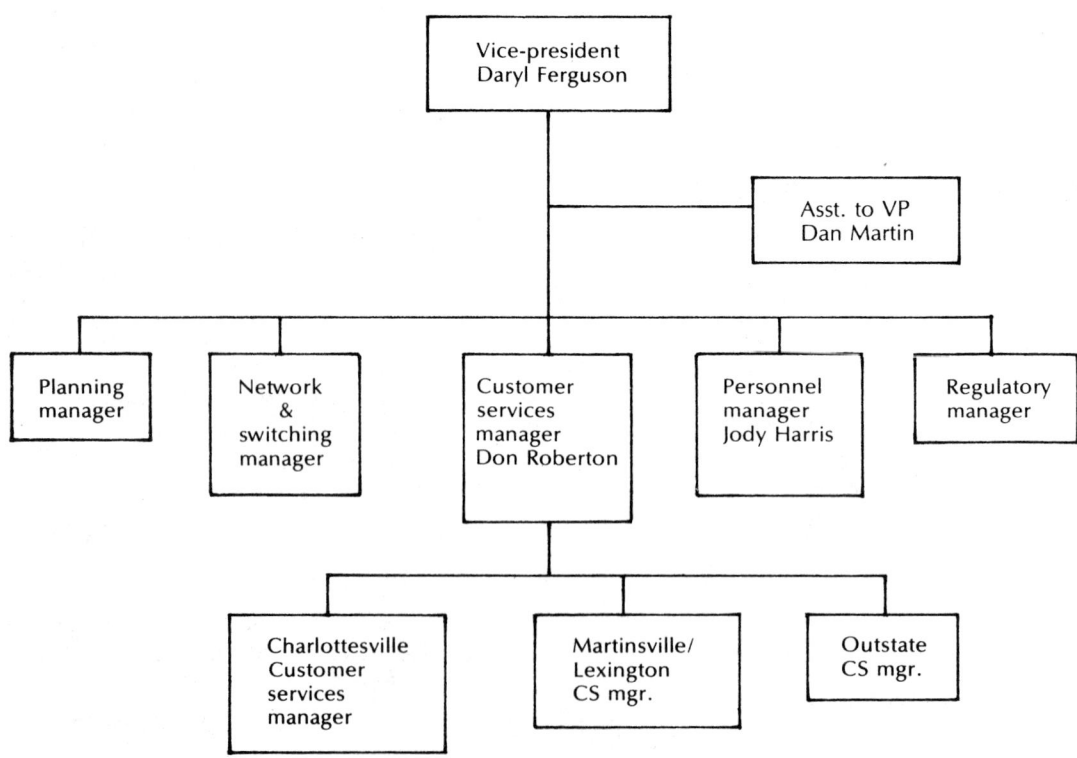

Ferguson brought a number of new managers when he came to Virginia. In particular the department heads of Customer Services and Network & Switching who between them have 96% of the hourly workforce were replaced by Mr. Ferguson.

The Virginia division had experienced problems in the past which had affected service to customers and management–employee relations. The division management had changed a number of times over the past 10 years. It seemed like as soon as the employees had become accustomed to one management, they were replaced by another team. Service suffered and the gap between management and workers had widened.

Mr. Ferguson and his new managers had made progress in improving the relationship between management and workers. In the winter of 1979, Mr. Ferguson and other managers started meeting with first line supervisors and hourly workers. These meetings became known as Skip Level Meetings and they had a positive effect on the workers. The workers aired their gripe or question, and the attending managers tried to give them an answer. The new attitude of the workers was that "this management cares but let's wait awhile longer before we trust them completely." Because of the success of the program, Mr. Ferguson decided to continue Skip Level Meetings provided they would only be held when scheduling of the managers and workers permitted.

Though progress had been made, there still remained some areas where improvements could be made. One particular area was in the communications and coordination at the lower levels between different groups. The Fall Rush Program demonstrated there were problems in this area that could be corrected.

FALL RUSH PROGRAM

In September of 1979 Mr. Ferguson received a phone call from a professor in the Sociology Department at the University of Virginia. He was calling to complain about Centel's service. Centel's work load typically increased 50% during the period August through September when students at the University of Virginia returned to school, so these types of complaints were not uncommon. It was during this conversation that the professor suggested a way that might help Centel improve service in the future to its customers in the Charlottesville area during the Fall Rush. He suggested to Mr. Ferguson that Centel organize two groups of employees from all areas of the company to meet during the spring of 1980 to discuss how Centel could better prepare for the Fall Rush. The groups would be composed of hourly workers and managers chosen by upper management. The professor would provide two sociology graduate students who would serve as facilitator for the two groups. Mr. Ferguson was impressed with the approach and gave the go-ahead for the program.

From January to March the two seven-member teams met weekly to review the results of the 1979 Fall Rush and analyze specific problem areas identified by division management. The first couple of meetings were unproductive as the team members argued over which group in the company was responsible for a particular problem. A number of times the facilitator in each group had to interject to get his team back on the right track.

After the first couple of meetings, the group began to be more productive. In March each group made a presentation of their analysis and recommendations to Mr. Ferguson and Mr. Roberton. The recommendations of both teams were well received. The two teams were then combined into one team that was to come

---

EXHIBIT 2
Centel's New Fall Rush Procedure for Incoming Students

August 1, 1980

Dear Student:

Welcome back to Charlottesville. Centel looks forward to serving your telephone needs, and to help start the semester out right, we've made some changes this year to make applying for service easier and faster.

Centel's temporary business office will be in a new location this year. We have leased space in the former Sears building (1105 West Main Street) and we'll be open at this site from August 11 through September 15, just to handle student applications. Our hours are 8:30 a.m. to 5 p.m., Monday through Friday. There is plenty of free parking at our new location, which is also on the University bus route.

There are several reasons why we need more space this year. We're taking a larger staff consisting of experienced service representatives, clerks, and storeroom personnel. They will be able to process your orders more quickly, give you a telephone, and in most cases, provide service at your residence in one to three days.

Our temporary office is air conditioned and more spacious than our permanent business office on Arlington Blvd., so you'll be served in comfort.

In order to accomplish our goal of providing you quicker and better service, we'll need your help. First of all, we expect all students to make applications for service at the temporary business office (TBO) location. (Only permanent-resident customers will be served at our Arlington Blvd. location.) Beginning August 11, phone or in-person applicants will be asked to go to the TBO. Secondly, while you're waiting (hopefully the wait will be short) we will ask you to complete your own Service Application Card which will save time when you get to the Service Representative.

There are some additional facts we'd like you to know about our operations this year. In approximately 2500 addresses where students are normally housed, we have left the number and equipment in place. This means that if you move into one of these locations, you will have the telephone number of the student who lived there previously. The advantage of this is that we'll have a good chance of providing same-day service. At locations not "dedicated," we still hope to be able to provide three-day service.

Also, our lease instruments are now limited to standard desk and wall models in black or white (rotary or Touch Call). We will, however, offer phones in a variety of colors for sale to students at a reduced rate. These phones will be refurbished (cleaned and repaired lease instruments that have been returned to the telephone company), but will carry a full one-year guarantee. You can save on your monthly bill by owning your own telephone.

Enclosed is a handbook that Centel has produced especially for students in our serving areas. We hope you'll take the time to read it—it will provide the answer to a lot of your questions. If you need additional information or have questions, please call the business office.

We hope to see you at our temporary business office.

Sincerely,

Larry L. Gorby

Larry L. Gorby
Customer Services Manager

up with one detailed plan for improving service during the Fall Rush. Work continued for another month at the end of which another presentation was made. A number of the recommendations were accepted and implemented in the summer of 1980. One of these was a letter (shown in Exhibit 2) sent to every returning U.Va. student detailing Centel's new Fall Rush operations.

At the conclusion of the fall rush, the Fall Rush Program was declared a tremendous success. The program saved Centel an estimated $88,000, but more importantly, Centel's image was greatly enhanced by the better coordination and service offered students. The members of the Fall Rush Program groups were also enthusiastic. One member commented that it was the first time division management had listened to the supervisors' and workers' suggestions.

QUALITY CIRCLES

The Fall Rush Program convinced Mr. Ferguson that an ongoing group participation program could definitely benefit Centel. He had heard about a program used by the Japanese called Quality Circles but was not sure if that was a program Centel could use. He asked his assistant, Dan Martin, a new MBA out of the Darden School at U.Va., to research major elements of the Japanese productivity system including Quality Circles and study some companies in the U.S. that had implemented a Quality Circle Program. Finally he wanted Dan to develop an implementation plan that could be initiated within the next six months if Centel chose to use Quality Circles.

Dan began his research by finding as many articles as he could on Quality Circles. As it turned out there were many due to the success of the Japanese and the new emphasis on productivity in American industry. After learning as much as he could from the articles, Dan called the American Productivity Center in Houston. From them he learned about three consulting firms on the West Coast which specialized in coming into companies and implementing Quality Circles. All three firms were established by the original Lockheed team that went to Japan to learn about Quality Circles and then returned to Lockheed and started their own program. Dan also contacted two companies on the East Coast which had implemented a QC Program. After visiting these companies he felt he understood what made Quality Circles work. He now needed to determine if circles would work at Centel.

Dan felt the best way to find out if circles would work at Centel was to talk to the managers and hourly people at all levels in Centel. He specifically concentrated only on the Charlottesville area because he felt it would be the best place to start a program with the division offices there and the success of the Fall Rush Program. If it turned out the program was successful in Charlottesville, it then could be expanded to other areas. Dan also talked to the IBEW Union manager. All the managers and the Union manager were receptive to such a program. Dan was really surprised the Union manager was for it because his research indicated that most Unions take a negative approach to such a program.

The two hourly workers Dan talked to had mixed feelings about Quality Circles. One felt such a program was needed because there were a number of times he had made suggestions to his supervisor and no one took any action. The other worker felt Quality Circles would just be another management program that would fail like all the others. Because the circles would be strictly voluntary, Dan was not worried by the last worker's comments. He knew only workers who wanted to participate would.

Dan Martin was convinced Quality Circles would benefit Centel, but what bothered him was the differences in a manufacturing environment where Circles were being used exclusively, compared to a service environment like Centel. Dan knew Quality Circles should be made up of people with common work-related problems. This is so everyone in the group would be able to contribute in analyzing the problem. In a manufacturing company Quality Circles are formed from one supervisor's work group because most of the group's problems are within their common work area. This could be an assembly line, a machine, or a procedure. In a service company like Centel this is not the case. Exhibit 3 shows the work flow in Centel's customer services department for getting one phone hooked up.

EXHIBIT 3
Service Order Flow

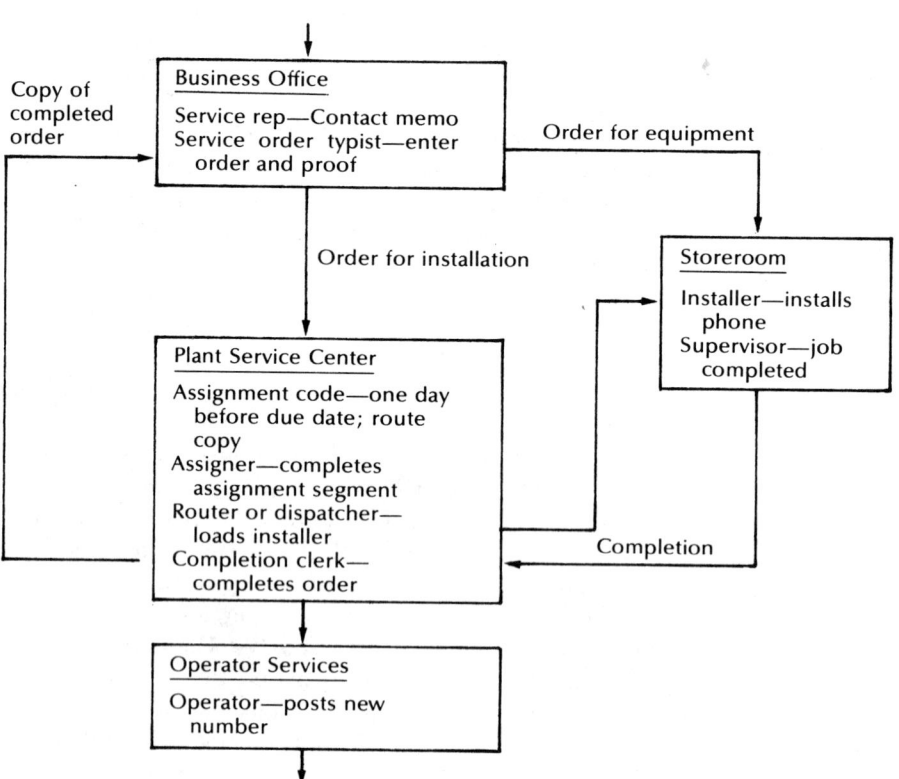

For the phone to be installed properly, it was important that each of the four groups coordinate their work with the other groups and communicate any problems. If one group had a problem then all the groups had a problem. Thus, in Centel the majority of work-related problems that had the greatest effect on service were *intergroup* rather than *intragroup* problems as in a manufacturing company.

MEETING

Dan knew Centel would eventually have Quality Circles made up of workers from different groups, but he was hesitant to recommend that approach at the outset. From his research he had determined that two of the most important characteristics of Quality Circles are that the groups choose their own problems to analyze and that all problems analyzed would be common to the group. With intergroup circles Dan was worried members might choose problems that were not common to all members. He knew this problem could be alleviated by allowing management to choose the problems to be analyzed, but that would undermine the whole concept of Quality Circles being the workers' program rather than a management-imposed program. One indication of this was that one worker who participated in the Fall Rush Program said he resented management telling him what problems to analyze. Dan felt once some workers had gotten experience in a Quality Circle made up of members from the same work group, they would better understand how to function in an intergroup circle. He knew from talking with a number of supervisors there were a number of problems that could be work-group analyzed.

Dan prepared the implementation plan shown in Exhibit 4 and sent it to Mr.

EXHIBIT 4
Quality Circle Implementation Plan

September 30, 1980

TO: Daryl Ferguson
FROM: Dan Martin
SUBJECT: QC Implementation at Centel

I recommend that Centel implement a pilot Quality Circle program in the Charlottesville offices of Customer Services and Network & Switching. I first would like to list my reasons for making such a recommendation, followed by some of the problems identified to me by some Centel managers. Finally, I will list the implementation program I recommend Centel use if they choose to have a Quality Circle program.

During the past month, I spent time talking to a number of Centel managers and the IBEW Union Manager in the Charlottesville area. In our meetings, I presented the QC concept and got their reactions to such a program. Also, I talked to these managers about their work environment and how compatible it was to a QC program. A number of strengths and weaknesses of the program as it pertains to Centel were identified.

I believe Centel should implement a pilot QC program in the Charlottesville area because:
1. Every manager and supervisor I talked to was favorable toward such a program. There were some problems identified, but all managers and supervisors said they would be willing to support

EXHIBIT 4, cont'd

such a program in their area under the right conditions. Also, the managers I talked to felt there were definitely a number of areas where employees could identify problems and make recommendations that would benefit Centel.

2. The IBEW Business Manager is in favor of the program and would like to see it implemented. Even though it is strictly voluntary, he was not sure if the hourly people would accept it, but he said the Union would take no action against the program.

3. The Fall Rush Program has made a favorable impression on the people involved in the program and on a number of employees who did not get to participate in the program now that management has used some of the recommendations of this program. According to first line supervisors, a number of employees feel the current management team will listen to employees' suggestions. Also, I believe the Fall Rush Program has established the idea of participative problem solving at Centel.

4. The Charlottesville area has closer contact with the division offices than any other Centel service area. The QC program will require a number of management meetings in the pre-implementation phase. These meetings will require less management time if the program is implemented in the Charlottesville area due to less traveling.

5. The skip level meetings have given employees a medium for airing grievances. Skip level meetings should be continued. This will help prevent Quality Circles being used by employees as a gripe session.

Some of the problems that will have to be addressed before Centel implements a Quality Circle program are:

1. What would be Centel's policy toward a Circle recommendation that eliminated someone's job?

2. What will Centel's policy be toward scheduling QC meetings? Will they be held during normal working hours or overtime? All the managers believed the program would benefit their area, but they could not see how they could schedule 8-10 people from one work group to meet for one hour each week and still meet their workload.

3. Since the normal workload goes up 25-50% during August and September, what would be Centel's policy toward circles meeting during the Fall Rush?

These were the problems identified by the managers I talked to. After the Steering Committee is formed, these should be the first issues they should consider after choosing a facilitator.

QC Implementation Plan

Below are the steps I recommend to implement a pilot Quality Circle Program at Centel. See the estimated timetable in Exhibit 1 and the estimated costs in Exhibit 2.

1. Hire a consulting firm to make an in-house presentation on Quality Circles to all managers in Customer Services and Network and Switching in the Charlottesville area. If scheduling is a problem the seminar can be presented at night or twice during the work day. I recommend the consulting firm Quality Circle Institute of Red Bluff, California, as a first choice and J.F. Beardsley and Associates of San Jose, California, as a second choice. They both have good programs, but the former is much cheaper.

2. Hire same firm to implement Quality Circles in Charlottesville offices of Customer Services and Network & Switching. The consulting firm will send preliminary information concerning the formation of the Steering Committee, criteria for selecting a facilitator, and information on the formation and training of Quality Circles.

3. Form the Steering Committee, composed of the department heads of Customer Service, Network & Switching, and Personnel, the Charlottesville Customer Services Manager, Union Representative, Facilitator (after he is chosen), and the Division Vice-President.

4. Have the Steering Committee select one full-time facilitator and either a second full-time or part-time facilitator. The second facilitator can be used as a substitute at the beginning and then as a full-time facilitator when the program grows.

5. Facilitators begin training with consultant. The Union representative can be included in the training, but he indicated to me at our meeting he was not interested in participating. The Steering Committee begins to meet regularly to prepare guidelines and objectives of Centel program. Consultant will help Steering Committee identify areas to consider.

6. Steering Committee, Facilitator, and Consultant Design Implementation Program for Centel.

EXHIBIT 4, cont'd

The program should identify departments that will have pilot circles, schedule for circle meetings, and schedule for group leader training.

Based on my study of the Charlottesville area, I recommend that a pilot program of six circles be initiated. I would put two circles in both the Charlottesville Customer Services Business Office and Plant Service Center. Because Centel desires to have them in Network and Switching also, I would organize two circles in Northern and Southern.

7. The facilitator should collect some pre-implementation data so as to later demonstrate a before and after comparison. I could not identify any data that Centel presently has to do this. Thus, I would recommend the Personnel Department administer a simple questionnaire to determine employees' attitudes in the Business Office, Plant Service Center, and Network & Switching.

8. The facilitator will next distribute Quality Circle literature to managers of the Business Office, Plant Service Center, and Network & Switching. Though I have already talked to most of these managers, it gives them an opportunity to review materials on circles and ask questions. It will then be up to the managers to select the pilot program circle leaders from the interested supervisory volunteers.

9. The Steering Committee will meet with the pilot program managers and circle leaders to discuss the program and answer any questions. This meeting is necessary to show middle managers and group leaders that the program has top management support.

10. The facilitator and consultant begin Circle Leader training. The Steering Committee and consultant make final review of circle policy, guidelines, and implementation plan.

11. Second level managers of pilot program departments conduct Quality Circle familiarization meetings with employees. The facilitator and possibly a representative of the Steering Committee should be there. Workers should be allowed to openly discuss the program and ask questions.

12. Circle leaders talk to each employee individually in their work groups to find out if employee is interested in voluntarily participating in the group.

13. The facilitator and circle leaders begin group training with training materials supplied by the consulting firm.

This concludes the pilot circle implementation plan. Circles will continue training for one hour each week during the first two months of the program. After two months, the circles will begin to identify problems in their work area and choose the ones they want to work on. The facilitator should schedule circle presentations to management on either recommendations or status once every three months. Members of the Steering Committee or pilot group managers should try and attend all or part of a circle's meeting at least once in the first three months of the program.

After the pilot program gets started, the Steering Committee needs to address the issue of circle expansion. How fast will circles be allowed to grow and in what areas are two primary considerations. Expansion should not be allowed until after approximately three months to give Centel management and employees a chance to experience the program.

The facilitator will meet with all the pilot circles during the first months to help the circle leader. After approximately three months, the facilitator should prepare a report for the Steering Committee on circle activities and any cost savings realized to date. Any problems in implementing the pilot circles should be identified in this report so the Steering Committee can make modifications to the program before future circles are added. Also, after three months of circle activities, the Steering Committee should meet with the managers and leaders of the pilot circles to discuss the attitudes of circle members, non-circle members, and middle management.

During the first six months, the facilitator will be able to contact the consulting group about any implementation problems and, if needed, have them send someone to Charlottesville. At the end of six months, the consultant will return to Centel to make an evaluation of the program and, along with the facilitator, establish goals for the program for the next year.

Once Centel has experienced some success with the pilot program, I would recommend the Steering Committee form two or three interdepartment groups between the Business Office, Plant Service Center, Storeroom, and possibly Operator Services. A number of people who took part in the Fall Rush Program said there are communication problems between groups that would be alleviated by intergroup interaction on problem solving. I do not recommend interdepartment groups initially because I feel the program must be accepted in its original form before making variations to it. Once employees become experienced

EXHIBIT 4, cont'd
Quality Circle Implementation Plan

in identifying and solving problems in their work groups, I feel they will be ready to tackle the more difficult task of interdepartmental problems.

I have tried to make my implementation steps as specific as possible. Once a consulting firm is retained and a facilitator hired more detail can be incorporated into the plan as Centel begins to get into the preliminary implementation phase. It will be up to the Steering Committee to add more detail and make modifications to the program as information becomes available.

EXHIBIT 4a
Implementation Timetable Guideline

Action	By whom	Approximate working days
Decision to start.	Division Vice President	0
Contact consultant to arrange for in-house seminar and implementation. Hopefully, seminar can be scheduled within next 20 days.	Assigned Individual	1
Receive and review preliminary information from consultant concerning organization of steering committee and choosing facilitator.	Assigned Individual	5
Form steering committee and initiate first meeting.	Assigned Individual	8
Steering committee selects facilitator and works on circle objectives and guidelines.	Steering Committee	18
Facilitator begins training with the instructor/consultant. Also, the two work on setting up implementation program to be presented to steering committee.	Facilitator	18
Facilitator collects preimplementation data for before and after comparison.	Facilitator	23
Distribute Quality Circle literature to pilot group managers.	Facilitator	28
Pilot group managers and supervisors meet with steering committee to discuss program and answer any questions.	Steering Committee and Pilot Group Managers	30
Select pilot program circle leaders from interested supervisory volunteers. Begin leader training.	Pilot Group Managers Facilitator	31
Managers conduct Quality Circle familiarization meetings with employees. Facilitator, Circle leaders, and a member of the steering committee participate as speakers.	Managers Facilitator	35
Leader contacts each employee to determine circle membership.	Leader	37
Leaders and facilitator begin weekly Circle meetings and initiate member training.	Facilitator Leader	38
Circles learn problem solving techniques from training sessions.	Facilitator Leader Group Members	78
Facilitator makes progress report to steering committee and arranges Circle presentation.	Facilitator	100
Steering committee decides on program expansion and makes revisions to policy/procedures.	Steering Committee	3 Months

EXHIBIT 4b
Cost Analysis—Quality Circles

A. One time costs:

Consultant seminar presentation	$ 500
Consultant implementation cost	3,950
Consultant expenses (estimate only)	4,000
	$8,450

B. On-going costs:
Full-time facilitator
Loss of production due to Circle meetings
Management expenses for participation on steering committee

Ferguson and his department heads. Mr. Ferguson called for a meeting with his department heads and Dan to go over the implementation plan. Mr. Ferguson and Mr. Roberton said they felt Centel should go right to intergroup circles. They felt the greatest problems to be addressed were in this area and that the Fall Rush Program had shown such a concept could work at Centel. They both felt they did not have the six months Dan had recommended before going to intergroup circles.

Dan and Jody Harris, the Personnel Manager who would be responsible for the program, did not agree. They felt Centel should get some experience with the QC Program as used by other companies before making any changes. Dan tried to point out the differences between the Fall Rush Program and Quality Circles and explain why he did not recommend intergroup circles to begin with. Mr. Ferguson, still unconvinced, asked Dan to reanalyze the situation and if necessary, come up with a new plan.

DECISION

Dan returned to his office and thought over what had transpired. He knew why Mr. Ferguson and Mr. Roberton wanted to use intergroup circles, but it bothered him that they did not have six months before forming such circles. Dan wondered if increasing productivity was their only reason for wanting to implement a Quality Circle Program? Dan felt a circle program should be started to increase worker participation and morale. Productivity increases are a benefit of the program and are a primary reason for management implementing such a program. If increasing productivity was the *only* reason Centel wanted to implement circles, Dan was worried what would happen if the program did not generate the magnitude of cost savings ideas the Fall Rush Program had. Whatever their reasons, Dan knew he would have come up with a new plan or be better prepared to defend his old plan to Mr. Ferguson next week.

Drug Distribution
at Victoria Hospital (R)

On February 1, 1983 John Hart, Director of Pharmacy at Victoria Hospital, London, Ontario, received an important memo from Mr. A. Thompson, President of Victoria Hospital Corporation. Mr. Thompson required an immediate evaluation of the recently tabled and much publicized recommendations of the Dubin Committee. The Ontario Minister of Health had appointed the Dubin Committee in June, 1982 to investigate the approximately 40 suspicious infant deaths on the cardiac ward of Toronto's Hospital for Sick Children between July, 1980 and March, 1981. In its report the Committee found fault with a number of areas in the Hospital including drug administration. The Committee specifically criticized the lack of control by the hospital's drug distribution system in detecting medication errors. After reviewing the Hospital for Sick Children's situation and Victoria Hospital's existing drug distribution systems, Mr. Hart wondered what action he could take to ensure patient safety in Paediatrics and the other wards at Victoria Hospital.

VICTORIA HOSPITAL CORPORATION

From 1887 until 1973 Victoria Hospital was managed by a Board of Hospital Trustees accountable to the Corporation of the City of London. In 1973 Victoria Hospital was incorporated under the provisions of the Corporations Act for the purpose of owning, controlling, and operating the Hospital. The Corporation had a sixteen member Board of Directors comprised of: the President, Vice-President, and Secretary of the medical staff, five individuals elected from the community, six people elected with the approval of various governing bodies, and two appointees of the Lieutenant-Governor of Ontario.

Victoria Hospital was London's oldest and largest hospital, with over 3,500 staff and over 550 doctors with admitting rights. It was also one of Canada's largest teaching hospitals, with 175 post-graduate medical students. It was a major treat-

Copyright © 1984, the University of Western Ontario.

Case material of the University of Western Ontario School of Business Administration is prepared as a basis for classroom discussion. This case was written by John Haywood-Farmer and David Johnston. The authors gratefully acknowledge earlier reports on Victoria Hospital by R. R. Britney, P. J. Kuzdrall, and J. Stanczyk of this School.

ment referral centre for southwestern Ontario providing emergency, general, specialist, and chronic medical care. Victoria Hospital served the public through two active-patient campuses and three chronic-care affiliated institutes. The South Street Campus (South Street) was located near downtown London. It contained 709 beds in 30 wards including 119 in the 5-ward War Memorial Children's Hospital which was the largest paediatrics centre in southwestern Ontario. The Children's Hospital was housed in a separate building at South Street. The 135-bed, 5-ward Westminster Campus (Westminster) was located in a suburb 3.5 km from South Street. These active-patient facilities were used by about 29,000 in-patients and newborn infants, and, including the Hospital's family medicine clinics, by about 230,000 emergency, one-day-stay, and out-patients per year. Bed occupancy averaged about 90% except in the Children's Hospital where it was about 75%. The average stay was about 9.0 days.

The Psychiatric Institute, the Veterans Care Centre, and Western County Medical Services were chronic care institutions with a total of about 525 beds that had become affiliated with Victoria Hospital during the 1970s.

In 1983 a new hospital was under construction at Westminster which would eventually replace South Street and provide similar bed numbers and improved health care and research facilities. Plans called for two eight-floor towers containing 350 beds to be completed by the mid 1980s and two more towers to be completed by the late 1980s, at which time the project would be finished. Mr. Hart was actively involved in planning the new Pharmacy at Westminster. Mr. Hart and pharmacy consultants were planning to have a central Pharmacy with Satellite Pharmacies on certain floors in the towers of the new facility. The Satellites would serve as home bases for clinical pharmacy work in sensitive wards such as Paediatrics. The Westminster facilities would give Pharmacy ample room to expand programs, increase staff, and improve service.

THE PHARMACY DEPARTMENT

The Pharmacy department administration, including Mr. Hart's office, was located at South Street. The department employed one Director, five Supervisors, and 53 other staff distributed as shown in the table below. Exhibit 1 is an organizational chart of the department.

	SOUTH STREET	WESTMINSTER	PSYCHIATRIC INSTITUTE
Staff Pharmacists	10	3	2
Pharmacy assistants	16 + 2 PT	4 + 1 PT	2 + 1 PT
Temporary Pharmacists	2	1	0
Clerical and Porter Staff	4 + 1 PT	4	0

The 1982 operating budget for Pharmacy was $3.2 million of which about 33% was for salaries, about 50% for drugs, and about 17% for other pharmaceutical supplies. The average annual salaries paid were: pharmacists, $30,000; pharmacy assistants, $14,000. The overall budget had kept up with the general rate of

EXHIBIT 1
Pharmacy Department Organization Chart

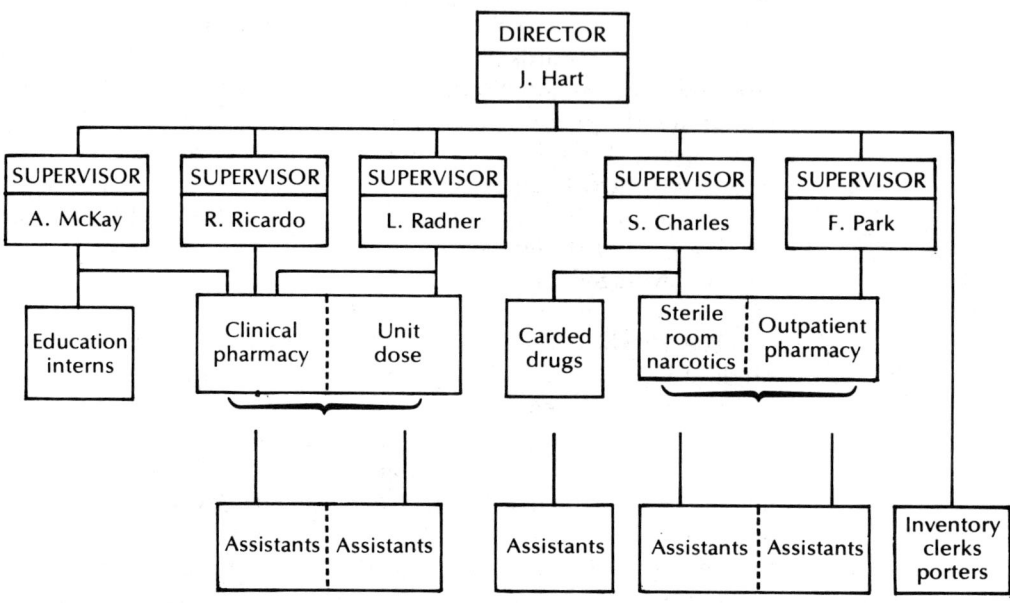

inflation but the prices of some drugs had increased as much as 30–40% during the last year. Mr. Hart was under strong pressure from the hospital's administration to reduce costs in response to government cuts in health care spending and the large deficits that Victoria Hospital had incurred in recent years.

The South Street Pharmacy occupied about 120 square metres of work area and about 250 square metres of storage space on the first floor. Conditions were crowded but no additional space was available. Westminster, with about 740 square metres devoted to Pharmacy, provided about 25% of South Street's storage needs and about 90% of its packaging requirements. Westminster also supplied pharmacy services to the affiliated institutions; South Street Pharmacy served only its own campus.

Pharmacy had a number of unique features compared to the average hospital pharmacy. During the summer months it hired up to six student pharmacists to replace pharmacy assistants and clerical staff on vacation. In addition, each year two pharmacists (residents) interned full-time for 12 months at Victoria Hospital, working both in Pharmacy, and monitoring drug administration and discussing pharmacy issues of mutual concern with nurses on the wards. The student pharmacists were included in Pharmacy's budget but the residents were funded separately. Neither group was included in the staffing numbers above but each required extra supervision from Pharmacy. The hospital tried to give its pharmacy residents a broad exposure to as many facets of hospital pharmacy as possible.

Scheduling the residents and ensuring their proficiency in each area further added to Pharmacy's administrative burden. South Street Pharmacy had an out-patient service which offered patients and staff prescription filling similar to that found in drug stores.

Pharmacy was open during the following hours:

	SOUTH STREET	WESTMINSTER	PSYCHIATRIC INSTITUTE
Monday to Friday	7:30 A.M.–8:00 P.M.	8:00 A.M.–6:00 P.M.	8:30 A.M.–4:30 P.M.
Saturday, Sunday	7:30 A.M.–6:00 P.M.	8:00 A.M.–5:00 P.M.	
Sunday Evening	7:00 A.M.–9:00 P.M.		

The staff worked eight-hour days scheduled within the above periods. Outside these hours a pharmacist was on call (on a rotating basis) and could be paged if a nurse requested emergency pharmacy assistance. Call-ins occurred about three times per week.

Mr. Hart, in common with the other professional pharmacists, held a four-year university degree in pharmacy. Pharmacy assistants usually had completed a one-year training program at a provincial community college. Mr. Hart had been Director of Pharmacy since 1975 after progressing through the various levels of responsibility in the department.

DRUG DELIVERY SYSTEMS AT VICTORIA HOSPITAL

Mr. Hart spent 70% of his time managing the five drug delivery systems used at Victoria Hospital and the remaining 30% purchasing for the department. Exhibit 2, prepared as part of a recent consulting report on Pharmacy's operations, shows how the Pharmacy managers spent their time. The budgetary pressures on Pharmacy led Mr. Hart to regard getting the best price from suppliers and keeping

EXHIBIT 2
Supervisor's Roles*

Function	F. Park	L. Radner	R. Ricardo	S. Charles	A. McKay	J. Hart	Total
General admin. committee			33.3%	40%	55%	70%	198.3%
Pharmacy prog.**	60%	100%		40			200
Clinical prog.	10			20	20		50
Education & research	10		66.7		25		101.7
Purchasing & mat'ls mgmt.	20					30	50

Notes:
*The numbers given are approximate percentages of time allocated to each program as reported to Mr. Hart. General administration includes efforts beyond the supervisory roles within each program.
**The Pharmacy Program includes out-patient services, Ward Stock, Unit Dose, Carded Drug, and sterile products distribution systems.

up with developments in the pharmaceutical industry as crucial to the successful operation of Pharmacy. Purchases and inventory records were kept on a Kardex file system and monitored by an inventory secretary on each campus. Mr. Hart was considering computerizing this function.

Normally drugs were given to a patient only on the order of a doctor although some drugs, such as laxatives, could be given without a doctor's permission. Prescriptions were kept in the patient's file at the ward nursing station and the prescription information was transcribed by nursing staff onto a medication record for each patient. Based on about 1.2 million individual drug doses prepared annually by Pharmacy, Mr. Hart estimated that at least 3 million doses had been dispensed at South Street and Westminster in 1982. He did not expect the number of doses dispensed to change. Pharmacy supplied about 2,000 different drugs.

Pharmacy used five drug delivery systems of which two—Ward Stock and Unit Dose—accounted for large portions of both drugs used and Pharmacy time. The systems are described below.

1. Carded Drug

The Carded Drug system was used to supply oral solid drugs to patients with relatively stable drug needs in the three affiliated chronic-care institutions. Pharmacy, upon receipt of a copy of a doctor's prescription, packed 35 doses of each drug in a blister pack heat-sealed onto a cardboard backing. After the prescription and the packaged drugs were checked by a pharmacist, the drugs were sent to the ward where they were administered by nurses. The cards had a double label system. The nurse removed half the label when the drug was administered and, after collecting a specified number of them, returned them to Pharmacy. The receipt of the labels signalled Pharmacy to refill the order.

2. Narcotics and Controlled Drugs

Drugs in these two categories were kept in a small locked room in Pharmacy and were very tightly controlled. Upon receipt of a copy of the doctor's prescription, Pharmacy supplied the appropriate drug to the ward where it was kept in a locked cupboard. Each ward had a Narcotic Disposition Sheet and a Controlled Drug Disposition Sheet upon which each administration of each dose of drugs in these classes had to be recorded with the signature of the nurse who prepared the dose. Sometimes signatures of two nurses were required. Each day, Monday to Friday, Pharmacy personnel counted the narcotics and controlled drugs on hand in each ward, reconciled them against the Ward Disposition Sheets, and replenished the supply if appropriate.

3. Ward Stock

Ward Stock was the traditional drug delivery system at Victoria Hospital and 21 wards at South Street (468 beds) were serviced by this system. As the name implies, each ward held an inventory of its commonly-used drugs in a drug cupboard at the nursing station. Pharmacy had a list of Ward Stock drugs authorized for each ward. Pharmacy purchased drugs in many types of containers from numerous suppliers. Drugs purchased in small containers were sent to the ward inventory in the manufacturer's labelled container. Drugs purchased in large containers were repackaged by Pharmacy in relabelled small containers before dispatch to the wards.

Drug inventories were taken in each ward three times per week by the night-shift nurse assigned to medication duties in each ward. The nurse estimated stock on hand and reviewed each patient's medication record. Based on her estimate of the inventory and the patients' future requirements, the medication nurse decided whether or not to place an order for a particular drug. Order quantities and order points were at the discretion of the nurse. The nurse recorded orders in the Ward Stock Requisition Book. Each ward had a drug basket and the medication nurse took it and the Requisition Book to Pharmacy at the end of her shift. Pharmacy prepared the order and delivered it to the ward later in the day by porter. Occasionally, for example when a ward drug supply inadvertently ran out, emergencies arose. Under such circumstances, the medication nurse obtained a rush order from Pharmacy by telephone or, rarely, obtained the drug from another ward. Telephone orders had to be followed by a written order within hours.

Each 12-hour shift had one medication nurse per ward who was responsible for preparing, delivering, and administering the correct dosage of the prescribed drug to each patient. After checking each patient's medication record, she counted or measured the correct amount of each drug. Pills, capsules, and some liquids for oral administration were placed in small disposable plastic cups. Other drugs were placed in syringes for intramuscular or bags for intravenous administration. Some preparations, such as diluting drugs for intravenous administration, required careful, time-consuming work. Chemotherapy and some other drugs were highly toxic to both the patient and the nurse who had to handle them.

The medication nurse placed the prepared doses on a cart along with the medication records and took them with her to the patient's bedside as she made her rounds. The medication nurse administered the prescribed drugs to the patient and immediately noted the fact on the appropriate medication record. Occasionally a prepared drug was refused or not needed by a patient. In such cases the drug was returned to the ward drug cupboard if it was hygienically possible.

Pharmacy kept a copy of the Ward Stock Requisitions. Each pharmacist was responsible for one or more wards. Every two months he or she would visit the ward to discuss inventory levels and potential problems with the medication nurse. Sudden excessive demand for a drug would prompt such a visit. Inventory levels varied considerably from ward to ward.

4. Individual Patient Prescriptions

Some patients in Ward Stock wards required drugs not held in the ward's inventory. In these cases, a ward nurse, acting on a doctor's prescription, ordered the drug from Pharmacy. Pharmacy filled the prescription, typically in a seven-day quantity, using a container whose label included the patient's name. The drug was taken to the ward where it was stored with, and administered like, Ward Stock drugs.

5. Unit Dose

The remaining nine South Street wards (232 beds) and all of Westminster's were served by the Unit Dose system under which Pharmacy prepared all individual drug doses for patients. Only small quantities of drugs required very quickly in emergency situations, relatively routine drugs such as aspirin, laxatives, etc., or drugs that could not be prepared in individual doses were kept in the ward drug cupboard. At South Street all intravenous solutions except specialty intravenous preparations were prepared by ward nurses, but at Westminster, Pharmacy had an intravenous admixture program in which Pharmacy made up most intravenous preparations.

In some cases Pharmacy was able to purchase individually packaged unit doses directly from the drug manufacturer but in other cases repackaging and relabelling were required. Despite a higher price, prepackaged unit doses were usually cheaper when repackaging costs were considered so that Pharmacy normally purchased them if possible. Pharmacy repackaged the individual doses in small, disposable, standard packages with standard labels. All of the regular repackaging and relabelling were carried out at Westminster. Pills and powders were sealed in transparent plastic packets. Liquids were measured into disposable vials, syringes, or intravenous bags. In some cases the containers had to be a special colour or completely opaque because the drugs were unstable when exposed to light. Except for a few cases in which drug instability prevented it, Pharmacy stored the prepared unit doses in labelled bins in Pharmacy. Pharmacists prepared doses of unstable or emergency drugs shortly before they were sent to the wards.

One copy of the doctor's prescription on file in the patient's medication record at the ward nursing station was sent to Pharmacy where it was entered into a master medication Kardex file for each Unit Dose ward. Acting on the prescription, pharmacists, and pharmacy assistants working under the supervision of pharmacists, assembled the necessary medication for each patient. Usually they were able to draw the required unit doses from the unit dose inventory but sometimes they had to make up doses to fill the order. Pharmacy assembled the orders to meet the regular daily 3:00 P.M. drug deliveries to the wards. In addition, Pharmacy immediately filled and delivered emergency requests for drugs to Unit Dose wards.

Unit Dose employed duplicate sets of locked drug delivery cassettes that contained 8, 12, or 16 standard drawers (about 6 × 10 × 28 cm) labelled with a patient's name and ward. At any one time one set of cassettes was in use on the wards and the other was being replenished in Pharmacy. When a pharmacy assistant finished assembling a day's drug supply for a Unit Dose patient, he or she placed the order in the patient's cassette drawer. A pharmacy assistant then took the filled cassettes to the appropriate wards on a cart that held up to 12 large cassettes and brought the empty cassettes back to Pharmacy. In emergency cases drugs were delivered to the ward by pneumatic tube, by hand delivery by porter, or to a ward nurse.

At the appropriate times the ward medication nurse took the drugs to the patients, checked the drugs against the medication records, administered the drugs to the patients, and recorded the administration in the same way as for Ward Stock drugs. If her check showed a discrepancy, the nurse called Pharmacy to resolve it. Surplus drugs were returned to Pharmacy in the cassette along with a completed form explaining the surplus.

Pharmacy had a locked two-sided cabinet at each campus into which small quantities of Unit Dose drugs were placed for emergency access by nursing supervisors at night. Almost all Unit Dose drugs were included in the night cabinet except controlled drugs, narcotics, study drugs, and unstable drugs. When a nursing supervisor took a drug from the night cabinet, she left some of the external packaging and a note explaining the circumstances. Only Pharmacy staff had access to the Pharmacy itself after hours.

THE GROWTH OF UNIT DOSE AT VICTORIA HOSPITAL

Mr. Hart had experienced some problems with the Ward Stock system. Thefts of some drugs had occurred because of the lack of inventory control. In addition, inventory tended to accumulate in ward drug cupboards, increasing the total hospital drug inventory and leading to increased obsolescence costs when drugs were destroyed after they had reached their expiratory dates. Mr. Hart estimated that about 10–20% of South Street's inventory of about $760,000 was held in ward drug cupboards.

The Unit Dose system with its tighter controls had largely overcome these problems. Victoria Hospital had been adopting Unit Dose on a ward-by-ward basis since 1976 after a pilot study in the early 1970s. The Westminster campus, when it was finished, would run entirely on Unit Dose. The system was introduced first into areas where Pharmacy needs were well defined and where no additional Pharmacy support was required to cover emergency requests for drugs. The conversion process at South Street proceeded as follows: 1976, 5th floor General Medicine wards; 1978, 3rd floor Surgery wards; 1980, 2nd floor Post-cardiac and Cancer wards. At that time nine of 30 wards at South Street and the five at Westminster had been converted.

Conversion stopped for a number of reasons. Pharmacy ran out of storage and dosage preparation space. Pharmacists generally resisted working the extended and awkward hours necessitated by Unit Dose. Pharmacists were in short supply in Ontario and Mr. Hart had had trouble hiring any. The net cost of converting South Street fully to Unit Dose was estimated to be a $210,000 annual increase in Pharmacy operating costs, mainly for two pharmacists and ten pharmacy assistants, as well as $50,000 for additional pharmacy equipment and fixtures, provided that space and pharmacists could be found.

The 1971 pilot study of the Unit Dose and Ward Stock systems at Victoria Hospital had concluded that under Unit Dose, drug administration time by nurses decreased from 164.5 to 158 hours per ward month with a corresponding increase in Pharmacy time from 4.5 to 84.5 hours per ward month. Under Unit Dose, nurses spent 7.5 hours per ward month extra giving drugs but saved 14 hours on drug preparation. Of the total extra time observed, 21.5 hours per ward month were attributed to increased checking of drug dosages, 13.5 by Pharmacy and 8 by Nursing. Several articles in the pharmaceutical literature had discussed Unit Dose costs. One,[1] for example, reported that under Unit Dose nurses spent an extra 8 seconds per dose in administering the drug but saved 93 seconds per dose in inventory management, record keeping, and drug preparation. The general consensus seemed to be that saved nursing time more than made up for increased pharmacy time. One author concluded, however, that:

> In spite of the research which demonstrates reduced nursing time requirements under unit dose, it is often not possible to reduce nurse staffing as a trade-off to increase pharmacy staffing to implement a unit dose system. The time saved in one nursing shift on one nursing unit is usually not enough to free a full-time equivalent. In my experience, nurses are able to assume other high priority activities (e.g., direct patient care and assessment) when freed from some medication system duties. Hospital administrators will want to know what nurses do with the extra time saved by implementing a unit dose system.[2]

Hospital and pharmacy professionals generally acknowledged that a properly running Unit Dose system could allow significantly improved patient safety. Several published studies reported error rates of 8–20% under Ward Stock and 3–5% under Unit dose. Nursing administrators at Victoria Hospital supported Unit Dose because it reduced medication errors and freed nursing time. Only a few of Victoria Hospital's nursing personnel had some reservations that the Unit Dose system could make nurses lax in carefully checking the drugs given to the patient. Younger nursing staff generally felt comfortable with Unit Dose, having been taught the system in nursing school. All nurses new to Victoria Hospital were required to attend a one-day briefing on the Hospital's drug delivery systems. Selected nurses received special certification training for up to a month to allow them to handle certain toxic and powerful drugs.

RECENT DEVELOPMENTS AT THE HOSPITAL FOR SICK CHILDREN

Beginning in July, 1980 the death rate on the cardiac ward at Toronto's 700-bed Hospital for Sick Children increased noticeably. Despite warnings from nursing staff that many of the deaths were quite unexpected, little was done about the situation until January, 1981 when the Hospital's Mortality Review Committee ordered closer monitoring of heart rates and display of drug dosage charts on

---

[1]H. J. Black and R. Upham, "Impact of Unit Dose Pharmacy Services on the Time Involvement of Registered Nurses With Medication Activities," The University of Iowa, 1971.

[2]C. Buchanan in *The Practice of Pharmacy: Institutional and Ambulatory Pharmaceutical Services*, D. C. McLeod and W. A. Miller, Eds., Harvey Whitney Books, Cincinnati, Ohio, 1981, Chapter 33, p. 407.

emergency cardiac arrest carts. After a short respite, the rate of suspicious deaths increased.

In March, 1981 an autopsy showed an exceptionally high level of digoxin, a powerful heart drug, in a dead infant's body. Similarly elevated digoxin levels were subsequently found in other corpses. After an investigation, police considered about 25 of the 40 cardiac ward deaths to be very suspicious. All had occurred while one nursing team was on duty. On March 25, 1981 police charged a member of that cardiac ward team with four counts of murder. These charges were later dismissed. The suspicious deaths apparently stopped when the charges were laid.

The atmosphere was highly charged and the subject of daily news reports. It was unclear whether or not the babies had died from digoxin over-doses and, if they had, it was not clear whether or not the drug had been administered accidentally, negligently, or on purpose. It was not clear if Hospital procedures were a contributing factor.

In June, 1981, in response to mounting pressure to determine the cause(s) of the deaths, to clear the Hospital's name, and to prevent a recurrence, the Ontario Health Minister appointed the Dubin Committee which was given a broad mandate to review the management of the Hospital. The Committee members were an Ontario supreme court justice, a medical school dean, a senior hospital administrator, and a nursing school director.

The Committee report, made public on January 28, 1983, made wide-ranging criticisms of virtually all areas of the Hospital and made 98 recommendations to overcome the deficiencies found by the Committee. Eleven of the recommendations related specifically to the Pharmacy.

Victoria Hospital already had procedures in place to satisfy most of the Committee's pharmacy-related recommendations but four were more troublesome. One was to provide more space for the preparation of intravenous solutions but such space was not available at South Street. Intravenous solutions usually had to be prepared just before use and were bulky to transport and store. Another was that Pharmacy put its own labels over manufacturer's labels on Ward Stock drugs. Mr. Hart knew that implementation of such a change at Victoria Hospital would require additional staff for very uncertain benefits. A third recommendation was that Pharmacy use automated systems wherever possible to improve productivity. Mr. Hart had unsuccessfully requested funds for such automation from the Hospital's budget for several years. He estimated that automation of purchasing and inventory control would cost about $50,000.

THE UNIT DOSE RECOMMENDATION

The Dubin Committee also recommended that the Hospital for Sick Children fully adopt a Unit Dose system which, it felt, would provide a better means of monitoring medication errors. The Committee expressed the view that Unit Dose was particularly important in paediatric care where standard adult doses could not normally be used. In such cases the standard dose had to be divided into fractional ones to accommodate the smaller body weight of a child. Children presented other problems in drug administration too. An infant's body chemistry differed from an adult's so that certain drugs, designed for and tested on adults, had different effects on children. Very young children could be seriously affected by contamination or careless administration of drugs. Also, children could offer little assistance to doctors, nurses, and pharmacists in diagnosing their drug needs or in protecting themselves from abuse. The Hospital for Sick Children had announced that it would convert to Unit Dose delivery and that it would ask the Ontario Ministry of Health for $1 million to help with the conversion costs. Only 10% of Ontario's hospitals used Unit Dose, mainly because of the higher costs it entailed. Mr. Hart was not sure if centralizing drug decisions away from the patient was the best choice for paediatric wards.

MEDICATION ERRORS AT VICTORIA HOSPITAL

The Dubin Committee's concern over medication errors prompted Mr. Hart to examine Victoria Hospital's incident reports. The Hospital staff or supervisors involved had to complete an incident report form (see Exhibit 3) for any irregular incident, such as accidents, falls, missing articles, drug-related errors, etc., which adversely affected patient care or well-being. Both Pharmacy and Nursing had responsibility for medication errors. Copies of each completed drug-related incident report were sent to the head nurse, the Hospital administration, and Pharmacy. Each month or so the Nursing–Pharmacy Administration Committee reviewed the reports for possible trends. Exhibit 4 shows a compilation of reports from June, 1982 to January, 1983.

Victoria Hospital normally allowed a nurse three minor errors before Nursing initiated a competency review. Major errors resulted in an immediate review. The Hospital had a progressive discipline procedure that progressed through the stages of verbal warning, written warning, suspension, and finally dismissal. There were no explicit written standards concerning what constituted an error or whether an error was minor or major. These classifications were based on judgment and circumstances.

Pharmacy served 110 beds in five paediatric wards including an Infant Intensive Care Unit. All were on the Ward Stock system. During the last five years, no life-threatening incidents resulting from medication errors had been reported on paediatric wards. In 1983, 50–70% of one clinical pharmacist's time was devoted to paediatrics to attend to the special needs of child patients. Paediatrics' nursing staff were dedicated to working closely with clinical pharmacists and to scrutinizing closely the administration of drugs.

JOHN HART'S CONCERNS

The cause of infant deaths at the Hospital for Sick Children had not yet been fully explained. Mr. Hart was faced with a larger question: Could Pharmacy and Nursing protect the Hospital and its patients from a fatal medication-related error? Mr. Hart wondered whether Unit Dose was the best alternative for better control of the drug delivery system not only in paediatrics, but throughout the Hospital.

EXHIBIT 3
Incidence Report Form

HOSP NO.		Ward	Room	Emer.☐	OPC☐	POF☐
Name				Last		First
Address						
Age	Sex	Birth D M Y date		Insurance No. OHIPetc.		
OHIP subscriber				Relationship to subscriber ( ) Self ( ) Spouse ( ) Child		
Doctor				Date		

VICTORIA HOSPITAL CORPORATION
LONDON, ONTARIO

INCIDENT REPORT
PREPARED FOR THE HOSPITAL SOLICITOR

A.   Incident involving: 1. Patient ☐   2. Outpatient ☐   3. Visitor ☐   4. Patient employee ☐

This includes: accidents, injuries, medication errors and articles missing or damaged.

B.   For accidents involving hospital personnel—see W.C.B. procedure.

Date of Incident	Patient Diagnosis:	AMBULATION PRIVILEGES	INCIDENT WITNESSED
Day Mo. Yr. Time _____ Hrs.	Has patient had surgery ☐ No ☐ Yes _____ Days Post-Op	☐ Unlimited ☐ Limited ☐ Requires assistance ☐ None	☐ No ☐ Yes _____ Name and Status

LOCATION OF INCIDENT	TYPE OF INCIDENT	(For Medication and Treatment Incident Only)	
Ward _____ Room _____ Other _____	☐ Fall ☐ Medication error ☐ Treatment error ☐ Loss of property ☐ Injury ☐ Damage to Hosp. prop. ☐ Other _____	TYPE OF INCIDENT ☐ Wrong Patient ☐ Wrong dosage ☐ Wrong time ☐ Wrong route ☐ Failure to give ☐ Other _____	EXPLANATION ☐ Improper patient identification ☐ Picked up wrong medicine cup ☐ Delay in recording medication ☐ Failure to notice order ☐ Misinterpreted order ☐ Misread label ☐ Error in computing dosage ☐ Error in transcribing dosage ☐ Order incorrect ☐ Other

PERSONNEL INVOLVED	PATIENT STATUS (before occurrence)	SAFETY DEVICES IN USE	
☐ Student Nurse (1st, 2nd) ☐ Nurse Intern ☐ Graduate Nurse ☐ Reg. Nursing Assist. ☐ Nursing Assist. Student ☐ Orderly ☐ Other _____	☐ Well oriented ☐ Sedated ☐ Appeared confused ☐ Appeared depressed ☐ Uncooperative ☐ Language barrier ☐ Other _____	(before occurence) ☐ Signal light within reach Yes ☐ No ☐ ☐ Bedside up-one ☐ two ☐ No ☐ ☐ Restraints Yes ☐ No ☐ ☐ Caution Signs Yes ☐ No ☐ ☐ Other _____	

STATE BRIEFLY WHAT HAPPENED:

Action Taken:

Patient Examined By:	X-Ray taken
☐ Charge Nurse ☐ Clinical Nurse Co-ordinator ☐ Nursing Administrative Assistant ☐ Physician Time _____ Date _____	☐ No ☐ Yes Region _____ Result _____

Date _____   Signature of Reporter _____

Physician's written comments (at time of seeing patient)   (This section must be completed by an M.D. for legal purposes)

Time _____ Date _____   _____ M.D.
                                                          Signature   (over)

EXHIBIT 3, cont'd

COMMENTS OF HEAD NURSE OR NURSE IN CHARGE:

————————————————   ————————————————
Date   Signature

COMMENTS OF CLINICAL NURSE CO-ORDINATOR OR NURSING ADMINISTRATIVE ASSISTANT

————————————————   ————————————————
Date   Signature

FURTHER INFORMATION OR STATEMENTS:

————————————————   ————————————————
Date   Signature

COMMENTS OF MEDICAL DIRECTOR:

————————————————   ————————————————
Date   Signature

```
                        ┌──────────┐
                        │  Report  │
                        └──────────┘
                             ▼
                        ┌────────────┐
                        │ Head nurse │
                        └────────────┘
                             ▼
┌──────────────────────────────────────────────────────────┐
│ Clinical nurse                         Nursing administrative │
│ coordinator           or                      assistant       │
└──────────────────────────────────────────────────────────┘
                             ▼
        ┌─────────────────────────────────────────────────────┐
        │ Director of nursing or associate director of nursing │
        └─────────────────────────────────────────────────────┘
                             ▼
                   ┌──────────────────┐
                   │ Medical director │
                   └──────────────────┘
                             ▼
                     ┌──────────────┐
                     │ Special file │
                     └──────────────┘
```

EXHIBIT 4
Reported Medication Errors From June 1982 to January 1983

Ward	System	Beds	I	II	III	IV	V	VI	VII	Total
South Street Campus Non-Paediatric Wards										
1	Unit	25	2	1	1	0	4	0	1	9
2	Unit	22	0	0	0	1	0	1	0	2
3	Unit	27	2	2	0	4	10	4	3	25
4	Unit	30	3	4	0	6	7	6	3	29
5	Unit	31	2	0	1	6	10	6	6	31
6	Unit	22	0	2	2	6	3	0	1	14
7	Unit	26	0	6	0	4	4	0	3	17
8	Unit	22	0	4	3	0	7	2	0	16
9	Unit	27	0	3	0	9	4	1	2	19
10	Ward	38	0	2	2	3	1	4	0	12
11	Ward	31	0	0	0	0	1	1	2	4
12	Ward	18	0	0	0	0	3	0	0	3
13	Ward	18	0	0	0	0	0	0	0	0
14	Ward	26	0	3	1	1	2	3	1	11
15	Ward	30	0	3	1	2	2	2	1	11
16	Ward	20	2	3	1	3	3	6	2	20
17	Ward	18	2	7	1	10	5	7	2	34
18	Ward	8	0	0	0	0	0	0	0	0
19	Ward	11	0	0	0	0	0	0	0	0
20	Ward	30	0	0	1	0	1	0	1	3
21	Ward	28	0	2	0	3	1	4	2	12
22	Ward	21	0	3	1	2	1	0	0	7
23	Ward	14	0	2	0	3	0	0	0	5
24	Ward	26	0	4	1	3	3	1	6	18
25	Ward	21	0	2	0	1	0	1	0	4
South Street Campus Paediatric Wards										
26	Ward	15	3	3	1	4	2	2	0	15
27	Ward	31	0	0	0	0	0	1	0	1
28	Ward	28	0	0	1	4	0	0	0	5
29	Ward	18	0	3	0	1	1	0	0	5
30	Ward	27	0	0	1	1	1	0	0	3
Westminster Campus Wards										
31	Unit	28	2	0	0	2	3	1	0	8
32	Unit	26	1	1	1	2	0	1	0	6
33	Unit	20	0	1	0	3	3	1	0	8
34	Unit	30	1	0	0	4	0	0	0	5
35	Unit	31	3	1	1	3	4	4	2	18
Other[b]	Ward		2	3	1	5	2	6	4	23
Ward unspecified[c]			5	12	1	8	15	8	7	56
TOTALS		844	30	77	23	104	103	73	49	459

Source: Incident Reports Involving Drug Therapy, seven summaries, June 1982–January 1983.

[a] Error types:
  I   Incorrect narcotic or controlled drug count
  II   Failure to sign or co-sign narcotic or controlled drug sheet
  III   Medication given to the wrong patient
  IV   Incorrect dosage administered
  V   Failure to give medication
  VI   Wrong medication given or medication given at wrong time
  VII   Other

[b] These units included service units without formal beds such as operating suites, delivery room, emergency, etc. They were administratively separate from the wards.

[c] These numbers included the 49 errors in one month's summary for which the ward was inadvertently omitted.

One significant change resulting from a conversion to Unit Dose would be a shift in legal responsibility for medication-related errors from Nursing to Pharmacy. Given the current restrictions on his space and budget, Mr. Hart wondered what alternatives he had. He was sure of one thing: a repeat of an incident similar to that at the Hospital for Sick Children would do irreparable damage to the stature of the Hospital in the community and would expose management and staff to hostile public scrutiny.

PART
IV

MANAGEMENT OF TECHNOLOGY

Kalen's Super Markets, Inc.

As ground was broken for a new Kalen's supermarket in June of 1981, the company's top management was in the process of deciding what type of checkstand equipment to buy for the store. Kalen's had installed scanning equipment in three stores in 1980 to decrease labor costs and improve their profit margin. After a year of experience, they were concerned because it appeared they were not receiving the full benefits of the system. In the next three months, they intended to make a thorough evaluation of scanning in order to reach a decision for the new store.

COMPANY BACKGROUND

Kalen's Super Markets, located in Louisville, Kentucky, was a family-run business with eleven stores in the greater Louisville area. Started by Joe Kalen in a five-hundred-square-foot store in 1937, the business had grown to serve 5.7 million customers in 1980 with sales of over $110 million.

Kalen's success was the result of offering customers quality food at competitive prices with the best service possible. Kalen's services included courtesy clerks to carry groceries, having a qualified meat cutter on duty at all times, an easy check-cashing policy, and night stocking to avoid cluttering aisles during the day. The stores were notable for immaculate appearance, friendly employees, wide aisles, restrooms, and a delicatessen and pastry shop. Kalen's was so devoted to its customers' needs that a particular store would often carry an item even if only one customer wanted it.

The company's emphasis on customer service had paid off handsomely through the years. Despite ranking third in number of stores in Louisville (behind Safeway's twenty-three and A&P's fourteen), Kalen's had a 21 percent share of market, compared with Safeway's 28 percent and A&P's 14 percent. In addition, earnings after taxes had averaged 1.5 percent on sales versus the industry average of 0.87 percent.

Kalen's "people orientation" also extended to its 1,300 employees. Excellent benefits, including an annual company picnic, bonuses for full-time employees, and opportunity for advancement resulted in a low turnover rate and no employees represented by unions.

The company was managed by James and Robert Kalen, sons of the founder. Both had attended college, and Bob had received an MBA from a well-known southeastern business school. The next level of management included a controller and eight supervisors, who were each responsible for a particular department such as meat, produce, or general merchandise. Most of the supervisors had not attended college but had worked their way up through the business, generally starting as clerks. As a group they had approximately 150 years of experience in the grocery business.

OPERATIONS

A supermarket is a low-margin business that depends on volume to make a profit. Although Kalen's had consistently managed to achieve above-average earnings, they were always looking for opportunities to reduce costs. Out of every one dollar in sales, approximately eighty cents went towards the cost of the merchandise, ten cents to pay for labor, and eight cents for utilities, advertising, taxes, and other miscellaneous items. Thus, the two logical areas for cost control were inventory and labor.

At any time, Kalen's would have approximately $3.5 million tied up in merchandise, either on the shelf, in the store's backrooms or in their central warehouse. Inventory carrying cost was estimated at 20 percent. Since this merchandise represented a good part of their net assets, it was important to see that stores were not overstocked. On the other hand, not enough merchandise or the wrong mix of products would result in stockouts, leading to lost sales and customer dissatisfaction. At each Kalen's store, the ordering function was performed by the night grocery crew who stocked the shelves. Each person in the crew was responsible for every product in one aisle of the store. Four times a week he or she would place an order with a wholesaler based on the stock on hand and what would sell. Since the crew were, for the most part, very experienced, they generally did a good job of managing the inventory. However, as each store carried over 12,000 items, measuring their performance with any precision was extremely difficult.

The second possible area for cost control was labor. At Kalen's the greatest portion of wages, 30 percent, was paid to the people manning the front end—that section of the store where customer purchases were totaled by cashiers and bagged by courtesy clerks. For every cashier there were, on average, 1.5 courtesy clerks, since they had to bag and carry groceries to customer cars. In addition, a front-end manager was responsible for authorizing checks, handling customer complaints, and making sure the front end ran smoothly.

Each cashier was stationed at a checkstand about 35 inches high and 8 feet long that consisted of a cash register and a conveyor belt to bring a customer's purchases to the cashier and then to the courtesy clerk (Exhibit 1). Depending on the sales volume, each store had eight to twelve checkstands.

EXHIBIT 1
Supermarket Checkstand: Customer Unload

Source: *Progressive Grocer*, May 1977. (Note: This is not a Kalen's Super Market.)

In eight of the stores, the customer unloaded purchases onto the conveyor belt. In three stores, over-the-end (OTE) checkstands were used; where the customer cart was wheeled directly to the end of the conveyor belt, the front edge of the cart was unlatched and lowered, and the checker unloaded merchandise with one hand and entered the price into the register with the other (Exhibit 2).

Cashiers used key-entry systems at eight Kalen's stores to total customer purchases. These systems consisted of a series of electronic cash registers (ECRs) With the exception of the newer scanning systems, the ECR link-up was the most sophisticated cash register system available. ECRs would automatically calculate and add in taxes, electronically weigh and price produce, record bottle refunds and coupons, and track sales of produce and other items through the use of a look-

EXHIBIT 2
Over-the-End Checkstand with Scanner: Checker Unload.

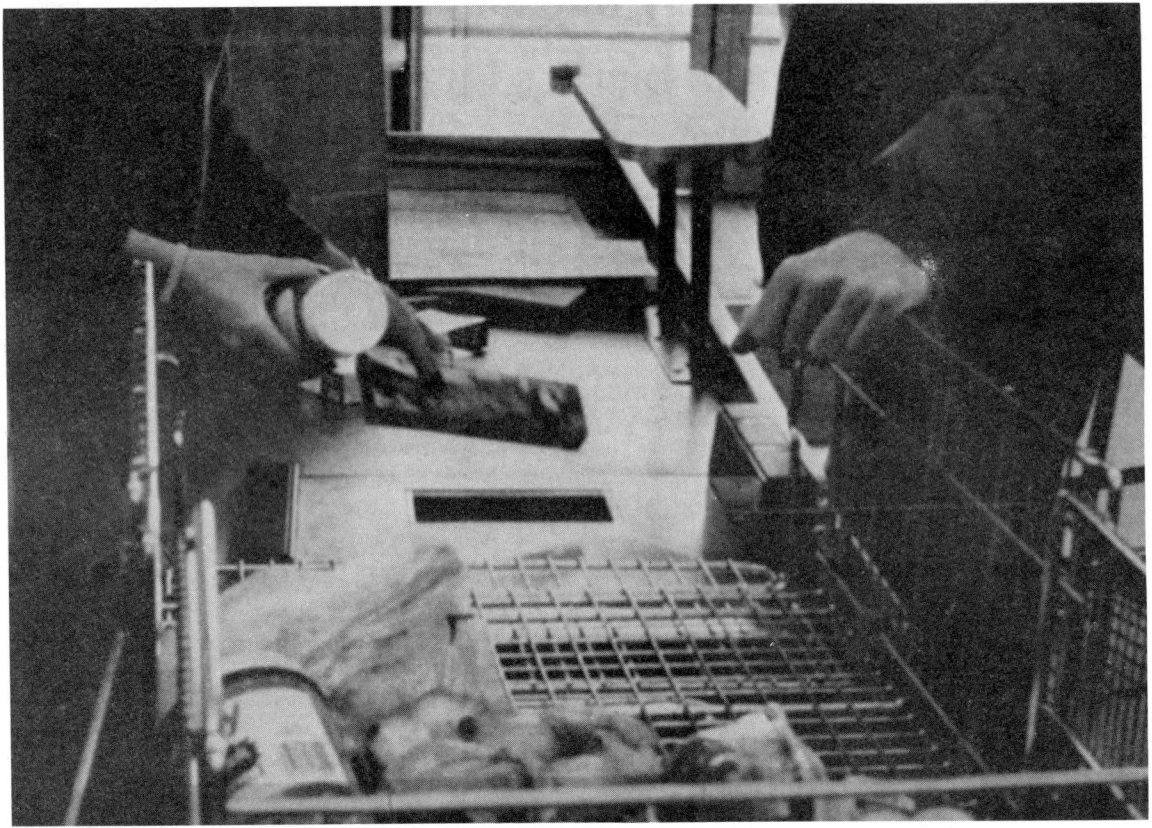

Source: *Supermarket Business,* February 1981

up code.[1] In addition, a cashier was able to enter item prices much faster than with a conventional cash register, since the ECR keyboard only had ten keys. The computer link-up allowed management to collect department and store sales daily and to monitor an individual cashier's performance in terms of speed. Kalen's had tested ECRs in 1974 and by 1978 had put them in all their stores.

USE OF SCANNING IN SUPERMARKETS

The factor that made the development of scanning possible was the Universal Product Code (UPC). UPC symbols are machine readable bar codes that identify

---

[1]Instead of entering the price, the cashier would enter a 2-digit code and the price was automatically supplied by the computer.

products with a ten-digit number consisting of a manufacturer code and a product code. This system of uniquely identifying products was developed by the food industry to allow the use of scanner-equipped checkstands by retailers and to provide detailed product-movement information to manufacturers.

Scanning equipment requires optical scanners built into the checkstand and an in-store computer to read the UPC symbols. As a cashier passes an item over the scanner, the scanner reads the code and sends it to the computer for price matching. This information is sent back to the terminal, where the price and a description of the product are printed on the sales receipt and simultaneously displayed on a view screen for the customer. Exhibit 3 illustrates this procedure and describes some benefits of scanning from a brochure distributed by Kalen's to its customers. One of the benefits was that the register tape provided more detailed information on purchases than other systems.

Scanning was first introduced to the supermarket industry in 1972 when the Kroger Company tested a prototype system for fifteen months in a Cincinnati supermarket. Although no UPC symbols existed at that time, Kroger used similar identification marking for the test. The results, while not totally conclusive, were generally promising. The test verified that cash savings could be achieved and checker productivity improved with scanning, but several benefits, such as better inventory and management control, were difficult to quantify. Nevertheless, on the basis of the test, many people predicted that scanning would revolutionize the industry.

Several obstacles had to be overcome, however, before the new technology would become common. The most obvious was the need for food manufacturers to change their packaging to include UPC codes. Retailers felt that until 65 percent of all items were coded scanning would not be feasible, since a cashier would have to key-enter so many uncoded prices.

In order to accomplish this task, a central agency was formed of food manufacturers, wholesalers, and retailers to administer the UPC program and see that it became an industry standard. Despite the several billion dollars in packaging equipment costs that the manufacturers had to absorb, they went along with the program since they would ultimately get more detailed product-movement information than ever before possible. Nevertheless, it was not until 1976 that 65 percent of grocery items were coded. By 1978 the percentage had risen to 80 percent, and by 1981 over 95 percent of grocery items included the UPC.[2]

BENEFITS OF SCANNING

Another problem which slowed the acceptance of scanning was the difficulty of quantifying many of the benefits of scanning, which could be divided into "hard" or "soft":

"Hard" benefits were generally related to the speed and accuracy of store

---

[2]This figure does not include random weight items such as meat and produce as well as many non-food items. Of the approximately 12,000 items carried by a typical Kalen's, only 74 percent were scannable in 1981.

EXHIBIT 3

Information on Scanning Provided to Customers

42 Years Of Trust And Confidence

For over 42 years, **Kalen's** has been striving to provide its customers with the best overall shopping experience by offering quality merchandise at the lowest possible prices and the utmost in service. Because we intend to maintain this trust and confidence, we are continuously alert for ways to keep our operating costs down. Over the years very few productivity improvements have taken place in the food distribution system.

Fortunately, this situation has changed and the grocery industry has provided a technological advancement that has the potential to significantly improve productivity in supermarket operations . . . the computer assisted check-out. We at **Kalen's** have considered carefully both the immediate and long term benefits to our customers and believe that the implementation of this front end system will further our commitment to hold the line on operating costs.

While the installation of this new equipment will not bring lower prices immediately, it does enable us to pursue cost-saving measures that eventually can produce savings for all food shoppers.

The largest savings will come from the elimination of price marking on each individual package. Instead, the price of each product will be clearly posted on the shelf, and you will also have a record of the individual prices on our new descriptive sales receipt (see back page). Elimination of individual item pricing will increase our productivity and help us offset the many inflationary pressures we face today. We estimate that on a typical eight person stock crew, price marking requires the full-time efforts of at least two crew members.

We realize that any change may cause concern for some people, but we are confident that the vast majority of **Kalen's** customers will be pleased with the new system. The result will be an even better food shopping experience at **Kalen's**.

Here is how the computer-assisted checkout works.

1. Each can, box, bottle, and bag has a Universal Product Code (UPC) Symbol that identifies each item.

For example, the first five digits represent the manufacturer, while the second five digits identify the specific item. Keep in mind that the price is not in the symbol. The symbol identifies the item, not the price.

2. The scanner in the checkout counter reads this code and sends it through a communication line to the "in store computer."

3. The "in store computer" matches the code information received from the checkout scanner with the price that is stored in its memory and sends the price back to the checkout terminal, where the price and item description are printed on your sales receipt and simultaneously appear on the terminal display.

Special Note:
Items not having a UPC will continue to be individually priced and recorded as before, for example: fresh meats, produce, and deli-pastry items

operations and provided savings in operating costs and thus improvements in gross profit. The three principal hard benefits that could be achieved were improved checker productivity, more efficient pricing, and a reduction in merchandise shrinkage.

In the Kroger test, checker productivity had greatly improved with scanning, because the cashiers did not have to enter prices manually and because price checks were virtually eliminated.[3] Kroger found that the average time required to process an order decreased from 3.82 minutes to 2.6 minutes with scanning. In a similar study done in 1976, Giant Food, Inc. calculated that the increase in checker speed with scanning translated into a $5,112 savings per month in a

---

[3]When an item does not have a price tag, the cashier must wait while a clerk checks the price.

EXHIBIT 3, cont'd

Using The UPC Symbols and Computer-Assisted Checkout Means:

Greater Accuracy

With the scanner reading the UPC symbols, the chance for error is reduced. Overrings and underrings are eliminated.

To make sure that each price in the computer matches each price on the shelf and/or item, we now have a pricing specialist who will coordinate pricing throughout the store. He will be checking and verifying prices on a continuing basis.

More Efficient Checkout

Elimination of time consuming price checks and searching for the price on a package will mean less customer time at the checkstand.

More Informative Sales Receipt

```
KALEN'S SUPER MARKET

    DM PINEAPPLE       .63 E
    LEMONADE PT        .16 E
    FH SPAG/MTBL       .73 E
    HH MUSTARD         .43 E
    JOY LIQUID         .65 A
    6 PACK COKE       1.99 E
    BATTERIES         1.55 A
    CIGARETTES        4.19 A
    YELLOW CORN        .19 E
    BROWN SUGAR        .69 E
    VEG OIL           1.03 E
    NAIL POL REM       .49 A
    MILK 1/2 GAL      1.00 E
    BUFFERIN          1.49 A
    YEL CAKE MIX       .33 E
    MINUTE RICE       1.25 E
    SOS PADS           .31 A
    TRIX              1.03 E
    FRENCH BREAD       .89 E
    TAX    .76 BAL 19.79
    CSH 20.00 CHG      .21
 05/13/80 12:55     7          8
 ** A PLEASURE  TO SERVE YOU **
```

A Complete Shopping List For Future Reference

Serving You Better With The Computer-Assisted Checkout

$140,000/week store. However, both studies compared cashier speed with scanning against cashier speed with mechanical registers. As noted earlier, ECRs also offered the potential to increase cashier speed due to the simplified keyboard. Therefore, the increase in checker productivity that could be realized from scanning depended on what type of equipment it would be replacing.

A second "hard" benefit was more efficient pricing. In non-scanning stores prices had to be applied to every item using a pricing gun to attach a gummed label. In scanning stores prices were identified by a shelf tag that appeared underneath the product. This tag shown in Exhibit 4 carried the name of the item, its size, price, and the unit price. The unit price was a price per standard measure which the customer could use to compare prices of different-sized items.

The only time that shelf tags had to be replaced was when they were damaged

EXHIBIT 4
Unit Price Shelf Tag

or a price changed. With item pricing, if a price changed, each item had to be taken off the shelf, the original gummed label scraped off, and the new price reapplied. Since Kalen's had price changes every week on over 400 items, shelf pricing provided a substantial labor saving.

Reduction in merchandise shrinkage, a third "hard" benefit of scanning, was principally derived from reductions in under-ring losses, which occur when cashiers ring up a lower-than-actual item price.

Under-ring losses are reduced in a scanning store because there are fewer opportunities for cashiers to make pricing errors. In a non-scanning store, checker errors can result in either an over-ring or an under-ring. Since customers will more often bring an over-ring to the attention of the checker, the result is a net under-ring loss.

The increase in pricing discipline also reduced under-rings. In a scanning store, prices are being checked constantly to ensure that the price in the computer matches the price on the shelf. Since the great majority of general price changes are increases, there are fewer incorrect prices to result in under-rings.

For example, at Dick's Super Markets in Wisconsin, the introduction of scanners yielded an estimated 0.6 percent of sales saving in shrinkage in a $150,000/week store. However, as Bill Brodbeck, Vice-President of Dick's stated, "These disciplines could be put into place in a non-scanning store and the same increase in gross profit dollars would occur. The question is, will or can the average supermarket put such practices into place without being forced to do so by a scanning system?" He estimated that no more than 60 percent of the improvement possible with scanning could be achieved in a non-scanning store.

The "soft" benefits of scanning were related to improved management information and control. Three areas where the detailed information provided by scanning was useful were labor scheduling, checker evaluation, and merchandising.

Since scanning systems recorded the time that customer transactions took place, labor schedules for checkers and baggers could be based on the number of items purchased per time interval rather than on dollar sales. This information could improve store operations by enabling managers to eliminate extra labor during slack shopping periods and improve customer service by adding labor at peak periods. However, many ECR systems were able to generate the same information.

Scanning could improve checker evaluations by providing scan reports on average transaction value, average customer purchase, coupon redemption, number of voids, and items per minute scanned. This information was generally used to eliminate "sweethearting," and to motivate cashiers to work faster. Sweethearting involves the cashier ringing up a lower-than-actual item price (i.e., underringing) or simply allowing items to pass the checkout stand undetected. Sweethearting was held in check because management could identify cashiers who consistently had a lower customer purchase than the average. Motivation was often improved by instituting a cashier performance system in which cashiers received feedback on their performance and rewards were given for increasing their speed.

Problems could crop up with the measurement of performance, however, since checkers could "beat the system." For example, to increase their item count they could scan each of 24 cans in a case of soft drinks. Another problem was the definition of performance. At many supermarkets, including Kalen's, the cashiers were encouraged to know the customers on a first-name basis, which slowed them down but was valuable public relations.

The third principal "soft" benefit of scanning resulted from using product-movement reports to make in-store merchandising decisions. Before scanning, retailers had to use warehouse-withdrawal information to make merchandising decisions. This information consisted of the number of cases for a given brand which were shipped to a particular store each month. While the information provided a rough guideline to the best-selling brands, it was not very precise or timely due to the effects of changing retail inventories, inter-store shipments, and product promotions. Also, these warehouse figures did not include Direct Store Delivery (DSD) items.[4]

With scanners, retailers were able to find out the exact quantity sold, in units or dollars, of any UPC-coded item and could also determine the gross profit. This information could be used for several purposes such as: (1) determining which brands should be dropped and which given more shelf space; (2) evaluating the effect of a change in location or visibility for a product category. Armed with accurate, by brand, and timely (weekly) sales information, retailers were able to make in-store merchandising changes that had never been considered prior to scanning because of lack of information.

Despite all the benefits of scanning, retailers were slow to adopt the new technology because of the uncertainty surrounding the acceptance of the UPC code and the difficulty of quantifying the soft benefits. By 1976, only 125 supermarkets had installed scanning. Since 1976, more scanners were installed in each year than the previous year but by mid-1981, still only 10 percent of the nation's 34,900 supermarkets had scanning.

---

[4]DSD products, such as drinks, snacks, ice cream, and cookies, were warehoused by brokers and manufacturers and stocked on the retail shelf by salesmen.

THE 1980 DECISION TO INSTALL SCANNING AT KALEN'S

The 1980 decision to install scanning equipment in three stores, two new ones and a remodeled store, had been made for three reasons. The primary reason was defensive. Giant Food, Inc., a 125-store chain headquartered in Washington, D.C., had committed in the late 1970s to install scanners in every store as soon as possible. Giant had three stores in Louisville, which Kalen's monitored closely since Giant emphasized many of the same sales features as Kalen's, such as cleanliness and customer service. Giant had stated that they would be able to lower prices as a result of scanning savings and Kalen's was concerned about the potential impact on their business. Management thought that to delay going with scanning would mean giving up their position of leadership in providing customer value.

Another reason for going to scanning was that it appeared to be a good investment. Kalen's anticipated that scanning equipment and maintenance would cost $50,000 more per store than the type of key-entry system presently in use in the stores. Based on information from equipment vendors and other retailers, however, they estimated scanning would decrease front-end labor costs by 10 percent and payback would come in two to two and a half years (Exhibit 5). To be conservative they did not consider any of the other possible savings.

The third reason for installing scanning at that time was to save money on hardware. It appeared that the technology would continue to become more expensive, so that, if they waited, the payback period would lengthen.

KALEN'S ACTUAL SCANNING EXPERIENCE

Kalen's actual experience with scanning was quite different from their projections. To begin with, they vastly underestimated the amount of support necessary to get the system working and keep it running smoothly. Getting price changes into the system, keeping shelf tags in the store up-to-date, maintaining the central item-price file in the computer, and getting the software to work properly were all tasks that turned out to be far more time consuming than originally anticipated. These tasks required the full-time services of a computer programmer, a scanning coordinator, a clerk, and a pricing specialist for each scanning store. Thus, the

---

EXHIBIT 5
Kalen's Calculations: Scanning Payback in 1979

Additional cost of scanning over ECRs:	$50,000 per store
Savings: 10% at the front end	
Front-end direct labor hours/week at a $200,000/week store	1000-1400 hrs./week
10% Reduction	100-140 hrs./week
1979 average wage	$3.73/hr.
1st year saving (1979)	$19,396*-$27,154
2nd year saving (1980) (assume wages increase 5%)	$20,384-$28,538
3rd year saving (1981) (assume wages increase 5%)	$21,424-$29,993

Source: Company records.
*(100 hrs./week) (52 weeks/year) ($3.73/hr.) = $19,396

original $150,000 estimate of additional costs for scanning turned out to be $373,000 in the first year. In addition to the extra cost, this emphasis on simply running the system prevented Kalen's from focusing attention on gaining the expected benefits. Moreover, the number of scanning vendors continued to increase and the scanning technology seemed to be improving. By the end of the first year, Kalen's management was very uncertain about scanning and decided to put an indefinite hold on new scanning installations until an evaluation could be made.

EVALUATION

Nelson Keegan, Kalen's controller, did a preliminary cost-benefit analysis of scanning, which is reproduced in Exhibit 6. His analysis identified four savings from the system:

The primary benefit came from the elimination of item pricing. Originally, management had decided to continue individual item pricing at the scan stores because they feared adverse consumer reaction. Some consumers felt that shelf pricing was inadequate since the price in the computer could be different from the price on the shelf. These consumers were vocal enough to get laws passed in several states by 1980 that made item pricing mandatory. Kalen's wanted to remove prices but also wanted to avoid at all costs taking a position that would align them against the consumer because that would hurt their image. However, since they appeared not to be realizing any front-end savings from scanning after eight months, they decided to remove prices in December, 1982 and, by doing it quietly,

---

EXHIBIT 6
Monthly Cost-Benefit Analysis: Scanning vs. ECR System

Additional costs of scanning (per month per store)	
Equipment rental	$1,236.90
Equipment maintenance	$ 590.96
Pricing specialist and additional help required for changing shelf tags	$1,488.00
Computer support supplied by wholesaler	$ 400.00
TOTAL	$3,715.86
Office support required for scanning stores (Fixed cost per month; will not change if additional scan stores are added)	$3,848.13
Identified benefits (per month per store)	
1 night stock clerk	$1,260.00
Price change savings	$ 506.25
Cost of labels and tags saved	$ 249.20
Savings from elimination of yearly price checks	$ 32.75
	$2,048.20
Benefits not yet calculated:	
Checker productivity	
Merchandising information	
Gross profit improvement (shrink reduction)	

Source: Company records.

suffered no adverse effect. With this move they were able to reduce the number of men on the grocery crew, who stock and price merchandise, by one man per scan store and also to save labor on price changes.

Another benefit resulting from dropping item pricing was an increase in pricing discipline. Because of the necessity of having a pricing specialist in each store to ensure that the shelf tags matched the prices in the computer, pricing

EXHIBIT 7
Cashier Speed: Items per Minute (IPM)

Store #85				#87				#88*[1]			
Week ending 5/9		Week ending 8/15		Week ending 5/9		Week ending 8/15		Week ending 5/9		Week ending 8/15	
OPER	IPM	OPER	IPM	OPER	IPM	OPER	IPM	OPER	IPM	OPER	IPM
140	27	121	28	16	40	16	33	281	24	276	25
121	24	118	27	39	29	23	33	262	23	281	24
131	24	142	27	30	28	39	33	271	23	258	22
146	23	140	26	35	28	44	30	276	23	259	22
143	23	131	24	44	27	47	30	279	22	262	22
118	23	120	23	20	26	48	30	254	21	277	22
132	23	129	22	23	26	15	29	256	21	280	22
133	23	133	22	34	25	30	29	258	21	283	21
126	22	144	21	27	25	20	28	268	21	279	21
124	21	119	20	15	25	27	27	270	21	264	20
116	21	124	20	33	24	35	27	272	21	270	20
137	21	132	20	19	24	50	26	280	19	272	20
115	21	137	20	48	24	37	25	283	19	274	20
141	21	116	19	41	24	42	25	282	18	260	19
144	20	127	19	46	22	33	24	253	17	273	19
130	19	122	17	51	22	34	24	269	17	254	18
127	18	148	16	25	21	40	23	273	17	268	18
145	16	117	14	18	21	51	22	264	16	265	17
123	13			38	21	22	21	265	16	267	16
				32	20	32	21	266	15	266	15
				21	18	52	20	255	14	269	15
				22	17	17	19	251	14	278	15
				50	16	18	19	267	14	251	12
				52	16	43	19	260	13	252	12
				40	15	19	18	252	12	263	10
				42	13	36	18				
				36	11	21	17				
						26	14				
						28	14				
						29	13				
AVG. 21.47		AVG. 21.39		AVG. 22.52		AVG. 23.7		AVG. 18.48		AVG. 18.68	

Source: Company records.
OPER = Operator Identification
[1] Checker Unload System
*Scanning Store

errors were greatly reduced. Before scanning, Kalen's checked all the prices in the stores once a year and generally found about 5 percent that were incorrect. In the scanning stores, prices were being checked constantly and, in a recent audit, were found to be 99.2 percent correct. The increased discipline carried over to the key-entry stores as well, since the incorrect price percentage had dropped to 2 percent in recent months.

| #89 | | | | #91* | | | | #92* | | | |
| Week ending 5/9 | | Week ending 8/15 | | Week ending 5/9 | | Week ending 8/15 | | Week ending 5/9 | | Week ending 8/15 | |
OPER	IPM	OPER	IPM	OPER	IPM	OPER	IPM	OPER	IPM	OPER	IPM
166	29	166	35	96	28	97	31	204	30	224	33
168	29	187	30	98	27	98	31	224	30	204	31
156	27	189	30	89	27	87	30	209	26	210	31
170	27	157	29	97	25	89	29	215	25	216	28
177	27	183	29	91	25	96	28	216	25	209	27
178	27	161	28	71	24	71	28	203	24	203	26
165	25	170	27	77	24	77	26	213	24	213	26
167	24	165	26	95	24	75	25	217	24	221	26
180	23	182	26	82	23	95	24	214	23	222	26
183	23	156	25	90	23	70	23	208	21	212	25
188	23	159	25	87	22	83	23	218	21	214	25
161	22	163	25	83	21	90	23	206	21	217	25
174	22	164	25	93	21	91	23	201	20	207	24
175	22	167	25	85	21	79	22	205	19	215	24
157	21	175	25	67	20	73	20	207	19	223	23
158	20	160	24	75	20	66	19	221	19	201	21
163	20	174	24	66	19	69	19	223	19	208	21
164	20	177	24	68	19	81	19	212	18	218	21
171	20	178	24	78	19	85	19	219	16	227	21
184	20	184	24	79	19	78	18	220	16	220	20
189	20	190	24	81	19	86	18	202	15	202	19
160	19	172	23	73	18	82	17	211	14	206	19
169	19	179	23	88	18	65	16				
172	19	180	23	65	17	84	15				
173	18	181	22	94	16	88	15				
181	18	186	22	72	14	72	14				
155	17	188	22			76	14				
162	16	169	19								
AVG. 22.04		AVG. 25.28		AVG. 21.27		AVG. 21.81		AVG. 21.32		AVG. 24.64	

Representative data from a 3-month sample. Cashier improvement program was underway in each store, beginning 5/16 and ending 8/15.

In order to determine what other benefits could be realized from scanning, Bob Kalen initiated studies in the summer of 1981 on checker productivity and merchandising benefits:

Since after a year of experience with scanning, Kalen's had seen no apparent front-end savings, a checker productivity program was initiated to raise the speed of the cashiers at the scanning stores without affecting the friendly, courteous atmosphere at the front end. At the time the program was started, cashiers at the scan stores were no faster than those at the key-entry stores, on the average. Carol Beth Martin, the training specialist assigned to the program, hypothesized three reasons for the lack of improvement of the scanning cashiers:

1) Cashiers were forced to spend time bagging when courtesy clerks were taking groceries to customer cars;
2) The older, more experienced cashiers resisted using the correct motion to scan items and tended to spend more time chatting with customers;
3) Because only 74 percent of items were scannable, the cashier's "scanning motion" was often broken.

To improve productivity the courtesy clerk-to-cashier ratio was increased to 2:1 at one of the scanning stores (#92) and Carol Beth instituted a program of refresher meetings and providing feedback on performance to the cashiers. After three months, Carol Beth had accumulated data on cashier speed from the three scanning stores and three key-entry stores. A sample of these data is presented in Exhibit 7. At this point she needed to decide if the cashiers at the scanning stores had indeed become faster and, if so, whether the increased speed would mean a decrease in labor hours.

In order to determine the extent of the merchandising benefits achievable with scanning, Bob Kalen hired an MBA summer intern to analyze the sales information generated by the three scan stores. The intern's primary objective was to quantify the benefit of using scanning sales information to make in-store merchandising changes. To accomplish the task, two controlled in-store tests were designed for, respectively, flexible bag snacks and cookies.

In the cookie area, the impetus behind the test was a merchandising idea that Bob had been reluctant to implement because of a lack of information. The idea was to create a special four-foot section in the cookie aisle which would contain reduced-price cookies. It was thought that this new section would increase total cookie sales because people would be attracted by the bargains. In a typical Kalen's, the specially-priced items were spread throughout the aisle rather than grouped. If the test were successful, all eleven stores would be reset to include a special section. The results of the test are reproduced in Exhibit 8.

The snack test was designed to settle a continuing disagreement between Kalen's store managers about merchandising flexible bag snacks. Several managers believed that using two secondary snack displays in the store increased total sales of snacks. Others believed that these extra displays merely transferred sales from the shelf to the displays and that no displays were required. To settle the argument and find the most profitable alternative, a controlled test was developed. The details of the test and the results are presented in Exhibit 9.

EXHIBIT 8
Merchandising Test: Cookies

Objective: Determine if a four-foot "special buys" section for cookies increases total cookie sales.

Test design: The test was conducted over a two-week period, August 3-15, at store #91. During the two weeks, no cookie items appeared in the ad and there were no secondary cookie displays allowed in the store. For the first week, the section was left unchanged with "special buys" scattered throughout the total 48-foot cookie section. For the second week, the section was reset to include a "special buys" section where four items were prominently featured as diagrammed. Customer count for the store was noted.

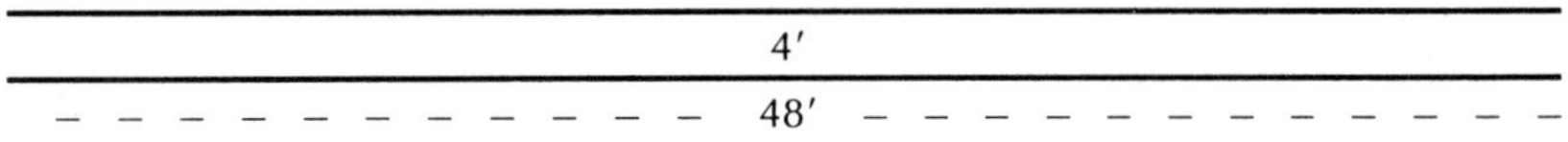

```
                              4'
 – – – – – – – – – –  48'  – – – – – – – – – –
```

Results: Manufacturer	Wk #1	Wk #2
Murray	$ 322.58	$ 310.56
FFV	101.31	76.06
Keebler	479.45	600.85
Nabisco	823.21	863.24
MaMa	89.95	50.53
Brenner	12.46	6.23
Sunshine	193.55	228.30
Royal Crest	39.04	48.16
Archway	111.00	77.43
Fireside	25.99	10.05
Jacks	8.31	12.66
Pepperidge Farm	109.99	105.23
Salerno	15.48	0
Richfood	—	—
TOTAL	$2,332.32	$2,389.30
Customer count	11,247	10,976

Source: Company records.
NOTE: Gross Margin is approximately 21% for the total cookie category.

After analyzing the results of the two tests, Bob Kalen and the intern were still uncertain as to what dollar benefit should be ascribed to scanning. Both realized that the sales increases were not directly attributable to the scanning information, but without the information, the changes probably would not have been made. Also, Bob knew that to achieve any further benefits would mean hiring a scan analyst to design tests and interpret the data and would also require management time if the scanning information was to be used properly.

Other benefits that had been cited by scanning-equipment manufacturers, such as the reduction in shrinkage, were impossible to measure precisely. Kalen's knew such benefits should show up in gross profit, but looking at the numbers in Exhibit 10, they were unsure whether scanning had made a positive contribution or not.

EXHIBIT 9
Merchandising Test: Flexible Bag Snacks

Objective: Determine the incremental dollar sales generated by secondary snack displays.
Test Design: The test was conducted over a two-week period, Ausust 3-15, in the three scan stores. During the two weeks of the test, no snack items were advertised, since this would have invalidated the results. During the first week, all three stores sold snacks only off the shelf (no secondary displays) in order to provide comparative data. During the second week of the test, Store #88 put up two secondary displays (Frito-Lay and Wise), Store #92 put up one display (Wise), and Store #91 again had no secondary displays. To ensure that the test was not biased by business conditions, customer count was noted.

Results:	#88		#91		#92	
Manufacturer	Wk#1	Wk#2	Wk#1	Wk#2	Wk#1	Wk#2
UTZ	$360.11	$327.67	$355.67	$400.53	$414.64	$473.87
Wise	268.37	313.28	407.72	249.21	379.69	466.40
Frito-Lay	1,410.44	1,715.85	1,657.33	1,803.50	1,377.47	1,522.05
Snyders	119.26	126.27	152.03	128.98	161.98	168.16
Charles	122.63	101.30	132.82	110.80	116.20	123.06
Gibbles	137.23	140.81	178.12	206.18	167.72	150.08
Keebler	12.75	17.00	18.70	13.60	6.80	12.75
Nabisco	96.63	87.42	112.22	59.97	97.53	108.70
Pringles	76.59	84.60	71.16	82.95	89.73	83.37
Richfood	37.05	22.44	47.50	40.84	43.70	38.23
Other	38.61	59.40	29.70	44.55	57.42	52.47
TOTAL	$2,679.67	$2,996.04	$3,162.97	$3,141.11	$2,912.88	$3,179.14
Customer count	9,443	9,376	11,247	10,976	9,282	9,000

Source: Company records.
NOTE: Approximate gross profit margin is 24% for snacks.

In addition to their own company data, Kalen's was able to get some information from other independent supermarket chains about scanning benefits. This information is presented in Exhibit 11.

THE NEW STORE

The new store was due to be completed in January, 1982. With 33,500 square feet, it would be the largest store in the chain and was expected to relieve some of the congestion at the Masterson Avenue Kalen's (#89) located only ½ mile away. The Masterson store was Kalen's leading store. In 1981, it had averaged almost $300,000 in sales each week, and its volume had grown at a rate of 25 percent each year since opening in 1975.

In the first year Kalen's management hoped to draw $100,000 per week from the Masterson store and to generate $50,000 of additional sales from competing supermarkets in the area. They estimated that, because of the overcrowding at

EXHIBIT 10
Gross Profit Margin Grocery and Frozen Food**

Store No.	1979	1980	1981
#81	17.01%	16.87%	17.37%
#82	17.19%	17.02%	17.13%
#83	16.83%	17.24%	17.35%
#84	17.90%	17.64%	17.65%
#85	17.01%	17.07%	17.06%
#86	17.56%	16.49%	17.18%
#87	17.81%	17.49%	17.66%
#88*	17.44%	17.72%	18.41%
#89	17.81%	18.68%	17.60%
#91*	17.61%	17.75%	17.51%
#92*		17.69%	18.15%
Company Total	17.39%	17.45%	17.57%

Years refer to Kalen's fiscal year which runs from July 31 to August 1. Therefore, 1979 figures are at August 1, 1979.
*Scanning stores: scanners installed spring 1980.
**Meat, produce, and general merchandise sales account for approx. 30% of sales volume. Gross profit margins for these departments have been excluded since scanning has little impact on them.
Data have been disguised.

EXHIBIT 11
Other Supermarkets' Evaluation of Scanning Benefits

Dick's Supermarkets (Platteville, Wisconsin)
Annual Savings in a $150,000/week store: (compared with Electronic Cash Registers)

Shrinkage savings	$46,800	(Estimated from improvement in gross margin)
Checker productivity	$35,755	(120 hrs./wk × $5.73/hr × 52 wks)
Shelf pricing	$16,800	(55 hrs./wk × $5.87/hr. × 52 wks)
Price change savings	$ 2,598	
Tracking of In-ad coupons	$ 2,400	(7 hrs./wk manual counting × $6.52 × 52 wks)

Easter's Supermarkets (Altoona, Iowa)
Annual Savings in a $125,000/week store (compared with Electronic Cash Registers)

Checker productivity	$ 4,178	(16.5 hrs./wk × $4.87/hr. × 52 wks)
Shrinkage savings	$ 0	(No improvement in gross margin figures)
Shelf pricing	$ 8,944	(43 hrs./wk × $4.00/hr. × 52 wks)
Price change savings	$ 1,820	(5 hrs./wk × $7.00/hr × 52 wks)

Giant Food, Inc. (Landover, Maryland)
Annual Savings in a $140,000/week store (compared with Mechanical Cash Registers)

Checker productivity	$61,344	(Calculated on basis of hourly wage, $6.40/hr., which includes fringe benefits.)
Shelf pricing	$32,940	
Reduction in Under-rings	$10,920	Estimated that under-ring losses amount to .2% of sales and that scanning will eliminate 75% of this loss.
Routine ordering benefit	$31,766	(Not in practice yet, but assumes savings of 31 hours × $8.54 × 52 wks).

Masterson, they were losing approximately $50,000 in business each week to neighboring supermarkets like the Safeway store that backed up to the new store.

In deciding what type of checkstand equipment to install in the new store, Kalen's was concerned about several factors. The primary one was customer acceptance. Since they planned to draw customers from the Masterson store, Kalen's wanted to minimize the confusion for those customers switching stores. Therefore, they decided to use the checker unload system in use at Masterson. Although this method was slower than customer unload, surveys done by Kalen's in 1979 had found that approximately 75 percent of customers strongly preferred the checker unload system.

With this decision made, Kalen's management had to make a decision on scanning. The Masterson store had a key-entry system, but the Safeway store had scanning and had removed item prices. In fact, in the greater Louisville area, 12 supermarkets out of a total of 90 were equipped with scanning. Despite the acceptance of scanning by most customers in Louisville, the future of shelf pricing was cloudy. The Kentucky State Legislature was soon to consider a bill that could make item pricing mandatory and thereby eliminate a large dollar savings for supermarkets.

Another issue in the checkstand decision involved the merchandising benefits of scanning. The customer demographics of the new store were very similar to those at another Kalen's scan store. Since these two stores were also approximately the same size and had the same layout, Kalen's was not certain that scanning was needed at the new store to provide merchandising information.

One of the biggest questions in the checkstand decision arose because of the rapidly evolving technology of the scanning equipment. In 1980, Kalen's had acquired a model 3650 programmable store system, the most advanced hardware and software package available from IBM, yet in mid-1982, a new system was due to be released that would provide 180° scanning capability and cost less than the old system. The new 3687 scanner would be the first to combine laser light with holography, enabling it to read UPC codes on the underside and vertical sides of items up to 4½ inches above the scanning window. While the exact price for the complete system was not known at this time, indications were that it would cost at least $12,000 less than the current 3650 Programmable Store System.

If purchased, a 3650 system would cost approximately $160,000 for a ten-checkstand system. However, Kalen's could lease several of the elements, which would reduce the purchase price to $120,000 and add a monthly lease payment of $1,512. Maintenance on this system would be approximately the same as with the 3687 at $1,338 per month. To buy a key-entry system similar to that at Masterson would cost approximately $75,000, while a combination purchase/lease agreement for it would cost $59,000 and $465 per month. Maintenance for the key-entry system would be about $730 per month.

Since Kalen's had no desire to be saddled with obsolete technology six months after their store opened, they negotiated with IBM to give them two other options. They could lease the key-entry system on a six-month renewable basis and then convert to the 3687 or they could lease the 3650 system and convert. Of course, if they did not want to convert when the 3687 was introduced, they could purchase either the key-entry system or the 3650.

THE DECISION

With the store opening only seven months away, Kalen's management needed to reach a decision. They liked the flexibility of the six-month lease arrangements but realized that they still needed to make a basic decision on whether or not to go with scanning.

Kalen's believed that the company would continue to be successful with or without scanning. However with many of their competitors—especially the large chains—installing scanners in greater numbers, they were concerned about falling behind the industry. Already some retailers were realizing benefits from scanning in areas such as automatic inventory reordering, scheduling stock crews, setting up new store layouts and shelf stocking patterns using the detailed item-movement data and even selling the detailed item-movement data to market research companies.

Shaw's Supermarkets, for example, a Massachusetts-based company, had set up a program making it possible for its 38 stores to restock automatically from its warehouse. As a result, inventory turnover at the stores was boosted by 20 percent. Ralph's, a supermarket chain in California, had formed a scanning analysis department in 1979 and were far ahead of the industry in terms of applications. If the national chains were able to lower their cost of doing business, Kalen's would be in trouble in future years.

On the other hand, Kalen's had to balance these purported benefits against the risks of a commitment to scanning. As Bob Kalen stated,

> "Our company has always been interested in new technology, but an independent really has to wait. We cannot afford to be pioneers when you are talking about spending a lot of money on equipment. We want to be progressive as a company, but we want to make sure we don't over-extend ourselves, jump in, and lose everything. We are not that complicated or sophisticated an organization. Is scanning really for us?"

Mead CompuChem
The Ethernet Decision

It was June, 1982. Howard Magid, vice-president of operations for Mead CompuChem, stared out his window at the threatening clouds. His plane reservations for a trip to the West Coast the next week had just been confirmed. Howard wondered what he would hear there from Finnigan Corporation and Hewlett-Packard. What these companies' engineers had to say might help Howard decide what should be done about the Ethernet project.

BACKGROUND ON MEAD COMPUCHEM

Mead CompuChem was a division of the Mead Corporation, a major forest products company. CompuChem was one of three divisions comprising Mead's Advanced Systems Group. The division was three years old, although the planning for it had gone on for several years before its start in 1979. The division was created to serve the growing market for chemical tests on water and soil samples. Because of various environmental regulations, companies that discharged effluent into bodies of water had to have water samples analyzed for the composition and concentrations of various known pollutants. Many of the soil samples came from hazardous waste dump sites; they were used to determine the composition of the material buried at the site. Rather than analyze the samples themselves, companies often contracted laboratories to do the analyses. Mead CompuChem serviced commercial customers as well as the Environmental Protection Agency. (Mead CompuChem's lab in Research Triangle Park, North Carolina, was just down the road from one of EPA's main laboratories.)

Since its start with four employees, the division had grown to 89 people at Research Triangle Park and another 16 at a newly opened satellite regional facility in Chicago. Sales had increased more than threefold in 1981 and were expected to double in 1982.

The concept at Mead CompuChem was to make a line flow process out of what historically had been treated as a small batch operation. Analyzing environmental samples for pollutants was not new. Traditionally, such analyses demanded the use of specialized machines called gas chromatograph/mass spectrometers (GC/MS). These delicate scientific instruments cost about $120,000 each. Typically, pollution analysis would be done by a Ph. D. chemist operating such an instrument and interpreting its results. Mead Corporation foresaw that with the increase in environmental regulations mandating pollution testing, this small-sample approach could be altered to make it a much more systematic line flow process. With specialization of duties and attention to the flow of materials, Mead CompuChem could do in three weeks and at much lower cost what it took traditional chemists six weeks to do.

A DESCRIPTION OF THE PROCESS

Mead CompuChem was strictly an analytical laboratory. It did not collect samples for its clients nor did it interpret the results. It simply provided the client with a chemical analysis of which pollutants occurred in the samples and in what concentrations. The client could order a variety of tests. For water samples, a deluxe test would detect and determine the concentrations of 128 "priority" pollutants—including acids, bases, pesticides, volatile chemicals, metals, cyanides, and phenols. The most popular analysis detected 113 organic chemicals that were priority pollutants. In addition, on a special quotation basis, CompuChem could provide analytical services to a customer's specifications.

To a client requesting sample analysis, CompuChem would send a patented container with decontaminated bottles and jars of various sizes in which to put the collected samples. The client would ship the container back to Mead CompuChem by air freight. Upon receipt of the container, documentation was initiated to indicate what kinds of analyses were desired, what procedures would be required, where the analyses and their preparation steps would be performed in the lab (there were 23 work stations), and the time each work station had to perform its task (without violating EPA-mandated analysis procedures or making the final report late to the client).

After the order had been entered into the computer routing and scheduling system, the samples had to be prepared for analysis. If a water sample was to include analysis of volatile chemicals, no preparation was required other than to refrigerate it. For all other tests, the sample had to be prepared by a process called *extraction,* which concentrated any chemicals in the sample so that they could be analyzed. The equipment in the extraction lab was designed to concentrate organic constituents from water and soil samples. Once extracted, the small vials of concentrated samples were ready for the gas chromatograph/mass spectrometry lab.

In an analysis by GC/MS, one to five microliters of a sample solution were injected into a gas chromatograph injection port. Here the sample was volatilized and entered the chromatographic column, where differences in the chemical nature of each compound in the sample caused a separation of compounds. Each compound entered the instrument's ion source (through a special pressure balancing interface), where it was bombarded by electrons. This bombardment caused the molecules to fragment into a characteristic pattern of smaller charged particles called ions. These ions were then separated according to their mass-to-charge ratio and detected in sequence by an electron multiplier. The signal generated by the multiplier was proportional to the abundance of each fragment ion and could be used to generate a "mass spectrum" for each compound in the sample. To identify the component, the instrument's computer data system compared the spectrum of the unknown material with a library of compounds. If the system could not make a match, a skilled chemist looking at a printed mass spectrum was sometimes able to identify which compounds produced specific peaks in that mass spectrum and the levels at which they were present. For some unknowns, however, the mass spectrum information was not sufficient to identify the compounds.

While reasonably simple in concept, the GC/MS technology was extremely sophisticated. Furthermore, the data produced by such an instrument was so voluminous (15 to 25 megabytes of data per day per instrument) that each of CompuChem's 18 GC/MS machines in Raleigh/Durham and each of its six machines in Chicago required its own minicomputer to accumulate the data and reduce it to a form that could be analyzed.

In a typical run, the GC/MS took about 45 minutes to perform the chemical analysis and to accumulate the data. During this time, the minicomputer could perform two distinct tasks—the foreground (or primary) task and the background task. The foreground task was always the accumulation of raw data for the run in progress. The background task could vary. Important background tasks included (1) "quantitation," whereby the raw data from the previous run underwent some calculations and were summarized; (2) printing; and (3) searches, whereby specific characteristics of the previous run were compared with a library of such characteristics in order to help identify the compounds. Occasionally, a sample was so complex that the background tasks on the previous run's data, particularly printing, could not be accomplished in the 45 minutes devoted to accumulating data on the current run. To give the minicomputer time to catch up, a new sample injection was postponed 15 to 20 minutes. This kind of delay was especially prevalent with semivolatile analyses, where it occurred for between 20 and 40 percent of the samples.

After a run had been made on the GC/MS, the run results were reviewed by an assistant manager, usually a shift later. The results as reviewed were sent to the report integration section, which collected all the analyses done for a client's order and integrated them into a single report. The resulting documents were then transmitted to the quality control section, which looked for any irregularities in each run and determined whether any problems existed. When there was a problem, the results could usually be corrected by reevaluating the original data, although sometimes samples had to be rerun. Quality control typically saw the results three to four days after they had been run. Once quality control approved the run, a final report was generated. Exhibit 1 presents a process flow diagram for CompuChem's operation.

The Research Triangle Park GC/MS lab housed 18 machines. They were run 24 hours a day on three shifts. Not all of them were necessarily busy during each shift; that depended partly on the volume and mix of work entering the lab. Two of the machines were used only for R&D. One shift of four machines was dedicated to product development—special analysis aside from the mandated environmental

EXHIBIT 1
Simplified Process Flow Diagram

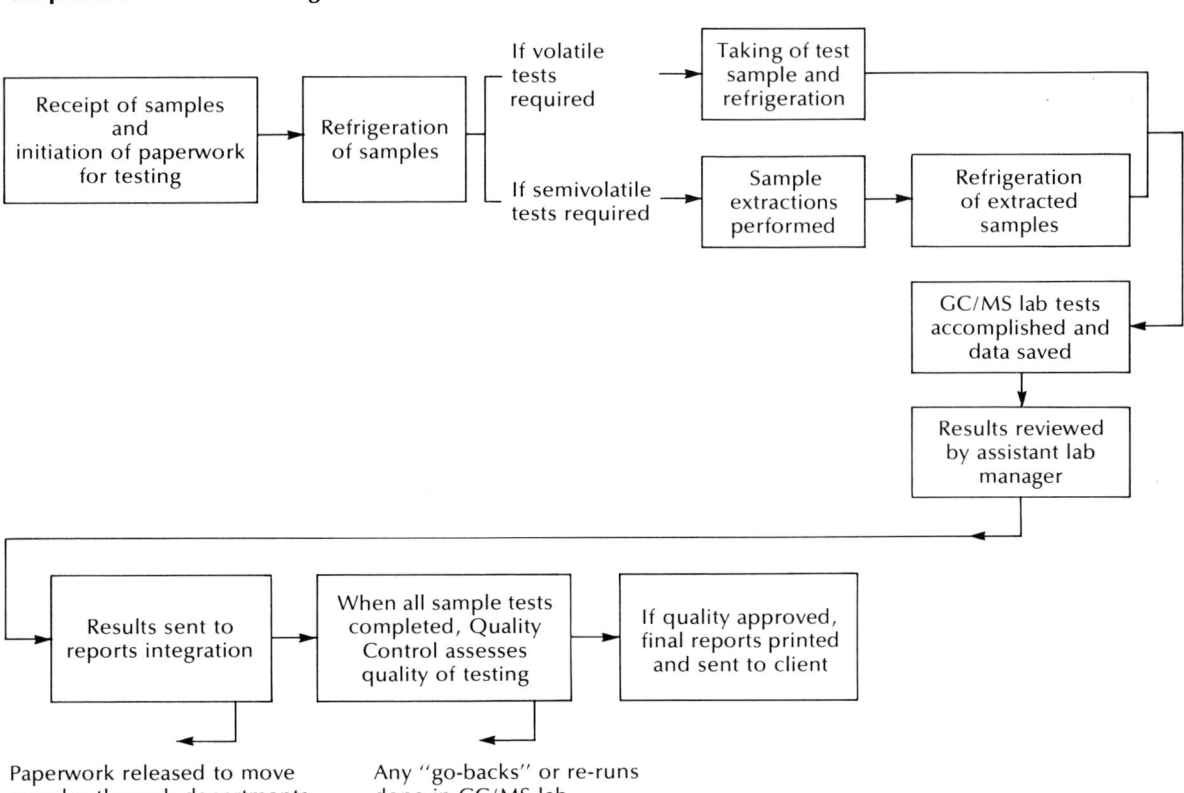

Paperwork released to move
samples through departments
or to further tests

Any "go-backs" or re-runs
done in GC/MS lab

work or the perfecting of new procedures before their introduction into the production laboratory; these machines could be pressed into service during the second and third shifts if they were needed because of work volume or downtime on other machines. The remaining 12 machines were used routinely for production. They were grouped into four stations of three machines each. Two stations concentrated on the analysis of volatiles, and two on the analysis of semivolatiles; samples for the latter had undergone preparation in the extraction lab.

At the start of each eight-hour shift, by EPA mandate each machine had to be "tuned." This tuning was almost an art and typically took about an hour. Tuning assured that the machine was operating properly and was detecting all that it should be detecting and that results would be reproducible by other machines in other laboratories. To tune a machine, the technician ran a standard solution of known compounds through the machine to see whether the machine detected all the compounds in this solution and at the correct concentration levels. A blank sample containing pure water, for example, would also be run to make sure that the machine was being completely purged of contaminants between runs.

A single technician handled three machines (a work station) at a time. Each of the machines would be set up for a particular type of procedure. Because a setup could take several hours, it was advisable to run together as many samples requiring the same procedure as possible. During any eight-hour shift, the technician in charge of a work station was exceedingly busy. The tasks might include retrieving a sample from the refrigerator, "shooting" it into the machine, monitoring data acquisition, initiating the software programs that reduce the data, monitoring the summary tables, starting the printing of the reports on the run, setting up the machine for different procedures, tuning a machine, performing an initial data review, or initiating preventive maintenance.

QUALITY CONTROL

Assuring that the GC/MS was operating properly and that the results it derived were accurate was a complicated endeavor. Not only did the machine need to be tuned every eight hours, but each sample had to be specially prepared. To calibrate the machine's results so that the concentrations of pollutants could be accurately determined, special concentrations of standard chemicals not normally occurring in nature were "spiked" into every sample. These special compounds at their known concentrations provided the standards with which to compare the pollutants in a sample. Naturally, it was desired that the GC/MS detect all the surrogates spiked into each sample. If, for example, the level of a particular surrogate was too low, something was wrong. Perhaps the instrument was faulty. Or perhaps something about the chemistry of the sample led the surrogate to be "lost" chemically.

Determining the cause and extent of any GC/MS failures was a key duty of the four workers in the Quality Control section. To be assured that all was well, the Quality Control section entered (1) pure blanks into the system, (2) blanks spiked with standard compounds, and (3) already analyzed samples spiked with known concentrations of particular compounds. About 10 percent of the volume run through the lab consisted of blanks, and one of every 20 consisted of a blank or a sample spiked with known concentrations of particular compounds. Given such care, most runs went smoothly and presented no problems. However, about 5 to 10 percent of all samples needed to be rerun because of problems, and about 5 percent required the reevaluation of the raw data produced by the machine.

In order to provide this capability of reevaluating raw data, all the runs done by the lab were saved on magnetic tape. This archive also permitted clients who had questions about the analysis to look at the data in raw form. Unfortunately, the GC/MS were not equipped to generate magnetic tapes. To generate a tape, the disk pack from a GC/MS had to be removed and placed on another computer system that would dump its contents onto a magnetic tape; the disk pack could then be replaced and reused. It took about 15 minutes to remove a disk pack, transport it to the tape back-up apparatus, locate another disk pack, put it back onto the GC/MS, and have the machine ready for a new analysis. Approximately every 5 to 10 runs, the disk pack was filled and required the back-up procedure.

Thus, for each machine in the lab, between 15 minutes and half an hour every shift were spent backing up the run results.

In addition to authorizing controls (blanks) through the GC/MS, the Quality Control section examined the outcomes of all the tests. Reports were not released without Quality Control's approval.

CURRENT PROBLEMS AND THE PROMISE OF ETHERNET

The effective utilization of CompuChem's resources suggested that the company was better off when (1) all of its GC/MS were tuned and accumulating data, as opposed to being untuned or processing/printing data; (2) all computerized information was used by computers only and printed out on high-speed printers, as opposed to forming the basis for manually typed reports and the manual use of computer-generated data; and (3) there was little lag in the availability of data by quality control or by other areas of the business. These points can be explained more completely:

1. *Machine availability*. The extreme complexity of the instruments used in the GC/MS lab and the need to have them tuned every eight hours placed real constraints on the business. Naturally, the greater the fraction of any shift a machine was devoted to running samples and accumulating data, the more profitable it and the lab were. Time spent tuning a machine and waiting for hard copy printouts to be developed was essentially unproductive. If machines could be tuned more quickly or if data processing by the GC/MS themselves could be avoided, then the lab could be more productive.

   In addition, the constant starting and stopping of the disk drives was beginning to cause the physical deterioration of the units. Seveal head crashes (i.e., hardware failures that lost all the data on a system by destroying the recording medium on the disk) were occurring each quarter, costing about $400 in hardware costs and two hours in lost machine time each, if the parts were in stock. In addition, each head crash destroyed the data from one or more runs and these samples had to be repeated. Thus, instrument downtime required for repairs was increasing and the mean time between failures was dropping.

2. *Use of machine-generated data*. At several points in the CompuChem process, computer-generated data were printed into hard copy reports and manipulated manually before a final report was sent to the client. It was recognized that the process would be more productive if, every time data were generated by the computer, they could be saved for subsequent computer use and not lost. Two segments of the process were particularly important in this regard:
   • The final reports that were sent to clients included data that the GC/ MS had generated. However, because these data were saved only on tapes or on hard copies, the final report could not easily use that information. Efficiency would be enhanced if the word processors that printed

the client reports could tap directly into the GC/MS-generated data. In that way, the report writing operators would not have to enter significant results manually into final reports.

- A computer system (the laboratory management system) scheduled jobs in particular labs and their work stations. However, the results of each step in the process had to be entered manually onto the laboratory management system and the paperwork for each job had to be reissued. If the output of one segment of the process could be saved on the central computer, then the data entry step could be eliminated and the paperwork describing each job's routing would not have to be reissued. This would save some effort in production control.

  In addition, because of manual transcription of data, erroneous information was sometimes placed on the various computer systems in the laboratory. If basic data could be entered only once and the results automatically accumulated in that file, adequate safeguards could be installed to ensure that the error rates were almost zero.

3. *Time lags for information.* Quality Control suffered a lag of three or four days before it could review a run's results. This lag imposed some extra cost on the system. For example, in about 5 percent of the cases, Quality Control ordered a "go-back," a re-analysis of the data accumulated by a GC/MS. All told, a go-back cost about an hour of various people's time. Some go-backs could be avoided if more hard copy were generated by each run, but the generation of this hard copy would consume operator time and GC/MS time. The time lag for Quality Control also raised concerns about the propagation of incorrect procedures or machine operation.

If such faulty operations could be identified early, savings would result. The technology called "Ethernet" showed promise of solving some of the problems inherent in CompuChem's current operations. Ethernet was a local area network technology developed by Xerox Corporation and licensed to others at a nominal fee. This technology permitted computers and other data processing equipment to exchange data at fantastically high speeds, on the order of 10 million bits per second. Theoretically, an Ethernet network could connect all of CompuChem's GC/MSs with other computers and peripheral devices such as tape drives and larger disk pack storage units. In such a system the GC/MS machines could "pitch" data to larger and faster computers that could "catch" the data and manipulate them faster than could the minicomputer within each GC/MS machines. The GC/MSs would no longer be stand-alone units but would be tied to each other and to a series of computers that could service the data much more efficiently. No longer then would the GC/MS minicomputers tie up instrument time merely processing and printing hard copy reports. No longer would disk packs have to be dismounted and remounted in order to save data on tape. No longer would quality control have to wait three or four days for the hard copy results of particular runs; instead, it could review a given shift's data within minutes of that shift's completion. In fact, quality control could even monitor a machine's performance as it was collecting data. Individual GC/MSs could pitch packets of freshly accumulated raw data onto Ethernet, which could then feed that data to a dedicated computer for quantitation, printing, search, and other analysis. The potential of Ethernet was exceedingly enticing. (See Exhibit 2 for a summary of the benefits anticipated with an Ethernet network).

EXHIBIT 2
Potential Savings from an Ethernet Network

Item	Present operation	Estimated benefit from ethernet*
Quality control		
1. Identifying GC/MS malfunction (occurs about once a month)	4 worker-days	Only one worker-day likely
2. Go-backs	5% of runs; 1 hour spent on each go-back	Go-backs eliminated; data already on-line
3. Reruns	About 5-10% of all runs	Savings probably less than 10% of current cost of reruns
4. Special requests for hard copy output by QC section	Occurs in about 10% of runs; requires about 1 minute of print time to produce	Special requests eliminated; data already on-line
5. Effort by QC section	Base case for comparison	Twice the checks could be accomplished in half the time
Product control		
1. Report integration	Paperwork on routing, procedures, and timetable reissued after each lab performs its tasks	Only one set of paperwork need be issued; all tracking could be done on-line
2. Scheduling	Done by lab managers and operators; slack in schedule estimated at 20% of capacity	Could be done entirely by computer; slack in schedule could be reduced
3. Final report	Clerks need to enter numerical results into word processing	Savings estimated at 70% of two clerks' time
GC/MS lab operations		
1. Instrument "up-time"	Instruments up about 60-70% of the time they could be available for data accumulation (i.e., tuned and functioning)	Instruments could be fully utilized for data accumulation once tuned
2. Archive function	About 16 worker-hours per day; inadvertent slack in shift schedule	4 hours per day; turnaround would improve (more runs per shift)
3. Reliability	Frequent handling of disk packs results in some problems with data integrity	Reliability would improve
4. Reviewer time	Recurring problems not caught early	Quick availability of data may eliminate these problems. Savings in worker-hours (by the reviewer of run results) estimated at 10-15%

*Estimates based on departmental information.

THE SITUATION WITH FINNIGAN

Finnigan Corporation was a small, but highly regarded, one-product company located in California's Silicon Valley. It had designed and produced all the GC/MSs used at CompuChem. To develop an Ethernet network, these machines had to be linked to an Ethernet cable with the appropriate hardware and software to permit each machine to pitch data onto the Ethernet network. (The development of Ethernet also meant configuring the Ethernet so that it was compatible with the HP3000 minicomputer whose planned use was as the "catcher" of the summary data the GC/MSs pitched. This problem was one Mead CompuChem had to address.) The hardware involved a modern board that permitted data to be transmitted outside the minicomputer built into each machine. The software was to organize the data into "packets" so that they could be pitched effectively onto the Ethernet network.

CompuChem's idea about using Ethernet was not new. In June 1981, CompuChem had approached Finnigan about the applicability of Ethernet. At that time an aggreement was reached that Finnigan would develop the modem and write the software. This agreement was very favorable to CompuChem: Finnigan agreed to install the required hardware and software with no advance payment and with the stipulation that CompuChem had no financial obligation if the network did not meet its specifications.

Finnigan had estimated that 90 days would be required to complete the task. However, it was eight months before Finnigan returned to CompuChem with a prototype. This prototype included a modem board and some software. The prototype did succeed in transmitting data from the previously stand-alone equipment to a computer that could catch the data. However, it took too long and thus was not acceptable. In fact, the old procedure of removing the disk pack and physically carrying it to another computer to be mounted and processed onto tape was faster than the Finnigan prototype. Finnigan acknowledged the failure of its prototype to meet requirements and promised to return with an improvement. In June 1982, four months after the unsuccessful debut of its prototype, Finnigan had yet to return with a workable system. Howard Magid did not know whether Finnigan was close to a solution or whether the company had abandoned hope of developing the software necessary to use an Ethernet network effectively. Although the financial agreement was favorable to CompuChem, the absence of a financial stake in the venture did significantly reduce CompuChem's leverage with Finnigan. Howard did have a favorable opinion of Finnigan's technical capabilities in general, however, and had faith in the leader of Finnigan's software efforts.

SHORT-TERM OPTIONS

Howard had identified four options:

1. *Wait for Finnigan.* If Finnigan was successful in remedying the present problems within a reasonably short time, then all was well. The hardware changes that Finnigan was making would probably cost CompuChem about $100,000. When Finnigan would succeed, however, was not known; it could be next week, or never. It was not clear either when CompuChem

would know that Finnigan had failed. Finnigan could, of course, state that it had abandoned the project, but Magid thought that unlikely. Rather, he thought that Finnigan would put this project on the back burner, claiming to CompuChem that it was working on it slowly but surely.

CompuChem did not require the use of the Ethernet network right away. The current economic recession had affected CompuChem's business. Sales for 1982 were originally forecasted to be three times 1981 levels, but in June it looked like sales would only double them. This decline offered the company some breathing space, for it was only with high volumes that the capabilities of the Ethernet system to augment capacity were seen most clearly. Although no one knew when the recessison would break, Howard thought that it would be autumn before volume picked up substantially and the lab would again clog up with work.

2. *Use what Finnigan had already done and jerry-rig the rest.* CompuChem could take the eight modems already developed by Finnigan, reimburse Finnigan for the $30,000–$40,000 that their development probably cost, and use those modems to link groups of two or three GC/MSs via "hard wiring" to minicomputers to process some of the data from each machine and to do the tape archive of each run. This option would abandon the Ethernet network in favor of a much less sophisticated approach. CompuChem would lose the ability to review data on-line, which quality control had wanted. However, the major features desired—keeping the machines up longer, saving the transfer of disk packs for archival purposes, and using computer-generated summary information directly in the preparation of final reports—would all be saved. This fix of the problem would be a custom job, but it would be fairly inflexible and would duplicate only a fraction of what Ethernet's total potential promised for the company over the years.

3. *Go to a third party and try to save the Ethernet concept.* Under this option, the modem hardware that Finnigan had already developed would be utilized, but CompuChem would try to save the concept of an Ethernet by going to a software expert to develop the software for linking the Finnigan GC/MSs to an Ethernet (e.g., placing the data into "packets" and making the network connection). In essence, this option would do for CompuChem all that Finnigan was supposed to do but apparently could not. This option would be more expensive than the first two, requiring about $100,000 for hardware and about $50,000 for software.

Both this option and the second one ran some risks. It could be that Ethernet and related technologies simply could not be married effectively with GC/MS. By choosing either option 2 or option 3, CompuChem risked throwing away lots of money. Another risk was associated with fixing any problems with the Finnigan instruments. If software deficiencies or errors were identified, Finnigan would provide remedial software to solve the problem. However, both options 2 and 3 called for modifications in the Finnigan software. Hence, any software problems might be seen as related to the adaptation of the software, not with anything that Finnigan had been responsible for. Thus it was safer to have Finnigan entirely responsible for all hardware and all software, because the company would ensure that the instrument was capable of meeting specifications. By choosing either option 2 or option 3, CompuChem risked losing Finnigan's expertise in solving any software problems that cropped up.

To make matters worse, a large portion of the program code for the instrument was undocumented. Modifications were difficult, if not impossible, without the close cooperation of the Finnigan "gurus" who understood the guts of the system.

4. *Do nothing.* CompuChem could abandon its search for a solution to this problem and run the operation more or less as it was. The cost of this option was opportunity costs, which were fairly negligible at low volumes but increased substantially as volume grew. Howard Magid felt that with high volumes an Ethernet network could save between $40,000 and $100,000 per year in staff costs in quality control, data processing, and elsewhere.

LONG-TERM CONSIDERATIONS

Mead CompuChem was currently depreciating the Finnigan machines it owned in three years. Thus, next year, in 1983, the first group of six Finnigan machines would be fully depreciated. CompuChem did not have to use Finnigan machines. Hewlett-Packard also made a GC/MS and was expected to announce its latest models in September. According to advance reports, these models would permit local area network communication (HP's own design, not Xerox's Ethernet) between machine and Hewlett-Packard minicomputer. Howard Magid viewed this as a favorable development because Hewlett-Packard had an excellent reputation and was considered by many to announce new machines only after technical problems had been solved. Thus, CompuChem could wait a year or so and start acquiring Hewlett-Packard equipment that would have a local area network already developed for it and serviced by the company. This approach was consistent with CompuChem's decision to purchase HP3000 minicomputers to drive the laboratory management system. Hewlett-Packard GC/MS equipment had not been originally chosen because the Finnigan equipment was easier to tune and operated more smoothly. It was hoped that the new Hewlett-Packard GC/MS would be closer to Finnigan's performance.

More fundamental to the long-term prospects of Mead CompuChem was the impending decision about the kinds of chemical tests that the company would perform in the future. Lee Myers, Mead CompuChem's president, thought it likely that the company would pursue larger markets than those spawned by environmental regulations. For example, markets for very esoteric testing in toxicology or chemotherapy could be entered easily. These markets, however, required higher volumes, quicker turnarounds (days, not weeks), and lower unit prices than the environmental analysis business, although their data needs for each test would be much less. If CompuChem were to enter this market, it would probably need analytical instruments different from GC/MSs. With an Ethernet network, however, even new instruments could be linked with GC/MSs and computers to provide a very flexible analysis system.

Lee Myers expected that this strategic decision for CompuChem would be made in the next six months. His goal was to have the environmental business be less than half of the division's total sales in three or four years.

Eddins, Inc., Instrument Division

It was late May 1981, and Sam Eddins, manager of the Design Assurance and Support Engineering [DASE] Department of Eddins' Instrument Division sat back in his chair and pondered the current situation. In the past several years because of changing markets and technologies, the division, located in Raleigh, N.C., had been developing an increasing number of new products and product options. Division managers expected this trend to continue, but Sam was concerned that the resources needed to develop new products were becoming scarce. Not only manufacturing capacity, but the availability of engineers, draftsmen, programmers, and toolmakers were all potential constraints on new product development. For instance, Sam had recently read that the average U.S. toolmaker's age was 55. More importantly, three times as many toolmakers retired each year as enter the labor force.

Sam wondered if it might be time to implement the long talked about next step in Computer Aided Design/Computer Aided Manufacturing [CAD/CAM] in Raleigh. Any requests for capital equipment for the upcoming year had to be submitted by year end, and Sam knew he had a number of preliminary tasks to complete before a request could be submitted.

COMPANY BACKGROUND

During the 1970s Eddins, Inc., had grown from a small battery manufacturer to a $1-billion-a-year, worldwide supplier of electrical and electronic products. The major elements of Eddins' strategy for the 1980s were:

1. Maintain and expand market and technological leadership in electrical and electronic products.
2. Focus research and development efforts in areas of rapid market growth and profit potential.
3. Allocate resources to building electronic products in markets with the most growth and profit potential.
4. Provide a stimulating professional and technical environment offering opportunity and satisfaction to employees.
5. Manage the company's financial resources to support future growth.

Eddins' electrical products had a well-established base, while many of the electronics products were recent developments or acquisitions. Growth within the electronics operations was concentrated on six targeted markets: high-speed minicomputers, factory automation, medical instrumentation, defense systems, electronic components/materials, and test and measurement.

The Instrument Division competed in the increasingly global test and measurement market. Although this overall market was growing at 15 percent per year, the division's segment, direct writing recorders, was only expected to grow at an average annual compound rate of 8 percent.

The division produced a full line of direct writing recorders (DWRs) and associated components. Exhibit 1 illustrates these products. DWRs used in both industry and laboratories, take analog input signals such as voltage, current, or frequency and condition them to drive a writing mechanism. The resulting hard copy provides permanent documentation of the original signals. The recorders are somewhat unique instruments in that they require significant electronic design (signal conditioning, drive circuits, etc.) as well as mechanical design (enclosures, paper mechanisms). In addition, each DWR was sold with a group of associated accessories (such as signal conditioning amplifiers) for specific customer applications.

The division products were regarded as top quality and, although priced at a premium, maintained a 60 percent share of the DWR market. Sales in 1979 for the Raleigh operation were approximately $35 million.

Hewlett-Packard (HP) was Raleigh's major competitor. HP produced a comparable product (features and price) but had only a 20 percent share of market. Watanobi, a Japanese competitor, had recently gained a 10 percent share with DWRs priced 20–40 percent below Raleigh and HP.

Although the overall DWR market was fairly stable at 8 percent per year growth, significant product changes were taking place. Digital array print technologies were replacing the old ink pen writing mechanisms, while microprocessor controllers were being added to the paper drive mechanisms. In addition, signal conditioning amplifiers were continually being developed to meet new customer applications.

CAD/CAM FUNDAMENTALS

Two basic types of CAD/CAM systems were available, mechanical and electrical/electronic.[1] Mechanical CAD/CAM systems facilitated the design and production of mechanical parts ranging from bolts to airplane wings. Electrical/electronic systems focused on the creation of printed circuit boards (PCBs) or integrated circuits (ICs). For either type, either large, general-purpose or very specific application systems could be purchased.

All CAD/CAM systems contained a central processing unit (CPU) that stored

---

[1]While it was possible to purchase the CAD or the CAM portions alone, this case will always refer to an integrated combination.

EXHIBIT 1
Examples of Direct Writing Recorders (DWR)

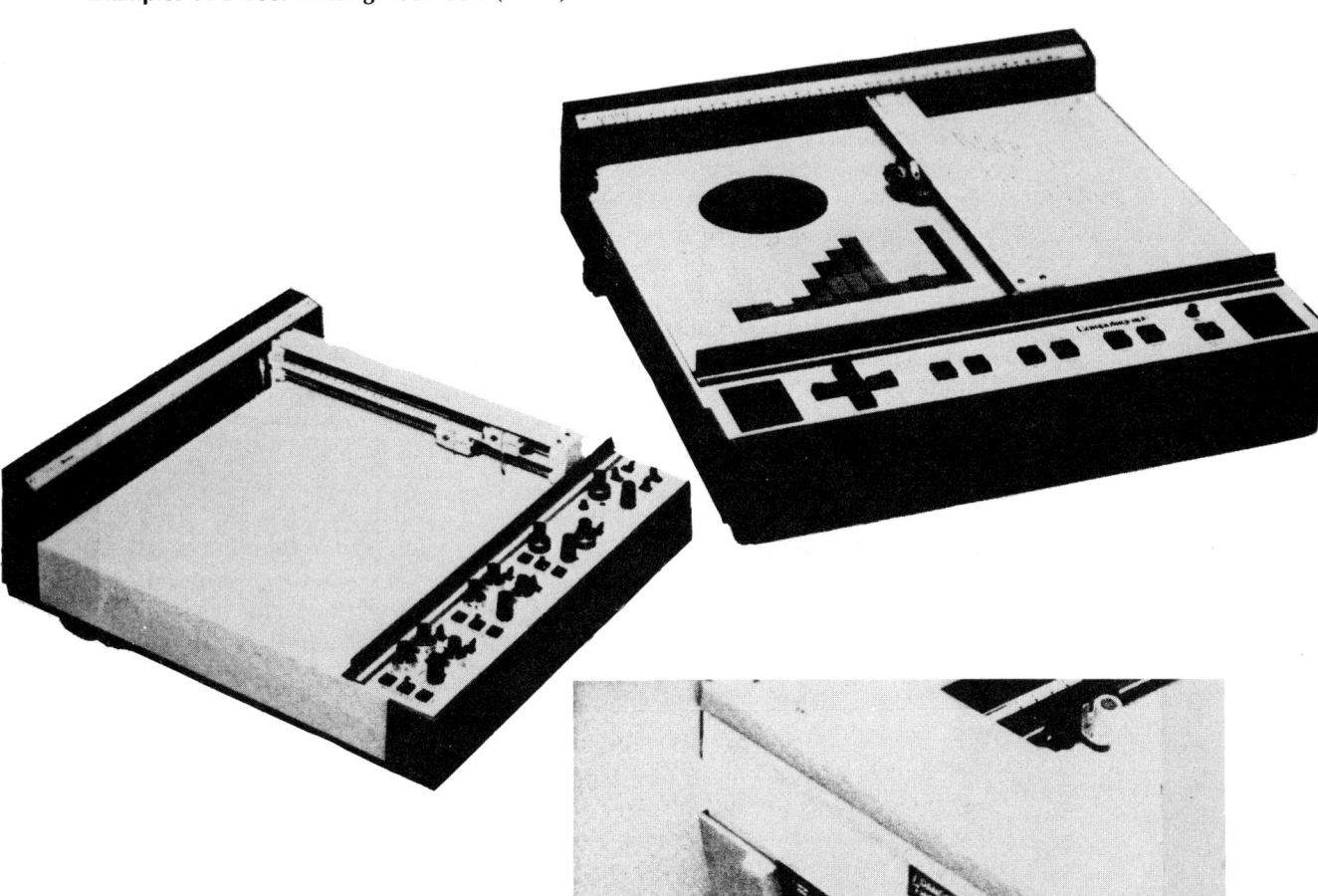

Main features
- A3 or A4 Format
- High specification—cost effective design
- Sensitivity from $50\mu V/cm$ to $20V/cm$—18 ranges
- Modern styling with smoked perspex dust cover
- Electrostatic paper hold-down
- Mute facility both axes
- Lockable controls—for constant calibration
- Timebase fitted as standard
- Optional plug-in personality module—for individual applications
- Long life high intensity L.E.D.'s for accurate paper alignment
- Uses a standard fibre tipped pen or Rotring option
- Systems and OEM versions available
- Electronic limits in both axes

The optional plug-in personality module can be fitted to all three versions of the 60000 range of recorders. It allows the user to build his own special input circuits onto the module thus extending the range of applications and making it an extremely flexible recorder.

and manipulated a common data base. This CPU might be a mainframe, mini, or micro-computer, depending on the application(s) it was to support.

Each system also contained one or more work stations for the operator(s). The work station, which might also have varying degrees of processing power, consisted of a graphics terminal through which the operator created, displayed, and changed drawings. Points, lines, or symbols making up a drawing were input to the graphics terminal with a function keyboard, joystick, thumbwheel, digitizing tablet, or any combination of these devices. Exhibit 2 illustrates the creation of a simple drawing; Exhibit 3 shows other CAD/CAM drawings.

Hard-copy documentation of the graphics screen was provided by either a pen plotter (for high-quality output) or an electrostatic printer (for quick output).

EXHIBIT 2
Creation of Part Drawing on CAD/CAM Graphics Terminal

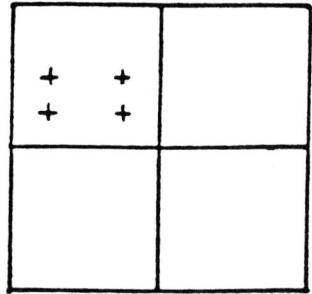

1. Screen is split into sections. Each section is a different view. Four points are defined representing the vertices on that face.

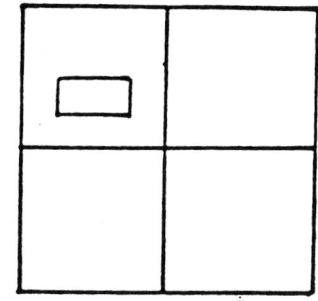

2. The points are connected with straight line elements outlining the top face.

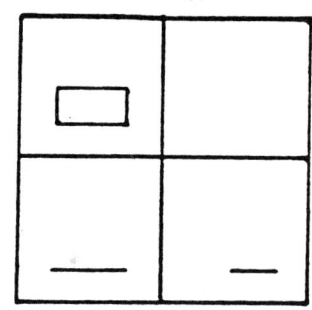

3. The image is projected into three views.

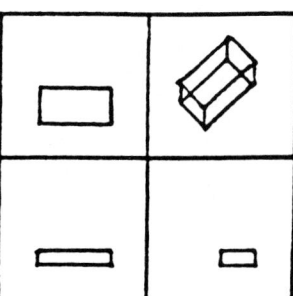

4. The face is projected into the third dimension.

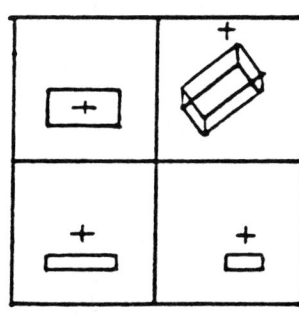

5. A point is specified above the block.

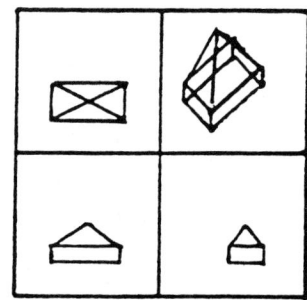

6. Line segments connect the point to the top corner of the block. Drawing is complete.

Source: *CAE Annual/1982.*

EXHIBIT 3
Examples of Mechanical CAD/CAM Drawing on Graphics Terminal

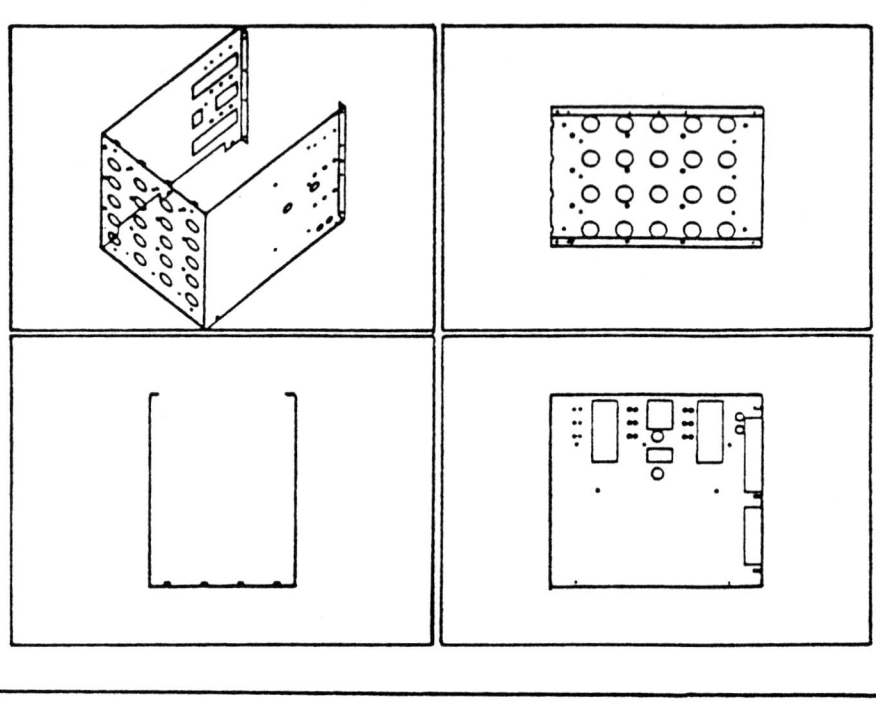

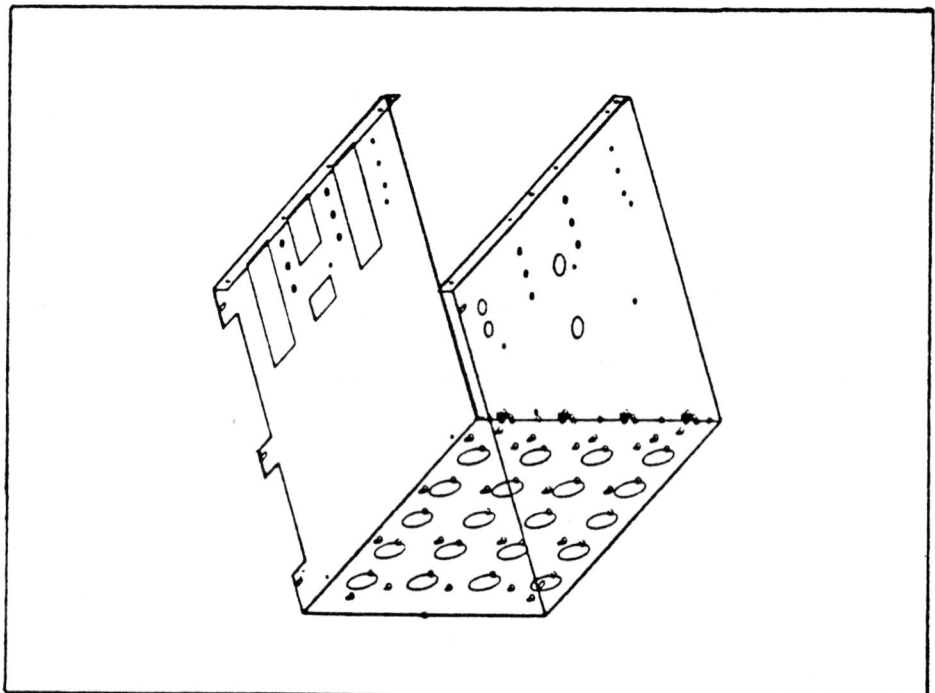

Source: Benchmark Test

Most CAD/CAM systems also contained an alphanumeric cathode ray tube (CRT) and keyboard for entering text (labels, titles, dimensions) or engineering data (material density, tensile strength, etc.) with a drawing. One hard-copy documentation device and one alphanumeric CRT and keyboard would service several work stations. Exhibit 4 illustrates the hardware components of a typical CAD/CAM system.

All drawings and data entered through these peripheral devices ended up in a common data base. In theory, then, CAD/CAM was the nucleus of a production and engineering data base, which included all information describing a company's products. CAD/CAM could affect functions in all departments of a company, including part definition, analysis, drawing, bill-of-material construction, sched-

EXHIBIT 4
Hardware Components of CAD/CAM System

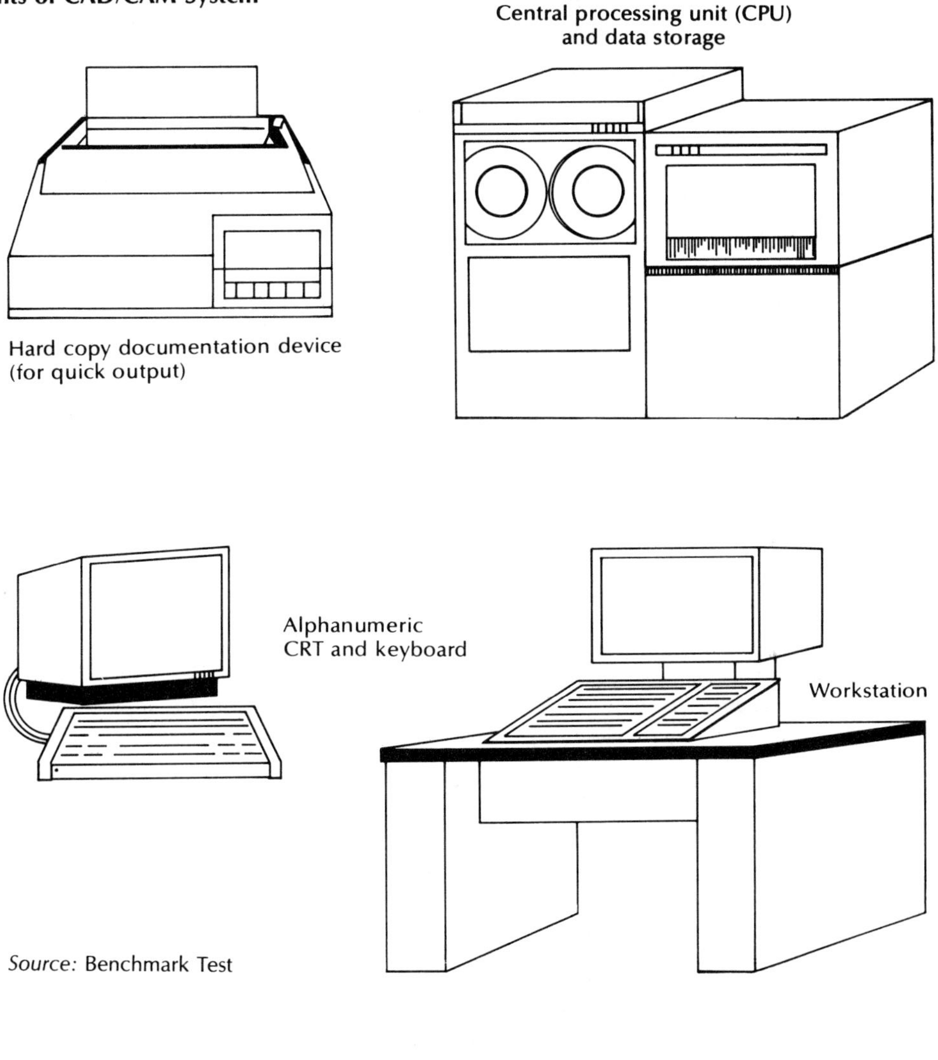

Hard copy documentation device
(for quick output)

Central processing unit (CPU)
and data storage

Alphanumeric
CRT and keyboard

Workstation

Source: Benchmark Test

uling, numerical control (NC), program generation, assembly, testing, inspection, and technical illustration. Exhibit 4 points out the potential of a fully integrated data base.

CAD/CAM AND THE FUTURE

As shown in Exhibit 5, CAD/CAM was a potentially large step in the direction of the "automated factory." It had significance particularly in the United States where yearly growth in output per hour had dropped from 3 percent in the 1960s to 1 percent by the mid-1970s to a negative figure in 1979.[2]

While the automated factory looked attractive on paper, however, it had proved to be a nightmare to implement. Massive amounts of information were required to run any such operation. CAD/CAM could take a portion of this data and provide for the orderly creation, manipulation, and distribution of it. If a factory was to become truly automated, however, all its systems—engineering analysis, master scheduling, machine scheduling, material requirements planning, machine control, testing, management information, etc.—had to be integrated with CAD/CAM. Because each of those systems operated somewhat independently, the objective of a highly integrated automated factory was a long-term goal.

BENEFITS OF CAD/CAM

Sam's extensive reading and experience had convinced him that CAD/CAM would have tangible benefits in reducing or preventing rises in direct labor and material costs. He was also aware that significant intangible benefits could be gained from CAD/CAM applications. These potential benefits included:

1. *Common Data Base*. Once a design was developed on a graphics terminal, it was stored in a data base and could then be used to perform additional tasks. Data could also be easily changed, and everyone had access to the same information.
2. *Advanced Product Analysis*. The CPU could manipulate huge amounts of data efficiently, which permitted the designer to conduct the kind of rigorous product analysis that was virtually impossible to perform manually. Analyses could range from value analysis of a single part to restructuring of entire product lines.
3. *Dynamic Drawing Manipulation*. Designers could sketch a three-dimensional drawing or model, make instantaneous changes, rotate the design to any position, zoom in on it, or cut a cross-sectional plane through it. This capability allowed a designer to evaluate many more designs than would normally be possible. The productivity and creativity of engineers could be substantially improved.
4. *Standardization of Drawings*. Frequently used symbols for particular drawings could be stored in the computer memory and recalled when needed. Generating these symbols with a push of a button instead of from scratch saved time per drawing and produced consistent drawings.

---

[2]"A CAD/CAM World?" *Barrons*, December 2, 1980, p. 4.

EXHIBIT 5
Potential of Integrated CAD/CAM

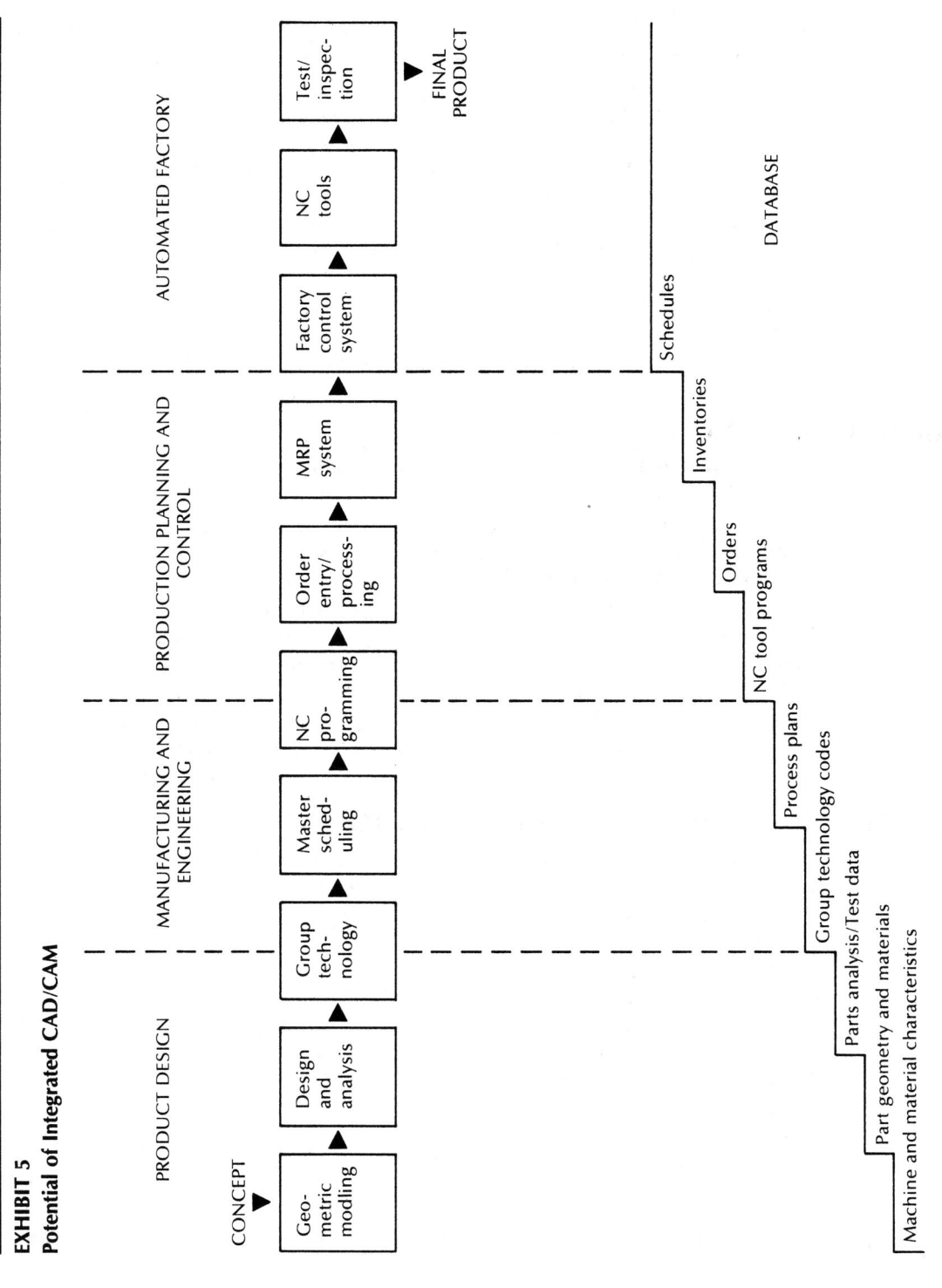

Source: *CAE Annual/1982.*

5. *Improved Product Quality*. By providing designers the opportunity to select the best of several alternative designs, CAD/CAM permitted a product's quality to be improved in the design phase. CAD allowed for sensitivity analysis and precise, rapid production of a selected design.

6. *Improved Market Response*. Reducing the design and production cycle times associated with new products, product options, or nonstandard products meant that perceived needs in the marketplace could be satisfied in a more timely fashion than before. As product life cycles became shorter and competition stiffened, these capabilities became increasingly important.

7. *Clean Drawings*. All data were stored in computer memory, so that new drawings could be created with the push of a button. Drawings that were damaged or needed major or minor updates could be quickly replotted to create a new master drawing.

THE RALEIGH OPERATION

The division's Raleigh operation, which had begun as Gifford Instruments in the 1930s, had been the market leader in direct writing recorders for years by the time it merged with Accuracy Corporation and later became part of Eddins in 1969. The Raleigh plant, which operated as a profit center, employed 260 hourly personnel and 315 salaried personnel; none were unionized.

The operation was currently running 1 shift 5 days a week. The average length of employment of salaried and hourly personnel combined was almost 12 years. The division general manager had been recently promoted from his position as director of engineering. Current DASE staffing levels were as follows: Manufacturing Department—1 senior engineer, 1 junior engineer, and 1 draftsman; Manufacturing Engineering—4 senior engineers and 5 junior engineers; Design Engineering and Drafting—2 senior engineers, 2 junior engineers, and 9 draftsmen.

AUTOMATION IN THE INSTRUMENT DIVISION TO DATE

In the Raleigh manufacturing operation, the key to success was the efficient transfer of the technology of a product into a finished, saleable product. Within the Instrument Division the most important function in producing DWRs was believed to be printed circuit board (PCB) creation. The second most important function was recognized as mechanical design and production of metal and plastic components.

In 1967 a master plan had been created to accommodate these priorities. The first phase of the plan was to establish a PCB department and fabricate PCBs inhouse rather than subcontract. As a result, PCB cost had been reduced 40–60 percent

In the second phase, a numerically controlled (NC) automatic component insertion system was brought in.[3] This system automatically placed components

---

[3]Numerically controlled systems consisted of a machine tool, a controller, and an instruction program. The instruction program was an input to the controller, which in turn controlled the machine tool.

EXHIBIT 6
Actual Productivity Gains of PCB CAD/CAM System

Technical activity	Before* CAD/CAM	After* CAD/CAM	Productivity ratio gain
Digital design time per component	2.5	1.5	1.7
Analog design time per component	3.0	1.1	2.7
Avg. design time per component	3.0	.8	3.7
Manuf. assembly drawing per PCB	14.0	5.0	2.8
Documentation assembly drawing per PCB	9.0	.5	18.0
NC programming (auto. insertion) per PCB	44.0	20.0	2.2
NC programming (auto. tester) per PCB	12.0	3.0	4.0
NC programming (drill) per PCB	80.0	16.0	5.0
Drawing changes per PCB	4.0	2.0	2.0
			Avg. 4.67

Source: Company records.
*Hours to complete listed technical activity.

(resistors, capacitors, transistors, etc.) on the blank PCB. The system resulted in reduction of component-assembly cost by 80 percent. A numerically controlled test system that automatically tested the PCBs for short or open circuits was also added. At the same time, several NC milling, punch, and drilling systems were purchased to facilitate plastic and metal component production.

The purpose of the third phase, which evolved over the years, was to purchase the best electronic CAD system for PCB design that was justifiable. Eventually two such systems were implemented, resulting in some of the productivity increases shown in Exhibit 6. These PCB CAD systems not only improved design and drawing efficiency (Raleigh was able to terminate five "rent-a-draftsmen"), but also bridged the gap from engineering to manufacturing: NC instruction programs for machine tools and test equipment no longer had to be produced manually. These programs could now be generated automatically by the post processor in the CAD/CAM system from data input by the designer.

Besides the PCB CAD/CAM systems and the NC equipment Raleigh had successfully implemented, other stand-alone systems such as MRP, VAX 11/780 engineering computer, order entry, and general management information systems. A simplified version of the current product development and production processes within Raleigh is given in Exhibit 7.

CURRENT SITUATION

Sam knew that, if the PCB CAD/CAM system was judged a success, then a fourth phase was to be added to the master plan. This phase would involve examining the feasibility of a mechanical CAD/CAM system. The new system would have profound effects not only on Sam's department but also on the entire operation.

In order to get a handle on the potential of the new system, Sam went back and checked the 1980 work activities. Since he believed 1980 was fairly representative of future years at Raleigh, he was able to determine which tasks would

EXHIBIT 7
Simplified Illustration of Product-Development and Production Process

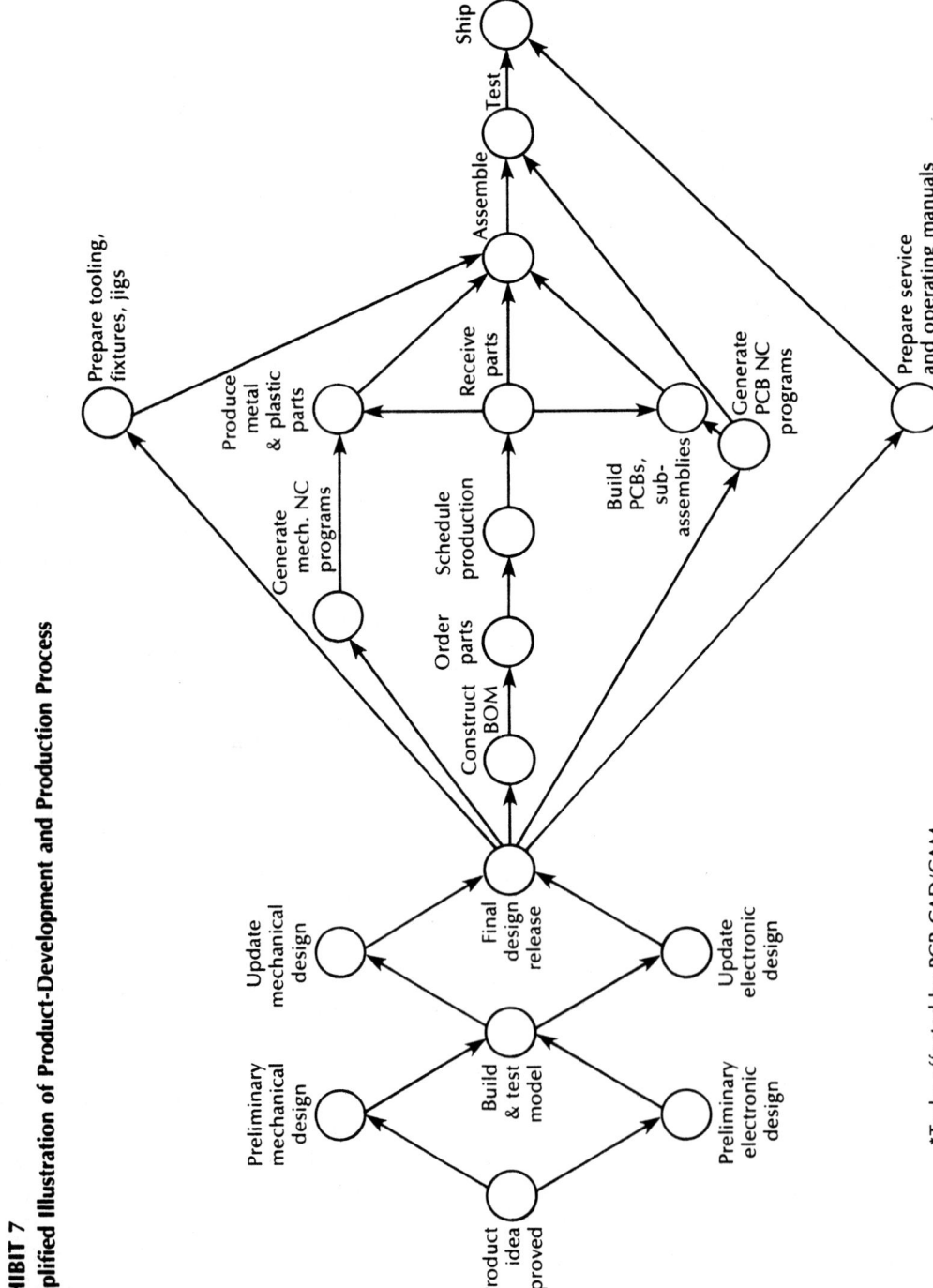

Source: Casewriter's observations.

*Tasks effected by PCB CAD/CAM

EXHIBIT 8
Expected Productivity Gains of Mechanical CAD/CAM System

Technical activity	Dept.*	Occurrences per year	HRS per occur-rence	Productivity ratio gain**
1. Flat pattern development	ME	390.0	8.0	4.0
2. Detail solid design	E	130.0	20.0	4.0
3. Detail sheet metal design	D,E	390.0	20.0	4.0
4. Assembly design	D,E	253.0	22.0	5.0
5. Plastic mold design	ME	14.0	120.0	4.0
6. Fabricate mold	M	14.0	200.0	3.5
7. Jig and fixture design	ME	300.0	40.0	6.0
8. Layout	D,E	15.0	80.0	10.0
9. Nesting development	ME	390.0	.5	5.0
10. Fabricate fixture	ME	300.0	5.0	3.0
11. Design changes (drawings)	D	1633.0	2.0	6.0
12. Design changes (tooling)	ME	200.0	2.0	5.0
13. Design changes (molds)	ME	40.0	9.0	3.5
14. Styling (industrial design)	D,E	15.0	80.0	10.0
15. Bill of material construction	M	253.0	12.0	20.0
16. NC programming	ME	130	7.0	3.0
17. Exploded views for manuals (vendor cost equals $20K)	N/A	N/A	N/A	N/A
				Avg. 5.05

Source: Company records.
*Department performing task:
M = Manufacturing
ME = Manuf. Engineering
D = Drafting
E = Design Engineering
**Estimated from industry data. The productivity ratio is in terms of hours *directly* affected by CAD/CAM on a before versus after CAD basis. For example, a 4.0 represents a 400 percent improvement in direct labor productivity. These ratios also assume 100 percent utilization of equipment and no learning curve effects.

be directly affected by a new mechanical CAD system. Those tasks, along with the responsible department and the total number of manual hours spent on the tasks last year, are shown in Exhibit 8. In addition, Sam was able to assign productivity gains expected to result from the mechanical CAD system.

Sam tabulated some preliminary costs for a system (to run on Raleigh's VAX 11/780 computer) that would accomplish the listed productivity gains. These costs could be broken down as follows:

- system and application software, hard-copy printer, hard-copy plotter, alphanumeric CRT, miscellaneous $175,000

- individual work station containing graphics terminal, function keyboard and thumb-wheels (per work station) .... $ 48,200

- yearly maintenance would equal 4 percent of the final system cost .... $175,000 + ($48,200) (number of work stations)

Operators of such a system would cost approximately $13.20/hour with 2,000 hours making up 1 man-year. This cost, which included labor and fringe benefits, was similar for manufacturing, manufacturing engineering, drafting, and design personnel.

DECISION

Sam believed that he had enough information to make some preliminary recommendations, but if he recommended pursuing the new mechanical CAD/CAM system, numerous questions remained, such as:

- How do we justify the system?
- Over what planning horizon?
- How much can we save per year?
- How many shifts should we run with the system?
- How many work stations do we need?
- How do we determine which vendor can best supply our needs?
- What are the key issues in implementing the system?
- What would be the impact of CAD/CAM on product development, the production process, and the workforce?
- How would we know if we were successful in implementing the system?

Finally, Sam wondered how this new system would fit in with the web of existing stand-alone systems and how it meshed with a long-term goal of attaining the "automated factory." He needed a well-organized management report addressing these issues as soon as possible.

INDEX